Globalization, Technology, and Competition

Globalization, Technology, and Competition

The Fusion of Computers and Telecommunications in the 1990s

Edited by
Stephen P. Bradley
Jerry A. Hausman
Richard L. Nolan

HARVARD BUSINESS SCHOOL PRESS
Boston, Massachusetts

97 96 95 94 93   5 4 3 2 1

Library of Congress Cataloging-in-Publication Data

Globalization, technology, and competition : the fusion of computers
 and telecommunications in the 1990s / edited by Stephen P. Bradley,
 Jerry A. Hausman, Richard L. Nolan.
   p.   cm.
   Includes bibliographical references and index.
   ISBN 0-87584-338-7 (alk. paper)
   1. International business enterprises—Management.   2. Information
technology.   3. Competition, International.   I. Bradley, Stephen P.,
1941–   . II. Hausman, Jerry A.   III. Nolan, Richard L.
HD62.4.G554   1993
658'.049—dc20   92-36104
                                                         CIP

The paper used in this publication meets the requirements
of the American National Standard for Permanence of Paper for
Printed Library Materials Z39.49-1984.

Contents

I. Globalization and Technology

  1. Global Competition and Technology   3
       Stephen P. Bradley, Jerry A. Hausman, and Richard L. Nolan

II. Organizational Structures for Global Strategies   33

  2. How Will Information Technology Reshape Organizations?
     Computers as Coordination Technology   37
       Thomas W. Malone and John F. Rockart

  3. A Framework for the Design of the Emerging Global
     Organizational Structure   57
       Robert G. Eccles and Richard L. Nolan

  4. On the Design of Global Information Systems   81
       Benn R. Konsynski and Jahangir Karimi

III. Creating and Restructuring Industries   109

  5. The Role of IT Networking in Sustaining Competitive
     Advantage   113
       Stephen P. Bradley

  6. Telecommunications and the Restructuring of the Securities
     Markets   143
       George A. Hayter

  7. The Coordination of Global Manufacturing   169
       Ramchandran Jaikumar and David M. Upton

  8. Quick Response in Retail/Manufacturing Channels   185
       Janice H. Hammond

IV. Strategic Response to Structural Change   215

  9. Information Technology and the Boundary of the Firm: Who
     Wins, Who Loses, Who Has To Change   219
       Eric K. Clemons

  10. Being Global and the Global Opportunity   243
       Pierre Hessler

  11. Saturn—The Making of the Modern Corporation   257
       Richard G. LeFauve and Arnoldo C. Hax

  12. Information Technology and the Global Virtual Corporation   283
       David B. Miller, Eric K. Clemons, and Michael C. Row

V. Competing with Technology   309

13. The Bell Operating Companies and AT&T Venture Abroad
While British Telecom and Others Come to the United States   313
Jerry A. Hausman

14. Seven Technologies to Watch in Globalization   335
Alan Hald and Benn R. Konsynski

15. Building the Broadband Society   359
William Marx, Jr.

About the Contributors   371

Index   381

Part One
Globalization and Technology

1
Global Competition and Technology

Stephen P. Bradley, Jerry A. Hausman,
and Richard L. Nolan

Globalization and Technology

By far the most significant drivers of strategic change in the world today, globalization and technological innovation, are accelerating at a pace that will make them even more important in the decade ahead. Globalization is proceeding differently in different industries, driven primarily by: increasingly similar demands of end users for global products; changing needs and capabilities of global customers; underlying economies of scale and scope in research, product development, and manufacturing; and the traditional differential costs of input factors (e.g., labor rates and raw materials in different countries). Technology enables firms within an industry to capture economies of scale and scope by going global; global firms rely on technological innovation to enhance their capabilities. Technology is thus both driven by, and a key driver of, globalization.

For an example of how globalization and technological innovation continually reinforce one another we need only look at the way information technology and telecommunications are reshaping competitive landscapes and radically changing how both individuals and firms work together throughout the world. A two-day colloquium held at the Harvard Business School to explore the impact of globalization and technology on business was attended by more than one hundred invited guests who discussed and debated 22 invited papers. The colloquium was organized around the theme that globalization and technology are dramatically influencing the structure of industries, the strategies of firms competing in these industries, and the organi-

Figure 1-1
Drivers of Change

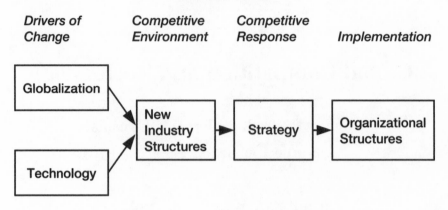

zational forms needed to support the new creative strategies of these firms. The structure of the colloquium is illustrated in Figure 1-1.

Globalization is an important emerging business mandate relevant to virtually all businesses. It is an Information Economy, as opposed to an Industrial Economy, business concept. Modern communications enable businesses to operate in multiple countries with diverse shapes and forms of organization and control. They make it possible to send information to any part of an organization instantaneously, enabling every part to know what every other part—and the organization as a whole—is doing all the time. Moreover, global businesses can link directly to their customers, suppliers, and partners around the world. Businesses capable of participating in global markets can operate in a much more robust manner than those constrained to narrower national markets. They can exploit national market niches that are too small to be efficiently served individually, but that collectively add up to an efficient scale. They can marshal scarce skills from multiple countries to work on a project or problem when the required skills cannot be found in one country or in the numbers needed.

Globalization of business has continued to the point that a new, more sophisticated set of management principles is emerging. Christopher Bartlett and Sumantra Ghoshal's research on the trend toward globalization and these new management principles is described in *Managing Across Borders*.[1] They advocate that transnational corporations attempt to maximize global economies of scale and scope while being locally responsive to customers in the countries in which they operate. As companies become more global, and especially when a transnational strategy is attempted, there develops a great demand for improved communications both in capacity and sophistication. There is no end in sight for this trend.

This book explores the impact of globalization and technology on the very fabric of the way business is conducted. In focusing particularly on information technology and telecommunications, it entertains such questions as:

- How is technology changing?
- How are industries affected by changing technology?
- How are companies responding to threats and opportunities created in their industries by technology?
- How are firms cooperating differently?
- How is the way individuals work and interact changing?
- How are activities coordinated across multiple locations and in multiple languages?
- How are information technology and telecommunications providers competing to enable this transformation?

We have drawn conclusions in three broad areas. First, we believe a new fusion of information technology and telecommunications is occurring that will radically affect all companies, whether or not they were significant users of technology in the past. These changes are being driven by the needs of increasingly global competitors, inasmuch as many key suppliers of technology are uncertain how to respond.

Second, this new fusion of technology is extremely dynamic and will change the fundamental structure of firms. Emerging "networked" structures are enabling more cooperative work. Transforming the organization to support networked structures for competing in the next decade will be a major challenge for most companies.

Third, the competitive strategies of firms are being and will be increasingly affected by the creation of new industries, restructuring of existing industries, and focus on gaining competitive advantage through the fusion of information technology and telecommunications. How to evaluate the requisite massive investments in technology will be a major concern for senior managers.

Our initial approach has been to explore different types of company demand for information technology and telecommunications. We have treated technology in the broadest sense to encompass the way different companies "work" in the course of providing goods and services. We have taken competitive strategies to be a manifestation of the way companies want to work to establish an advantage in the marketplace. We conclude that there is, indeed, a demand for a fusion of information technology and telecommunications that is different than the traditional demand for separate computing and telecommunications services. End users correctly perceive that a fusion of these technologies is required to satisfy their needs. Companies investing in technology are indifferent to whether their needs are met by a single supplier in bundled fashion or by multiple suppliers with one supplier, or the company itself, providing the integration. Their urgent concern is to find practical methods for meeting increasingly intense user demands.

Next, we assessed how the fusion of information technology and telecommunications will affect the competitive environment. We conclude that technology will result in the creation of many new industries and, more important, the fundamental restructuring of many existing industries. Restructuring in this context refers to the changing bases of competitive advantage in an industry and the fundamentally different ways in which buyers, suppliers, and rivals compete, cooperate, and, in general, interact with one another. Entry and mobility barriers will be eliminated in many industries and created in relatively few. As a result, the competitive strategies of most companies will have to respond to threats and opportunities created by new technology. Some companies will succeed and others fail, as the sources of competitive advantage are modified or changed altogether. Companies will have to make substantial additional investments in technology simply to avoid strategic jeopardy. For the most part, these investments will be an absolute strategic necessity, but will not lead to any sustainable competitive advantage. In other words, companies will have to make these investments merely to remain competitive in the future.

Finally, we examined the competition to supply needed technology. Although both traditional computer and telecommunications companies seem to recognize the demand for fused services, they are not currently structured to provide them, nor is it clear that they will be able to successfully restructure to do so. Software clearly is playing a critical role in developing fused services, but traditional suppliers seem not to have any unique competitive advantage in software, and some have critical weaknesses in this area. Certain key suppliers, such as AT&T and NEC, are trying to develop the relevant technologies and software to provide complete solutions. IBM, through alliances with a variety of partners, is apparently attempting to do the same. But many computer companies, software developers, systems integrators, and specialized hardware suppliers seem to be betting that they can focus on part of the customer's needs and deliver superior value. It remains to be seen how this strategy will play out.

Our 1987 colloquium and resulting book, *Future Competition in Telecommunications,* took stock of the state of competition in telecommunications in the United States as a result of the 1984 Modified Final Judgment (MFJ) executed by Judge Harold Greene of the Federal District Court of the District of Columbia.[2] The MFJ established a framework for deregulation of the telecommunications industry, whereby AT&T agreed to divest its Bell operating companies (BOCs). In 1988, we judged the effort to establish competition in telecommunications in the United States was only a partial success. Integration of computers and telecommunications was dramatically altered. Since then, the information technology industry, which has been characterized by 25% to 30% per year price/performance increases, has begun to be integrated with the telecommunications industry, and we now seem to be on the threshold of a new surge of competition resulting from the fusion of these industries' products and services. The entry of the Bell operating companies, which received governmental permission to provide information services in 1991, is likely to intensify competition and give rise to more new service offerings. We view increased competition among companies that are aggressively transforming themselves into viable global competitors as healthy and beneficial.

The increase in competition seen in the United States has also occurred in some countries overseas. Both the United Kingdom and Japan have privatized their formerly government-run telephone companies, and both countries now permit competition in provision of long-distance services. Many other countries have allowed for competition in the provision of data services, equipment purchases, and cellular services. Yet most of these other countries—France and Germany, for example—still restrict the provision of long-distance services both within their countries and internationally. The restriction of competition protects the very high prices charged by the national telephone companies for domestic and international long-distance services. The immediate prospects for change here are not high. While pressure by the U.S. government on international long-distance prices and the harmonization of the European Community (EC) may provide some impetus for lower prices in the future, the near-term regulatory situation in most industrial countries outside the United States, Canada, the United Kingdom, and Japan will continue to limit competition in favor of high service prices.

As we examine the industry landscape of computers and telecommunications in the early 1990s, we find that the new global marketplace and competition are technologically enabled by the hardware networking technologies. Equally important, we find that network organization constructs have progressed as well, facilitated by greatly improved software. The net result is that hardware and software technologies exist to enable the global network organization form. We also recognize that technology alone is insufficient to make the global network organization "happen." There must also be a process involving people and organizational change, and we recognize the importance of this process. However, to provide perspective to companies that are trying to transform their organization with technology, we have focused on leading-edge firms and practices. Indeed, another work on the implementation, or transformation, process is warranted.

User-Driven Demand for New Services

Simply stated, the "new services" being demanded by end users are the integration of computing and telecommunications. But a simple statement belies the actual complexity. Richard Nolan's Stages Theory, which identifies a series of S-shaped curves that involve organizational learning on major computer-based technologies, can be used to describe the demand for information services.[3] Figure 1-2 depicts three S-shaped curves of 15

Figure 1-2
Stages Theory

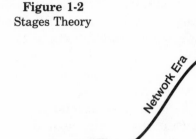

Copyright © 1992 by Richard L. Nolan

to 20 years' duration, which correspond to the DP (data processing) Era, the Micro Era, and the Network Era. These curves roughly describe the demand for computer-based technologies, including telecommunications, at the level of the firm.

The DP Era

The DP Era, about 1960 to 1980, was dominated by industry products that supported mainframe computing. Minicomputers, although prevalent in this era, were managed in a centralized manner similar to mainframe computers. The demand, or "internal market," within firms for mainframe computing was the automation of low-level clerical and factory work. The application paradigm was "automation," where the computer was applied to making the existing organization more efficient. Most often, existing processes and procedures were automated; rarely was the fundamental functional hierarchical organizational structure significantly changed. Following about 10 to 15 years of investment, a critical mass of automation would be achieved, at which point a number of firms would downsize their blue collar and clerical work forces by as much as 20% to 30%, leading to a lower overall cost structure in the industry. Downsizing of the work force at the factory and clerical levels seemed to begin in most industries in the mid-1970s and continued aggressively throughout the 1980s.

With the demand for mainframe computing tailing off in the mid-1970s, as reflected by the slowing of growth in firms' DP Era S-curves, the computer industry began to address the demand for computer-based technology in the middle of the organization. Because the middle consisted of professionals, such as engineers, accountants, and managers, this demand was fundamentally different from that for computing at the bottom of the organization. The DP Era paradigm of automation was generally attempted at this level, and it usually failed. Work done by mid-level professionals tended to be too complicated and esoteric to automate in the same way that clerical and factory work had been automated.

The Micro Era

A new paradigm introduced to address the problem of mid-level professionals was distinguished from automation by Shoshana Zuboff, who coined the term "informate."[4] The objective of informating, unlike that of automating, is not to replace professionals with computing, but to use computing to leverage the work of professionals. The microcomputer, with associated innovations such as programmer-less programming (e.g., spreadsheets, word processors, computer-aided design [CAD], and so forth) and graphic user interfaces, fueled the Micro Era. With a critical mass of professionals today equipped with microcomputers, we are seeing the beginnings of an aggressive and permanent downsizing of the work force in the middle of the organization, similar to what we saw at lower levels in the mid-1970s and throughout the 1980s.

In the Micro Era, computers, particularly microcomputers, have satisfied another less well-understood demand in the organization. Microcomputers have increasingly been incorporated directly into the products and services of firms. Many automobiles today incorporate as many as 15 microcomputers. Credit cards are being equipped with chips that can record data and communicate with computer networks. And an astonishing array of products, from consumer electronics, major appliances, copiers, and toys to lighting, security systems, and environmental controls, have been made "smarter" by including microprocessors in their design.

The Network Era

Investments in computers in the three main areas or markets described above—automating clerical and factory work, informating information workers, and supporting the development of intelligent products and services—are the basis of the emerging demand for networks. This book is aimed at fostering a better understanding of the radical changes emerging in the Network Era, as depicted in Figure 1-2. We have observed computer-based networks evolving in each of the demand areas discussed above. Wide-band networks have evolved from the base of automated systems. Local area networks (LANs) initially employed to electronically link teams of professionals (e.g., engineers, accountants, and executives) have been connected to wide-band networks to enable local groups of professionals to interact with geographically dispersed groups via their workstations. Products, such as automobiles and airplanes, are designed by globally networked groups that collaborate daily, passing "blueprints" back and forth around the world and talking about them over the telephone or via video conferencing or electronic blackboards.

Even the computers incorporated in products are being integrated into networks, and then further integrated into a firm's other electronic networks. For example, when executives at Ford of Europe discovered that their engineers had incorporated multiple independent computers into an automobile, they concluded that it made sense to integrate these computers into a network in order to better control and monitor the car's performance. It was a small technical step to collect these data and provide a plug-in download to the computers at Ford repair shops. It was not even a very big technical step to hook up the Ford repair shop computers to Ford engineering headquarters to assist in dealing with the most troublesome repair problems. These steps toward nested, integrated electronic networks of computers have a profound impact on the structure of organizations and the service value provided to customers.

Although many companies have already made major investments in computers and local area networks, most have not yet adequately addressed the design, management, and global exploitation of these electronic networks. This will become an increasingly critical factor in how firms compete in the 1990s.

New network services will make it possible for companies to be effectively managed and to compete anywhere, anytime. A top executive can hold a meeting with senior executives who remain in Tokyo, London, New York, and Des Moines in virtual reality—as if all were in one place. The meeting might take the form of a video conference, with visuals and documents shared via a computer network. Already it is possible to schedule, monitor, and coordinate the production of multiple factories in a number of countries from a single location. The same should be possible for retail outlets, training facilities, and most other operations.

Organizational Impact

The demand for integrated services involves the way companies want to "work," indeed, must work in order to be world-class competitors. The demand for tools that enable people to work differently is associated with the evolution of new organizational structures. The predominant form of organization in the Industrial Economy, the divisionalized functional hierarchy, is characterized by a set of management principles centered around the notion of a hierarchy: chain of command, span of control, paper-based memo communications, and so forth. This organizational structure is slowly giving way to an alternative structure, termed the "network" structure, characterized by an alternative set of management principles: point-to-point electronic-based communication, teams, and strategic alliances. The network structure is more appropriate for leveraging information technology.

Thomas Malone and John Rockart's term "coordination technologies" (see Chapter 2) goes beyond the simple definition of new services as the integration of computers and telecommunications. The notion of coordination technologies directly addresses the rationale for such integration, which is to enable people to cooperate more effectively and efficiently in the conduct of their work. Malone and Rockart contend that trends toward cooperative work are engendering a re-definition of provider companies' products and services, which can now best be described as coordination technologies.

Richard Nolan and Robert Eccles (see Chapter 3) characterize most organizations as operating informal network organizational structures that float on top of formal functional hierarchies. Such network structures are more effective for structuring work with regard to emerging information technologies, and these informal structures are slowly but surely being formalized. Technologies such as E-mail, phone-mail, relational databases, neural networks, parallel processors, imaging, and object-oriented programming are especially important for enabling more effective organizational structures. Functional hierarchical structures are slowly fading into the background.

Benn Konsynski and Jahangir Karimi (see Chapter 4) build on the work of Bartlett and Ghoshal as they discuss how information technology is being used in emerging global structures. They contend that interorganizational systems (IOSs) play an important role in enabling cooperation and coordination among companies, as well as affecting the competitiveness of nations.

Competitive Strategy and Technology

The fusion of information technology and telecommunications is creating new industries, restructuring existing industries, and radically changing the way firms compete. In the past, large investments were made in technologies to support competitive strategy. But truly massive investments will be required in the future. Many firms are making strategic commitments to technology with the stated objective of gaining significant competitive advantage in their industry. Stephen Bradley (see Chapter 5) points out that a few of the firms that make such commitments will achieve their objective; most, however, will likely not realize a sustainable competitive advantage, but rather only a brief competitive edge that will be rapidly dissipated by industry forces, particularly the responses of competitors.

Changing Industry Structures

New industries are being created and existing industries restructured by the accelerating pace of globalization and technological innovation. We have for a long time had value-added/managed data networks, such as those of EDS and General Electric Information Systems (GEIS). Community networks have developed naturally as private infrastructure has become substantially more cost effective or when special performance characteristics (e.g., security) were lacking in the public infrastructure. Société Internationale de Telecommunications Aeronautique (SITA), the community network that supports data communications among nearly all international airlines, was initiated and continues to be effective because of economies of scale in delivering high-performance services to its customer owners. More recently, new information-driven industries have begun to emerge at an ever-increasing pace. Examples include a wide spectrum of applications, ranging from news retrieval services, such as Dow Jones and Lexus/Nexus, to information networking services, such as Prodigy (the IBM–Sears joint venture), and video text systems, such as that provided by France's Minitel to its telephone subscribers.

Most "new" industries created over the years have provided services that complement services offered by existing industries or have substituted for existing, less efficient services. They have tended to be stand-alone industries that attract new entrants and exploit economies of scale or scope. But today the fusion of information technology and telecommunications is permeating most industries and often restructuring the underlying basis of competition. The integration of these technologies and their complex application to the essence of the underlying activities that make up a business are becoming permanent facets of participation in almost any industry. Where once information technology and telecommunications were inputs to or substitutes for specific activities within a firm or industry, the integration of these technologies is becoming the very basis for executing, coordinating, measuring, and communicating about activities within firms. To illustrate the fundamental change that has taken place, we examined financial services, manufacturing, and retailing.

The most striking example of the new technology restructuring a financial services industry is provided by George Hayter's description (see Chapter 6) of the International Stock Exchange (ISE) in London. Major triggering events were the almost complete deregulation of the exchange and the introduction of new technology. Deregulation permitted broader membership in the exchange, ended fixed commissions, and sharply increased the number of firms competing for customer business. New technology in the form of the stock exchange automatic quotation (SEAQ) system greatly increased the efficiency of the market by making information readily available to all regardless of physical location. The changes were dramatic. Virtually all trading moved off the floor to trading rooms with complete access to support staff, information resources, computer models, and customers. Turnover from foreign securities accounted for more than half the turnover on the ISE, compared to less than 5% for New York and 2% for Tokyo. Substantial business shifted to London from other European exchanges, notably those of Paris and Stockholm. On the other hand, the members of the ISE did not fare as well. The efficiency of the market virtually eliminated exchange members' operating margins, and London firms suffered extensive losses with essentially no prospect for a return to traditional profitability.

The second broad area in which technology is restructuring industries is manufacturing. As the forces for globalization have intensified competition, many manufacturing industries have become extensive users of information technology and telecommunications. With many markets increasingly demanding similar products worldwide, it is essential that the major firms in an industry be active participants within each of the three major markets of North America, Europe, and the Pacific Rim. Thus, in industries such as medical imaging we see the major competitors General Electric, Siemens, and Toshiba active in one another's "home" bases of operations. This pattern holds for automobiles, computers, reprographics, power generation equipment, and engineering plastics, as well as for many other industries. In each of these industries, information technology and telecommunications play an essential role in coordinating and controlling remote locations, increasing efficiency in decentralized operations, and standardizing products and processes throughout the world to meet the needs of both local and global customers.

The use of technology to support traditional global industries is well documented. But important changes are taking place in manufacturing technology that may radically restructure many industries once again. Ramchandran Jaikumar and David Upton (see Chapter 7) report on the widespread adoption of programmable machines and computer-aided manufacturing (CAM) that promises to have far-reaching consequences for factory operations and, in turn, industry structure. The manufacturing cell, essentially a factory within a factory in which a small group of machines performs the entire manufacturing process, is becoming the dominant manufacturing configuration in many industries. Manufacturing cells are designed to be highly flexible, highly reliable, and require very low overhead. They are, in effect, reducing the minimum efficient scale of manufacturing operations. In addition, increased standardization in the communication link between design and manufacturing through the use of standardized computer-aided design (CAD) is reducing the need to collocate engineering design and high-volume manufacturing. These two factors together substantially reduce economies of scale in manufacturing, while simultaneously reducing the capital required to participate in manufacturing. Moreover, these small flexible manufacturing units can be physically and organizationally independent from the design, engineering, and marketing functions.

With entry barriers lowered, it is likely that new firms will enter manufacturing in these industries, and markets for flexible manufacturing capacity will emerge. This is precisely what has happened with the Prato textile system in Italy, which has realized dramatic performance improvements measured in greatly improved cycle times, reduced in-process inventory, greater capacity utilization and product variety, and enhanced quality. Other industries with important manufacturing activities, from toys to printed circuit boards and semiconductors, are beginning to operate in a similar manner. In the future, we can expect an acceleration of this trend toward markets for flexible manufacturing capacity enabled by the integration of information technology and telecommunications.

The restructuring of the manufacturing activity in the textile industry has implications for how developments in information technology and telecommunications are restructuring the retail industry. Janice Hammond (see Chapter 8) describes time-based competition, or quick response, in the retail industry that is rapidly becoming the norm. A quick response strategy involves three key components: consumer testing to select specific products for specific markets, an effective information architecture that accommodates all suppliers in the channel, and a short-cycle replenishment system. The first step in implementing a quick response system is to establish effective partnerships with all suppliers and develop standards for universal product codes (UPCs), electronic data interchange (EDI) communications, and shipping container bar codes. The second step involves implementing point-of-sale (POS) data analysis of trends, computer-aided design to facilitate timely design decisions, and flexible manufacturing technologies. It has been estimated that a quick response system in the apparel industry utilizing existing technologies can cut total channel time from 125 to 30 days and, in the future, perhaps to 10 days. Implementing quick response systems in the apparel industry alone could save more than $12 billion annually.[5] The Limited and Benetton appear to be leading other retailers in this area.

Undoubtedly the biggest force in retailing in the United States today is the discounter Wal-Mart, which is rapidly changing the face of retailing through creative relationships with a number of its suppliers. Major investments have enabled Wal-Mart to pump its more than 2,000 stores' cash register data into a mega database, from which it can now download vendors' weekly POS data to their computers.

A number of Wal-Mart's vendors are overwhelmed by this capability, but others are responding. Milliken and Seminole Manufacturing (in apparel), General Electric (in light bulbs), and Procter & Gamble (in a variety of products) are accepting the data, analyzing them, and using them to their competitive advantage. Wal-Mart increased Milliken and Seminole Manufacturing's unit sales for apparel by an estimated 31% and inventory turns by 30% when it implemented a quick response system. For GE, Wal-Mart provides daily inventory status reports by warehouse via EDI, and GE plans inventory levels for each warehouse, cuts its own purchase orders, and continuously ships full truckloads, while measuring its performance against Wal-Mart's inventory turns and out-of-stock rates. GE saves inventory carrying costs through better planning, reduces transaction costs, and has substantially fewer stock-outs. Wal-Mart saves by allowing GE to incur planning and ordering costs, has increased working capital productivity, and reduced lost sales. The bottom line, substantial cost savings in the value system that are shared by the partners in the relationship, is typical of what can be achieved by implementing quick response systems.

The undeniable conclusion is that the fusion of information technology and telecommunications is radically restructuring entire industries, from financial services to manufacturing to retail. The new technology is not only making firms more efficient in carrying out their traditional activities, but fundamentally changing the form of competition in many industries. The restructuring is pervasive, changing forever the ways in which people work together, suggesting substantially different organizations to support their efforts, and shifting the basis of the strategies pursued by firms in these industries to new concepts of competitive advantage.

Changing Firm Strategies

The restructuring of existing industries made possible by the integration of information technology and telecommunications is being driven largely by the strategies of firms attempting to gain advantage over the competition in their industry (see Eric Clemons, Chapter 9). Firms pursuing competitive advantages based on establishing a low-cost position, effectively differentiating products and related services, or competing effectively in time are making massive investments, estimated to be as much as 50% of their total investments, in information technology and telecommunications. In competitive strategy, these investments are largely internal to the firm, in cooperative strategy, they are designed to more effectively link a firm's strategy with that of its suppliers, buyers, and, in some instances, its rivals.

In competitive strategy, we first consider technological applications within the single business, then turn to the interrelationships among businesses. Federal Express, an example of a single business case, makes elaborate use of technology to support its vision—"to be a premier high-quality logistics carrier of time-sensitive goods on a worldwide basis." The company uses information about a package and its location as a key differentiator, and makes this information available directly to customers.

Sony Corporation, a truly global company with sales balanced throughout the world and facilities located in 25 countries, has made a large investment in information technology and telecommunications designed to speed up operations, reduce inventories, and improve quality and customer service. The technology yields cost savings, but these are not always analyzed, as the emphasis is on time-based competition for its own sake.

In terms of interrelationships among businesses in the same firm, vertical relationships are usually designed to reduce transaction costs. Information technology and telecommunications are being used to manage many vertical relationships designed to gain or defend a competitive advantage. Caterpillar Tractor Company is committed to a $1.8 billion project, called "Plant with a Future," designed to globalize and modernize its manufacturing facilities and processes. Flexible cell-based manufacturing processes are being combined with computer integration across their manufacturing facilities worldwide. Because it is stretching the limits of the information technology currently available, Caterpillar has run into some difficulties with the project. Asea Brown Boveri (ABB) is attempting to change the basis of competition in power generation by bundling products and services that have traditionally been provided by specialized suppliers, such as General Electric (turbine generators) or Combustion Engineering (boilers). Through extensive acquisitions, ABB has become a completely vertically integrated provider of power generation capabilities. Coordinating the newly acquired disparate parts of ABB to facilitate local responsiveness requires effective use of information technology and telecommunications.

Horizontal interrelationships among businesses in the same firm are generally employed to capture economies of scope. Often they involve leveraging specialized assets through some form of distribution channel. Merrill Lynch's competitive strategy to be first to introduce a cash management account (CMA) is an example of this type of horizontal relationship. The CMA, a consolidated asset management account that includes checking and brokerage accounts, credit and debit cards, and money market and mutual funds, presents customers with one interface to a full line of Merrill Lynch services.

A discussion of horizontal relationships enabled by technology would be incomplete without reference to NEC. NEC's strategy epitomizes the main thesis of our colloquium and this book. Its "C&C" (computers and communications) strategy has been the foundation of its success. In 1985, NEC was one-tenth the size of IBM but number ten in computers, one-seventh the size of AT&T but number seven in telecommunications, and two-thirds the size of Texas Instruments but number two in semiconductors. Overall, the company was number five, and by 1988, it had moved to number three. NEC realized economies of scope from managing its horizontal interrelationships at the same time that IBM's Rolm acquisition in telecommunications and AT&T's initial attempt to go it alone in computers were failing. NEC coordinates and facilitates its interrelationships in a global environment with the integrative computers and communications technology it espouses. Although a key provider of the technologies that enable globalization, IBM has only recently evolved into a truly global form. Pierre Hessler of IBM (see Chapter 10) provides an introspective view of what "being global" means for the traditional international company.

Increasingly, information technology and telecommunications are being used to foster cooperative strategies with buyers, suppliers, and even rivals. On the buyer side, American Hospital Supply is the classic example of an interorganizational information system forming the basis of long-term competitive advantage. By recognizing that acquiring and tracking the information needed to bill patients and insurance companies accurately accounted for half the cost of hospitals' purchasing supplies, American Hospital was able to grow from a $300,000 company to a $3 billion company in less than 10 years and significantly reduce Johnson & Johnson's dominance. However, after they were acquired by Baxter-Travenal, they did not continue to invest in their leadership position and much of their competitive advantage was lost. In another example, Westinghouse is linked to its electric utility customers through information technology products in managed maintenance and regulatory compliance.

On the supplier side, we have already remarked on Wal-Mart's extensive use of technology to link to its suppliers and gain an advantage in the process. Ford and Xerox are well known for quality programs that make extensive use of technology to provide close linkages with a limited number of suppliers worldwide. The new Saturn Corporation of General Motors, which is described by Skip Le Fauve and Arnoldo Hax (see Chapter 11), is an example of a quality-driven cooperative strategy. Rosenbluth Travel, described by David Miller, Eric Clemons and Michael Row (see Chapter 12), is an excellent example of cooperation among rivals. They initiated a global alliance of partners to provide common services throughout the world; the key to the alliance is the use of information technology and telecommunications to create a global virtual corporation.

Sustaining Competitive Advantage

With the creation of new industries and the restructuring of many existing industries, massive investments will be made in information technology and telecommunications. The key question that arises is whether any of this investment will afford the firms making it a sustainable competitive advantage. We believe that many of the firms justifying these investments on the basis of gaining competitive advantage will be disappointed.

Firms that invest in technology in an attempt to gain a competitive advantage ultimately want to lower their cost of doing business or improve customer perception of the performance of their products and services, that is, to differentiate their approach. In both cases, the notion of competitive advantage is not absolute but relative to the competition. Investments intended to lower a firm's costs usually rely on capturing economies of scale or scope, reducing transaction costs, exploiting linkages among various business activities, or managing interrelationships with other businesses in the firm. Investments intended to improve differentiation, on the other hand, usually call for responding more effectively to buyer needs for improved quality, performance, features, service, or cycle time. A firm that is first with an investment in technology often creates a brief competitive advantage, only to be surprised when the competition matches or improves upon its initiative.

Why is it so difficult to sustain competitive advantage? The four key threats to the sustainability of competitive advantage identified by Pankaj Ghemawat are imitation, substitution, holdup, and slack.[6] Investments in information technology and telecommunications are often easily imitated. The fruits of these investments are usually not patentable, nor are they very difficult to copy, and outside expertise is readily available to help a company copy and improve on the ideas and innovations of other companies. Competitive advantage may thus only stem from being first. The Rosenbluth International Alliance, for example, might be imitated, in which case Rosenbluth would find itself once more in the position of trying to out-hustle the competition to come up with the next innovation. The approach of trying to outperform the competition with each successive innovation was a difficult strategy for the U.S. semiconductor industry against the Japanese, and it may not work for Rosenbluth in the travel industry against American Express and other global players.

Substitution is a threat to the kind of technology investments that are difficult to imitate and to the continuous improvement efforts that keep a first mover ahead of its competitors. Given Federal Express's emphasis on continuously improving its positioning and taking advantage of economies of scale in marketing and operations, it is difficult to imagine one of its competitors overtaking it in the overnight package delivery business. Even DHL's extensive international presence seems to be vulnerable to incursions by Federal Express. But fax and EDI are substitutes for much of the company's core business, and they are already beginning to dissipate Federal Express's competitive advantage.

Holdup can occur when other parties exert power, usually control of scarce resources, to extract a portion of the returns from an investment in technology. The relationship that developed between Merrill Lynch and Michael Bloomberg is illustrative. Bloomberg developed a sophisticated trading support system that depended on timely bond price information that was not widely available. Merrill Lynch provided the information in return for a minority interest in the company and an agreement to restrict access to certain Merrill Lynch competitors. The threat of appropriation is present in almost all value-added information services. It is the detailed knowledge of the industry to which the services are to be provided, and the specific information assets themselves, not the delivery system, that often capture most of the profits. This is a potential threat to Prodigy once alternative channels of distribution emerge. It is also the reason that AT&T will probably not gain a great deal of profitability from joint ventures in value-added information services. The regional Bell operating companies (RBOCs) might, given their superior though not exclusive access to the end users in their regional monopolies.

The final threat to the sustainability of competitive advantage is organizational slack. This occurs most often in firms that develop leading market positions in their industries and then become complacent. Over time they become inefficient by adding unnecessary layers of management, inadvertently slowing the product development cycle, failing to continuously improve costs, and becoming less responsive in providing service. Xerox was a prime example of this phenomenon in the early 1980s but turned itself around through its "Leadership Through Quality" program which made effective use of networking. IBM and General Motors are currently wrestling with similar problems.

So prevalent are the threats of imitation, substitution, holdup, and slack that gaining competitive advantage through investment in information technology and telecommunications seems highly unlikely. Why then are so many firms making massive investments in these technologies? The answer may be that some are seeking the elusive first-mover advantages discussed above. More often, it is simply that these investments are perceived correctly as strategic necessities. To survive in the future, firms must meet or beat the competition in delivering value to the customer. With industries being fundamentally restructured by the integration of information technology and telecommunications, it is often absolutely essential that these investments be made to avoid genuine strategic vulnerability.

Technology-Based Supplier Competition

Changing industry structures that are driving new competitive responses and new organizational forms and mechanisms are precipitating a restructuring of the traditional industries that have supplied various technologies (see Jerry Hausman, Chapter 13). Although users perceive a fusion of information technology and telecommunications, the extent to which suppliers will have to be full-service providers is not clear. AT&T and NEC appear to be taking an integrated approach, but other computer companies, systems integrators, software suppliers, and specialized hardware suppliers are betting on an unbundled approach to this complex market. Regardless of how this turns out, all suppliers are being radically affected by the changing structure of their industry or segment. Who will be best positioned for the upcoming competitive fight is still an open question.

Information Technology Providers in Hardware

Computer hardware providers in the United States and abroad are facing extremely difficult business conditions. The two largest international computer manufacturers, IBM and Digital Equipment Corporation, have both massively reduced employment levels and have experienced very large losses in recent years. Nixdorf of Germany has been bought by Siemens, ICL of the United Kingdom has been bought by Fujitsu, and Bull of France is in limbo, awaiting yet another rescue by the French government and its taxpayers. Although some of the current financial distress arises from the ongoing recession and the cutback in capital spending by firms, the longer-run secular trend for hardware producers is not favorable. The computer hardware industry has significant overcapacity, which has led to the expected response of fierce price competition, low margins, and continued capacity contraction.[7]

Similar business conditions prevail in the telecommunications hardware industry. PBX prices have been steady or fallen over the past five years, and industry sources report that almost no PBX providers currently are making money on their products. A relatively static technology and overcapacity have, as in computer hardware, led to fierce price competition and low margins. The central office switch market, at least in the United States, where it is open to competition much more than in either Europe or Japan, has witnessed a 50% decrease in price per line over the past five years. Again, lack of technological innovation and overcapacity have significantly increased competition.

Two competitive strategies, successful in the 1970–1985 period, are no longer valid. The first, product differentiation—"no one ever got fired for ordering IBM"—has simply ceased to be important. Until about 1989, large U.S. corporations bought their personal computers (PCs) from IBM, or perhaps Compaq, if they were adventuresome. Today, companies such as Dell, Gateway, Northgate, and Zeos provide PCs to even the largest U.S. companies. The significant investment IBM made in "account control" in the 1970s and 1980s is no longer enough to provide a return to shareholders. The second strategy, actually a variant on product differentiation, is customer lock-in. Customers' millions of dollars of investment in nonportable IBM mainframe software forced them to remain loyal to IBM for some time. This strategic advantage continues, but it is rapidly diminishing in importance. Competitors such as Amdahl and Hitachi now offer IBM-compatible mainframes, which has led to significant price discounting, and customers are also conscious of the importance of avoiding lock-in for the future. Indeed, IBM's "data channel" strategy for its PS2 PCs has to date been almost a complete failure. Neither customers nor software providers will allow themselves to be overly dependent on a single manufacturer's hardware.

The basis of competition has changed the industry in a profound way. Instead of account control and customer lock-in, open architecture reduces customer switching costs and increases competition. Rather than choosing to solve their problems by using a single vendor, customers now purchase equipment and software from numerous companies and rely on effective systems integration. Systems integration, in turn, depends on a skilled personnel base and software to combine the various vendors' equipment into a reliable network. The hardware solution, with its reliance on ever-larger and -faster machines, is applicable to an ever-shrinking range of situations faced by competitive firms. Thus, the outlook for IT and telecommunications hardware manufacturers is not favorable.

These hard times for IT and telecommunications hardware manufacturers have led some analysts to conclude that only software producers will succeed in the future.[8] Intel, whose earnings and stock price are both at all-time highs, is a prominent exception. To date, Intel has repulsed the challenges of both the Japanese in microprocessors and Advanced Micro Devices (AMD), which is cloning Intel 386 series chips. Intel's 486 chip is in wide use, with a 586 series chip expected soon. Although the "IBM standard" has vanished, an argument exists for the existence of an Intel standard, with Motorola and RISC technology providing the current competition. Intel technology now has a huge embedded base of users, with a corresponding base of barely portable software. Can Intel's success continue? The technological innovation in Intel microprocessors has been astounding, surprising both minicomputer and mainframe producers. The prediction common a few years ago of migration to two types of computers—PCs and workstations, and supercomputers—now appears incorrect. Only PCs and workstations and massively parallel machines, all powered by microprocessors, may exist in the future.

IT Software Providers

Software producers have been the great success stories of the PC revolution. Microsoft, Lotus, Borland, and such network software producers as Novell have garnered large market shares, sustainable competitive advantage, and large embedded bases of users. We find it surprising that IBM, which built its mainframe success in large part on customer lock-in through software, ceded its strategic advantage to Microsoft in its haste to introduce PCs in 1981. The future is not assured for PC-based software manufacturers, since the competing UNIX framework, which allows for much greater portability, has been adopted by most workstation manufacturers. Although with the convergence of PCs and workstation price and technology, UNIX-based workstations could overtake PC technology, we believe this outcome to be unlikely at least in the next five to ten years. To some extent, the fate of software producers is tied to Intel's future successful technological innovation. Software producers that create user solutions to problems without incurring an intermediate layer of high cost and ill-managed technical personnel should continue to be successful given the significant barriers to entry created by user familiarity with software. As with Intel in hardware, the innovative nature of software products should allow for continued profitable margins.

The Producer/User Interface

Such industry players as IBM and Digital, recognizing the increased importance of software in creating customer solutions, have focused attention on customer demands, created by globalization and networks, for both computer and telecommunications networks. The solution to globalization and network demands is almost surely a software solution. These same companies have also decided that they must take the lead in providing examples that show that the networked global solution will work. According to IBM's Pierre Hessler (see Chapter 10) and AT&T's William Marx, Jr. (see Chapter 15), both corporations are attempting to create global organizations that will use the products and services they are trying to sell to customers.

The products and services provided by IT companies are designed to facilitate global competition by enabling low-cost, seamless, high-speed transmission of information throughout the world. Major competitors, as IT producers have long realized, will operate in a global marketplace. A key question for network providers is whether they can export their local expertise to foreign markets. AT&T has determined that the software demands for exporting its switching systems to foreign countries would involve a redesign effort of the order of magnitude of designing an entirely new switch. We expect that software companies striving to provide network solutions will encounter similar problems. Telecommunications networks are still operated primarily by national governments, which tend to view them as a source of subsidy for other industries rather than as a strategic necessity for global competition in the long-awaited Information Age.

In principle, national and international standards could solve many compatibility problems. But in practice, we doubt that standards will provide a feasible solution. The glacially bureaucratic pace of standards setting renders it incapable of keeping up with technology.

Standards and Open Systems

The changes that have occurred in the telecommunications and computer equipment industries during the 1980s have had two interacting effects: a paralysis in standards formation, and a move toward open systems less dependent on standards. First, we consider standards. For many years, there existed a de facto IBM standard for mainframe computers. With the IBM 360/370 operating system (and microcode) closed and the large investments many corporations had in nonportable software, competitors needed access to the 360/370 OS to compete. Early entrants, such as RCA (with its Spectra 70 series), as well as more recent entrants, such as Amdahl and Hitachi, were required to design their mainframe computers to be compatible with IBM 360/370 software. Peripheral suppliers, too, such as Memorex, Telex, and Storage Technology, designed their hardware to be compatible with the IBM standard. In telecommunications, at least in the United States, AT&T, which controlled 80% of all access to domestic lines, set standards through its manufacturing arm, Western Electric, that were used throughout the industry.

With the demise of the mainframe over the past five years and the growing importance of personal computers and workstations, the era of IBM-set standards came to an end. To some extent, IBM continues to influence standards in PCs, but Microsoft and Intel play a more important role. In workstations, no single company has a dominant influence on standards, and in telecommunications equipment, standards setting has become extremely cumbersome since the breakup of AT&T in 1984. Bellcore, the joint research arm of the Bell operating companies that commenced operation at the time of divestiture, might have assumed AT&T's standards-setting role in the United States but for limitations imposed by the Modified Final Judgment on the BOCs with respect to R&D and manufacturing. Internationally, too, standards setting has been less than successful. ISDN, for instance, was designed as an international telecommunications standard. Companies in North America are currently attempting to agree on a North American ISDN standard because international standards have been so slow to be adopted and have already been superseded by technological change in some areas.

Standards can improve economic efficiency by allowing manufacturers to produce at lower cost. Economies of scale create lower average manufacturing costs when output increases, and production of computers and telecommunications equipment is characterized by significant economies of scale. If the same central office switch platform can be used in North America, Europe, and Asia, important scale economies can be realized. Standards can likewise increase economies of joint production, also called economies of scope. For example, because central office switches and MATSOs, the control devices for cellular telephone networks, have similar features, economies of joint production are to be expected.[9] But standards can also retard technological advance, and can be used in an anticompetitive manner. Indeed, numerous competitors and the U.S. government complained about certain standards practices of IBM and AT&T during the 1970s.

In the absence of essentially single-firm standards setting, we expect standards to become less important in the future because of the difficulty of gaining agreement among numerous competitors or nations. Lack of a streamlined standards formation process and the rapidity of technological change make it increasingly likely that standards formation will occur too late to matter. Despite the losses of economies of scale and scope that may attend the decreasing importance of standards, customers (and competition) may well be better off in a "post-standards" world.

In a world without standards, we expect customers to demand open systems so as not to be locked into a given supplier's technology. Open systems will undoubtedly lead to increases in innovation and in the entry of niche suppliers that will spur competition. The unfortunate outcome of the de facto standards world of IBM and AT&T was that both companies managed the pace of technology to optimize profitability and avoid jeopardizing their installed base. Because in an open-system world no company will be able to manage the pace of technology, it is likely that the speed of technological change will be greater.[10] Moreover, software solutions, rather than hardware solutions, will become increasingly important as the means of technology integration. A greater separation between hardware and software producers, with competition between the two groups to produce customer solutions, is likely to lead to more and better solutions than an environment in which one company packages its hardware with an essentially closed software system. The growing importance of software should also be a better fit with the global marketplace, in which software will have to be modified to meet local requirements in the absence of international standards. Given software's increasingly important role in providing integration and functionality, we believe the overall demise of standards is unlikely to affect markets or customers adversely.

Emergence of Information Intensity

The shift from the importance of hardware to software in the computer/telecommunications industry has accelerated the emergence of a number of diverse information technologies: multimedia, video-conferencing, portable computers, and telephone. The net effect is to increase the "information intensity" in organizations. Alan Hald and Benn Konsynski (see Chapter 14) describe the trends creating increased information intensity and discuss the key technologies associated with it.

The Future IT Industry Structure

The future structure of the IT industry is likely to reflect competitors that achieve core competence in three areas: software, networks, and customer solutions. Currently, systems integrators (e.g., EDS and Andersen Consulting) and software companies (e.g., Microsoft and Novell) have a distinct advantage over traditional IT hardware providers. Both can work across multiple hardware platforms and design customer solutions based on readily available and competitive hardware from numerous manufacturers. Traditional hardware providers such as IBM may be constrained to rely on proprietary product offerings based on a single platform. Large computer manufacturers, such as IBM, and telecommunications providers, such as AT&T, thus face a critical challenge—to transform their existing organizational structures so as to focus on software and network integration that will provide customer solutions. IBM, Digital, AT&T, and many other industry participants, realizing the scope of this challenge, have made acquisitions and formed partnerships and joint ventures. Whether industry transformation will occur remains an open question, but without such transformation, software providers and systems integrators will reap the commercial benefits of future IT developments.

At the Harvard Business School colloquium that gave rise to this volume, Michael Porter claimed, based on research reported in *The Competitive Advantage of Nations,* that the converged IT industry will not be viable unless fierce competition exists in the competitor's home market. We can infer from Porter's approach that currently only the United States is situated to succeed, given the failure to date of the Japanese in software and networks and the "country champion" approach that persists in most European countries. Thus, according to Porter's thesis, countries will be required to develop a critical mass of competitors domestically in order to survive globally.

We disagree with this analysis. The same forces of globalization and networks that we see transforming the IT industry are likely to transform competition among IT providers as well. Software development knows no national boundaries, and transmission of computer code and data is becoming faster and cheaper by the moment. Porter's analysis may well be applicable to hardware production, which may depend on a thriving and competitive domestic industry to achieve the requisite interaction among design, engineering, and component supply. But software solutions and network integration, unlike traditional manufacturing, do not require low-cost inputs to be successful. On the contrary, they use relatively high-cost, human capital inputs in the form of highly educated individuals. Thus, we do not see a sustainable competitive advantage for the United States in the new IT industry, given newly available inputs from Eastern Europe and the former Soviet Union as well as the competition from European countries. Software development and the creation of customer solutions should be the ultimate exportable commodity, inasmuch as transportation costs will be near zero and governments will be unable to distort trade or protect inefficient domestic industry (since quotas and tariffs will be unenforceable). We thus envision global competition in the IT industry without the necessity of a large domestic market supporting numerous competing providers.

Notes

1. Christopher A. Bartlett and Sumantra Ghoshal, *Managing Across Borders* (Boston: Harvard Business School Press, 1989).

2. Stephen P. Bradley and Jerry A. Hausman, eds., *Future Competition in Telecommunications* (Boston: Harvard Business School Press, 1989).

3. Richard L. Nolan, "Managing the Computer Resource: A Stage Hypothesis," *Communications of the ACM,* 16, no. 7 (July 1973); and Richard L. Nolan, "Managing the Crisis in Data Processing," *Harvard Business Review* (March–April 1979): 115–126.

4. Shoshana Zuboff, in *In the Age of the Smart Machine* (New York: Basic Books, 1984).

5. Janice H. Hammond, "Quick Response in Retail Channels," Harvard Business School Working Paper 92068 (1991).

6. Pankaj Ghemawat, *Commitment: The Dynamic of Strategy* (New York: Free Press, 1991).

7. Andrew S. Rappaport and Shmuel Halevi, "The Computerless Computer Company," *Harvard Business Review* (July–August 1991):69–80.

8. Ibid.

9. All MATSO manufacturers, with the exception of Motorola and Novatel, a Canadian manufacturer, also manufacture central office switches.

10. Although we think this outcome is likely, certain economic theorists, beginning with Joseph Schumpeter, have argued that competition over technology will not necessarily increase the pace of technological change.

Part Two
Organizational Structures
for Global Strategies

Introduction

In his colloquium presentation Christopher Bartlett of the
Harvard Business School expanded on *Managing Across Borders,* his seminal work with Sumantra Ghoshal of INSEAD,
which deals with the emerging organizational model of the
transnational firm.[1] The transnational firm has an organizational structure that facilitates the simultaneous achievement
of three objectives—global efficiency, national responsiveness,
and the ability to develop and access knowledge on a worldwide
basis. Because these objectives often conflict with one another,
many firms pursue them selectively rather than simultaneously. Bartlett emphasized that simultaneous achievement
of these objectives will effectively define the successful global
company. Indeed, that management is being required to perform
at a higher level of sophistication than once thought possible,
and that new technologies are essential to achieving these
higher performance levels, were among the major themes of the
colloquium.

Globalization and technology are mutually reinforcing drivers
of change. Competition has been, and continues to be, a force
for management exploitation of the full potential of the global
market. This pressure to exploit the global market has turned
up a powerful enabler in information technology. Application of
existing technology, resulting in the realization of partial benefits of globalization, leads management to demand more sophisticated technology. The newer technology required to meet this
more need-specific demand enables further globalization. This

33

cycle has shaped the emergence of both new technologies and new organizational structures.

The emerging organizational structures, which take the form of dense, information-intensive networks, are beginning to make the traditional divisionalized functional hierarchy obsolete. The dimensions of global competition are encouraging management, traditionally slow to forsake known for unknown structures, to adopt these newer structures at a quicker pace. The informal networks that are overlaying traditional divisionalized functional hierarchies will be formalized over time and will eventually replace them.

A word such as "network" may be too simple to reflect the variety of these new organizational structures; nevertheless, that term captures their essence. Network, in contrast to hierarchy, connotes interconnected parts without an established chain of command. Interconnectedness also connotes efficiency, in that communication among different parts of the organization moves quickly.

The three chapters in this section afford readers a preview of the theory and process of designing the new network organizational structures essential to "becoming global." The principal message of the authors of these chapters is that the global organization is emerging in a form quite different from the traditional functional hierarchy, a form that facilitates organizational performance at higher, more sophisticated levels and enables the effective resolution of conflicting objectives such as global efficiency and local service response to narrow, niche markets.

Reshaping Organizations with Computer Technology

Massachusetts Institute of Technology professors Thomas Malone and John Rockart pose the question: "How will information technology reshape organizations?" Their examination of the first- and second-order impacts of improved technology on organizations led them to conclude that technology makes markets vastly more efficient. Thus, many transactions previously conducted most efficiently within the firm now can be conducted more efficiently outside the firm through new markets, as evidenced not only in the creation of electronic markets, but also in the wider use of outsourcing. They further conclude that the costs of both internal and external coordination are very important and must be explicitly managed in emerging global organizations.

Designing the Emerging Global Organization

Harvard Business School professors Robert Eccles and Richard Nolan have been students of the evolving network organization from different perspectives. The results of Eccles' studies of the network organization in the investment banking industry, conducted with Dwight Crane, also of the Harvard Business School, are reported in *Doing Deals*.[2] The authors' conclusion that the industry is, indeed, evolving toward a network form of organization includes identification of such key characteristics as the organic form of the structure. Nolan has been a consultant for organizations making the transition from traditional to network structures. Eccles and Nolan have blended their academic research and consulting experience into a framework for the design of the emerging global network organization structure. This framework consists of a series of core infrastructures that provide the basis for shared resources and common utilities. Within these infrastructures, self-designed, project-oriented teams "do the work" of the firm in acquiring resources to serve markets and customers.

Eccles and Nolan present only one of several possible approaches for designing the evolving global network organization, but it identifies a number of key elements that must be incorporated in any effective approach, among them the ability to create high levels of market responsiveness and efficiency, and to create a highly flexible, organic structure that can expand to meet any opportunity and rapidly contract when an opportunity has been identified.

Eccles and Nolan conclude that traditional approaches to organizational design are too laden with obsolete institutionalized concepts, such as centralization versus decentralization, to be effectively used in the design of the global network organization. General managers, they argue, must look to new concepts and new approaches.

Global Information Systems in the Transnational Context

In the concluding chapter of this section, Benn Konsynski of Emory University and Jahangir Karimi of the University of Colorado expand on the transnational structures described by Bartlett and Ghoshal, then focus on the design of global information systems within the context of the transnational organization.

They describe the evolution from information systems contained almost entirely within traditional firm boundaries to interorganizational, and even national, information systems, such as the Singapore government's port management system. The authors attempt to reconcile Malone and Rockart's probing of information technology's impact on the firm with Eccles and Nolan's conceptual design framework. They describe extant cases of global information systems that provide a preview of emerging applications of information technology that may soon become commonplace.

Notes

1. Christopher A. Bartlett and Sumantra Ghoshal, *Managing Across Borders* (Boston: Harvard Business School Press, 1989).
2. Robert G. Eccles and Dwight B. Crane, *Doing Deals: Investment Banks at Work* (Boston: Harvard Business School Press, 1988).

2

How Will Information Technology Reshape Organizations? Computers as Coordination Technology

Thomas W. Malone and John F. Rockart

Introduction

About one hundred and fifty years ago, business in America and elsewhere began to experience a change more profound than any since the end of the Middle Ages. That change was called the Industrial Revolution. We are now in the early stages of another business change that may prove to be at least as significant.

In the early 1800s, as documented by Chandler[1] and others, America was a nation of small shops, family farms, and individual craftspeople. Merchants and other agents facilitated market transactions among these small entrepreneurs, the functions performed today by banks, brokers, distributors, and insurance companies. Then, about 1840, the world began to change. Factories, railroads, and steam engines allowed materials to be produced and moved more rapidly and cheaply, and over greater distances, than had ever been possible. Entire new industries, such as the railroads, came into being, and vast wealth was created. Almost all businesses were affected by the possibilities of the new technologies. To take advantage of economies of scale in production and transportation, huge new organizations were created, each containing tens of thousands of employees and numerous layers of professional managers.

Businesses are again beginning to change dramatically, a key driver this time being the development of new information technologies. Computers and communication networks allow us to move, store, and process information faster, more cheaply, and over greater distances than ever before. These new technologies have already led to the creation of new industries (such as the computer industry), to the accumulation of new wealth, and to changes in almost all kinds of business.

But there is a critical difference this time. The Industrial Revolution of the last century was driven by changes in the economics of production and transportation. Although information technologies do affect these processes, the primary changes in the revolution under way today are being driven not by changes in *production* but by changes in *coordination*. Whenever people work together, they must communicate, make decisions, and allocate resources. They must arrange to have the right things in the right places at the right times. They must decide what to do and who will do which parts of it. These coordination activities are performed by managers, clerks, salespeople, buyers, brokers, accountants, and, to some degree, by almost everyone who works.[2]

It is in these heavily information-based activities that information technologies have some of their most important uses, and it is here they will have their most profound effects. The very term "computer" suggests that we usually think of computers as machines for "computing," that is, for taking in information, performing calculations or other manipulations, and presenting the results. This image of computing fails to capture the essence of what computers are really used for today in almost all industries, and how they will be used in the future.

Many of the most important uses of computers today, for tasks such as order entry, inventory control, and accounting, are actually ways of helping large groups of people coordinate their activities. As computers are increasingly connected to one another, there will be many more ways these systems can be used to help groups of people coordinate. In short, we suspect that in the next few decades computers and computer networks may well be remembered not as a technology used primarily to compute things, but as a technology used primarily to coordinate things—that is, as "coordination technology."

We believe that by dramatically reducing the costs of coordination and increasing its speed and quality, these new technologies will enable us to coordinate more effectively, to coordinate previously isolated activities, and to evolve new, coordination-intensive business structures. One possible outcome of the Information Revolution in many industries may be a return to the small organizations of the pre-Industrial Revolution era. Because new technologies make it easier for people to coordinate across firm boundaries and over wide regions, we are already seeing the emergence of networks of firms that work together flexibly to produce products that would previously have been produced by a single large firm. The makers of automobiles and computers, for example, today outsource extensively to produce more and more of the components in their products. Some products, such as the fabrics woven in the mills of Prato, Italy, are produced by networks of thousands of small firms. Eventually, we may see extreme versions of this structure, in which computer networks coalesce many independent contractors into "virtual organizations" almost overnight to solve a problem or produce a product in a matter of days.

In the Industrial Revolution, the firms that triumphed were those organized to take advantage of mass production and transportation technologies. In the Information Revolution, the firms that benefit most will be those that take advantage of new coordination technologies to better integrate the work of people within companies and to link companies more effectively to one another.

An Analogy: The Effects of Improved Transportation Technology

To understand what is likely to happen as the costs and capabilities of information technology continue to improve dramatically, let us consider an analogy with transportation technology. Like information technology, transportation technology is a pervasive factor of production. Also like information technology (although not to the same degree), transportation technology improved significantly in both cost and performance over the last century and a half. Using simple notions from economics, we can analyze the changes that occurred in three categories: substitution, increased use, and new structures.

A first-order effect of reducing transportation costs with trains and automobiles was simply substitution of the new transportation technologies for the old. People began to ride in trains and cars more and on horses and in horse-drawn carriages less.

As transportation technology improved, people began to use

it as more than a substitute for earlier forms of transportation. A second-order effect of reducing transportation costs was to increase the amount of transportation people used. When trains and cars made travel cheaper and more convenient, people began to travel more. They commuted farther to work each day; they traveled more often and farther for business meetings; and they were more likely to visit faraway friends and relatives.

Greatly increasing the amount of transportation people could feasibly use eventually led to a third-order effect: the creation of new "transportation-intensive" structures. People began to live in distant suburbs and shop in shopping malls—both examples of new structures that depended on the widespread availability of cheap and convenient transportation.

Effects of Improved Information Technology

What analogous effects might information technology have? First, information technology reduces the costs of production processes in many industries. Robotics and numerically controlled tools, for example, have been substituted for manual equipment and operators and have dramatically improved the costs and quality of some manufacturing processes. But effects on production tend to be highly industry-specific.

More significant, all industries will be affected by dramatic reductions in the costs of coordination. Our transportation analogy leads us to expect three types of effects, outlined below.

First-order effect: substitution. A first-order effect of reducing coordination costs with information technology is to substitute information technology for human coordination. For example, thousands of clerks were eliminated from the back offices of insurance companies and banks when data processing systems were first installed. Similarly, scores of factory "expediters" have been eliminated by computer-based systems that track the progress of each job in the factory and indicate which is to be given priority at each workstation.

More generally, it has long been predicted that computers will bring about the demise of middle management because the communication tasks performed by middle managers can be performed less expensively by computers.[3] Although this prediction went unfulfilled throughout the 1960s and 1970s, it began to be borne out in the 1980s, as many companies eliminated layers of middle managers and "flattened their hierarchies."

In addition to coordination within organizations, technology can also substitute for human effort in coordinating between organizations. For example, the jobs of many stockbrokers and trading specialists are being changed dramatically (and sometimes eliminated altogether) by trading systems that match buyers and sellers electronically, independent of location. Such a system was installed on the London Stock Exchange, and within weeks the floor was virtually deserted as trading moved to electronic terminals around the world.[4]

Second-order effect: increased demand. A second-order effect of reducing coordination costs is to increase overall the amount of coordination. Airline reservations systems in wide use today, for example, make it easy for travel agents to consider more flight possibilities for a given customer and have led to an explosion of special fares and price adjustments. American and United, the two airlines that provide the largest systems, have benefited significantly from the fees they charge for this interorganizational coordination service and from their access to information that allows them to adjust their fare schedules dynamically based on up-to-the-minute information about demand.

Otis Elevator Company, which significantly increased the amount of coordination involved in its elevator maintenance operation by installing a nationwide system called Otisline to manage its repair force, is another example. With Otisline, trouble calls are received by highly trained, multilingual operators at a national 800 number. The operators record problems in a computer database and electronically dispatch local repair people. This real-time availability of data on continentwide elevator problems has vastly improved the management of repair activities. If, for example, a particular part has failed in the last week on eight of 100 elevators of a particular type installed in 1982, Otis can preemptively replace that part on the other 92 elevators. Although such national correlation of data was always possible in principle, the amount of communication and coordination it required previously made it infeasible in practice. Now, together with other capabilities of the Otisline system, this additional coordination has played a major role in reducing maintenance calls by nearly 20% and significantly increasing customer goodwill.

The second-order effect of increasing demand may occasionally overwhelm the first-order substitution effect. For example, in one case we studied a computer conferencing system that was used to help eliminate a layer of middle managers. Several years later, however, almost the same number of new positions (for different people at the same grade level) had been created for staff specialists in the corporate staff group, many of whom were helping to develop new computer systems.[5] When we asked what these new specialists did, we were told that they undertook projects that "we wouldn't have been able to consider before." One interpretation of this outcome is that the managerial resources no longer needed for simple communication tasks could now be applied to more complex analysis tasks that once would have been left undone.

Third-order effect: new structures. A third-order effect of reducing coordination costs is to encourage a shift toward the use of more coordination-intensive structures. Some 10,000 Frito-Lay route salesmen, for example, use hand-held computers to record sales for each of 200 grocery products as they are delivered to each customer on their route.[6] Every night the stored information is transmitted to a central computer, and information on changes in pricing and promotions are sent to the hand-held computers for use the next day. Each week, the centrally stored information is summarized, combined with purchased competitive data, and made accessible to some 40 senior executives through an executive information system (EIS).

The availability of this data has enabled Frito-Lay to decentralize decision making from corporate headquarters to four area heads and some 30 district managers. These managers are expected to utilize the data not only to monitor how well they are doing against sales targets, but also to recommend changes in sales strategy to top management. This entire coordination-intensive structure has been possible only in the past few years, as hand-held computers, EIS software, computer cycles, and telecommunications capability have improved significantly and dropped dramatically in cost.

Many of the most interesting new coordination-intensive structures involve links between different organizations. The American textile industry, for example, as illustrated in Figure 2-1, is implementing a series of electronic connections all along the value chain from suppliers of fibers (such as wool and cot-

Figure 2-1
Electronic Linkages on the Value Chain for Men's Slacks

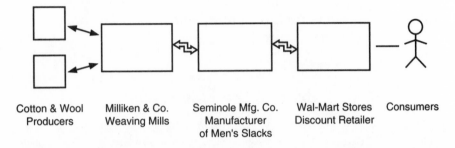

| Cotton & Wool
Producers | Milliken & Co.
Weaving Mills | Seminole Mfg. Co.
Manufacturer
of Men's Slacks | Wal-Mart Stores
Discount Retailer | Consumers |

Note: One of the first large-scale experiments with electronic linkages in the apparel industry returned the value chain for men's slacks from weaving mill to retail store. Wal-Mart experienced 30% increases in unit sales and inventory turnover rate.

ton), through the mills that weave these fibers into fabric, to the factories that sew garments and, ultimately, to the stores that sell them to consumers.[7] When networks like this are fully implemented, the sale of a sweater in New York will trigger shipping and production activities all the way back to the wool warehouse. This new multiorganization structure will thus reduce inventory costs throughout the value chain and make the entire industry more responsive to changes in consumer tastes. Wal-Mart has already established parts of a similar system with electronic connections to Procter & Gamble and several other major suppliers. In doing so, it has eliminated significant parts of its own purchasing groups and contracted with its suppliers to replace products as they are sold.

Sometimes technology helps create interorganizational networks, not only among buyers and suppliers, but also among potential competitors. For example, members of the Rosenbluth International Alliance, a consortium of travel agencies around the world, share customer records, services, and software and provide toll-free English-language help lines in every major country.[8] This consortium, led by Rosenbluth Travel in Philadelphia, can manage all travel arrangements for international trips and for meetings of people from many parts of the globe.

The textile firms near Prato, Italy, illustrate a related kind of interorganizational alliance.[9] There, the operations of a few large textile mills were broken apart into many small firms, coordinated, in part, by electronic connections. This network of firms is able to adjust flexibly to changes in demand, sometimes shifting orders from an overloaded firm to one with spare capacity. It also benefits from the entrepreneurial motivations of the owners of the small firms.

Greater Use of Markets

Information technology, as these examples illustrate, is already facilitating the emergence of new, coordination-intensive structures.[10] What do these changes mean for the organizations of the near future?

One surprising result of our research is the prediction that information technology will precipitate an overall shift toward proportionately greater use of markets, rather than internal decisions within firms, to coordinate economic activity.[11] To understand why, consider that all organizations must choose between making the goods or services they need internally, or buying them through market transactions with external suppliers. General Motors, for example, must decide whether to make tires or buy them from a tire manufacturer. As Figure 2-2 summarizes, market transactions often require higher coordination costs than internal coordination within a firm.[12] For example, to buy something in a market, you may need to compare a number of potential suppliers, negotiate contracts, and perform formal accounting for the money that changes hands. But a market purchase has the advantage of allowing the buyer to benefit

Figure 2-2
Relative Costs for External Market Transactions
and Internal Hierarchical Coordinations

Coordination Mechanism	Production Costs	Coordination Costs
Markets	Low	High
Hierarchies	High	Low

Note: Buying something from an external supplier instead of making it allows a firm to exploit economies of scale and realize other production cost advantages, but usually requires higher coordination costs related to finding a supplier, accounting for payments, and negotiating contracts.

from the supplier's economies of scale and to choose the best product currently available as needs change.

By this reasoning, an overall reduction in the unit costs of coordination should reduce the disadvantages of market purchases. This, in turn, should lead to markets becoming more desirable in situations in which internal transactions were previously favored. Thus, we should expect the widespread use of information technology to lead to more "buying" instead of "making" (that is, to less vertical integration) and to smaller firms.

Exceptions to these predictions might be found in industries in which reductions in production costs are greater than reductions in coordination costs. Also, some coordination technologies might improve internal coordination more than market coordination. But in the long run, for most industries, we expect overall decreases in the costs of coordination to lead to more market-based coordination. We expect to see, for example, more electronically mediated alliances (such as that of Rosenbluth International) and increasing use of electronic markets to choose suppliers (e.g., the airline reservations systems). We also expect large firms to make much greater use of transfer pricing and other market-like mechanisms to coordinate internal activities.

More efficient markets. One important implication of this argument is simply that information technology helps make markets more efficient. No longer do buyers have to exert great effort to compare products and prices from many different suppliers. An electronic market can easily and inexpensively collect and distribute such information. This suggests that electronic markets are especially likely to appear in industries where the benefits of electronic search are greatest. For example, as Arthur Warbelow points out, factors that encourage electronic markets include: widely scattered buyers and sellers, large price differences, and rapidly changing product availability.[13]

The observation that market efficiency will increase also suggests that firms whose strategic advantage rests on market inefficiencies may be threatened. For example, the availability of an electronic network for the London Stock Exchange greatly reduced the cost of matching buyers and sellers and also dramatically reduced the profits of brokers and specialists who previously had a monopoly on performing this function.

Many other kinds of brokers, distributors, and retailers are similarly vulnerable. Consumers, for example, can now bypass retail stores entirely using computer-based systems like Comp-U-Card and Compu-Store to buy household goods and services at substantial savings. Electronic markets can also make it easier to evaluate product quality. We suspect that it is only a matter of time before networks contain extensive comments and evaluations from previous buyers of products sold electronically—a kind of instantaneous, on-line *Consumer Reports.*

Outsourcing more, but with fewer companies. Another implication of increasing market efficiency is that firms may focus on the few core competencies that offer them strategic advantage in the marketplace and buy, rather than make, most of the other products and services they need. In the past few years, for example, both Ford and Chrysler have significantly increased the proportion of components they purchase externally.

This increasing use of external suppliers does not always mean, however, that firms should use a greater *number* of suppliers. In fact, in many industries, there has been a decrease in the number of suppliers used. In one study, for instance, the average number of suppliers for automobile firms decreased by 25% between 1983 and 1988,[14] and Motorola has reduced its supplier base from 10,000 to 3,000 in the past few years.[15] In other words, firms can benefit by outsourcing more, but especially by outsourcing through close relationships with a smaller number of suppliers.[16] As Yannis Bakos and Erik Brynjolfsson point out, this makes sense because by doing so a firm can increase the incentives for its suppliers to invest in quality improvements.[17]

Continuing competitive advantage. A related implication is that single innovations in information technology are seldom, in themselves, likely to be a source of continuing competitive advantage. Contrary to original expectations, systems such as American Hospital Supply's link to customers do not usually "lock in" customers to one vendor in the long run. Eventually, customers are likely to gravitate to other electronic systems that make markets more efficient by offering a choice among several vendors. Similarly, a bank ATM system that can be imitated by competitors soon becomes a competitive necessity rather than a competitive advantage.

One way to maintain continuing competitive advantage from

information technology is to innovate so rapidly that even would-be imitators are always a step behind. Another is to use information technology to leverage some existing structural advantage. Barclays de Zoete Wedd, a British stockbroker, has been able to obtain continuing benefit from an electronic stock trading system because it was already the market maker for far more stocks than any of its competitors.[18]

Adhocracies

Another coordination-intensive organizational structure likely to become much more common in the future is what some management theorists call a "networked organization," or (more picturesquely) an "adhocracy."[19] This organizational form is already common in organizations such as law firms, consulting companies, and research universities, which must readjust continually to a changing mix of projects, each requiring a somewhat different combination of skills and resources. This structure makes heavy use of rapidly shifting project teams and highly decentralized networks of relatively autonomous entrepreneurial groups. People communicate laterally throughout the organization to manage interdependencies in projects, without relying so much on traditional hierarchical decision making (see Figure 2-3).

The large amount of unpredictable lateral communication makes this organizational structure extremely coordination-intensive. New electronic media, such as electronic mail, video-conferencing, and electronic bulletin boards, enable it to work much more effectively. Computer networks, for example, can be used to find and coordinate people with diverse knowledge and skills from many parts of an organization. New computer-based technologies are particularly useful for this purpose because they can transfer information not only faster and more cheaply, but also more selectively. For example, systems now exist to help people find, filter, and prioritize their electronic mail based on topic, sender, and other attributes.[20] Technologies such as these can help combat information overload. Together, these capabilities enable new coordination technologies to help speed up the "information metabolism" of organizations, that is, the rate at which organizations can take in information, move it around, digest it, and respond to it.

Figure 2-3
Corporate Structures

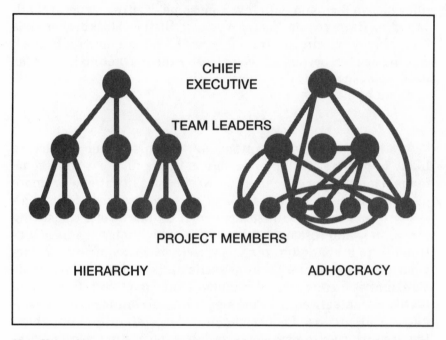

Note: Hierarchies are a common organizational form today in part because they provide an "economical" way of coordinating large numbers of people: by bringing diverse information to central points for decision making. Adhocracies rely much more heavily on unplanned lateral communication throughout an organization. As the costs of communication decline and the need for flexibility increases, adhocracies will become more common.

Incentives for information sharing. One of the important implementation questions in using technology to support an adhocracy is how to provide incentives that encourage people to share information. For example, in a study of how one large consulting firm used a group computer conferencing system, Wanda Orlikowski found that there were surprising inconsistencies between the intended uses of the system and the actual incentives in the organization.[21]

At a simple level, for instance, an important part of the performance evaluation of professionals in this organization was based upon their billable hours. Professionals were not allowed, however, to bill the hours they spent learning to use the conferencing system. Should we be surprised, therefore, that many people did not take the time to learn this somewhat complex system?

At a more subtle level, Orlikowski observed that this organization (like many others) was one in which people were rewarded for being the "expert" on something—for knowing things that others did not. Was it any surprise, therefore, that many people were reluctant to put the things they knew into a database where everyone else could easily see them?

These observations do not, of course, mean that conferencing systems like this one cannot be useful in organizations. What they do mean is that we must be sensitive to subtle issues like incentives and organizational culture in order to obtain the full benefits of such systems.

Global Organizations

Since information technology clearly makes it easier for people to interact over long distances, it (along with advanced transportation technologies like jet airplanes) facilitates the emergence of truly global organizations. All the organizational structures we have discussed so far can occur not only on a local scale, but also on a global scale. For example, many of today's global corporations increasingly use adhocracy-like project teams with participants from all over the world to design new products and plan new strategies. Similarly, worldwide electronic markets for foreign currencies and other financial instruments exemplify an increasing globalization of markets for many kinds of goods and services.

Together, these new technologies are leading to a world where different national economies and different subsidiaries of the same corporation are no longer quasi-independent, autonomous entities. Instead, as is obvious to even casual readers of world news, our global economies and companies are becoming increasingly interdependent. Fortunately, as the increasing global integration of today's largest companies illustrates, the same technologies that have helped create these global interdependencies can also help manage them.

Centralization and Decentralization

Plentiful information poses two potential problems of organizational power. First, some people worry that managers might become Big Brothers that use information to exert strong centralized control over those who work for them. Alternatively, others worry that if power were decentralized throughout the organization, workers might use their newfound powers to serve their own narrow interests, leading to organizational chaos.[22]

In practice, neither of these two dark visions has materialized. What appears to be happening is a paradoxical combination of centralization and decentralization. Because information can be distributed more easily, people lower in the organization can now become well enough informed to make more decisions effectively. At the same time, upper level managers can now more easily review the decisions made at lower levels. Senior managers thus retain (or even increase) centralized control over decisions, and lower level decision makers are aware that their decisions can be routinely spot checked by senior managers.

At Phillips Petroleum, for example, the critical decision of what price to set for petroleum products was originally made by senior managers, based primarily upon recommendations of staff analysts several levels down in the organization. When the firm deployed an executive information system, senior managers began to make some of these decisions directly, based upon the "global" information provided by the system. But they soon discovered that passing this information on to local terminal managers, who could also take into account local information concerning competitors' prices, would produce sounder pricing strategies in each area of the country. The pricing decision was thus decentralized, adding significantly to the company's bottom line.

Another way of understanding this paradoxical effect is to realize that the new technology does not just redistribute power: it can provide a sense of greater power for everyone. For example, several insurance companies' agents already carry laptop computers when they visit customers' homes. The agents use these computers to fill out applications and do instant projections of premiums and benefits. It then takes several weeks to transmit new applications back to headquarters, have them reviewed by underwriters, and issue new policies. Soon, however, the underwriting rules for certain routine policies will be included in the laptop computer, making it possible for agents to issue policies in customers' homes.

These systems will empower the agents, enabling them to control the time and place at which the underwriting decisions are made and to make sales immediately. But the power of the central underwriters will be increased, too. The underwriting rules they create will be consistently applied in the laptops, allowing the underwriters to devote more time to analyzing interesting, and potentially more profitable, nonroutine cases.

Emerging Organizational Structures

The changes we have discussed so far require no great predictive leaps; they are already happening. But what will happen as information technology continues to improve? What other kinds of organizations might emerge in the globally interconnected world these new technologies make possible?

Answer Networks

One possibility is "answer networks," networks of experts available to answer questions in different areas. One might turn to these networks with such questions as "How many bars of soap were sold in Guatemala last year?" or "What are the prospects for room-temperature superconductivity in consumer products by 1995?" Answer networks would involve massive databases and layers of human experts in many different topic areas (see Figure 2-4). Some questions could be answered easily from information in a database. Others would be referred to progressively more knowledgeable human experts. Depending on how much an inquirer was willing to spend and how quickly an answer was wanted, a reply might range from a newspaper clipping to a personal response from a Nobel laureate scientist. Limited services of this kind exist today (e.g., product hot lines and library reference desks), but computer networks and databases will make such services less expensive, more valuable, and therefore, more widely used.

Overnight Organizations

A related possibility is that we will use electronically mediated markets to assemble "overnight armies of intellectual mercenaries." These might take the form of large numbers of consultants who earn a living doing short-term projects over a network. One could, for whatever job was to be done (e.g., evaluating a loan or designing a lawnmower), quickly assemble a

Figure 2-4
Answer Network

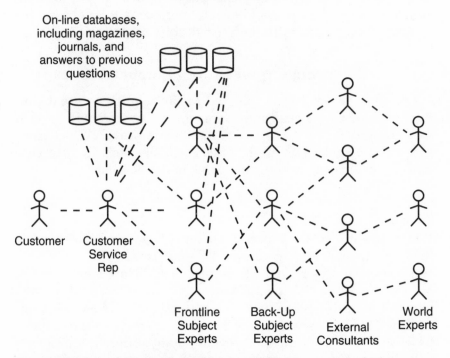

On-line databases, including magazines, journals, and answers to previous questions

Customer   Customer Service Rep

Frontline Subject Experts   Back-Up Subject Experts   External Consultants   World Experts

Note: One kind of organization that will become much more common in the future is an "answer network." Callers will interact with customer service representatives who are connected to massive computer databases and layer upon layer of experts.

team by advertising electronically and/or consulting a database of available people. This database might contain not only peoples' skills and billing rates, but also unedited comments from others who had used their services. Although consulting firms and advertising agencies do such things now, pervasive networks will enable teams to be assembled more quickly, for shorter projects, and from many different organizations.

Internal Labor Markets

Markets for services might be used within an organization as well. Rather than rely on supervisors to allocate the time of people who work for them, extensive internal markets might be developed for the services of people and groups. A department with a small programming project, for example, might advertise internally for a programmer. Even if not in real dollars, "bids" received from prospective programmers would reflect their skill levels and availability, and "payments" to these programmers would reflect how valuable they had been to other parts of the organization.

Computer-Mediated Decision Networks

Another likely structure is one that integrates input from many people in making complex decisions. In deciding, for example, where to locate a new plant, many kinds of facts and opinions are useful. Today such decisions are often made after incomplete discussions with only a few of the people whose input might be valuable. In the future, we may use computer networks to organize and record the issues, alternatives, arguments, and counterarguments in graphical structures that illustrate their interrelationships, thereby enabling many different people to review the parts of the argument they know or care about and contribute their own knowledge and opinions. Someone in a remote part of an organization might be aware, for example, of a planned highway that would completely change the desirability of a proposed plant location. As inputs are collected, people can vote on the plausibility of different claims. Then, using all the information displayed in the system, a single decision maker or group can make a decision.

Conclusions

To conclude, let us project even further into the future. Imagine, for instance, that storing, transmitting, and processing vast amounts of information become almost free and instantaneous. All the information now stored on paper anywhere in the world can be searched and retrieved at almost no cost. Video connections to any person or archival store on the globe are essentially free. What will our organizations look like in this context?

One obvious characteristic of this world will be that automated and human filtering services are extremely valuable. People who can creatively analyze, edit, and act upon information in ways that cannot yet be automated will become even more valuable when the information available to them is vastly increased.

What we do in such a world of information will also depend on what else is important to us. When trains and automobiles reduced the constraints of travel time, other values became more important in determining living patterns. As Kenneth Jackson has documented, for example, American values about the importance of owning one's home and the moral superiority of rural life played a large role in determining the nature of American suburbs.[23]

Similarly, when the costs of information and coordination are no longer a barrier to getting what we want, other things we value will become more important in determining what our lives are like. But what do we really want that information technology might help us achieve? Consider the following traditional Middle Eastern story about people's desires.[24]

> THE FOUR MEN AND THE INTERPRETER
>
> Four people were given a piece of money.
> The first was a Persian. He said: "I will buy with this some *angur*."
> The second was an Arab. He said: "No, because I want *inab*."
> The third was a Turk. He said: "I do not want *inab*, I want *uzum*."
> The fourth was a Greek. He said: "*I* want *stafil*."
> Because they did not know what lay behind the names of things, these four started to fight. They had information but no knowledge.
> One man of wisdom present could have reconciled them all, saying: "I can fulfill the needs of all of you, with one and the same piece of money. If you honestly give me your trust, your one coin will become as four; and four at odds will become as one united."
> Such a man would know that each in his own language wanted the same thing, grapes.

The travelers all wanted the same thing, but they had different names for it. Although we use different names for the things we want (money, power, fame, love), there may be deeper needs that all of these desires are attempts to fill.

New kinds of information technology will almost certainly help satisfy some of our obvious desires for things like money. But to use the new technology wisely, we will need to think more carefully about what it is we really want. New organizational structures, for example, may be particularly good at satisfying needs for nonmaterial things, such as challenge and autonomy. And perhaps, as the story suggests, all these desires are themselves manifestations of still deeper desires that technology-mediated organizations might help to satisfy, if only we can recognize them.

Acknowledgments

Adapted from "Computers, Networks and the Corporation," by Thomas W. Malone and John F. Rockart, copyright © 1991. All rights reserved. (*Scientific American*, 265, no. 3, September 1991: 92–99.) A previous version of this chapter appeared as T. W. Malone and J. F. Rockart, "Information Technology and the New Organization," *Proceedings of the Hawaii International Conference on Systems Sciences (HICSS)*, Koloa, Hawaii, January 7–10, 1992.

Preparation of this paper was supported by the MIT Center for Coordination Science and the MIT Center for Information Systems Research.

Notes

1. A. D. Chandler, Jr., *The Visible Hand: The Managerial Revolution in American Business* (Cambridge, Mass.: Harvard University Press, 1977).

2. T. W. Malone and K. G. Crowston, *Toward An Interdisciplinary Theory of Coordination* (Massachusetts Institute of Technology, Center for Coordination Science Technical Report 120 (1991).

3. H. J. Leavitt and T. L. Whisler, "Management in the 1980s," *Harvard Business Review* (November–December 1958): 41–48.

4. E. K. Clemons and B. W. Weber, "London's Big Bang: A Case Study of Information Technology, Competitive Impact, and Organizational Change," *Journal of Management Information Systems*, 6, no. 4 (1990): 41–60.

5. K. G. Crowston, T. W. Malone, and F. Lin, "Cognitive Science and Organizational Design: A Case Study of Computer Conferencing," *Human Computer Interaction*, 3 (1987): 59–85.

6. J. Linder and M. Mead, "Frito-Lay, Inc.: A Strategic Transition (A)." Harvard Business School Case 9-187-065 (1986); N. A. Wishart and L. M. Applegate, "Frito-Lay, Inc.: A Strategic Transition (B)." Harvard Business School Case 9-187-123 (1987); and L. M. Applegate and N. A. Wishart. "Frito-Lay, Inc.: A Strategic Transition (C)." Harvard Business School Case 9-190-071 (1989).

7. J. H. Hammond and M. G. Kelly, "Quick Response in the Apparel Industry." Harvard Business School Case 9-690-038 (1990).

8. E. K. Clemons and M. C. Row, "Information Technology at Rosenbluth Travel: Competitive Advantage in a Rapidly Growing Global Service Company," *Journal of Management Information Systems* (in press).

9. M. J. Piore and C. F. Sabel, *The Second Industrial Divide* (New York: Basic Books, 1984); and R. Johnson and P. R. Lawrence, "Beyond Vertical Integration: The Rise of the Value-Adding Partnership," *Harvard Business Review* (July–August 1988): 94–104.

10. V. Gurbaxani and S. Whang, "The Impact of Information Systems on Organizations and Markets," *Communications of the ACM*, 34, no. 1 (1991): 59–73.

11. T. W. Malone, J. Yates, and R. I. Benjamin, "Electronic Markets and Electronic Hierarchies," *Communications of the ACM*, 30 (1987): 484–497;

T. W. Malone, "Modeling Coordination in Organizations and Markets," *Management Science*, 33 (1987): 1317–1332; and T. W. Malone, and S. A. Smith, "Modeling the Performance of Organizational Structures," *Operations Research*, 36, no. 3 (1988): 421–436.

12. O. E. Williamson, *Markets and Hierarchies* (New York: Free Press, 1975).

13. A. W. Warbelow, "Electronic Market Access Forums in Non-Homogenous Markets: An Exploratory Study of Environmental, Market Structure, and Managerial Considerations." Unpublished D.B.A. thesis, Harvard Business School (1992).

14. S. Helper, "How Much Has Really Changed Between U.S. Automakers and Their Suppliers?," *Sloan Management Review* (Summer 1991): 15–27.

15. J. R. Emshwiller, "Suppliers Struggle to Improve Quality as Big Firms Slash Their Vendor Rolls," *The Wall Street Journal* (August 8, 1991): B1, B2.

16. E. K. Clemons and S. P. Reddi, "The Impact of Information Technology on the Organization of Production: The 'Move to the Middle' Hypothesis." University of Pennsylvania, Wharton School Working Paper (1992).

17. J. Y. Bakos and E. Brynjolfsson, "When Quality Matters: Information Technology and Buyer-Supplier Relationships." Massachusetts Institute of Technology, Center for Coordination Science Technical Report (1992).

18. E. K. Clemons and B. W. Weber, "Barclays de Zoete Wedd's TRADE: Evaluating the Competitive Impact of a Strategic Information System," in *Proceedings, 23rd Hawaii International Conference on Systems Sciences* (January 1990): 137–146.

19. A. Toffler, *Future Shock* (New York: Bantam Books, 1970); and H. Mintzberg, *The Structuring of Organizations* (Englewood Cliffs, N.J.: Prentice-Hall, 1979).

20. T. W. Malone, K. R. Grant, F. A. Turbak, S. A. Brobst, and M. D. Cohen, "Intelligent Information-sharing Systems," *Communications of the ACM*, 30 (1987): 390–402.

21. W. J. Orlikowski, "Learning from Notes: Organizational Issues in Groupware Implementation." Massachusetts Institute of Technology, Center for Coordination Science Technical Report 131 (1992).

22. J. Pfeffer, *Power in Organizations* (Marshfield, Mass.: Pitman Publishing, 1981); and D. Mechanic, "Sources of Power of Lower Participants in Complex Organizations," *Administrative Sciences Quarterly*, 7 (1962): 349–364.

23. K. T. Jackson, *Crabgrass Frontier: The Suburbanization of the United States* (New York: Oxford University Press, 1985).

24. Idries Shah, *The Way of the Sufi* (London: Octagon Press, 1980): 103.

3

A Framework for the Design of the Emerging Global Organizational Structure

Robert G. Eccles and Richard L. Nolan

To compete in a global economy requires an organization that is managed on a global basis. Global management entails balancing the general or universal with the specific or particular. Shared resources and common management practices provide a general or universal infrastructure for obtaining economies of scale and scope, effective innovation, and shared learning; specific or particular localized resources and management practices enable the organization to adapt to globally diverse local environments along such dimensions as consumer tastes, work force characteristics, and government regulation.[1]

Bartlett and Ghoshal's "transnational" organization is an integrated network of assets and resources that can achieve global efficiencies and national responsiveness simultaneously, and that possesses the ability to develop and exploit knowledge on a worldwide basis.[2] They contrast the transnational organization with prevailing models of multinational, global, and international organizations that sacrifice certain competitive capabilities to achieve others. Their notion of a transnational organization suggests that managers who must compete on a global basis must be able to operate at levels of sophistication previously not thought possible.

Building on Bartlett and Ghoshal's research, a Nolan, Norton & Co. research study identified the key characteristics of a global organization.[3] These are depicted in Figure 3-1 as a series of creative destructions moving from the attributes of the non-transformed organization (i.e., operating in the Industrial Econ-

Figure 3-1
Becoming Global

Today	Business Attributes to be Transformed	Global
Geographic Concept		Business Concept
Centralization/ Decentralization		Any Place
Mechanistic		Holistic
Isolationism		Low Boundaries
Not Invented Here		Networks of Trust
Geographic Presence		Cultural Fit
Central Controllers		Core Connectors
Replication of Resources		Economies of Scale
Stove Pipes		Great Communications
Short-Term Focus		Long-Term View

Source: J. L. Daniels and N. C. Frost, "On Becoming a Global Corporation," *Stage by Stage* 8, no. 5 (November–December 1990).

omy) to the transformed organization (i.e., operating in the Information Economy). These characteristics were summarized from research conducted at ten of IBM's major global customers that had undertaken significant initiatives in developing global strategies. They represent a general consensus of the senior management interviewed on outcomes they were striving to achieve from their various global initiatives. (Pierre Hessler, in Chapter 10, comments further on this research.)

Bartlett and Ghoshal are among a growing number of scholars who see the need for and evidence of new models of organization.[4] Our contribution to this literature examines the global economy as opposed to Bartlett and Ghoshal's particular definition of global companies, since our aim is to highlight the role of information technology in creating global organizations. We consider Bartlett and Ghoshal's work among the best current thinking on managing in a global environment, but they ignore the role of information technology. We build on their work by focusing on global companies to create a more general theory of a new model of organization.

Our central point is that managing a global company requires two levels of design. The first level, that we call "superordinate design," is the responsibility of very senior management. This level is concerned with putting in place the infrastructure of assets, resources, and management practices that will be utilized by individuals throughout the company to perform the second level of design, which we term "self-design." Self-design involves individuals using the infrastructure to build relationships to accomplish what needs to be done. Richard Nolan and Alex Pollock described the notion of two levels of design as a "network floating on top of a hierarchy."[5] Although we believe that both levels are necessary, much current thinking argues that the hierarchical level might eventually be eliminated.

We begin by briefly sketching the role of information technology in the current economic transition. This transition is forcing companies to engage in a series of new business mandates that culminate in the need to become a global organization. We then discuss the organizational characteristics of the global organization. The concept of design is developed by describing seven organizational infrastructures. While other combinations can be developed for infrastructures, the seven we chose are inclusive of the key shared activities, and serve as the foundation for self-designing activities around strategy, structure, and systems. We conclude with some thoughts about how to most effectively manage these two levels of organizational design and discuss the changed role of senior management.

Impact of the Computer on Traditional Organizational Structure

In the Industrial Economy, the predominant organizational structure was the divisionalized functional hierarchy. Max Weber formally defined the hierarchy for organizing people to carry out activities directed toward organizational objectives.[6]

Start-up or small organizations have tended to be characterized by flat hierarchies. As they grow in size and complexity, these organizations migrate to functional hierarchies. General Motors' CEO Alfred Sloan was instrumental in operationalizing Weber's theoretical statements of bureacracy in business;[7] Du Pont introduced the idea of "divisionalization";[8] longtime consultant to General Motors, Peter Drucker, developed and documented the principles of management derived from the Theory of Bureaucracy.[9] General Electric later introduced the idea of strategic business units (SBUs).[10] Divisionalization and SBUs retain the principles of the functional hierarchy, but break the organization into centralized functions to be carried out by corporate, and decentralized functions to be carried out by operating, units.

Although it served business well for decades, this form of organization began to break down in the 1960s with the infusion of computers into organizations. Figure 3-2, based on analyses performed for Nolan, Norton & Co. clients, illustrates the change in the shape of the organization and communications from 1960 to 1980 and the conceptualization of organizations as informal networks floating on formal hierarchies.

One of the main reasons, if not the main reason, for the breakdown of the divisionalized functional hierarchy form of organization is the impact of the computer, a machine that enables information to be processed in a revolutionary manner in terms

Figure 3-2
Evolution of Organizational Structures

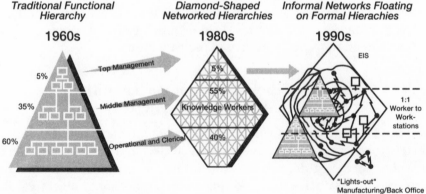

Source: Richard L. Nolan, unpublished presentation given at the "CEO Symposium" at the Harvard Business School on January 7, 1992.

of speed, storage, access, analysis, and geographical distribution. The development of computers first influenced the lower levels of traditional organizations, and more recently, has influenced the middle levels of organizations. The DP Era resulted in the automation of routine transaction processing, which led to downsizing the number of workers at the lower part of the organization. The Micro Era resulted in leveraging knowledge work of middle managers, which led to an overall breakdown in traditional communication channels and following the chain of command. Electronic networks emerged to the point that shadow networks are an important part of current organizations.

Further, the computer and its associated economics have made the cost of capturing information insignificant. Information capture has become a by-product of the cash register. When transactions are recorded, the information is captured in a medium that is cheap, and one that can be easily replicated and transmitted anywhere for pennies. With organizational information resources growing at an exponential rate and the pace of competition becoming increasingly dynamic, the organizational design principle of controlling the flow of information became obsolete.

Before computers, information was managed much as other scarce resources. In the functional hierarchy, the principal information medium was paper—memoranda, documents, reports— which was expensive to source, develop, and distribute.

The advent of the computer vastly changed the economics of information in the firm. With the cost of obtaining, refining, and distributing units of information trending toward zero, continued management of information as a scarce resource is inappropriate. Unlike other resources, information is not lost when it is used. Quite the contrary, wide use and distribution increase the value of information.[11]

In the information-rich global marketplace, organizations designed to control and channel information by strictly hierarchical principles cannot compete effectively. Modern organizational design must consider the proliferation of information in a manner that capitalizes on the existence of masses of information.

The computer imparted an economic value to information in much the same way that the refinery imparted an economic value to crude oil. The functional hierarchy as a form of organization existed before the advent of the computer. As the computer matured—from narrow mainframe forms to more robust forms made possible by the microcomputer—the assumptions of existing functional hierarchies for dealing with information flows and decision making came to be seen as constraining.[12] Ancillary forms of organization that better capitalized on the capabilities of the computer subsequently emerged around the formal hierarchy. In many organizations, these ancillary forms have become dominant in key areas of decision making, such as new product development, major capital investment, and responses to major competitive threats.

Analysis of these ancillary forms of organization led us to characterize them as emerging networks,[13] enabled by the capabilities of modern information technology.[14] These networks can be thought of as groups of workers (within as well as outside the formal organization) that employ a wide variety of information technologies to facilitate frequent, fast, robust communication toward a common purpose. Networks are less stable and more organic than functional hierarchies; during the process of accomplishing a shared purpose, workers in the network may change, and once a shared purpose is achieved, the network may be disbanded. New networks are regularly and instantaneously formed.

The focus of much recent attention by academics and managers, network organizations are designed by the people who constitute them. Who works with whom, and how, is not prescribed by higher management. Instead, individuals who need to get things done seek out and form working relationships with others who have the relevant expertise and commitment. From the perspective of senior management, the emergent network structure is self-designed.

Self-designed networks are best thought of as floating on top of functional hierarchies, or, more generally, designed infrastructures. Individuals access people and other resources—which are, in a sense, held or stored in the underlying infrastructures—as needed to accomplish their objectives.

A New Framework for Organizational Design

Most prevailing organizational design approaches were conceived for Industrial Economy environments. Our approach is proposed in light of the fast-paced, ever-changing environment of the Information Economy, in which business operations are entirely dependent on computer systems. In this context, we contrast key ideas of our proposed approach with those of traditional approaches.

First, traditional approaches are based on the assumption that senior management can design the total organizational structure. Certain business functions are centralized and others decentralized to divisionalized or lower business units. In contrast, we propose that only key, high-level infrastructures can be explicitly designed by senior management. Day-to-day decisions and operations related to getting work done are too dynamic and depend on fast response to diverse customer requirements; these decisions are best left to knowledge workers in self-designed networks.

Second, traditional approaches implicitly embody restrictions on the flow of and access to information. Decentralization in this context is a kind of necessary evil. Modern information technology—which can make information about an event available to everyone the instant it occurs—has abolished these information constraints.[15] Micromanagement, though rendered possible by this development, is undesirable because it undermines the effective exploitation of the potential value of knowledge workers—that is, stifles innovation and commitment.

Third, traditional approaches are based on a sharp, formal articulation of objectives and strategy. Subsidiary organizational units are provided with derivative narrow objectives. Our approach calls for the articulation of business visions that are fuzzy in comparison, but rich in statement of intentions and desired outcomes. These visions are analogous to John F. Kennedy's famous statement of vision in response to Russia's *Sputnik* satellite. Kennedy's vision was to put a man on the moon by the end of the decade. The proposal represented a stretch objective, the time dimension was definite, and accomplishment of the objective had a clear criterion. Subsidiary units are encouraged to make things "happen" by interpreting general information of the vision and taking actions to achieve the result.

We propose that organizational structures be created through the design of key infrastructures; these structures should support and nurture, transient and organic self-designed networks built upon and existing "on top" of underlying infrastructures.

Superordinate design. Superordinate organizational design consists of establishing the major shared infrastructures in which the organization will operate. These infrastructures, although they must be flexible, are the points of stability in which the organization operates and by which groups of knowledge workers can effect coordinated outcomes.

Although designing self-designed organizations might appear to be a contradiction in terms, what we mean is the designation of the bounds of action within the shared infrastructures, leaving actions relative to achieving specified outcomes to the discretion of the networks of knowledge workers. To operate in an environment of high uncertainty, the transformed global organization must rely on innovation and continuous learning by participating knowledge workers. And if this innovation and continuous learning is to be possible, knowledge workers must be given significant flexibility to act and modify procedures and approaches developed to serve customers in the marketplace.

Senior management is responsible for designing the infrastructures that knowledge workers use to create the networks necessary for getting things done. These infrastructures include human and financial capital as well as management practices and tools. We have identified seven superordinate designed infrastructures.

1. Core competencies and expertise infrastructure. C. K. Prahalad and Gary Hamel introduced the concept of "core competencies" that "coordinate diverse production skills and integrate multiple streams of technologies."[16] Core competencies and the expertise on which they are built are the basis of an organization's competitive advantage. They are what the organization must do better than any of their competitors to enjoy viability and profitability, and can range from the design and manufacture of small gasoline engines (e.g., Honda) to national electronic order entry (e.g., American Airlines). Thus, the firm must focus on core competencies, nurture their development, and innovate to continuously improve them. It is important for managers to have a clear understanding of these competencies. This is especially important and especially difficult, in a highly diversified company. Unless a company's core competencies are explicit and incorporated in its strategy, it is unlikely that the whole will be equal to the sum of its parts.

Senior management is responsible for identifying and articulating an organization's core competencies and ensuring that the skills and processes upon which they are based are continually developed and renewed. Continuous learning and innovation programs, up-to-date skills inventories, and targets for improvement are among the ways in which superordinate design of core competencies occurs.

Information technology contributes to the development of core competencies and expertise in several ways. Relational databases enable an organization to cumulatively build knowledge bases relevant to creating, nurturing, and maintaining core competencies. Multimedia workstation-based just-in-time training facilitates the renewal and growth of expertise upon which core competencies are developed.[17] And global telecommunications capabilities enable knowledge workers to share knowledge relevant to developing and utilizing the core competencies of the firm.

2. Shared knowledge and databases infrastructure. Core competencies, such as collective learning, depend upon shared knowledge, some of which can be captured in information data. More generally, Bartlett and Ghoshal identify "joint development and worldwide sharing of knowledge" as one of the key organizational characteristics of the transnational corporation.[18] Senior management must ensure that mechanisms exist to capture and make available throughout the organization knowledge developed in geographically dispersed parts of the global company. For example, appropriate tax advice and regulatory tax authorities' case decisions are extremely important knowledge to be shared among a public accounting firm's tax partners worldwide so as to ensure that clients operating in different countries are consistently and properly served.

In order to protect data integrity, specific databases must be maintained in designated parts of the company. For these databases to be available to other parts of the firm, common database standards and communications protocols must be established. Thus, data become an example of "dispersed and interdependent assets and resources,"[19] the organizational characteristic that supports the strategic capability of global competitiveness in the transnational corporation. Accomplishing this requires large relational databases, data administration software, and full penetration of workstations (i.e., one workstation for each knowledge worker).

3. Human assets and structural contour infrastructure. The knowledge and learning that form the basis of a firm's competitive advantage are ultimately generated by and reside in individual human beings within the firm. Developing a firm's human capital through recruiting, socialization, and training is part of senior management's superordinate design responsibilities.[20] So are decisions regarding the broad structural outline of the firm and the physical location of its human assets. Bartlett and Ghoshal point out that achieving the strategic capability of multinational flexibility requires "differentiated and specialized subsidiary roles."[21]

The functions and divisions that exist, and their physical locations, in turn affect the development of human capital. In recruiting, information technology can be used to develop computerized screening mechanisms and simulations, videos, and programmed exercises for training programs. Information technology also affects the broad structural contours of the firm in terms of levels, locations, and connections among knowledge workers.

4. Project tasking and team assignment infrastructure. The broad structural outline of a firm exists primarily for organizing its human assets and may have very little to do with how work actually gets done. The human assets and structural contour are the functional hierarchy on top of which float the shifting, self-designed networks of relationships that make practical use of the human assets available. And although senior management is not explicitly responsible for creating these networks, it is responsible for providing the tools for doing so. Thus, people must know how to locate assets, as through computerized organizational charts that contain information on workers' backgrounds and skills. They must also know who is available, for how long, and under what terms. Technologies such as E-mail, phone-mail, and computerized calendars can be employed to identify available resources and project management software to help managers control tasks and resources within the networks they assemble.

5. Performance measurement infrastructure. Senior management is responsible for establishing performance measures to assess how effectively individuals, functions, divisions, and processes are being utilized. These measures are equally useful to the people who use these assets. Measures of quality, customer satisfaction, innovation, human capital development, and market share are becoming as common as traditional measures of financial performance.[22] These measures can be evaluated by comparing them to previous period and competitors' results, projected (budgeted) expectations, and best practices through competitive benchmarking. Another useful way of measuring performance is through peer evaluations conducted by those who participate in the networks. Information technology, notably in the form of executive information systems that combine internal and external sources of data, is playing an increasingly central role in performance measurement. Interorganizational systems that connect a company with its suppliers and customers facilitate the flow of information together with the flow of goods and services.

6. *Resource allocation infrastructure.* Resources, financial and otherwise, must be allocated to individuals, projects, functions, divisions, and businesses. Three of the most important examples of the resource allocation component of the infrastructure for which senior management has superordinate design responsibilities are annual and capital budgets and compensation. All three of the underlying processes for these classes of resources direct the allocation of substantial financial resources based upon expected returns as determined by previous performance and anticipated future opportunities. While senior management may not make all of the specific decisions regarding the allocation of these resources, it is responsible for establishing the processes by which the decisions are made. Information technology is used to gather and analyze information relevant to these resource allocation decisions, and to maintain an accounting of resource allocations and inventories.

7. *Information and telecommunications technology infrastructure.* The information and telecommunications technology architecture supports all of the applications that facilitate the other six components of the infrastructure. Senior management is responsible for establishing principles to select information technology resources (hardware, software, and applications) useful to the firm, determine their location and management, and guide their development and sourcing. It is this technology architecture that supports the generation, storage, and transmission of knowledge; it forms a framework for the superordinate design of core competencies and expertise, shared knowledge

and databases, human assets and structural contours, project tasking and team assignment methodologies, performance measurement, and resource allocation.

Self-design. The self-designing activities that enable work to get done are performed by knowledge workers who utilize the superordinate-designed infrastructures to enable them to accomplish their tasks.

The distinction between superordinate design and self-design should not be confused with the difference between centralization and decentralization. Superordinate design is a senior management responsibility, and some centralized decisions must be made to execute it, but its primary purpose is to provide the resources, tools, and processes that knowledge workers need to accomplish work that meets customers' needs. Nor is self-design decentralized decision making, even though knowledge workers are responsible for making an increasing number of decisions. The purpose of self-design is to shape the organization in whatever ways are necessary to allow workers to make and execute decisions. We can illustrate this difference by examining the self-design of structure, systems, and strategy—three areas that in traditional organizations are usually a senior management responsibility—and the role of the superordinate-designed infrastructure therein.

1. Structure. Organizational structure is the most apparent and perhaps most discussed variable in "new model" competitive organizations in an Information Economy. The most popular term used to describe the structure of these types of organizations, "network," connotes a structure that is neither a typical functional nor a typical divisional hierarchy; instead it is intermediate between a hierarchy and a market. Concomitant with the blurring of boundaries between units established in the structural contour is the blurring of boundaries between the firm and its suppliers, customers, and even competitors through strategic alliances, joint ventures, value-added partnerships, and other such "soft" forms of managing external relationships.[23]

The network does not totally replace the hierarchy, but operates off it. The underlying hierarchy is the relatively stable part of the infrastructure, which contains resources accessed on a task-by-task, project-by-project basis to form local networks. These networks support the relationships that form and dissolve as tasks and projects originate and are completed. The network structure is designed by anyone who needs to get something done, whatever his or her level in the functional hierarchy. Because the overall network structure is an aggregation of many local networks, it is extremely complex and constantly shifting: a static hierarchical structure is not replaced by a static network structure. No one person, at any level in the organization, has a total picture of what the network structure looks like. Because it is constantly changing, it is as much a process as it is a structure.

Four components of the superordinate-designed infrastructure are especially important in creating self-designed network structures. The most obvious is the human assets and structural contour, which contains the people with whom the designers and/or knowledge workers form working relationships. The project tasking and team assignment methodologies are used to identify who is available and under what terms, and the shared knowledge and database component identifies the resources that are needed and where they reside. The information technology and telecommunications architecture component plays a central role, since the people who make up the network may be located anywhere in the world.

2. Systems. Like structure, management control systems have historically been designed by senior management, usually in the finance function. But unlike structure, systems have been slow and difficult to change. It is relatively easy to redraw the boxes on an organizational chart, but until recently changes in systems required a horde of programmers, already backlogged with projects, working for months or years on a large mainframe computer. By the time the systems were redesigned to reflect the altered reporting structure, the latter had already changed again, perhaps several times. To the extent that managers and knowledge workers designed their own systems, they were typically simple and often manual reports using data generated by functional processes.

The shared knowledge and databases and information technology and telecommunications architecture components of the infrastructure make it possible for anyone with a workstation to design and redesign his or her own systems. Shared databases provide crucial data that can be combined with local and external data ported in through telecommunications networks and analyzed and displayed on individual workstations. The power of these workstations and the software that resides in them enables individuals to easily create and change a wide variety of systems without relying on financial and systems analysts. This same technology also makes it possible to connect individually generated systems that have wider applications.

3. *Strategy*. Strategy, too, has historically been the responsibility of very senior management, often assisted by strategic planning staff and external consultants. Lower level managers and knowledge workers have been responsible for implementing strategy. This approach to strategy formulation worked when markets were large and relatively stable. But the nature of the strategy formulation process is changing as markets change. More and more companies now pursue strategies that offer customized products and services for local and even "micro" markets, involve a large service component featuring direct, real-time interaction with customers who have rapidly changing requirements (because *their* customers' requirements are changing too), and are based on unpredictably changing technologies. Individuals closest to customers are in the best position to identify their needs and to evolve strategies for meeting them.

This grass roots strategy formulation process utilizes the core competencies and expertise, shared knowledge and databases, and resource allocation components of the infrastructure.[24] The broad parameters within which the strategy formulation process takes place are established by senior management, but the strategy is self-designed by the people who implement it. The resulting corporate strategy is emergent.

From Decision Making to Decision Framing

The foregoing suggests some dramatic changes in the role of an organization's most senior managers, among them, a shift from decision making to decision framing. In the divisionalized functional hierarchies of the Industrial Economy, senior management makes the "big" decisions that establish the context for the smaller decisions made at lower levels in the organization. Whether they involve spending levels or strategic commitments, the farther one goes down the hierarchy, the smaller the decisions become in terms of both scale and scope.

In the Information Economy, big decisions may be made at any level of the organization. In contrast to the Industrial Economy, effective decision making occurs where the information and expertise resides, not always where the authority for the magnitude of the decision is in respect to the traditional functional hierarchy. Senior management is often aware of these decisions, but not always, since only time can reveal how "big" a decision is. When it is aware of these decisions, senior management may ratify them, or even be involved in making them, but other knowledge workers in the firm are always involved as well.

Instead of the primary responsibility for making big decisions, senior management becomes responsible for framing the context in which big decisions are made by developing the superordinately designed infrastructure. This infrastructure puts in place the information, resources, tools, and processes that knowledge workers need to make the best decisions possible in a highly uncertain and rapidly changing world.

There is thus an important shift in how we formulate the allocation of decision rights.[25] We should view it not in terms of a hierarchical continuum of centralization and decentralization based on the scale and scope of the decision, but rather in purely categorical terms. Because decisions that affect elements of the infrastructure, no matter how small, should still be made by senior management, some senior management decisions will look almost trivial in terms of their financial impact. All other decisions, no matter how big, should be made by workers in the firm who have the knowledge, perspective, and expertise required—often including, but in no way limited to, senior managers. This may result in very "low level" people making decisions that can have substantial financial impacts.

Implementing this categorical decision rule requires considerable analytical clarity about what the elements of the firm's infrastructure are and whether a decision affects the infrastructure, as well as great discipline in maintaining the distinction between infrastructure and all other decisions. Most senior managers will be tempted to fashion rationales for why a particular decision they are reluctant to let others make is an infrastructure decision. This temptation must be avoided if the distinction between superordinate design and self-design is to be maintained. Failure to do so will reinforce the divisionalized functional hierarchy appropriate to the Industrial, but not to the Information, Economy.

The first step to achieve the requisite clarity and discipline is for senior management to define explicitly the elements of the infrastructures, using the framework suggested here or some adaptation thereof. This emphasis on explicitness might seem contradictory to the spirit of self-design; it is not. Its purpose is as much to show what is not contained in the infrastructure as to show what is.

This is not to say that senior managers cannot participate in decisions at the self-design level. Because they are also knowledge workers, to not involve them would simply be to reinforce a hierarchical distinction that would confound decision making: decisions about superordinate design would come to be regarded as "centralized," and those about self-design as "decentralized." This would prevent the organization from moving away from a divisionalized functional hierarchy to a network floating on top of one.

The key point here is that very senior managers, up to and including the CEO, are also members of the network. But their participation in decisions about self-design is in the role of knowledge worker, not in the role of senior manager, and occurs at the invitation of the person or persons in the best position to mobilize the resources needed to make the best decision. If not invited, they cannot invite themselves to participate, even if they are reasonably certain that those involved are about to make a bad decision. Those responsible for self-design must be given the opportunity to make and learn from their own mistakes. Learning cannot occur if knowledge workers are prevented from collecting data for making and seeing the consequences of their decisions.

The network organization has the greatest impact on decision making. The framework for decision making becomes much more elaborate and important. Decisions are classified as infrastructure decisions and operational decisions.

As described earlier, infrastructure decisions are primarily the province of senior management, and shape what the organization is, and how it conducts business. They are made within the context of the infrastructures, including the process of forming self-designed organizational units. Operational decisions are mainly the responsibility of the knowledge workers participating in the self-designed networks. Operational decisions implement and execute strategy, and are made by those with the information and skills most relevant to a particular decision, and who can make the decision in the most timely manner possible. This gives the network organization a high level of responsiveness to changing market conditions and considerably increases the overall decision-making activity.

In contrast to a functional hierarchy, the frequency of decision making is dramatically increased and results in a corresponding decrease of the impact of individual or isolated decisions. This facilitates organizational learning, as well as a higher level of efficiency in carrying out the work of the firm. Of course, the feedback loop on the consequences of decisions is a vital performance management infrastructure in the network organization.

This mode of decision making requires new management principles for guiding decision making to the right knowledge worker, as well as a highly disciplined process for ensuring that decisions are made in a timely manner. The performance measurement infrastructure must incorporate monitoring for the timeliness and quality of decision making to ensure accountability.

Senior management cannot, of course, sit idly by if poor decisions continue to be made by individuals who, in pursuing "autonomy" (a useless concept in the model we are proposing), or for any other reason, fail to involve senior managers when they should. A critical senior management function is to intervene when patterns of ineffective decision making are detected, and to execute remedial action, which might involve altering infrastructures or reassigning knowledge workers (including firing).

Senior management's response must not be to inject itself forcefully into decisions, but rather to examine the infrastructure in order to determine what needs to be changed. The focus of senior management's attention should be on information, capabilities, tools, and processes, not on the particular operational decisions being made.

The Changing Role of Senior Management

This somewhat conceptual description of senior management's role can be made more concrete in terms of its consequences for line and staff roles. Like the difference between centralization and decentralization, the distinction between line and staff is irrelevant in this new model of organization, in which staff functions become part of senior management's job.

Senior management becomes truly general management since it no longer makes specific decisions regarding line functions.

We already see evidence of this in the diminishing size of the large corporate staffs that were once the hallmark of what were considered the most sophisticated and best-managed companies. Historically, staff functions were populated by professionals, many of them MBAs, who performed the analyses and even made the decisions for the line functions. These staff functions in strategic planning, finance, information systems, and human resources were a primary mechanism that senior management used to make or second-guess the decisions properly belonging to lower-level line managers. Rather than improving the quality of decisions, these staff functions often had the effect of stifling initiative and erecting barriers to its exercise. Self-design can hardly occur in the context of large corporate staffs.

Recently, these staffs have begun to disappear, their functions being merged directly into the responsibilities of firms' senior management and knowledge workers. The most dramatic example is that of large strategic planning staffs, the haven of so many recently minted MBAs who every year produced large volumes of charts and numbers as part of their companies' strategic planning processes. Such exercises are useless and even harmful when strategy formulation is a grass roots process based on the initiatives of knowledge workers who identify and pursue opportunities in the external marketplace. When this is the case, senior management's responsibility shifts from spending weeks reviewing strategic plans to ensuring that the requisite core competencies and expertise, shared knowledge and databases, and human assets and structural contour exist to permit knowledge workers to formulate strategies and change over time. Documentation is replaced by action. Nevertheless, firms need to monitor the validity of their actions by examining marketplace results; as problems appear, senior management must take corrective action to alter infrastructures, or to alter the human resources operating within the infrastructures.

Less dramatic, but equally clear, is the decline in the size of financial staffs, particularly in accounting departments. (Eventually the same thing will happen in treasury departments, as information technology plays an ever-larger role in mediating capital flows, and in tax departments where expert systems will manage companies' tax liabilities.) Workstations and software

are precipitating a dramatic decrease in the number of financial analysts who prepare periodic and ad hoc reports. Managers at all levels can now prepare such reports themselves, using decision support and executive information systems. As the number of managers comfortable with and adept at using this technology increases—and there are large generational effects here—the number of financial analysts will decrease. At the same time, the performance measurement and resource allocation elements of the infrastructure, traditionally the province of the finance function, will become more directly the responsibility of senior management.

Similar changes will occur in information systems and human resources, although here the transition is at an earlier stage of evolution. As sophisticated software and object-oriented programming makes information technology more powerful and user-friendly, large staffs of systems analysts and programmers will become unnecessary. Each knowledge worker becomes, in effect, his or her own programmer, in much the same way that advances in telecommunications have made individuals their own telephone operators.

The emerging paradigm shift in systems development—from large-scale projects to develop massive programs that run on mainframe computers to perpetually evolving prototyping to create virtual systems that use the underlying information technology architecture as a platform—will also reduce the size of information systems staffs. Other trends that will serve to reduce these staffs are the consolidation of small numbers of extremely large and powerful mainframe computers at data centers to provide firms' underlying technology platforms, and the growing reliance on outsourcing.

The implications of the fusion of what were formerly activities performed by information systems professionals into the daily work of everyone in the firm are seen in the changing structure of the information systems department. Historically part of the finance function, information systems was a large department that focused on applications designed to support the work of financial analysts. It reported at least two or three levels down from the CEO and was typically headed by a career information systems professional who started out as a programmer.

Today, the information part of the job is being separated from the technology part. The latter is being absorbed into knowledge workers' workstations, consolidated data centers, and small emerging technologies groups that explore leading-edge technologies for future applications. The chief information officer (CIO) is now truly an information, instead of an information technology, officer. Consequently, the CIO is as or even more likely to come from a function other than information systems, and reports directly to the CEO, making him or her truly a member of the senior management team.

This does not absolve senior management of responsibility for the technology part of information systems. The information and telecommunications technology element of the infrastructure is as important as other elements and the entire senior management team must develop the knowledge needed to become more involved in making decisions about it. The current generation of senior managers, most of whom are in their fifties or sixties, will on the whole find this proposition threatening or boring or both. But it cannot be avoided. Future generations of senior managers, who will have grown up with information technology, will accept it more readily. Moreover, the necessary knowledge is about what various technologies do and how they can be used, not about how they work. The latter will appropriately remain the concern of technology specialists, inside and outside the firm.

The most backward function in this evolution is human resources. Many managers perceive it to be their biggest impediment. One manager termed the function "inhuman nonresources" because of its focus on maintaining personnel statistics rather than developing human capital, and its tendency to cite reasons, regulatory and otherwise, why something cannot be done. At the same time, managers in other functions have hidden behind human resource systems and policies as a way of avoiding direct responsibility for performance appraisals, compensation, and promotions. Dealing directly with people in a candid but nonabusive way is invariably the hardest part of a manager's job.

Eventually, human resources record keeping will have to be separated from developmental activities, perhaps in the same way the information and technology aspects of information systems are being separated. The result will be that everyone in the firm will have more direct responsibility for the people they work with—subordinates, peers, and superiors (since development should not be based on hierarchy)—and that senior management will have more direct responsibility for the human capital and structural contour element of the superordinately designed infrastructure.

Despite lip service to the notion that "our people are our most important asset," the current generation of senior management may find this proposition distasteful.[26] In the future, senior management will have to spend at least as much time on human resource issues as on strategic, financial, and operating issues. As for information systems, they will have to develop the requisite knowledge, since few senior managers have any direct and meaningful experience with the human resource function. (We cannot think of a single company in which human resources is the function of choice for fast-trackers on the way to the top, although we can think of examples for every other function.) Of course, the needed knowledge must concern a transformed human resource function that focuses on human capital development, the area of business about which knowledge is least developed.

Perhaps the degree of senior management involvement we are suggesting for information systems and human resources seems excessive. It should not. In an Information Economy, after all, competitive success is based upon getting the right information to knowledge workers. It only stands to reason that information and human resources must be at the top of senior management's priorities. Rhetorical acknowledgment of the importance of people and information must be accompanied by practical involvement in the elements of the infrastructure that support and develop these assets. This will require a dramatic change in how senior management allocates its time and attention.

Conclusion

The dynamics and complexities of the global competitive environment challenge most traditional management approaches. The traditional approach to organizational design is proving to be a major problem in designing effective global organizations. In this chapter, we have proposed an alternative to traditional organizational design, and one that explicitly incorporates a role for information technology to facilitate key aspects of global competition, including knowledge sharing, frequent communications, and speed of responsiveness.

Our proposed levels of design approach should not be confused with centralization versus decentralization. Our two levels emphasize qualitatively different but related tasks. Framing the issue as centralization versus decentralization implies a continuum of decision-making responsibility arrayed against a hierarchical organization. We suggest a different language to analyze the management task. Rather than frame the management task in terms of decisions, which is the consequence of focusing on centralization versus decentralization, we should frame it in terms of superordinate designed infrastructures that provide the context for self-designed networks carrying out the work of the firm. The first step in making this new language a part of how people think and talk about a company is for management to delineate clearly each of the seven infrastructures.

Our proposed two levels of design approach also redefines senior management's role. Specifically, infrastructures definition and design become a key senior management responsibility. Senior management must resist the temptation to involve itself in operational decisions. Assumptions about who is, or is not, the right person to do things need to be set aside; people need to be permitted to take initiative.

Finally, our proposed two levels of design approach requires continuous monitoring and benchmarking of performance in order to sustain management control. Control should not be exercised hierarchically. Better to exert control indirectly, letting people in the organization decide whether to commit themselves to the initiatives proposed by others. In general, good ideas will gain sufficient support if their backers are skillful in using the infrastructure. Ideas with less merit will not, and will ultimately dissolve. Performance monitoring and benchmarking will provide information for the infrastructure and resource alterations required to keep the organization globally competitive.

We recognize that knowledge of designing effective global organizations is in an embryonic state. Our purpose in this chapter is not to propose "the" way to design the global organization, but to suggest an alternative to the traditional organizational design approach, which is proving inadequate to the task.

Notes

1. See C. K. Prahalad and Yves L. Doz, *The Multinational Mission: Balancing Local Demands and Global Vision* (New York: Free Press, 1987).

2. Christopher A. Bartlett and Sumantra Ghoshal, *Managing Across Borders* (Boston: Harvard Business School Press, 1989).

3. Nolan, Norton & Co., "A Research Study of Global Companies and Their Requirements for Services in the 1990s," sponsored by IBM, 1991.

4. Others include Robert G. Eccles and Dwight B. Crane, whose study of investment banks describes self-designing network organizations; Eccles and Crane, *Doing Deals* (Boston: Harvard Business School Press, 1988); Shoshana Zuboff, who advanced the notion of the informated organization in *In the Age of the Smart Machine* (New York: Basic Books, 1984); and Peter F. Drucker, "Management and the World's Work," *Harvard Business Review* (September–October, 1988): 65–76.

5. Richard L. Nolan, Alex J. Pollock, and James P. Ware, "Creating the 21st Century Organization," *Stage by Stage,* 8, no. 4 (July–August 1988): 1–11.

6. Max Weber, *The Theory of Social and Economic Organization,* T. Parsons, ed., translated by A. M. Henderson and T. Parsons (New York: Oxford University Press, 1947).

7. See Joseph L. Massie, "Management Theory," in *Handbook of Organizations,* James G. March, ed. (Chicago: Rand McNally, 1965).

8. See William Travers Jerome III, *Executive Control: The Catalyst* (New York: John Wiley, 1961), Chapter 13.

9. Peter F. Drucker, *The Practice of Management* (New York: Harper & Row, 1954).

10. See "General Electric Co., Background Note on Management Systems—1981." Harvard Business School Case 9-181-111 (1981).

11. For a discussion of managing information as a resource see Rashi Glazer, "Marketing in an Information-Intensive Environment: Strategic Implications of Knowledge as an Asset," *Journal of Marketing* (October 1991): 1–19.

12. See James D. Berkley and Nitin Nohria, "The Virtual Organization: Bureaucracy, Technology, and the Implosion of Control," Harvard Business School Working Paper 92-033, for a discussion of how hierarchy served as a virtual computer and how the advent of the computer opens up new possibilities of organization.

13. Eccles and Crane, *Doing Deals,* 133–141.

14. Nolan and Pollock, "Creating the Network Organization."

15. Lynda M. Applegate, James I. Cash, Jr., and D. Quinn Mills, "Information Technology and Tomorrow's Managers," *Harvard Business Review* (November–December 1988): 130–131.

16. C. K. Prahalad and Gary Hamel, "The Core Competence of the Corporation," *Harvard Business Review* (May–June 1990): 79–91.

17. For a discussion of just-in-time workstation-based training, see Harry M. Lasker's "Continuous Learning Systems," *Stage by Stage,* 10, no. 2 (March–April 1990): 19–22.

18. Bartlett and Ghoshal, *Managing Across Borders,* p. 67.

19. Ibid.

20. See A. Edstrom and Jay R. Galbraith, "Transfer of Managers as a Coordination and Control Strategy in Multinational Corporations," *Administration Science Quarterly,* 22 (1977): 248–263.

21. Bartlett and Ghoshal, *Managing Across Borders,* p. 67.

22. Robert G. Eccles, "The Performance Measurement Manifesto," *Harvard Business Review* (January–February 1988): 45–53.

23. See R. Johnson and Paul R. Lawrence, "Beyond Vertical Integration— The Rise of Value-Added Partnerships," *Harvard Business Review* (July– August 1988): 94–101. Also see Yves Doz, Gary Hamel, and C. K. Prahalad, "Cooperate with Your Competitors and Win," *Harvard Business Review* (January–February 1989): 133–134.

24. Eccles and Crane, *Doing Deals.*

25. For an economic perspective on the problem of allocating decision rights, see Michael C. Jensen and William H. Meckling, "Specific and General Knowledge, and Organizational Structure," presentation at Nobel Symposium no. 77, Saltsjobaden/Stockholm, August 18–20, 1990.

26. See *The Wall Street Journal* (April 29, 1991) for a survey of annual reports that give human resources short shrift while claiming it to be the firm's most important asset.

4

On the Design of Global Information Systems

Benn R. Konsynski and Jahangir Karimi

To compete effectively at home or around the world, firms must increasingly coordinate their activities on a global basis. Coordination and partnership across complex networks of organizationally and geographically distinct entities dispersed worldwide is becoming a primary source of competitive advantage. Global strategies today frequently involve cooperation with coalition partners as well as among a firm's own subsidiaries.

A global firm's value-chain activities are influenced by two environmental forces: national differentiation (i.e., diversity in individual country markets), and global integration (i.e., coordination among activities in different countries). The benefits associated with globalization derive not from the policies and practices of individual countries, but rather from the manner in which the activities in the global industry value chain are performed by a firm's worldwide systems. These systems involve partnerships with independent corporate entities that may entail the interchange of information and management processes across both legal organizational and national boundaries.

Globalization trends demand evaluation of the skills that organizations need to participate effectively in changing markets. Encouraged by recent globalization initiatives, many firms are leveraging new information technologies to change their coordination and control systems, management and operating processes, and organizational processes. Innovations in information technology in recent decades have greatly reduced coordination costs by reducing the time and cost of communicating information and, together with changes in market structures, have shifted competition from a national to a global scope. What is lacking in many global firms is a clear strategy for aligning their global information technology architectures with their evolving global business strategies. The challenge for many global firms is not to find the organizational structure that provides the best fit with their global strategies, but to build and manage decision-making processes that can respond appropriately to multiple changing environmental demands.

With global strategies evolving from multinational to transnational, decision making is no longer concentrated at corporate headquarters. Today's global firm must be able to transfer a great deal of complex information to diverse locations in its integrated network of operations. European companies have begun to see the power and simplicity of more centralized systems for managing their subsidiaries, while Japanese companies are increasingly supplementing traditional, time-consuming, case-by-case negotiations with more formal systems, routines, and policies. For their part, American managers are evincing renewed interest in shaping and managing previously ignored informal processes and value systems in their firms.

In this chapter, we first examine the structure and strategy and role of information technology in the global enterprise. We then look closely at how the themes of the chapter play out both in the corporate sector and, in light of a number of recent cases that suggest ways in which nations, acting as enterprises, can achieve competitive advantage through information technology, in the public sector. Our corporate example is Du Pont. In the public sector, we examine activities associated with trade documentation handling in Singapore (TradeNet), Hong Kong (TradeLink), Australia, Norway, and the United Kingdom, among other nations.

Strategy and Structure in the Global Enterprise

Clearly, no single model will suffice to characterize the nature of strategy and governance in the global enterprise. We review the basic categories of global organizational structures identified by Bartlett and Ghoshal, whose framework we have found to be useful for exploring differences among global competitive strategies, organizational structures, and information architecture needs.[1]

A firm that differentiates its products to meet local needs and respond to diverse national interests is said to embrace a multinational strategy (see Figure 4-1). Such a firm delegates considerable operating independence and strategic freedom to its foreign subsidiaries. Under this decentralized organizational structure, highly autonomous national companies are often managed as a portfolio of offshore investments rather than as a single international business. These subsidiaries focus on local markets. Coordination and control are achieved primarily through personal relationships between top corporate management and subsidiary managers rather than enforced by written rules, procedures, or formal organizational structure. Strategic decisions are decentralized, and top management is concerned primarily with monitoring the results of foreign operations. This classic strategy/structure model was adopted by most European-based companies that expanded prior to World War II. But much changed for European companies in the 1970s, as the EEC reduced certain tariff barriers and American and Japanese firms began to enter local markets.

A firm with a pure global strategy may seek competitive ad-

Figure 4-1
Multinational Strategy with Decentralized Organizational Structure

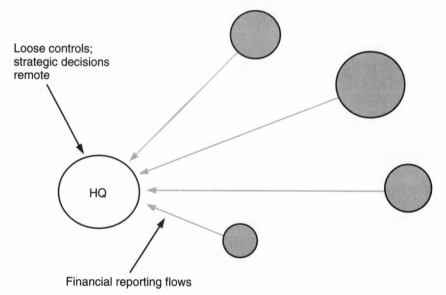

vantage by capitalizing on economies associated with standardized product design, global-scale manufacturing, and centralized control of worldwide operations (see Figure 4-2). The key parts of a firm's value-chain activities, typically product design or manufacturing, being geographically concentrated, are either retained at the center or are centrally controlled. This centralized organizational structure is primarily characterized by one-way flows of goods, information, and resources from headquarters to subsidiaries. Key strategic decisions for worldwide operations are made centrally by senior management. This export-based strategy was common in Japanese-based companies that relied on highly coordinated activities among subsidiaries in the postwar years. Toyota, for example, initially capitalized on a tightly controlled operation that emphasized worldwide export of fairly standardized automobile models from global-scale plants in Toyota City, Japan. Lately, growing protectionist sentiments and lower factor costs have led Toyota, among other companies, to establish production sites in less-developed countries in order to sustain its competitive edge.

A firm pursuing an international strategy transfers knowledge and expertise to remote environments that are less ad-

Figure 4-2
Global Strategy with Centralized Organizational Structure

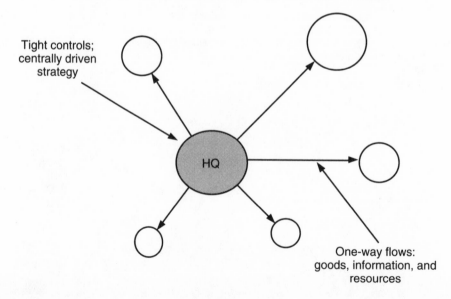

Tight controls; centrally driven strategy

HQ

One-way flows: goods, information, and resources

vanced in technology or market development. Subsidiaries' dependence on the parent company for new processes or ideas requires greater coordination and control by headquarters under this coordinated federation organizational structure than under the classic multinational strategy (see Figure 4-3). The international strategy/structure defines the managerial culture of U.S.-based companies, which have a reputation for professional management that implies a willingness to delegate responsibility while retaining overall control through sophisticated systems and specialist corporate staffs. International subsidiaries are more dependent on the transfer of knowledge and information under this structure than are subsidiaries under a multinational strategy, and the parent company makes greater use of formal systems and controls in its relationships with subsidiaries.

A firm pursuing a transnational strategy coordinates a number of national operations in a way that preserves its ability to respond to national interests and preferences (see Figure 4-4). National subsidiaries are viewed not as implementers of centrally developed strategies, but as sources of ideas, skills, capabilities, and knowledge that can benefit the company as a whole. It is not unusual for companies to coordinate product develop-

Figure 4-3
International Strategy with Coordinated-Federation
Organizational Structure

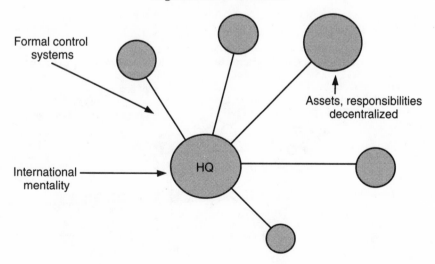

Formal control
systems

Assets, responsibilities
decentralized

International
mentality

HQ

ment, marketing approaches, and overall competitive strategy across interdependent national units. Under this integrated network organizational structure, top managers are responsible for coordinating the development of strategic objectives and operating policies, logistics between operating divisions, and the flow of information among divisions. During the 1980s, global competition forced global firms to become more responsive nationally. Today, these firms face a growing need for worldwide coordination and integration of activities upstream in the value chain (e.g., inbound logistics and operations) and greater national differentiation and responsiveness downstream (e.g., in marketing, sales, and services). In consumer electronics and branded packaged goods, for example, global companies are being forced to replace exports with locally manufactured goods and develop more locally differentiated products. Increasing numbers of firms are responding to these demands by adopting transnational strategies.

Another form of coordinated federation, the interorganizational design, consists of two or more organizations that have elected to cooperate in order to combine their strengths and overcome individual weaknesses. There are two modes of interorganizational design: equity and nonequity collaboration. Equity collaborations are seen in joint ventures, minority equity investments, and franchises. Nonequity collaborations are seen in forms of licensing arrangements, marketing and distribution agreements, and interorganizational systems (IOSs) for linking

Figure 4-4

Transnational Strategy with Integrated-Network Organizational Structure

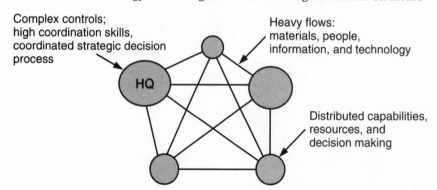

companies to suppliers, distributors, or customers. In the airline industry, for example, achieving economies of scale in developing and managing a large-scale reservation system is now beyond the capacity of medium-sized airlines. Consequently, in Europe two major coalitions have been created, the Amadeus Coalition, which uses software built around Continental and Eastern Airlines' System One computer reservation system, and the Galileo Coalition, which makes use of United Airlines' software. Even the largest carriers, acknowledging their inability to individually manage large-scale reservation systems, have joined coalitions.

Increased global competition during the 1980s produced a virtual explosion in the use of interorganizational designs by both global and domestic firms. In 1983 alone, the number of domestic joint ventures announced in communications and information systems products and services industries exceeded the sum of all previously announced joint ventures in those sectors. Research suggests that interorganizational designs can lead to: "vertical disaggregation" of functions (e.g., marketing, distribution) typically conducted within the boundaries of a single organization performed independently by the organizations within the network; the use of structurally independent organizations, or "brokers," to link different organizational units into business groups for the performance of specific tasks; and the substitution in traditional organizations of "full disclosure information systems" for lengthy trust-building processes based on experience.

The Role of Information Technology in the Global Enterprise: The Global Information System

Global firms' applications of information technology are increasing in both service and manufacturing industries, as dramatic changes accelerate information technology capability and availability and improve organizational skills in deployment. The earliest investments were in industries with established protocols and formalized transactions—international banking, airlines, and credit authorization. But with rapid improvements in communications and information technology during the 1980s, more and more activities of global firms were coordinated using information systems. Concurrently, patterns in the economics of information technology development began to change.

Existing and nearly completed public national data networks and public or quasi-public regional and international networks in virtually all developed, and a few developing, countries have spurred rapid growth in data-service industries (e.g., data processing, software, information storage and retrieval, and telecommunication services).

Today, global firms rely on data-service industries and information technology not only to speed up message transmission (e.g., for ordering, marketing, distribution, and invoicing), but also to improve corporate management and control by improving corporate functions such as financial control, strategic planning, inventory control, and changing the manner of production (e.g., by employing computer-aided design [CAD], computer-aided manufacturing [CAM], and computer-aided engineering [CAE]). More and more global firms' processes for planning, control and coordination, and reporting depend on information technology.

Organizations must begin to manage the evolution of a global information technology architecture that forms an infrastructure for the coordination needs of a global management team. Country-centered, multinational firms must give way to truly global organizations that will carry little national identity. General management's challenge is to build and manage the technical infrastructure that supports a unique global enterprise culture. The business dimensions of value added through information systems support in the global enterprise include:

- management control linkages,
- process coordination for manufacturing and marketing,
- effective resource sharing and allocation,
- operations flexibility,
- leveraging economies of scale and scope,
- business processes rationalization,
- compliance with legal and social responsibilities, and
- broad access to regional competencies and opportunities.

A global information system (GIS) is a distributed information-processing system that crosses national boundaries to support multinational and global enterprises.[2] Traditional information systems designs, because they evolved in response to different technology and regulatory opportunities and pressures, are often inappropriate for the new global systems architectures. A GIS needs to support both flexibility in and coordination among a firm's diverse activities in the new international markets.

Strategic control is defined as "the extent of influence that a head office has over a subsidiary concerning decisions that affect subsidiary strategy." As resources such as capital, technology, and management become vested in regions and subsidiaries, head offices no longer rely on control over these resources to influence regional or organizational strategies. The nature of head office strategic control over subsidiaries shifts with time, requiring new forms of administrative control mechanisms, such as those provided by improved information management strategies. Global strategic control is a key element of the GIS's role in facilitating the integration of a firm's value-chain activities while accommodating the variance that is often required in the global management process.

Many CIOs find it difficult to fully understand the scope of their international operations. Consequently, basic questions about equipment inventory, software installations, and human resource skills and talents available on a global basis often go unanswered.

Among the differences between domestic distributed systems and GISs is that the latter cross national boundaries and hence are exposed to wide variations in business environments, availability of resources, and technological and regulatory environments.[3] We explore these variations briefly below.

With respect to the business environment, there are, from the perspective of the home base country, differences in language, culture, nationality, and professional management disciplines among the subsidiary organizations. Differences in local management philosophy often result in business/technology planning responsibilities being fragmented rather than focused in one budgetary area. The complexity of business/technology planning and monitoring, control, and coordination functions frequently demands unique management skills.[4]

The predictability and stability of available infrastructure in a given country is a major issue when considering the country as a hub for a global firm. "It is a fact of life that some countries are tougher to do business in than others," observed Richard Carlye.[5] Regional economic dependence on particular industry and cross-industry infrastructure may be informative. Singapore has provided, through TradeNet, a platform for fast, efficient trade document processing;[6] Hong Kong's unique position as gateway to the People's Republic of China and its historic free port policies are reflected in its developing the TradeLink platform;[7] and Lufthansa, Japan Airlines, and Cathay Pacific, among other airlines, are trying to pool their global information technology infrastructure to deliver a global logistics system. At the same time, global banks are exploring the influence of their information technology architectures on the portfolio of financial instruments they can offer on a global basis.[8]

Resource availability can vary due to import restrictions or to lack of local vendor support. Since very few vendors provide worldwide service, many firms find that operational risk limits their choice of vendors for an individual project. Finally, the availability of telecommunications equipment/technology, e.g., LAN, private microwave, fiber optic, satellite earth stations, switching devices, and other technologies, varies among countries and geographic regions.

Changes in government, economy, and social policy can lead to critical changes in telecommunications regulations, which in turn can impose serious constraints on the operation of GISs. Price, service availability, and cross-border data-flow restrictions also vary widely from country to country.

In most countries, the PTT (post, telephone, telegraph) sets prices based on traffic volume rather than fixed-cost leased facilities. Doing so increases the PTTs' revenues and, at the same time, prevents global firms from exploiting economies of scale. The nature of a global enterprise's internal infrastructure system may also influence its ability to leverage regulation.[9]

Regulations that restrict the use of leased lines or the import of hardware and/or software limit GIS options in different countries (e.g., restrictions on connections between leased lines and public telephone networks, on the use of dial-up data transmission, or on the use of electronic mail systems for communication). It is not unusual for a company to build its own "phone company" to reduce dependence on government-run organizations.[10] Hardware and software import policies can also make local information processing uneconomical in some countries (e.g., both Canada and Brazil impose high duties on the import of hardware, and France, Saudi Arabia, and Israel have software import valuation policies).[11]

Transborder data flow (TBDF) regulations in part govern the content of international data flows.[12] Examples include requirements to process certain kinds of data and maintain certain business records locally, as well as the freedom to "transmit in," which is offset by limits on interactive applications that "transmit out." Although the content of TBDFs is regulated for purposes of privacy protection and economic and national security, such regulation can adversely affect the economics of GISs, forcing global firms to decentralize their operations, increase operating costs, or avoid certain applications.

International, national, and industry protocols and standards play key roles in permitting global firms to leverage their systems development investments. Although telecommunications standards vary widely from one country to another in terms of the technical details of connecting equipment and agreements on formats and procedures, conversion of the world's telecommunications facilities into an integrated digital network (IDN) is well under way; most observers agree that a worldwide integrated digital network and the integrated services digital network (ISDN) will soon become reality.[13] The challenge is not one of technology, which already exists; rather, integration depends on creating, and getting all countries to agree to, the necessary standards. Telecommunications standards are set by domestic governments or international agencies, by major equipment vendors (e.g., IBM's Systems Network Architecture [SNA], Wang's Wangnet, and Digital Equipment Corporation's DecNet) and by a group of firms within the same industry (e.g., SWIFT [Society for Worldwide International Funds Transfers] for international funds transfers and cash management, EDI [electronic data interchange] for transmitting formatted business transactions, such as purchase orders between companies,[14] and SQL [structured query language] for coordinating data across many databases).

Design and Management Strategy

The information systems concerns of global firms involve analyses of how similar or linked activities are performed in different countries. Global information systems are employed to manage the exchange of information, goods, expertise, technology, and finances.

GISs allow the many business functions that play a role in coordination—logistics, order fulfillment, finance, and so forth—to share information about the activities within the firm's value chain. In global industries this capability permits a firm to:

- be flexible in responding to competitors in different countries and markets,
- respond in one country (or region) to a change in another,
- scan markets around the world,
- transfer knowledge among units in different countries,
- reduce costs,
- enhance effectiveness, and
- preserve diversity in products and production locations.

Although many global firms have an explicit global business strategy, few have a corresponding strategy for managing information technology internationally. Many firms have information interchange protocols across their multinational organizational structures, but few have global information technology architectures. A global information management strategy is a necessary response to industry globalization (i.e., the growing globalization trend in many industries and associated reliance on information technologies for coordination and operation) and national competitive posture (i.e., the collection of separate domestic strategies in individual countries that may contend with global industry strategies and transcend multinational coordination). Whereas Procter & Gamble must contend with the need to address its global market in the branded packaged goods industry, Singapore requires improved coordination and control of trade documentation to compete more effectively in the cross-industry trade environment vital to its economic health. Each approach recognizes the growing information intensity in expanding markets and each, in turn, must meet the challenges occasioned by the need for cross-culture and cross-industry cooperation.

Table 4-1 presents the alternative information-systems management strategy options that result from the evolution of the global business environment and technology. New information technologies support closer integration of adjacent steps in the value-added chain through the development of electronic markets and electronic hierarchies, thus changing coordination

Table 4-1
Alignment of Global and Information Management Strategies

Business Structure	Coordination/ Control Strategy	Coordination/ Control Mechanism	IS Structure
Multinational/ Decentralized Federation	Socialization	Hierarchies: managerial decisions determine the flow of materials and services	Decentralization: stand-alone databases and processes
Global/ Centralized Federation	Centralization		Centralization: centralized databases and processes
International and Interorganizational/ Coordinated Federation	Formalization	Markets: market forces determine the flow of materials and services	IOS: linked databases and processes
Transnational/ Integrated Network	Co-opting		Integrated architecture: shared databases and processes

mechanisms.[15] The result, an increase in the proportion of economic activities coordinated by markets rather than by hierarchies, helps explain why global firms are shifting from multinational, global strategies to international (interorganizational), transnational strategies.

Managing across corporate boundaries has much in common with managing across national borders. Managing strategic partnerships, coalitions, and alliances has forced managers to shift their thinking from the traditional task of controlling a hierarchy to managing a network.[16] As explained earlier, managers in transnational organizations must gather, exchange, and process large volumes of information. Formal strategies and structures cannot support such information processing needs. Given the widespread distribution of organizational units and the relative infrequency of direct contacts among those in disparate units in a transnational firm, top management has a better opportunity to shape relationships among managers simply by being able to influence the nature and frequency of contacts among them using an appropriate information-systems management strategy.

A firm's information-systems management should include senior management policy on a corporate information systems architecture (ISA) that guides systems development, facilitates integration and data sharing among applications, and supports the development of integrated, corporate systems based on a corporatewide data resource.[17] A corporate ISA for a global firm is a high level map of the information and technology requirements of the firm as a whole. It comprises network, data, and application and technology architectures. Network and data architectures, because they are the highway systems for a wide range of traffic, are generally considered to be the key enabling technologies in the international environment.[18]

A new GIS management strategy must address, through appropriate ISA design, organizational and structural issues related to the coordination and configuration of value-chain activities. Key components of a GIS management strategy are a centralized and/or coordinated business/technology strategy for establishing data communications architecture and standards, a centralized and/or coordinated data management strategy for creating corporate databases, and alignment of global business and GIS management strategies.

Network Management Strategy and Architecture

A network architecture defines where applications are executed and databases are located and identifies the communications links needed among locations; it also sets standards to ensure that other ISA components are interrelated and work together. The architecture is important for providing standards for interconnecting very different systems instead of enforcing communality among systems. At present, network architecture potential is determined more often by vendors than by general industry or organizational standards.[19]

Architecture. Research on international business suggests that the structure of a global firm's value chain is key to its strategy; its fit with environmental requirements determines economic performance. But GIS environments are external to global firms and hence cannot be completely controlled. Consequently, services provided by GISs must be globally coordinated, integrated, and standardized, as well as tailored to accommodate national differences and individual country markets.

Deciding on an appropriate network architecture is a leading management and technology issue. Research in the global banking industry found that an international bank that provides a wide range of global, electronic wholesale banking services has some automated systems that need to be globally standardized (e.g., global balance reporting systems) and others (e.g., global letter of credit systems) that need to be tailored to individual country markets.[20] The research also suggests that appropriate structures for GISs may vary with product and service portfolios; a uniform strategy of centralization or decentralization may not be appropriate for all GIS applications. Moreover, the research found that international banks cannot expect to optimize the structure of environmentally diverse information systems with a uniform approach to GIS architecture, since such an approach may limit the product and service portfolios called for by the bank's global business strategy. An asymmetrical approach, structuring each system to suit the environmental needs of the service delivered, although more complex, can significantly improve the operational performance of international banks. Such an approach may, however, significantly increase coordination costs.

Business process standards. Use of standards is an important strategic policy, as many companies today limit the number of intercompany formats they support. Given the success in developing and adopting global standards in specific narrow areas (e.g., EDIFACT), one might argue that it is becoming more difficult to make "standards mistakes" than was the case several years ago. Companies can use standards to broaden their choice of trading partners in the future. In the absence of uniform data and communication standards at the international, national, and industry levels, no single product can address more than a fraction of the hardware and communications protocols scattered throughout a firm.

Whether set by governments, major computer and communication vendors, or through cooperative arrangements within an industry, standards are critical to the operation of GISs. Because standards are key to the connectivity of a set of heterogeneous systems, explicit senior management policy promoting adoption of and compliance with standards is important. One central policy governing key standards, (e.g., EDI, SQL) should include a management agenda for promoting understanding of both the standards and the standards-setting process within industry, national, and international environments.[21] Such a central policy accomplishes several objectives: it reduces costs, avoids vendor viability, achieves economies of scale, reduces potential interface problems, and facilitates transborder data flows. Consequently, decisions about the components of network architectures and standards involve a move toward centralized, corporate management coordination and control, whereas decisions regarding traffic volume require decentralized planning and conformity to data communications standards.

Data Management Strategy and Architecture

Data architecture defines the arrangement of databases within an organization. Although every organization that maintains data has a data architecture, in most organizations this architecture is more the result of the evolution of applications databases in various departments than of a well-planned data management strategy.[22] Data management problems are amplified for large global firms with diverse product families. For a global firm with congested data highways, problems associated with getting the right data, in the right amount, to the right people, at the right time multiply as global markets emerge.[23]

Lack of a centralized information management strategy often results in corporate entities (e.g., customers and products) having multiple attributes, coding schemes, and values across databases.[24] This makes linkages or data sharing among activities difficult at best; establishing linkages requires excessive time and human resources, and costs and performance of other data-related activities within the value chain are affected. These factors make important performance data unavailable to top management for decision making, eroding the firm's competitive position and introducing significant obstacles to its future competitive advantage.

Strategy/architecture. To improve coordination among a global firm's value-chain activities, a data architecture design should be based on an integrated data-management strategy that mandates creation of a set of corporate databases derived from the firm's value-chain activities. A recent study has pointed out the significance of a firm's value-chain activities in deploying IT strategically, although no specific information management strategy is proposed.[25]

Whereas departmental data are often used primarily by departments within the functional area that comprises a value-chain activity, corporate data tend to be used by more than one functional area within value-chain activities.

Corporate databases should be based on the business entities involved in value-chain activities rather than on individual applications. A firm must define: (1) appropriate measures of performance for each value activity (e.g., sales volume by market and period), (2) corporate entities by which performance is measured (e.g., product, package type), (3) relationships among the entities defined, (4) entities' value sets, coding schemes, and attributes, (5) corporate databases derived from the entities, and (6) relationships among the corporate databases. For example, for a direct value-adding activity, such as marketing or sales within a firm's value chain, the corporate databases might include micromarketing, brand profitability assessment, promotion monitoring and adjustment, and so forth.

Given this data management strategy, corporate databases are defined independently of applications and are accessible by all potential users. Such a strategy enables senior management to integrate and coordinate information with the value-adding and support activities within the value chain, identify significant trends in performance data, and compare local activities to activities in comparable locations.

A data management strategy creates an important advantage for a global firm inasmuch as activities identified in the firm's strategic planning are used to define its corporate databases. The critical creation of linkages between strategic business planning and strategic information systems planning is possible under such a strategy because the activities that create values for customers also create the data that the firm needs for its operations. A data management strategy does not, however, imply that all application databases should be replaced by corporate databases. Application databases should remain (directly or indirectly) as long as the applications exist, but there should be a disciplined flow of data among corporate, functional, and application databases.

A recent survey of American companies indicates that significant problems encountered with global networks are technical in nature, related primarily to the lower quality (e.g., slower effective data transfer speeds) and reliability of foreign telecommunications services.[26] The survey further suggests that these technical problems are exacerbated by politically imposed constraints that restrict firms' options for managing their global network. One IS executive's advice was that companies beginning to develop a global network should not assume that the only difference between a global and a domestic network is size. Survey respondents also expressed concern about lack of adequate top-management support for dealing with problems involved in running a global network; IS executives believed that top management was not adequately concerned about, and did not fully comprehend, the issues and problems involved in managing such networks. The survey also suggests that both management policies (e.g., the creation of corporate standards and help centers) and firm characteristics affect the successful operation of a global network. Firms that have established help centers to deal with the issues involved in international data transfer appear to be more satisfied with their networks than firms that do not have such centers.

Alignment of Global Business and GIS Management Strategies

One challenge facing management today is the need to align business strategy and structure with information systems management and development strategy. Appropriate design of critical linkages among a firm's value-chain activities results in an effective business design involving information technology and improved coordination with coalition partners as well as among the firm's own subsidiaries. Previous research has emphasized the benefits of establishing appropriate linkages between business strategic planning and technology strategic planning.[27] Among these are proper strategic positioning, improvements in organizational effectiveness, efficiency, and performance, and fuller exploitation of the information technology investment.

Establishing the necessary alignment requires involvement and cooperation, and entails the development of a new set of responsibilities and skills for both the general manager responsible for planning and the senior information technology manager. The general manager's new responsibilities include:

- formal integration of regional needs into a global strategic business plan in line with the global strategic IS evolution plan;
- examination of the business process requirements associated with global centralized and/or coordinated network, technology, and data management strategies;
- review of the global network architecture as a key enabling technology for the firm's competitive strategy and assessment of the impact of network alternatives on business strategy;
- awareness of key technologies and participation in standards and standards-setting processes at the industry, national, and international levels; and
- championing of adoption and diffusion in the rapidly expanding use of industry, national, and international business and technical standards.

For the senior information technology manager, critical new responsibilities include:

- awareness of the firm's business challenges in the changing global environment and involvement in leveraging the firm's information technology in its global business strategy;
- preparation of a systems development environment that recognizes the long-term, companywide perspective in a multiregional and multicultural environment;
- planning development of the firm's application portfolio on the basis of current business and future global strategic posture;
- ensuring that the business purpose of strategic systems development projects is clear in a global business context;
- recommendation and selection of key technologies and standards for linking systems across geographic and cultural boundaries;
- automation of linkages among internal and external activities within the firm's value chain and selling them to others;
- designing corporate databases derived from the firm's value-chain activities and accounting for business cultural differences; and

- facilitating corporate restructuring by building flexibility into business services.

International GIS initiatives require more than mere technical capabilities. The ability to operate effectively with foreign cultures, sensitivity to the demands and intrigues of top management, and a comprehensive view of business processes are examples of the skills needed internationally within the systems development function.[28] Many CIOs do not understand how IT can transform operations globally. Their entrenched, nonintegrated business processes and systems, because they were not designed to be cross-functional, much less cross-national, naturally resist a global IT strategy. Moreover, old systems carry the baggage of diverse technology and incompatible applications, which makes it even more difficult to build common global systems. A major New York bank that began to replace incompatible systems with a global network in the mid-1970s is still at it.

One crucial problem is the complex logistics of major international projects. The complexity of international systems-development efforts often makes even relatively straightforward projects more expensive, time-consuming, and risky than domestic initiatives. Time zone differences make coordination and planning of international projects difficult to manage and the fatigue of international travel often wears down even the most energetic and cooperative of teams.

In the face of cultural and linguistic differences between project leaders and team leaders, communications can suffer and assumptions can replace dialogue. Fear for one's job and loss of influence, resistance to relocation, and country-based reward and recognition systems often pose additional barriers.[29] Project management under these circumstances involves special skills that are not always readily available.

Cooperation of country managers is often key to successful execution of global initiatives. Without a shared global vision of the business, the CIO will find it impossible to sustain a global IT strategy. Even in the global enterprise, the central problem is that managers are generally responsible for their local authorities and not for those of other regions or functions. In most multinational corporations, the international dimension is often neglected because management responsibilities are strongly tied to regional business performance. In these cases, "international" is often the poor boy on the block.

Global Systems at Du Pont

Du Pont's implementation of MIS GIS functions has received wide recognition in its industry. Thomas Mead noted: "Analysts factor the company's ever-widening information architecture into their calculations when explaining why the company has expanded annual earnings nearly $1 billion between 1986 and 1989, a year when net income approached $2.5 billion on nearly $36 billion in revenue. About 40% of those revenues, moreover, come from outside the United States."[30]

Du Pont is organized into nine major departments (entities) worldwide in a matrix organizational structure. The company's business strategy has been to locate IS resources within those entities in order to be more responsive to end users by affording them complete control of resource allocation, and involve management more in decision-making processes. Seventy-five to eighty-five percent of Du Pont's managers (approximately 46,700) have desktop computers in their offices or homes.

Du Pont's global business strategy. Du Pont's objective is to be a great global company by meeting its financial commitments and dealing with market and business opportunities around the world. Based on the strategy defined by the company's chairman, business managers now want access to information around the world for scheduling plants and inventories worldwide, knowing where orders are placed, being able to interface with customers, and so forth. Achieving this global strategy requires that more data be available more quickly and more accurately on a worldwide basis than ever before.

Du Pont's global IS strategy. Du Pont's global business strategy has set four objectives for IS: to have a worldwide, functionally sufficient, reliable and secure IS infrastructure at a lower cost than the competition; to stimulate and enable (via education of both upper management and business management) the company's businesses to use information technology; to introduce new technology faster than the competition; and to have stewards for overall IS activity.

Du Pont's network infrastructure. Du Pont has made a strategic decision to constrain its technology base. General purpose computers, for example, are limited to IBM 370s, Digital VAXs, and HP systems that run MPE operating systems. This has enabled Du Pont to leverage its resources by remotely supporting business processes. The company is also running pilot programs in open system architecture and plans to adopt an open architecture in order to take advantage of operating systems and communications protocols around the world.

Du Pont's network infrastructure is composed of layers. At the bottom layer, of basic telecommunications transport, the company has aggressively adopted Tariff 12 (a sophisticated network service offered by common carriers such as AT&T and MCI Communications). To reduce costs, Du Pont has introduced its own multiplexers for co-transmitting voice and data, fiber-optic cable to Europe with company-owned multiplexers, and satellite circuits to the Far East to be replaced soon by fiber-optic cable. The next layer, basic networks, is composed of three data networks, one voice network, and one video network. The data networks are IBM's SNA, DEC's DecNet, and HP's X.25. The next layer accommodates the respective operating systems for IBM, DEC, and HP, and the top layer is composed of basic utility programs, such as electronic mail.

The network management function is shared with suppliers. Although Du Pont has outsourced some network management activities, service providers do not have complete control. "They don't know your computing environment so you don't want them to manage the data network, you want them to manage the transport," observed Ray Cairns, the Du Pont CIO.[31]

Du Pont's data management strategy. Du Pont plans to consolidate six data centers worldwide into four—two in the United States, one in Singapore, and one in Europe. By limiting its technology platforms, the company is able to remotely support its data centers and thereby achieve much greater flexibility in moving systems around the world. For example, it operates its European data center (a clone of the major data center in the United States) without systems programmers.

Du Pont's competitive edge. Du Pont's network and data management strategies have significantly improved coordination between the company and its diverse constituencies. Externally, Du Pont is electronically linked to customers and suppliers (800 companies have limited access to Du Pont's databases and/or deal with Du Pont electronically). Automating the interface with customers to facilitate purchasing and with suppliers to make them an important part of Du Pont's business system has given the company a competitive advantage; it has done so by raising switching costs and supporting structural changes that make it possible to share information with existing businesses, introduce and control new distribution channels, and exert influence over suppliers.

Internally, Du Pont has automated routine activities by facilitating communication among professionals in its value chain (e.g., between manufacturing and marketing). Du Pont's U.S. organization has led intercompany computing, closely followed by the European organization. In the Far East, progress has been slower. Cairns noted, "There are still some cultural problems about managers and professionals having PCs on their desks, so we have to overcome that. And you have the language barrier, too."[32]

Du Pont has approximately 800 PC-based AI systems used for manufacturing, marketing, scheduling, and similar applications. By limiting these systems to standard platforms, the company has been able to train end users to build them. Du Pont was the first chemical company to acquire a Cray Supercomputer, and has implemented dedicated executive information systems that enable top managers around the world to download, on a daily basis, certain information that can facilitate coordination on key strategic decisions.

Review of Du Pont's GIS initiative. Du Pont is an example of a global company with a transnational business strategy and an integrated network organizational structure. Recognizing the challenges facing Du Pont in the global business environment, its CIO has successfully aligned the company's GIS management strategy with its global business strategy by articulating a clear strategy for building an integrated global network infrastructure to support voice, data, and video; developing corporate databases and data centers around the world; establishing and enforcing corporate standards for key technologies; automating the linkages among the company's value-chain activities; effecting corporate restructuring through consolidation of data centers and limits on technology platforms; and championing strategic IS projects in divisions in which business was poor and such projects were at risk.

The Public Sector Role in GIS Design

Government policy plays a significant role in influencing the application of information technologies for establishing unique industry relationships. In the cases cited, government contributes through a range of interventions, from declaration of standards to operation of the facilitating market information mechanisms. Government-prescribed information technology standards and protocols are playing a critical role in the formation of these new arrangements. The Norwegian government's TVINN system for automated clearance and control in the Norwegian customs department, for example, is significant in two respects. One, it was a very early arrival on the trade-related EDI scene, having come on line in August 1988, four months before the Singapore TradeNet system. And, two, inasmuch as it is not a comprehensive trade-related system, but rather one that focuses only on customs, it represents only an intermediate solution to the trade documentation problem.

The decision to build an EDI system was made in 1985, whereupon the Norwegian government's customs department assumed the lead for the project. The Norwegian computer consulting and design firm, Avenir, managed the development of the TVINN system in a time frame similar to that for TradeNet. But unlike TradeNet, which is essentially fully automatic, rarely requiring human intervention, TVINN was designed to permit routine intervention by customs officers monitoring the documentation process to modify the process as necessary. Like TradeNet, the project has been very successful, and the customs department claims significant labor savings, improved accuracy, and faster turnaround.

One might conclude from the Norwegian case that public policy dominates public-sector GIS design decisions, but in most initiatives the authors have studied, the private sector has played an essential, often leading role. Generally speaking, private sector competition is more likely to yield innovative and effective GISs than government monopoly. Nevertheless, the public sector, through intergovernmental coordination, must often take the lead to facilitate the timely creation of a GIS. We believe the public sector (single and multiple government) should take the initiative through policy and regulation under the following conditions.

1. When cross-industry conflicts develop because of incompatible business procedures that must be standardized but that no individual entity wants to bear the costs of standardizing. The public sector usually must intervene to find ways to facilitate standardization and to ensure that the costs of compliance with national standards are fairly borne by the parties that will benefit.
2. When the competitive posture of a nation or region is threatened or when particular windows of opportunity exist that must be exploited quickly.
3. When key elements of a GIS capability require the construction or use of "natural monopolies," such as those exploited by regional telephone networks or specialized governmental data resources.
4. When key intergovernmental activities that can be influenced by the GIS require the actions of a government agency.

There can be little doubt that GISs have a significant impact on trade policies. There is also little doubt that governments will wish to take an active, and often leading, role in the creation of trade-related GIS systems. The inevitable involvement of customs and possibly other government agencies in the trade process makes this a certainty. But what about other GISs that do not necessarily involve government agencies? We can expect that governments will play a major role in any systems that relate to transborder flows of goods and information. Governments have an abiding interest in ensuring that systems built to facilitate business among competing companies are not designed or used in ways that give any global firm unfair competitive advantage. This principle has been enforced with much controversy in the United States, where airline companies that own and operate computerized reservation systems have come under government orders to alter the ways their systems perform in order to eliminate systematic unfair competitive practices facilitated by systems designs. We can expect similar concerns to arise with respect to GISs in other global markets. Public sector agencies are likely to view GISs as "common carrier" networks like those of telephone companies. Although GISs emerged as private systems, governments will probably demand an ongoing role to ensure that key social objectives are upheld in the functioning of the systems.

Summary and Conclusions

Changes in technologies and market structures have shifted competition from a national to a global scope, resulting in a need for new organizational strategies and structures. Traditional organizational designs, having evolved in response to a different set of competitive pressures, are generally not appropriate for these new strategies. New organizational structures need to achieve both flexibility and coordination among firms' diverse activities in new international markets.

Globalization trends have resulted in a variety of organizational designs that have engendered both business and information management challenges. One of these, the global information-systems management strategy, includes the following key components: a centralized and/or coordinated business/technology strategy for establishing data communications infrastructure, architecture, and standards; a centralized and/or coordinated data management strategy for designing corporate databases; and alignment of global business and GIS management strategies. Such a GIS management strategy is appropriate today because it facilitates coordination among a firm's value-chain activities and business units, and provides the firm with the flexibility and coordination necessary to deal effectively with changes in technologies and market structures. It also aligns information systems management strategy with corporate business strategy by providing a foundation for an information technology architecture.

Coordination challenges emerge as barriers to effective cooperation for true global performance rather than multiregional interchange. The evolution of global strategies from multinational to transnational suggests that decision authorities and decision making no longer emanate from a central corporate headquarters. Today's global firm must carry a great deal of complex information to diverse locations in its integrated network of operations.

Globalization, together with the competitive posture of the global enterprise, defines the competitive posture of nations and city-states.[33] The issues related to coordination and control in the global enterprise also involve the nation-state in a review of the alignment of its cross-industry competitive posture.[34] It is incumbent on governments to seek the level of intervention that strengthens the competitive position of the state in the global business community.

The challenges to general managers in the emerging global economic environment extend far beyond the information technology infrastructure. The information intensity associated with markets (products, services, and channel systems) and coordination across geographic, cultural, and organizational barriers will force global general managers to rely to a growing extent on information technologies to support their management processes. The proper alignment of the evolving global information-management strategy and the global organizational strategy is important to the positioning of the global firm in the global economic community.

Notes

1. C. A. Bartlett and S. Ghoshal, *Managing Across Borders: The Transnational Solution* (Boston: Harvard Business School Press, 1989).

2. M. Buss, "Managing International Information Systems," *Harvard Business Review* (Special Series 1980).

3. J. King, "Centralized versus Decentralized Options," *Computing Surveys* (December 1983): 319–345.

4. P. G. Keen, *Competing in Time: Using Telecommunications for Competitive Advantage* (Cambridge, Mass: Ballinger, 1988).

5. R. E. Carlye, "Managing IS at Multinationals," *Datamation* (March 1, 1988): 54–66.

6. J. King and B. Konsynski, "Singapore TradeNet: A Tale of One City," Harvard Business School Case 1-191-009 (1990).

7. J. King and B. Konsynski, "Hong Kong TradeLink: News from the Second City," Harvard Business School Case 1-191-026 (1990).

8. A. S. Mookerjee, "Global Electronic Wholesale Banking Delivery System Structure," Harvard University Ph.D. dissertation, 1988.

9. R. O'Callaghan and B. Konsynski, "Banco Santander: El Banco en Casa," Harvard Business School Case 9-189-185 (1989); A. Warbelow, J. Kokuryo, and B. Konsynski, "Aucnet: TV Auction Network System," Harvard Business School Case 9-190-001 (1989); and A. Warbelow, O. Fjeldstad, and B. Konsynski, "Bankenes Betalings Sentral A/S: The Norwegian Bank Giro," Harvard Business School Case 9-191-037 (1990).

10. Carlye, "Managing IS at Multinationals."

11. "Special Report on Telecommunications: The Global Battle," *Business Week* (October 1983).

12. J. Basche, "Regulating International Data Transmission: The Impact on Managing International Business," The Conference Board, Research Report 852, New York, 1984.

13. J. Martin and J. Leben, *Principles of Data Communications* (Englewood Cliffs, N.J.: Prentice Hall, 1988); and W. Stallings, *ISDN: An Introduction* (New York: Macmillan, 1989).

14. J. V. Hansen and N. C. Hill, "Control and Audit of Electronic Data Interchange," *MIS Quarterly,* 13, no. 4 (December 1989): 403–413.

15. T. W. Malone, J. Yates, and R. I. Benjamin, "Electronic Markets and Electronic Hierarchies," *Communications of the ACM,* 30, no. 6 (June 1987): 484–497.

16. R. G. Eccles and D. B. Crane, "Managing through Networks in Investment Banking," *California Management Review,* 30 (Fall 1987): 176–195; B. Konsynski and F. W. McFarlan, "Information Partnership: Scale Without Ownership," *Harvard Business Review* (September–October 1990): 114–120; W. Powell, "Hybrid Organizational Arrangements," *California Management Review,* 30 (Fall 1987): 67–87.

17. W. H. Inmon, *Information Systems Architecture* (Englewood Cliffs, N. J.: Prentice Hall, 1986).

18. Keen, *Competing in Time.*

19. Ibid.

20. Mookerjee, "Global Electronic Wholesale Banking."

21. P. G. Keen, "An International Perspective on Managing Information Technologies," ICIT Briefing Paper 4101 (1987).

22. D. L. Goodhue, J. A. Quillard, and J. F. Rockart, "Managing the Data Resource: A Contingency Perspective," *MIS Quarterly,* 12, no. 3 (September 1988): 372–391; V. Romero, *Data Architecture: The Newsletter for Corporate Data Planners and Designers,* 1, no. 1 (September–October 1988): 7–18.

23. Carlye, "Managing IS at Multinationals."

24. Goodhue, Quillard, and Rockart, "Managing the Data Resource."

25. H. R. Johnston and S. R. Carrico, "Developing Capabilities to Use Information Strategically," *MIS Quarterly,* 12, no. 1 (March 1988): 36–48.

26. P. T. Steinbart and R. Nath, "Problems and Issues in the Management of International Data Communications Networks: The Experience of American Companies," *MIS Quarterly,* 16, no. 1 (March 1992): 55–76.

27. H. R. Johnston, and M. Vitale, "Creating Competitive Advantage with Interorganizational Information Systems," *MIS Quarterly,* 12, no. 2 (June 1988): 152–165; and W. R. King, "Strategic Planning for IS: The State of Practice and Research," *MIS Quarterly,* 9, no. 2 (June 1985): vi–vii.

28. E. M. Roche, *Managing Information Technology in Multinational Corporations* (New York: Macmillan, 1992).

29. D. Robey and A. Rodriguez-Dias, "The Organizational and Cultural Context of Systems Implementation: Case Experience from Latin America," *Information and Management,* 17, no. 4 (November 1989): 229–239.

30. T. Mead, "The IS Innovator at DuPont," *Datamation* (April 15, 1990): 61–68.

31. Ibid.

32. Ibid.

33. King and Konsynski, "Singapore TradeNet," and King and Konsynski, "Hong Kong TradeLink."

34. Konsynski and McFarlan, "Information Partnership," and M. E. Porter, "The Competitive Advantage of Nations," *Harvard Business Review* (March–April 1990): 73–92.

Part Three
Creating and Restructuring Industries

Introduction

Just as occurred in the transition from the Agrarian to the Industrial Economy, new industries are being created and old industries restructured as we make the transition from the Industrial to the Information Economy.

Clearly structural change does not occur overnight. It is an evolutionary process, which reaches critical junctures that have major implications for firms. Initially, the services of new industries complement those of existing industries by expanding capabilities or substitute for less efficient services. As this process gains momentum and new competitors enter and tailor their emerging strategies to be more congruent with market forces, network structures within and across organizations multiply. Since these network structures accommodate information technology more effectively, they are more efficient, which puts pressure on older industries to restructure. Part of the current downsizing phenomenon can be attributed to such restructuring. The mutually reinforcing incorporation of information technology and restructuring around networks give rise to new ways of competing, such as just-in-time lean production, outsourcing, strategic alliances, electronic markets, and so forth.

But the most fundamental change lies in the concept of the firm. In the Industrial Economy, firm boundaries were strong and known, and there was a clear delineation between internal and external activities and transactions. Networking possibilities, both internal and external, blur these boundaries. The networked firm takes on new and different attributes. It can, for example, rapidly marshal resources that it does not actually own. Former Citibank chairman Walter Wriston captured the essence of this phenomenon with his observation that information about money is more valuable than money itself,[1] by which he meant that firms that can identify where money is available for the lowest cost and match this resource with the best opportunities are more important to the economy than traditional banks that serve local markets.

The extended boundaries enabled by the hundreds of electronic networks being formed daily are an important aspect of the new, albeit not yet fully refined, concept of the firm. The importance to the general manager of networks and the redefinition of the firm is that managing a network organization is fundamentally different from managing a traditional hierarchy. Many old management principles are no longer applicable, and new ones must be developed and learned.

The authors of the chapters in this section examine the impact of information on the restructuring of global industries. Their principal message is that eventually every industry will have to be restructured around the electronic networks that are redefining the concept of the firm in terms of boundaries and the way firms fundamentally compete.

Sustaining Competitive Advantage with IT Networking

Professor Stephen Bradley, a member of the Competition and Strategy interest group at the Harvard Business School, has examined the impact of globalization and technology on the structure of industries and the competitive response of firms to structural change. Here, he specifically evaluates electronic networking's role in sustaining competitive advantage. Bradley concludes that among electronic networking's dramatic impacts are the creation of new industries and, even more important, the restructuring of the very foundations of existing industries. Firms are investing in technology to facilitate restructuring or responding to technology to compete more effectively.

Bradley also finds that few of the general managers making extraordinary investments in electronic networking are fully aware of how their investments will pay off. He contends, in fact, that given their almost herd instinct to invest in order to not be left behind, it is important that general managers be selective and attempt to understand whether their investments are justified as strategic necessities, likely to yield a sustainable competitive advantage, or prone to fail and not pay off at all.

Telecommunications and the Restructuring of the Securities Industry

George Hayter was a player in the computerization and resulting restructuring of The London Stock Exchange, the October 1986 event that became known as the "Big Bang." Hayter tracks the migration of trading away from the exchange floor to computer screens in the "war room" linked to the exchange by telecommunications. The notion that extensive computerization of an industry changes everything was borne out in this instance. Indeed, Hayter, writing five years after the event, reflects on how many of the changes came as complete surprises and speculates on how the wholesale electronic networking of other industries might proceed.

Coordinating Global Manufacturing

Through their studies of transformations in a number of manufacturing industries, Harvard Business School professors Ramchandran Jaikumar and David Upton have concluded that in some cases worldwide manufacturing capacity can be allocated by competitive market forces through the use of information technology linked with cell-based manufacturing technologies. This linkage enables firms to become less vertically integrated as manufacturing capacity becomes, in essence, a commodity that can be accessed almost anywhere in the world using networking technology.

Coordinating Retail Channels

Harvard Business School professor Janice Hammond has studied business logistics and, particularly, channel coordination in the retailing industry—an ideal setting in which to examine technology's impact on the coordination of the interrelated value chains of the firms that make up the vertical stages of an industry from material acquisitions to end market. Networking in this context is clearly the primary enabler of the management concept of "quick response." Hammond traces the evolution of quick response in retailing and the role information technology has played in creating the essential networks that enable it, identifying in the process the potential for vast savings for firms that are able to respond to the technology challenge and simultaneously shift from a product to a customer service orientation.

Note

1. Walter Wriston, *Risk and Other Four-Letter Words* (New York: Harper & Row, 1986).

5

The Role of IT Networking in Sustaining Competitive Advantage

Stephen P. Bradley

The integration of information technology and telecommunications, termed IT networking, is having a dramatic impact on the structure of industries, on the competitive strategies of firms in these industries, and on the way firms cooperate within and across industries. In many cases, IT networking is changing the very fabric of how firms perform their core activities. In attempting to gain or enhance their competitive advantage, firms are making extraordinary investments in IT networking without being entirely sure of how these investments will ultimately pay off. Here we investigate the significance of the massive investments that have been, and will continue to be, made in IT networking, and question whether these investments will promote or enhance competitive advantage or merely turn out to be strategic necessities that enable a firm to survive to compete in the future.

Many firms are making strategic commitments to IT networking technology in order to gain significant competitive advantage in their industries. They are seeking not simply to improve efficiency by automating existing operations or leveraging individuals and groups, but to achieve a substantial advantage in the eyes of customers relative to the competition. Some will succeed, but most are likely to be disappointed, achieving not a sustainable competitive advantage but rather a brief edge, which is rapidly dissipated by industry forces or rendered obsolete by competitive responses. The problem will stem not from lack of creative ideas about how to use the technology, but rather from inadequate understanding and analysis of the logic that underlies the sustainability of competitive advantage.

In today's rapidly changing environment, nearly all firms are experiencing a strategic necessity that compels them to invest in IT networking technology. Customers are looking for and expecting better service in terms of shorter lead times, just-in-time inventory, quality assurance programs, flexibility, rapid response, and so forth. Electronic data interchange (EDI) with customers and standardized interfaces for computer-aided design (CAD) or computer-aided engineering (CAE) are becoming requirements in many industries. To support these new market demands, firms must cultivate faster, leaner, and more responsive organizations. IT networking technology within the firm is often seen as critical to improving the organization's ability to respond. For most firms, the demand for substantial improvements in organizational response and effectiveness requires closer relations with a smaller, more responsive group of suppliers. The host of demands made by customers are in turn passed on to these suppliers in the effort to meet the new performance requirements.

There is widespread awareness that failing to invest in IT networking today is likely to place a firm in strategic jeopardy. Competitors may invest first without fully understanding the strategic implications or evaluating the financial impact of their investment, and other firms may copy these investments lest they be left behind in a rapidly changing industry. In the face of dramatic industry changes, firms are making massive investments in IT networking, justifying them not on a traditional return on investment basis but on the assumption that they will somehow gain a significant competitive advantage in their industry. Most firms, as we shall see, do not realize a competitive advantage from their investments, and those that do find it difficult to sustain.

We focus here on the decision to invest in IT networking with a view toward improving management's understanding of the likely competitive advantage to be gained and the financial returns to be obtained. To illustrate how the technology is being implemented and the nature of the competitive advantages sought, we first present a taxonomy of the strategic applications of IT networking. We then present a framework for analyzing the likelihood that these investments will yield sustainable competitive advantage, become strategic necessities, or fail to achieve any of the benefits sought. Finally, we briefly relate this analysis to an approach for evaluating financial returns from alternative investments in IT networking technology.

Taxonomy of Strategic Applications

The taxonomy of strategic applications of IT networking is given in Table 5-1. The main categories of the taxonomy include investments designed primarily to affect (1) industry structure, (2) competitive strategy within a firm, and (3) cooperative strategy between the firm and other firms in the same or a related industry.

Industry structure cannot, of course, be separated from competitive or cooperative strategy, since changes in industry structure often result from specific competitive and/or cooperative strategies of existing competitors or new entrants to the industry. Even when structural change is driven by factors other than the competition, industry rivals must still adapt their competitive strategies to this change. Inasmuch as some strategic investments in IT networking are clearly made with the intent of creating a new industry, as opposed to significantly restructuring an existing one for competitive advantage, it is useful to focus on industry structure independently.

Industry Structure

The accelerating pace of globalization and technological innovation is driving both the creation of new, and the restructuring of existing, industries. The strategic implications of these two circumstances differ significantly.

Creating new industries. Whenever a new technology breaks on the scene, there is usually the opportunity to create new

Table 5-1
Taxonomy of Strategic Applications

Industry Structure	Competitive Strategy	Cooperative Strategy
New industries created	Within a single business	With buyers
Existing industries restructured	Among vertical businesses	With suppliers
	Across horizontal businesses	With rivals

businesses that provide the technology to those firms that can benefit from it at the outset but are unable to provide it themselves. Information technology and telecommunications have provided a host of such new industries.

Value-added/managed data networks such as those of Electronic Data Systems (EDS) and General Electric Information Systems (GEIS) emerged because the originating firms possessed some proprietary expertise and because there were clear economies of scale in delivering related services to multiple customers.[1] Both companies initially developed as time-sharing networks that provided high-powered computing, proprietary software applications, and data access to multiple users initially within the same organization and later across organizational boundaries. Today, with computing and data access having largely been brought back in house, these networks primarily provide efficient communications support for applications such as E-mail and EDI, while overcoming problems associated with differing local standards.

Community networks have emerged naturally when private infrastructure either became substantially more cost-effective or provided special performance characteristics (such as security) that were unavailable from the public infrastructure. Société Internationale de Telecommunications Aeronautique (SITA), the community network that supports data communications among nearly all international airlines, was initiated and continues to be effective because of economies of scale in delivering high-performance services to its customer owners. Since individual airlines can carry out many of the functions on their own proprietary networks, low-cost efficient operation is essential to the community network's survival.[2] Similar networks include SWIFT, developed to provide security and exploit economies of scale for international funds transfer in the banking industry, and RINET, initiated in 1987 to support the exchange of transaction data between trading partners in international insurance and reinsurance. In all three examples, cooperative endeavors are economically more efficient because they avoid unnecessary duplication of network services.

New value-added information service industries, covering a wide spectrum of applications, are emerging at an ever-increasing pace. News retrieval services such as Dow Jones and Lexus/Nexus provide real-time access to huge databases of articles on economic, business, social, and legal issues. Users accessing these databases via personal computers can identify articles of interest by searching for combinations of key words contained in specific publications or classes of publications, and print out short abstracts or the entire text. This process of seeking and refining information can be time-consuming and cumbersome and incur substantial duplication. An alternative service, Oxford Analytica, abstracts news from a variety of sources and makes it available electronically in a concise form. Other videotext systems, such as that provided by Minitel to France's telephone subscribers, offer news, weather, and information about products and services. Videotext systems for U.S. homes are more likely now that the regional Bell operating companies (RBOCs) have won the right in court to provide value-added information services.

Prodigy, an IBM-Sears joint venture in value-added information service, provides a wide variety of information services, including national and international news and weather, stock and bond quotations, access to an airline reservation system, product and service information, electronic mail, a bulletin board, and much more. For a low monthly fee, subscribers can have five separate accounts on the system and limited electronic mail access to all other subscribers. Many of the services available incur an additional cost. This evolving industry exploits economies of scope by bundling services that previously were offered individually.

Many other new information-service businesses are rapidly being created; video-conferencing, for example, has a potentially huge market. The competitors developing this technology, such as Picturetel in the United States, are forming alliances with players, such as IBM and Japan's NTT, that possess complementary resources. Another emerging service, centralized remote meter reading for electric, gas, and water utilities, will likely soon be widespread in the United States because of competitive pressures from the RBOCs, cable television, home monitoring and control systems companies, and others. In addition, supermarket point-of-sale (POS) data are providing an incredible level of detail on transactions, enabling such firms as Information Resources, Inc., to assess advertising and promotion effectiveness practically in real time along as highly refined a market segmentation as desired. Software applications, such as

Tactician, are enabling companies, such as GTE and Sears Roebuck, to bring POS data analysis capability in house using IT networking.

Most of the "new" industries created over the years, and those being created today, provide complementary services to existing industries; they either expand capabilities or substitute for existing less efficient services. They tend to stand alone, attract additional entrants, and exploit economies of scale or scope. For all of these newly created industries there is a question as to whether the benefit from being first in the market will accrue to the original innovators or be bid away by second-cycle innovators that bring additional economies of scale or scope or complementary resources to bear on the competitive dynamics of the newly created industry.[3] In restructured industries, technology, almost by definition, will have differential impacts on competitors, creating winners and losers among existing players and new entrants alike.

Restructuring existing industries. More important in the long run than the creation of new industries is that IT networking, which has the potential to restructure the underlying bases of competition in entire industries, is beginning to permeate so many existing industries. Information technology and telecommunications are less and less inputs to, or substitutes for, specific activities within firms or industries; the integration of these technologies is beginning to govern the way in which firms' activities are carried out, coordinated, measured, and communicated. To illustrate the fundamental change that has occurred, we briefly examine the impact of these technologies on financial services, broadcasting, manufacturing, and retailing.

London's International Stock Exchange provides a striking example of new technology restructuring a financial services industry.[4] The triggering events were near-complete deregulation of The Exchange and the introduction of new technology. Deregulation permitted broader membership, ended fixed commissions, and sharply increased the number of firms competing for customer business. By making information readily available to all regardless of physical location, The Exchange's automatic quotation system greatly increased the efficiency of the market. The resulting changes were dramatic. Virtually all trading moved from the floor to trading rooms with complete access to support staff, information resources, computer models, and customers. Moreover, foreign securities came to account for more than half of the London Exchange's turnover, compared to less than 5% for the New York and 2% for the Tokyo exchanges, and a substantial volume of business shifted to London from other European exchanges, notably those in Paris and Stockholm. Members of the London Exchange did not fare nearly so well, as the efficiency of the market virtually eliminated their operating margins; London firms suffered extensive losses with essentially no prospect of a return to traditional profitability.

Other financial service industries are also being restructured. Firms, such as Reuters and Dow Jones, support stock trading operations with real-time information, transaction products, trading room systems, and decision support models. Dow Jones's Dow Vision service, for example, includes text-based information, real-time market data, and decision support information. American Express, with its real-time network linking it to establishments it serves, and creative image-based billing systems for, and aggressive cross-selling to, customers, is largely responsible for the restructuring of the credit card industry. Such competitors as Visa and MasterCard have had to follow suit to the extent possible. There is also the much-discussed impact of automatic teller machines (ATMs) on retail banking. Once a regional competitor provided the capability, then other competitors within the region had to provide equivalent capability. When nationwide access to ATMs became a competitive necessity, national and international networks emerged. The next wave is likely to be home banking via personal computer and modem. The brokerage business is likely to undergo a similar radical transformation as discount brokers, such as Fidelity and Charles Schwab, introduce systems for direct purchase and sale of securities and other investment vehicles that reduce costs while improving service to clients. As these systems become more widespread and provide 24-hour access to international markets, their share of transactions is likely to increase significantly.

Another industry in the process of being radically restructured is broadcasting. By the mid-1980s, all three major networks had been purchased by large companies—ABC by Capital Cities Communications, NBC by General Electric, and CBS by Lowes—seeking apparently endless streams of cash to be derived largely from advertising revenues. Not long after these companies made their investments, cable expanded its position. Cable News Network (CNN), in particular, has had a devastating effect on the economics of network news broadcasting. Ted Turner was named *Time* magazine's "Man of the Year" in 1991 for CNN's role as a truly global news organization in terms of both its reporting and dissemination of the news.[5] The Gulf War highlighted CNN's new power in the industry. Telecommunications and information technology have reduced barriers to entry, enabling not only CNN, but the Fox Network, Turner Broadcasting, and other "super stations" to enter an industry previously thought to be impenetrable. Movie channels, such as Home Box Office and Showtime, and channels targeted at specific audiences—sports channels and the Disney Channel, for example—are likewise commanding substantial audience share. The VCR and movie rental businesses have also had a negative impact on the broadcasting industry. The end of the three major networks' oligopoly is directly attributable to technology's role in lowering entry barriers. "Interactive" television will likely accelerate the decline of the three major networks.

Many manufacturing industries have also responded to the intensification of competition by becoming heavy users of information technology and telecommunications. With markets increasingly demanding similar products worldwide, the importance of the triad—that is, the notion advanced by Kenichi Ohmae that it is essential for major firms in an industry to be active participants in each of the three major markets in North America, Europe, and the Pacific Rim—has become evident.[6] Thus, in industries like medical imaging we see such major competitors as General Electric, Siemens, and Toshiba active in one another's home bases of operations. The same is true in automobiles, computers, reprographics, power generation equipment, engineering plastics, and many other industries. Information technology and telecommunications play an essential role in helping firms in such industries coordinate and control remote locations, increase efficiency in decentralized operations, and standardize products and processes throughout the world to meet the needs of local as well as global customers.

The use of technology to support the rapid pace of globalization in manufacturing industries is well documented. Important changes in manufacturing technology may radically restructure many of these industries once again. The widespread adoption of programmable machines and computer-aided manufacturing has far-reaching consequences for factory operations and, in turn, industry structure. The manufacturing cell, a small group of machines that perform the entire manufacturing process— essentially a factory within a factory—is becoming the dominant manufacturing configuration in many industries. Manufacturing cells, which are designed to be highly flexible and reliable and require low overhead, in effect reduce minimum efficient scale for manufacturing operations. In addition, greater standardization in the communication link between design and manufacturing as a consequence of using CAD has reduced the need to collocate engineering design and high-volume manufacturing. Together, these factors substantially reduce both economies of scale and the capital required to participate in manufacturing. Moreover, small flexible manufacturing units can operate independently, physically and organizationally, of the design, engineering, and marketing functions.

With entry barriers lowered, it is likely that new firms will enter manufacturing in such industries and thus create markets for flexible manufacturing capacity. This is precisely what has driven dramatic performance improvements—in terms of cycle times, in-process inventory, capacity utilization, product variety, and quality—in the textile industry in the Prato region of Italy.[7] In this region, a myriad of small cooperating firms were created by the disintegration of a few large firms. Other manufacturing industries, from toys to printed circuit boards to semiconductors, are beginning to operate in a similar manner. We can expect an acceleration in this trend toward markets for flexible manufacturing capacity made possible by the integration of information technology and telecommunications.

Developments in IT networking are effecting a similar restructuring in the retail industry. Time-based competition, or quick response, is rapidly becoming the norm in retailing. A quick response strategy involves three key components: consumer testing to select specific products for specific markets; an effective information architecture that involves all suppliers in the channel; and a short-cycle replenishment system. The first step in implementing a quick response system is to establish an effective partnership with all suppliers and standards for electronic data interchange communications, universal product codes for product marking, and shipping container bar codes. The second step is to begin to use point-of-sale data to analyze trends, computer-aided design to facilitate timely design decisions, and flexible manufacturing technologies to ensure quick response. It has been estimated that a quick response system in the apparel industry based on existing technologies could cut total channel time from 125 days to 30, and perhaps to as little as 10, and could save more than $12 billion annually.[8] Two retailers that appear to be leading in this industry are The Limited and Benetton.

Wal-Mart, the discounter that is rapidly changing the face of retailing, utilizes IT networking extensively throughout its operations.[9] The company's nearly 2,000 stores are linked to both their headquarters and hub and spoke warehouse systems; store managers' decision making on inventory planning, product mix selection, pricing, and so forth is supported by technology; and POS scanners increase productivity and capture information for planning and control. Warehouse operations are also technology driven, with EDI links to headquarters, stores, and vendors. Since 1986 Wal-Mart has facilitated communication throughout the organization by a satellite hook-up, which supports weekly video-conferencing between headquarters and various warehouse and store locations. Extensive use of IT networking has not only enhanced productivity and efficiency, but also helped to empower employees at the local level. Competitors such as K mart and Target, forced to play catch-up in an attempt to match Wal-Mart's organizational efficiency, are making substantial investments in IT networking.

There is no question that IT networking is radically restructuring entire industries, including financial services, broadcasting, manufacturing, and retailing. The new technology is making firms more efficient in carrying out traditional activities at the same time that it is fundamentally changing the form of competition in many industries. Industry restructuring has become pervasive as the ways in which people work together are changed forever, business processes required to support their efforts are substantially changed, and firms' strategies are fundamentally altered to reflect new concepts of competitive advantage.

Competitive Strategy

The restructuring of existing industries enabled by IT networking is being driven largely by the strategies of firms that are attempting to gain competitive advantage in their industries. These advantages are believed to lie in establishing a low-cost position in an industry, effectively differentiating products and related services in the eyes of customers, or increasing speed of response (a form differentiation) relative to other competitors. With these objectives in mind, firms are making massive investments, perhaps as much as 50% of their total capital investments, in information technology and telecommunications. These investments are largely internal to a firm pursuing a competitive strategy, whereas a firm pursuing a cooperative strategy makes such investments in order to link its strategy more effectively with those of its suppliers, buyers, and, in some instances, rivals. In considering competitive strategy, we first review technological applications within a single business, and then interrelationships among vertical and horizontal businesses.

Within a single business. Many single businesses are using IT networking to lower costs, improve differentiation, or reduce lead times to market. Elaborate use of technology supports Federal Express's vision of being "a premier high-quality logistics carrier of time-sensitive goods on a worldwide basis."[10] Its worldwide information network, termed COSMOS for "Customer, Operations and Service Master On-line System," uses bar codes, scanners, and hand-held computers to capture data at every state of operation in order to provide rapid communications, efficient logistics management, and real-time tracking of packages. "Information about package status is one of our differentiators," a Federal Express manager explains, referring to the firm's attempt to gain a competitive advantage by making this information easily accessible to customers via computer.

Sony Corporation, a truly global company with sales balanced throughout the world and facilities located in 25 countries, has invested substantially in information technology and telecommunications to speed operations, reduce cycle times and inventories, and improve quality and customer service as a means to maintain its competitive edge. Its emphasis being on time-based competition almost for its own sake, Sony does not always analyze the cost savings that result from the technologies it has implemented.

A major challenge for Digital Equipment Corporation (DEC) which operates in more than 60 countries and employs more than 110,000 people, is to maintain a positive corporate culture that attracts the best individuals worldwide and encourages them to contribute to team efforts aimed at developing new products, finding software solutions, or defining a market approach. DEC's strategy of making extensive use of IT networking, including regular use of an "electronic blackboard" for research and development projects, has led several observers to characterize the company as the forerunner of the "global networked organization."[11]

Among vertical businesses. Vertical relationships among businesses in the same firm are usually employed to reduce transaction costs among the respective businesses.[12] Many firms are using information technology and telecommunications to manage such relationships in order to gain or defend a competitive advantage.

Asea Brown Boveri (ABB), which grew out of the 1987 megamerger of Brown Boveri of Switzerland and Asea of Sweden, is attempting to capture economies of scale while remaining highly responsive locally. ABB is perhaps the best example of the "transnational" company, a notion advanced by Bartlett and Ghoshal.[13] Having become, through its extensive acquisitions, a completely vertically integrated provider of the required capabilities, the company is attempting to change the basis of competition in power generation, transmission, and distribution by bundling products and services traditionally provided by specialized suppliers (e.g., General Electric for turbine generators, and Combustion Engineering, now a part of ABB, for boilers). Thirteen key executives and one hundred employees at its Zurich headquarters coordinate the federation of businesses that make up ABB, using IT networking to facilitate local responsiveness. A centralized management information system, dubbed Abacus, gathers data on 4,500 profit centers, compares actuals with budgets, makes forecasts, and aggregates data by business segments, countries, or companies within countries to permit a variety of analyses.[14]

Consider General Electric's global medical imaging business, which incorporates at least five major technologies, including magnetic resonance, nuclear medicine, CT scanning, ultrasound, and X-ray. GE has major operations throughout the world: in the United States, headquartered in Milwaukee; in Japan through a majority joint venture with Yokagauwa; in Korea through a joint venture with Daewoo; and in Europe through Compagnie General Radiologie (CGR), which GE acquired from France's Thomson in 1987. To manage the exceedingly complex task of coordinating the development of products, engineering, manufacturing, marketing, distribution, and services for this vast global business, GE makes extensive use of computer-aided design and engineering, integrated via IT networking.

Caterpillar Tractor Company is committed to a $1.8 billion project, termed "Plant with a Future" (PWAF), aimed at globalizing and modernizing its manufacturing facilities and processes.[15] The project combines flexible cell-based manufacturing processes with computer-integrated manufacturing (CIM) across the company's worldwide manufacturing facilities. The effort has involved moving a substantial part of Caterpillar's manufacturing out of the United States, where almost all of the firm's manufacturing took place prior to 1985. In addition, the company has begun to source on a worldwide basis and has reduced somewhat its vertical integration. This entire project is being coordinated through IT networking. Because it is pushing the frontiers of information technology currently available for CIM, Caterpillar has run into some difficulties with the project. Nevertheless, the company has successfully fended off its largest global competitor, Komatsu, which retains a highly vertically integrated manufacturing structure largely concentrated in Japan.

Across horizontal businesses. Horizontal interrelationships are employed among businesses in the same firm to capture economies of scope. Often, such relationships involve leveraging specialized assets through some form of distribution channel or specialized technologies across various businesses.

Schlumberger is active in a variety of businesses—including oil field development, automatic semiconductor testing, and manufacture of meters for measuring the consumption of gas, electricity, and water—that involve acquiring and converting data for rapid and efficient use by clients. The company believes that the competitive edge provided by "more reliable, faster transmission of data" is key to its various businesses.[16] The wide use of IT networking within Schlumberger has had the added benefit of greatly reducing travel time for professionals and disruptive relocations for R&D personnel.

Merrill Lynch's competitive strategy, which involved being first to introduce a cash management account (CMA), is another example of horizontal relationships. A CMA is a consolidated asset management account that can include checking and brokerage accounts, credit and debit cards, and money market and mutual funds. It presents a customer with one interface to a full line of Merrill Lynch services by integrating and combining what were previously separate lines of business. The approach's impact on Merrill Lynch has been dramatic. When the inevitable financial cycles lead a client to move assets to another market or instrument, it is not necessary for the client to leave the CMA since all likely alternatives are available directly from the account. Merrill Lynch's objective is thus to capture a client's assets initially and maintain the relationship by providing outstanding service and effectively erecting enormous psychological switching costs to leaving the CMA.

Finally, NEC's well-known "C&C" strategy, which stands for "computers and communications," has been the foundation of its success. In 1985, NEC was number ten in computers, far behind the leader, IBM, number seven in telecommunications behind AT&T, and number two in semiconductors behind Texas Instruments. However, in the three businesses taken together it was number five and, by 1988, had grown to number three by internal development.[17] At the same time, IBM's Rolm acquisition in telecommunications, and AT&T's attempt to go it alone in computers, were failing. NEC coordinates and facilities horizontal interrelationships in a global environment, using the integrative technology it espouses.

Cooperative Strategy

Information technology and telecommunications is increasingly being used to foster cooperative strategies with buyers, suppliers, and even rivals. Some have gone so far as to suggest that, in the long run, cooperative strategy may be more important than competitive strategy.

With suppliers. Perhaps the most dramatic examples of the value of cooperative strategy come in the area of changing supplier relationships. In industry after industry, supplier relationships are changing from highly adversarial to increasingly cooperative. Instead of trading off multiple suppliers against one another on an annual basis, many firms are relying on fewer suppliers and establishing long-term relationships with those suppliers based on mutual trust.

Wal-Mart—through creative relationships with suppliers ranging from Milliken and Seminole Manufacturing in apparel to General Electric in light bulbs to Procter & Gamble in a variety of products—is rapidly restructuring retailing. In the case of Milliken and Seminole Manufacturing, Wal-Mart increased unit sales by an estimated 31% and inventory turns by 30% by implementing a quick response system.[18] Wal-Mart uses EDI to give GE daily inventory status reports by warehouse, and GE plans inventory levels at each warehouse, cuts its own purchase orders, and continuously ships full truckloads. GE's performance is measured on the basis of Wal-Mart's inventory turns and out-of-stock rates. The company's inventory carrying and transaction costs have been substantially reduced, and it has significantly fewer stock-outs. The savings Wal-Mart realizes by having GE handle planning and ordering have increased working capital productivity, and the company has greatly reduced lost sales. Wal-Mart downloads weekly POS data to other vendors by SKU, reporting sales volumes, prices, location, and timing from its more than 2,000 stores. A number of these vendors are redesigning their manufacturing and replenishment processes to reduce the costs of their own and Wal-Mart's logistics operations. The bottom line is substantial cost savings in the entire value system, which are shared by the partners in these relationships.

Ford and Daimler-Benz are well known for quality programs that make extensive use of technology to achieve close linkages with a limited number of suppliers worldwide. Ford sole sources certain components for as much as five years or even for the life of a vehicle. To be selected, suppliers must be part of a preferred group that interfaces with Ford via EDI and uses a particular CAD/CAE system. The resulting relationships are highly cooperative, with cost transparency and sharing of cost savings resulting from supplier reengineering of the component or process.

This is a substantial change from the adversarial relationships that characterized the U.S. auto industry in the past.

Xerox has used its "Leadership through Quality" program to similarly change its relationships with suppliers.[19] It has reduced its supplier base in reprographics from more than 5,000 worldwide in 1981 to fewer than 300 today, while greatly improving communications and trust with suppliers. Changing supplier relationships—which have been accompanied by a 90% reduction in the incidence of defective parts and a 67% reduction in vendor inventory levels—are but a small part of broader changes instituted by the company, which brought it not only the prestigious Baldrige Award in 1989, but also net improvements in operating efficiency of approximately $2 billion annually.

For an example of cooperative strategy that involves both suppliers and buyers, we turn to Benetton, which operates approximately 5,000 retail stores in more than 75 countries.[20] Benetton has been described as a "vertically de-integrated company"; it sources most of its manufacturing operations from more than 200 dedicated suppliers and sells through retail outlets largely owned and managed by outside investors. The company makes extensive use of IT networking and CAD/CAE technologies to plan and coordinate activities among its numerous partners. Because they involve proprietary technology and yield economies of scale, purchasing and certain dyeing and cutting operations are performed in house. Retail distribution is coordinated by some 75 agents worldwide, who function as independent entrepreneurs. These arrangements have enabled Benetton to provide quick response, flexibility, low cost, and excellent service.[21]

With buyers. Historically, cooperative supplier relationships have been initiated much more often by firms sourcing a product or service than by suppliers. As cooperative relationships have increasingly proved to be highly effective for both partners, many suppliers have begun to pursue such relationships directly. Often, the initial motivation has been to lock in buyers by introducing switching costs, but the relationships that have proved to be most effective over the long term have developed into more trusting partnerships.

American Hospital Supply was the classic example of an interorganizational information system that formed the basis of a long-term competitive advantage. Because it recognized that half the cost of purchasing supplies for hospitals was tied up in acquiring and tracking the right information so that the proper amounts could be accurately billed to patients and insurance companies, American Hospital Supply was able to grow from a $300,000 company to a $3 billion company in less than 10 years, while consolidating the industry and significantly reducing the dominance of Johnson & Johnson. The latter eventually came up with an effective response, but by then, American Hospital Supply had built considerable customer loyalty. American Hospital Supply only began to lose its competitive advantage after it was acquired by Baxter-Travenol and its capabilities were eroded by a pattern of underinvestment.

Information technology-based products and services for managed maintenance and regulatory compliance are essential to electric utilities, particularly in the nuclear segment of the industry. Typically, they are the responsibility of in-house maintenance groups. But Westinghouse leveraged its industry-specific expertise and its ability to benchmark performance across the industry in order to achieve an advantage over in-house providers. The company has used IT networking to realize economies of scale in delivering these services, while introducing substantial switching costs, particularly with respect to captive maintenance providers. One of its systems involves a centralized diagnostic center employing expert systems linked directly to its customers' equipment with sensors.

Recently, businesses have begun to forge links directly with their ultimate customers. Japan's National Bicycle Company, for example, makes many of its bicycles to order.[22] Customers are measured on a machine in the dealer's showroom, which is part of a computer-aided design system. Customers also select the specific make and model of brake, derailer, chain, tires, and other options, including color and personalized name, if desired, and the order is electronically placed directly with the manufacturer, which can produce a made-to-order bicycle three hours later. The company, having determined that this response is too rapid, holds the order for a week so that the customer can have the joy of anticipation.

The bicycle example has been widely reported as an exciting exception, but it may soon be the rule in many industries.

Saturn Corporation, General Motors' first new nameplate in 50 years, essentially does much the same thing. A Saturn customer, aided by a salesperson at a computer terminal, places an order for a car with a unique set of options and choice of colors directly into the Saturn plant's production planning and inventory control system. Made-to-order rather than made-to-inventory may be the next great leap in retailing; it is here now in some industries.

With rivals. Many firms have established cooperative relationships with firms that are both partners and rivals, depending on the circumstances. Although sometimes intended to reduce rivalry in an industry, these relationships are for the most part initiated to enhance an existing competitive advantage or form an alliance to thwart a specific competitor.

To get at the notion of firms that are rivals in one business and partners in another, General Electric CEO Jack Welch poses a modern-day "riddle of the sphinx" asking, "Who is my customer in the morning, my rival in the afternoon, and my supplier in the evening?" The answer: several large diversified global companies, such as Toshiba in Japan and Hyundai in Korea. GE buys semiconductors, competes in medical imaging, and supplies power generation equipment to Toshiba; it is a partner in electric motor manufacturing with Hyundai (through a joint venture, KIMCO), to which it also sells, and from which it buys, a variety of other products. These large global players interface often through GE's GEIS value-added network.

Large engineering and construction companies, such as Bechtel, often form bidding consortia that involve construction subcontractors and architectural engineers. The same companies may be rival bidders on other occasions, particularly when the bidding can be unbundled. To coordinate and plan complex projects often involves extensive use of IT networking, project planning technology, computer-aided engineering, and so forth. The consulting industry works much the same way, forming consortia to prepare proposals, conduct bidding, and carry out projects that involve substantial amounts of diverse and specialized expertise. Proposals and bids are often prepared on a commercially available network, eliminating the need for the cooperating parties to meet face to face. The same consulting companies may simultaneously be bidding aggressively against one another for other projects. In some instances, they are simultaneously bidding on the same project as part of a consortia and as individuals.

Perhaps the most surprising pair to adopt a new cooperative strategy is IBM and Apple.[23] One might have suspected that these traditional rivals would never cooperate, but with software firms, such as Microsoft, extracting substantial industry profits, IBM and Apple have initiated a cooperative strategy in personal computers. Under a recent agreement, IBM is to provide a stamp of approval for Apple communication products, which the IBM sales force will then market, while Apple is to base future generations of high-end personal computers on IBM's proprietary RISC technology, the RS6000 microprocessor. (To maintain good relations with its current microprocessor supplier, Apple entered into an agreement whereby Motorola is to serve as a second source for the new generation microprocessors.) Through a joint venture called Taligent, IBM and Apple will co-develop the next generation operating system (referred to within Apple as "Pink"), which is to run on Apple's installed base of Motorola microprocessors, IBM's RS6000, and Intel's x86 series. This cooperative approach is aimed at setting standards and capturing future returns by providing essential software that would otherwise likely have been provided by Microsoft. Another joint venture, Kaleida, was formed to develop multimedia technologies to provide full-motion video on PCs. Such cooperation would have been unheard-of only a few years ago.

Sustaining Competitive Advantage

With the creation of new industries and the restructuring of many existing industries, massive investments will clearly have to be made in information technology and telecommunications, but how much of this investment will yield sustainable competitive advantage? Many of the firms justifying their investments on the basis of gaining a competitive advantage are, as we suggested earlier, likely to be disappointed.

When firms invest in technology in order to gain competitive advantage they are attempting to lower their cost of doing business, improve the performance of their products and services in the eyes of the customer, or improve their speed of response. In each instance, the competitive advantage sought is not absolute but relative to the competition.[24] The investment may be designed to lower costs within the firm by capturing economies of scale or scope, reducing transaction costs, exploiting linkages between various activities of the business, or managing interrelationships with other businesses in the firm. On the other hand, the investment may be designed to increase differentiation by responding more effectively to buyer needs for improved quality, performance, features, service, or cycle time. By being first with an investment in technology, firms often create a brief competitive advantage, only to be surprised when competition matches or improves on their initiatives.

Why is it so difficult to sustain a competitive advantage? Pankaj Ghemawat has identified four key threats—imitation, substitution, holdup, and slack—that a firm must address to sustain a competitive advantage.[25]

Threat of Imitation

In most instances, investments in information technology and telecommunications can be imitated fairly easily, at least by firms of comparable size. Indeed, development of a capability built around information technology often triggers competitors to acquire or develop a similar or superior capability. Most new IT-supported capabilities are neither patentable nor difficult to copy; vendors, consultants, and systems integrators are readily available to help a firm copy and improve upon any idea. In economic terms, the scarcity value of an investment is bid away by increasing its supply. To gain advantage from an innovation, a firm must introduce it early and keep ahead of the competition.

Automated teller machines were initially believed to have the potential to yield sustainable competitive advantage in retail banking. But as the benefits of ATMs quickly became apparent, all banks recognized that they needed to provide the service. Citibank, which inaugurated ATM service in New York City, was quickly followed by every other bank. Citibank's market share went up briefly, but the advantage did not last. While it incurred the substantial cost of being first, the other banks, seeing the need to provide the service, distributed their costs by forming a consortium to implement a competing ATM network, NYCE. The speed of imitation quickly dissipated Citibank's competitive advantage. Had they not quickly followed suit, the other banks would have certainly been at a competitive disadvantage.

In contrast, Merrill Lynch's cash management account was difficult to imitate for three reasons. One, the software needed to integrate the various services provided by the CMA was fairly complicated, and its development was kept secret. Two, Merrill Lynch already offered, in unbundled form, much of the full line of services that had to be provided to support a CMA. Three, substantial switching costs related to setting up accounts, becoming familiar with the process of moving money among instruments, and understanding and working with the statements of account transactions were associated with the CMA. The difficulty of imitation and the creation of switching costs not only gave Merrill Lynch a substantial lead on the competition, but also enabled it to sustain its competitive advantage.

Threat of Substitution

Substitution is the most pernicious threat to the sustainability of competitive advantage. To guard against imitation, modern firms constantly monitor the competition and make the strategic commitments needed to stay ahead. It is much more difficult to know what to monitor in the case of substitution, as it is often unclear where the threat will come from or what can be done about it once it is identified. Whereas imitation increases the supply of a good or service, thus reducing its scarcity value, substitution reduces demand for the good or service.

Even when technology investment is difficult to imitate and continuous improvement keeps an early mover ahead of competitors, competitive advantage may not be sustainable. Even Federal Express, which places considerable emphasis on continuously improving its position and taking advantage of economies of scale in marketing and R&D, has found fax and EDI, which can substitute for much of its core business, dissipating its competitive advantage. In the not-too-distant future, we may see all documents delivered via EDI, in color with graphics or even animation. High-quality hard copy, if needed, will be printed locally. Recognizing the threat of substitution to its overnight package delivery service, Federal Express is aggressively soliciting shipments, such as spare parts, that cannot be transmitted electronically.

Threat of Holdup

When other parties exert power, usually over the control of scarce resources, to extract a portion of the returns from an investment in technology, we have the threat of holdup. Holdup thus occurs when key specialized assets needed to gain competitive advantage are not owned or controlled by the firm seeking the advantage. It relates only to capturing the value from a strategy, not to creating the value.

The notion of holdup is illustrated by the relationship that developed between Merrill Lynch and Michael Bloomberg.[26] Bloomberg developed a sophisticated trading support system, which depended on timely bond price information that was not widely available. Merrill Lynch agreed to provide this information in return for a minority interest in the company and an agreement to restrict access to certain of its competitors. Merrill Lynch, because it had the complementary specialized assets needed to implement the system, was thus able to extract a substantial portion of the value of the service. Nearly all value-added information services are subject to the threat of appropriation. The detailed knowledge of the industry to which a service is to be provided, or the specific information assets, or both, typically capture more of an innovation's returns than the delivery system.

It is threat of holdup that will probably deny AT&T much of the return from joint ventures in value-added information services.[27] These returns are likely to be captured instead by firms with industry-specific expertise in the particular services. The RBOCs may fare no better in these businesses, despite access to the customers in their regional monopolies, because they are required to provide equal access to other vendors of value-added information services.

Threat of Slack

Slack describes a condition wherein a firm fails to capture all possible value from its competitive position because of inefficiency, complacency, arrogance, paternalism, and so forth. Because all firm activities must be performed in a superior, if not "world-class," fashion, many firms have begun to competitively benchmark the performance of key activities, overhead structures, balance sheet productivity, and so forth, not only against the best in their industry, but against the best in the world.

Ghemawat presents a dramatic example of organizational slack in his description of Xerox in the 1980s.[28] Xerox considerably improved its competitive position between 1980 and 1990 through its now well-known "Leadership through Quality" program. The cornerstone of this program, an effort to competitively benchmark all aspects of its operations, revealed that Xerox was at a 40% manufacturing cost disadvantage, its product development cycle was twice as long and involved twice as many people as that of competition, its overhead rates were way out of line, and its quality was perceived to be substantially lower than that of the competition. Xerox subsequently embarked on the program of competitive benchmarking that evolved into its "Leadership through Quality" program. The results were extraordinary: 40% reduction in new-product development costs, 30% reduction in development cycle time, 30% increase in "customer satisfaction index," 50% reduction in "significant customer problems," 67% reduction in production lead times, 67% reduction in machine defect levels, and so on. The bottom line, as pointed out by Ghemawat, is that there had to have been extraordinary organizational slack at Xerox to have made such savings possible.

Today, analysts find at General Motors, in particular, as well as at other U.S. automobile manufacturers, the same sorts of organizational slack. In *The Machine that Changed the World,* James Womack, Daniel Jones, and Daniel Roos document the success of Japanese lean production methods and make a strong case for restructuring all the competitors in the industry.[29] Though General Motors has, with the support of its subsidiary, EDS, made massive investments in information technology and telecommunications, it has by no means fully adopted lean production. In fact, for the most part, the company appears to have made these investments as an overlay to existing organizational structure and management practice. Most observers believe that General Motors must effect a massive downsizing and fundamentally alter the way it carries out its mission if it is to see any real change. At the Saturn and NUMI (a joint venture with Toyota) plants, General Motors has made its first attempts at eliminating organizational slack, but the methods used there have not as yet penetrated the rest of the organization to any great extent. It appears that Ford, particularly Ford Europe, is substantially ahead of GM in the effective use of IT networking and restructuring to eliminate organizational slack.

Many companies in other industries are facing the same problems. IBM is only now finally beginning to aggressively restructure itself and redefine the way it serves customers. No longer is an account management team, armed primarily with extensive knowledge of the capabilities of IBM products and completely dedicated to a single account, an effective approach. Customers are seeking solutions to specific problems that require a high degree of specialized industry or technical expertise. IBM needs to develop and share this scarce expertise across a variety of account teams. To identify, enhance, and continue to develop the requisite skills, new strategies must be conceived, new organizations established, and new incentives created in a mutually consistent way. Like General Motors, IBM, despite extraordinary resources and talent, is a long way from eliminating organizational slack.

On the other hand, General Electric seems to have gotten the message under the leadership of Jack Welch; the company has moved aggressively to restructure the way it does business, with the goal of maintaining and improving its competitive position in the many industries it serves. To increase the efficiency and productivity of all types of activities at every level of the organization, GE has become a leader in "business process redesign."[30] Under a broad program referred to as "Work-Out," General Electric has begun to implement a continuous improvement program (although this was not an objective when the program was initiated). IT networking, though a relatively small part of this effort, is often the vehicle that facilitates the redesign of business processes.

Competitive Advantage versus Strategic Necessity

The threats of imitation, substitution, holdup, and slack may seem so prevalent as to suggest that gaining competitive advantage through investment in IT networking technology is rather unlikely. Why, then, are so many firms making massive investments in this technology? In many cases, the answer is that firms are seeking elusive early-mover advantages, but more often, it is simply that they perceive such investments, whether correctly or not, as strategic necessities. To survive in the future, firms must meet or beat the competition in delivering value to customers. Competitors fear that not to follow suit is almost surely to grant competitive advantage to an early mover.

Early-Mover Advantages

The keys to gaining and defending early-mover advantage lie in creating entry barriers to ward off new competitors, building mobility barriers against existing competitors, and raising switching costs. Ghemawat identifies five forms of early-mover advantage: private information, size economies, relationships, response lags, and competitor retaliation.[31]

Private information, or specific expertise, is often a key entry or mobility barrier. Wal-Mart's initial expertise was in making the discount store format successful in small rural towns at a time when its competitors, focused on larger towns and suburban communities, were unsure of how to compete effectively in smaller communities. Wal-Mart's unique hub and spoke warehouse system, supported by information technology, was key to its success in rural areas and provided a low-cost basis for expanding into suburban areas.

Size economies, including economies of scale and scope as well as experience or learning, can also be important. Federal Express was the first overnight package delivery service to achieve minimum efficient scale in sorting operations, thus giving it a substantial cost advantage. By the time competitors achieved equivalent scale, primarily through industry consolidation and mergers, Federal Express had implemented a real-time package tracking information system that was too expensive for competitors to copy, given their relatively smaller market shares.

Relationships and contracts can be key, as evidenced by General Electric's relationship with Wal-Mart, which, although not an enforceable contract, provides such mutual benefit that it is unlikely to be displaced so long as service quality and performance are continuously improved. Microsoft's early relationship with IBM around the DOS operating system for personal computers so solidified its early-mover advantage that when IBM decided to go it alone with a new operating system, OS/2, it was unsuccessful in breaking the bond.

Response lags are probably the most effective barriers to imitation. Imitation invariably requires time for implementation, which defers its impact. By the time an imitator has acted, an early mover often has moved on to the next innovation, as seen in the example of Federal Express. Caterpillar Tractor has incurred some risk in its program of worldwide computer-integrated manufacturing, which will take more than five years to complete, because it believes that it will take Komatsu substantially longer to imitate the approach and consequently, in all likelihood, the latter will not follow suit.

Although threats of retaliation can sometimes protect early-mover advantages, IT networking examples are essentially non-existent. AT&T, despite a variety of threats, was unsuccessful in keeping MCI and Sprint out of the long-distance market. But once the competition entered and AT&T was largely deregulated, it continued to successfully defend its leadership position by exploiting economies of scale in marketing, particularly media advertising.

Strategic Necessity

We now examine the examples discussed to determine which are likely to yield sustainable competitive advantages, which fall into the category of strategic necessity, and which will prove to be poor investments overall.

Many of the examples in newly created industries can be understood by analyzing early-mover advantages. Prodigy, for example, can probably sustain its competitive advantage if it can secure a large enough installed base before it encounters a significant competitive threat. Prodigy has a significant lead, and substantial response lags exist. By continuously improving its services, it can create natural switching costs. For Dow Jones and Lexus/Nexus, on the other hand, investments in IT networking can be categorized as a strategic necessity; competitive advantage is difficult to defend in the information retrieval business due to relatively low switching costs. Moreover, the business is vulnerable to a substantial threat of substitution from CD rom technology. Oxford Analytica, in particular, will have to adopt the latter technology, as new competitors have already introduced it.

In industries restructured by IT networking, some early movers will be able to sustain a competitive advantage, but most will be forced to invest in the technology simply to compete. Because Wal-Mart's investments in IT networking clearly contribute to a sustainable competitive advantage, its strongest rivals, K mart and Target, will have to make similar investments in order to survive. Hence these investments are strategic necessities. Given sufficient response lag on the part of its competitors, Wal-Mart will likely be able to advance to a higher level of competitive advantage. In broadcasting, on the other hand, where IT networking is clearly a strategic necessity, the technology will continue to reduce entry barriers and increase competition.

Federal Express's competitive strategy, reinforced by size, particularly economies of scale in operations and marketing, and by experience, seems to have yielded a sustainable competitive advantage. In the longer term, however, substitution of fax and EDI may well erode its competitive advantage in the overnight package delivery business. ABB's investment in IT networking would seem to be a strategic necessity, as it is essential for coordinating the company's simultaneously global and local strategy, but it is unlikely to yield much in the way of competitive advantage. Similarly, in financial services, Reuters and Dow Jones need IT networking to provide their information and decision support services, but it is not likely to be a source of competitive advantage. As American Express's lead in IT networking has largely been matched by Visa and MasterCard, the basis of competition is switching to other sources of competitive advantage. Citibank VISA, in particular, has been able to successfully undermine American Express by emphasizing, in its advertising, its much wider acceptance by merchants.

Cooperative strategy may provide many opportunities for sustaining competitive advantage. As the GE–Wal-Mart partnership illustrates, once an effective cooperative strategy has been established, all incentives are directed toward making the partnership work. Failure of a partnership requires that a new partnership be formed and effective relationships established, which invariably involves disruption costs and lost time, and often involves loss of expertise as well. Xerox, with its "Leadership through Quality" program and fewer than 300 suppliers, has a strong incentive to make its various partnerships work. The same holds true for Ford, Benetton, and most of the other examples of cooperative strategy.

The lead in operating systems that has enabled Microsoft to "hold up" the computer industry has forced IBM and Apple to play catch-up with their joint venture to develop Pink, the operating system destined to compete with the next generation of Windows. Microsoft's competitive advantage appears to be sustainable for some time, given the size of its installed base and the response lags of its major competitors. In the long run, IBM and Apple can sell their new operating software bundled with the hardware, thereby achieving economy of scope, and perhaps recapture the initiative from Microsoft. But this is a highly risky strategy, given that the large installed base of Windows' users presents significant psychological as well as actual switching costs.

Strategic Investments

The most common complaint heard from senior executives discussing IT networking is that they have made massive investments in information technology in the past and have rarely, if ever, been able to measure the return on investment. What is the basis for these complaints? Is it that most of the investments made in information technology and telecommunications have been poor investment decisions? This is undoubtedly the case in some instances, but more often this sense of frustration derives from reliance on traditional capital budgeting evaluations.

The capital budgeting exercise attempts to justify investments based either on the cost savings relative to current operations or the additional cash flow generated by increased market share or increased margins. Evaluation is made in terms of a simple project investment, largely independent of the overall business strategy. What is needed is a more strategic evaluation of such investments, in the spirit of Alfred Rappaport's *Creating Shareholder Value.*[32] An investment in information technology and telecommunications should be evaluated not as a series of isolated projects, but as a required part of a coherent strategy for a business or collection of businesses. Alternative strategies, not projects, should be evaluated against future scenarios that include a significant loss of competitive position if all requirements of the strategy, including investments in IT networking, are not undertaken. This type of strategy evaluation highlights the need to invest in IT networking even when it is a strategic necessity rather than an attempt to gain a sustainable competitive advantage.

Notes

1. *Global Networking Study,* 4, Nolan, Norton & Co. and KPMG Peat Marwick, 1990.

2. Ibid.

3. Ralph E. Gomory, "From the 'Ladder of Science' to the Product Development Cycle," *Harvard Business Review* (November–December 1989): 99–105.

4. Eric K. Clemons and Bruce W. Weber, "Turmoil, Transparency, and Tea: Valuing the Impact of IT on London's Stock Exchange," in *Strategic and Economic Impacts of Information Technology Investment: Perspectives on Organizational Growth and Competitive Advantage,* R. Kauffman, R. Banker, and M. Mahmood, eds. (Idea Group Publishing, 1992), pp. 202–235.

5. *Time,* "Ted Turner, Man of the Year," January 1, 1992.

6. Kenichi Ohmae, *Triad Power* (New York: Free Press, 1985).

7. Ramchandran Jaikumar and David Upton, "The Coordination of Global Manufacturing," Chapter 7, this volume.

8. Janice H. Hammond and Maura G. Kelly, "Quick Response in the Apparel Industry," Harvard Business School Case 9-690-038 (1990).

9. George Salk, Philip Evans, and Lawrence E. Shulman, "Competing on Capabilities: The New Rules of Corporate Strategy," *Harvard Business Review* (March–April 1992): 57–69.

10. *Global Networking Study.*

11. Ibid.

12. Oliver Williamson, *Markets and Hierarchies: Analysis and Antitrust Implication* (New York: Free Press, 1975).

13. Christopher A. Bartlett and Sumantra Ghoshal, *Managing Across Borders: The Transnational Solution* (Boston: Harvard Business School Press, 1989).

14. *Global Networking Study.*

15. Christopher A. Bartlett and Susan Ehrlich, "Caterpillar, Inc.: George Schaefer Takes Charge," Harvard Business School Case 9-390-036 (1990).

16. Ibid.

17. John R. Wells, "NEC Corporation," Harvard Business School Case 9-386-129 (1983).

18. Hammond and Kelly, "Quick Response in the Apparel Industry."

19. Melvyn A. J. Menezes and Jon Serbin, "Xerox Corporation: Customer Satisfaction," Harvard Business School Case 9-591-055 (1991).

20. Ibid.

21. *Global Networking Study.*

22. Susan Moffat, "Japan's New Personalized Production," *Fortune* (October 22, 1990): 132.

23. David B. Yoffie, "Apple Computer 1992," Harvard Business School Case 9-792-081 (1992).

24. Moffat, "Japan's New Personalized Production."

25. Pankaj Ghemawat, *Commitment: The Dynamic of Strategy* (New York: Free Press, 1991).

26. Eric K. Clemons and Michael C. Row, "Sustaining IT Advantage: The Role of Structural Differences," *MIS Quarterly,* 13, no. 5 (September 1991): 274–292.

27. Joseph Baylock, Stephen P. Bradley, and Eric K. Clemens, "Enhanced Communications Services: An Analysis of AT&T's Competitive Position" in *Future Competition in Telecommunications,* S. P. Bradley and J. A. Hausman, eds. (Boston: Harvard Business School Press, 1989), pp. 277–300.

28. Ghemawat, *Commitment.*

29. James P. Womack, Daniel T. Jones, and Daniel Roos, *The Machine that Changed the World* (New York: HarperCollins, 1991).

30. Thomas A. Steward, "How Jack Welch Keeps the Ideas Coming at GE," *Fortune* (August 12, 1991).

31. Ghemawat, *Commitment.*

32. Alfred Rappaport, *Creating Shareholder Value* (New York: Free Press, 1986).

6
Telecommunications and the Restructuring of the Securities Markets

George A. Hayter

Every generation and every field of endeavor perhaps believes itself to be living in a period of unprecedented change. In letters unearthed in ancient Egypt, parents lament the unruly and disrespectful behavior of the younger generation and the unrelenting introduction of new ways of doing things. Yet if ever there was an example of a stable civilization, surely it is ancient Egypt. Perhaps our perception is altered by a sort of perspective effect, with immediate events seeming to move faster than less recent or historical events, rather as a railway passenger sees trees close to the track moving past more rapidly than more distant objects. Or perhaps as the structure of society becomes more complex and intricate, there is simply more to change and adapt in a given period.

World Financial Markets

Whatever the cause, few can fail to perceive that at the present time the world financial market is rapidly restructuring. Markets are coming and going and merging with one another, new instruments are being devised and traded, and linkages between markets are being established and dissolved.

What is the nature of the changes that are having an impact on and transforming the old, familiar scenery of financial markets? This chapter explores the effects of the telecommunications revolution on world financial markets and examines particularly how these markets have had to adapt and change, some slowly and some very quickly. London's Big Bang is taken as a case study of how the market has changed there, and used to outline the opportunities and challenges that face securities industry participants around the world.

The Pressure for Change

Changes in the securities industry are commonly attributed to communications, deregulation, and internationalization. The present analysis suggests that in fact the prime driver of change in the industry has been recent improvements in communications technology. That we are seeing accelerated political change in Eastern Europe at the same time is not coincidence. Improved communications is a root cause of these changes. It has been impossible for states to maintain a blackout on international communications, particularly via television and radio, in countries in which people can afford these commodities and speak and comprehend familiar languages. Change will occur more slowly in the enormous agrarian heartland of communist China, where mass communication is not yet a liberalizing force or a window to the world outside. Change in China, when it comes, will emanate from the coastal trading cities, which have good external communications and enjoy contact with more developed and democratic societies.

Communication is fast, cheap, and universally available in developed countries, and it is getting faster, cheaper, and more pervasive all the time. Those in the communications industry see no immediate prospect for a slowing in this trend. Digital communication, in particular, has begun to transform the way information, including pictures and voice, is transmitted around the globe. The union of communications technology and computers makes it possible for information to be stored, forwarded, replicated, processed, transformed, and re-transmitted in infinite and kaleidoscopic variety. The advent of communications satellites and fiber-optic cable has brought communications companies and their users an information bandwidth undreamed-of when the first undersea cables were laid earlier in this century. Many thousands of telephone conversations can now be transmitted over a single optical fiber the width of a human hair.

The Impact on Markets

What does change in the securities industry mean for financial markets? Perhaps of greatest importance is that market information is now available immediately and physical distance is no longer a barrier to its reception. For professional traders, this means fewer arbitrage opportunities, as prices in related markets level out rapidly and price-sensitive news and company information is available as quickly as prices. News of the victory at Waterloo took days to reach London; then, a competitive trading advantage could accrue to being a few hours ahead of other traders. Today, the best that can be hoped for is a few seconds' lead on the competition, and soon that advantage will be down to milliseconds. Traders must be faster and smarter, but the principles remain the same. Already in some markets a trader needs a computer to spot opportunities in time to act upon them ahead of the competition.

Although the problem is entirely academic to longer-term investors, it is noteworthy that transmitting information by satellite can confer a disadvantage on some traders. The round-trip communication delay for a signal to and from a satellite in geostationary orbit 22,500 miles above the earth amounts to about 250 milliseconds, compared to about 80 milliseconds needed for a terrestrial signal to travel halfway around the world. Thus, the speed of light and electricity is becoming a factor in competition between traders and a concern to operators of financial markets.

It has been argued that there are three ways a market can respond to these changes. One, the market can ignore them. In due course, this will give rise to a re-clustering of securities traders very close to the computer systems of the markets from which their price signals emanate. Firms closest to the source of the signal will always have the competitive advantage.

Two, exchanges could preempt this trend by offering the same computer room as their own signal transmitter to ensure that all traders are operating on a "level playing field." This would have the interesting effect of transforming an exchange from a physical trading floor for people to a virtual trading floor for computers, *within a single generation!* Traders could be located wherever they chose, presumably close to their customers, linked to their trading systems by communications that need operate only at the speed of human response.

Three, an exchange might create a global equality of information by introducing delays into its price signal to nearby participants to compensate for the transmission delays experienced by remote players. Designers of the Chicago Board of Trade AURORA system have considered this solution.

Another effect of faster communication is increased volatility and closer coupling of world markets. On a daily basis now, we can see the ripple effect of market trends running from time zone to time zone, interrupted only by weekends and public holidays. We have seen instances of near panic in a market rapidly transmitted to the next time zone, passing in a westerly direction around the globe for a day or two until stability was restored at a new, lower level. Market falls, of course, tend to be much more acute than upward adjustments: the greed/fear cycles work that way. Whereas greed takes hold gradually and feeds progressively upon itself, there tends to be an element of caution as the upward cycle gathers momentum. The collapse of markets caused by fear, on the other hand, operates very rapidly, like swimmers racing from the water at a shark scare. Sawtooth price trends have been dramatically compressed by faster communications. The well-documented market collapse of 1929 occurred over a period of several weeks. The more recent market collapse of 1987 took only two or three days, but the pattern was very familiar—a series of downward swoops, each followed by a partial and temporary recovery.

The application of information technology has also driven down the unit cost of trading, and this, combined with access to better and more reliable information, has driven up the volume of trading in many markets, particularly the foreign exchange market, in which annual trading volumes are some 20 times greater than required to fund international trade. This ratio has grown steadily over the years, presumably driven also by increasingly volatile foreign exchange rates.

Lagging the effects I have described is the more recent but rapid growth in cross-border trading—investors and intermediaries of one country trading in the securities of and with their counterparts in another. This trend is still in a very early stage.

How the Markets Have Responded

Widespread and general change in the behavior of markets and their participants has led to some striking changes in market mechanisms and their structures. For a London observer, this would have been difficult to miss, as the changes have been quite abrupt. But they are becoming apparent, and proceeding at a measured pace, around the world.

The equities exchanges, perhaps the most visible markets, provide a good illustration of what has been going on. Physical trading markets operating on trading floors mostly came into existence before widespread use of the telephone, when a floor was the only practical means of supporting multidirectional communication. Interesting exceptions to the established practice are the financial options and futures markets, which rely, in the main, on an open outcry, pit trading system. These markets are modeled directly on earlier commodities markets—the established means of trading has simply been adapted to new instruments.

A physical trading floor integrates the processes of price discovery, trading, and regulation, and good communication is a natural by-product. Indeed, price discovery generally occurs in the act of trading, rather as in an auction. Regulation is self-imposed in the sense that rules of fair play evolve and become codified through routine face-to-face contact between and interaction among individuals on the trading floor. Traders who regularly deal less than fairly with their counterparts soon find themselves disadvantaged on the floor. Market officials can maintain more or less effortless supervision of the physical trading market simply by being present and serving as referee when asked. A floor market can be self-policing.

Floor markets go hand in hand with an exclusive membership concept. Only certain individuals are permitted to enter the trading floor and anyone who wants to trade is obliged to do so through these people. Admission to the floor may be through ownership of a "seat" or employment by a member firm, and there may be more than one class of operator on the floor performing different functions. Operational rules governing relationships among these individuals and how they may trade are codified in a rule book or code of practice, which is enforced by peer pressure and supported by market officials.

This convenient approach is breaking down as an indirect consequence of improved communications technology. First to go was price information, which could be collected on the trading floor and transmitted immediately to ticker machines, printers, and, later, to TV screens off the market floor, and eventually around the world. When only the people on the trading floor had a clear, up-to-date, uncluttered view of the market, they enjoyed an exclusive information advantage. But when it became possible for good quality prices to be seen and used by almost anyone, this information had to be controlled if the interests of members were to be preserved. As a result, most markets have maintained a two-tier information structure: one tier is made available to the general public and off-floor professionals, while access to the other is restricted to those on the trading floor. Some markets employ a three-tier information structure that reflects and supports the three layers of this highly structured industry. The New York Stock Exchange, for example, makes available to professionals an intermediate tier of information, while providing the general public only delayed price information.

More recently, we have seen in the United States the introduction of "order routing" systems, interconnected webs of networks owned by the great "wire house" brokers that focus on the stock exchanges themselves. These networks enable orders bought and sold by brokers' branch offices across the country to be routed to the stock exchange of choice and the priced and confirmed execution details to be transmitted back for client notification. Order routing networks have become the physical battlefield upon which the competitive war for order flow has been fought between exchanges. Automatic execution of small, off-network orders, providing fast execution at a guaranteed price, was first offered in Chicago by the Midwest Exchange, and later by the Pacific Exchange. Other exchanges followed, including New York and NASDAQ.

Another major impact of information technology has been the introduction of electronic trading or trade support. Broadly, these systems fall into two categories: what one might call "order-driven systems," built to mirror electronically the continuous auction market process in exchanges where liquidity is provided essentially by the priced incoming buy and sell orders from investors; and what have become known as "quote-driven" or dealer markets, evolved from less formally structured markets in which dealers intermediate each broker's trade.

The first serious order-driven system was Toronto's CATS system, introduced in the early 1970s, which now executes about half the total value of turnover on the Toronto Stock Exchange and will soon cover the whole market. Equities exchanges in Europe, including Madrid, Paris, Copenhagen, and Brussels, have adopted similar systems. The Cincinnati Stock Exchange, an early U.S.-based attempt to go completely electronic, has never attracted significant levels of trading.

Order-driven systems build up a compound "limit order book" from priced incoming buy and sell orders that sets a best buying and best selling price for each stock. Additional "market liquidity" can be provided by designated intermediaries, who are permitted to trade for their own accounts. Trades can be executed either at the best price in the book, or at a better price (inside the best price or in larger size) through the participation of an intermediary. Many local variations exist on this general theme.

The order-driven market mechanism, though it maintains a close relationship between price discovery and trading, requires that some market users be prepared to submit priced limit orders for retention by a central computerized market system. This is not a universal practice and is not attractive for larger orders, which tend to move market price and, hence, must be "worked" more carefully. Nor is it useful under illiquid or volatile market conditions, as investors tend to be cautious about putting firm prices on their orders when the market is likely to move suddenly.

Quote-driven or dealer markets typically operate via telephone (or on a trading floor, as in the London jobbing market prior to the Big Bang of 1986). Examples of such markets include the U.S. Treasury bond and NASD "over the counter" markets, Eurobond market, foreign exchange market, and all gilts—United Kingdom and foreign equities trading in London. Prices in this type of market are quoted by dealers, called "market makers," who compete with one another as principals trading for their own accounts. In the London equity market, for example, 15 or more market makers typically "bid" and "offer" prices in a specified size (number of shares) in competition with one another. This was done by word of mouth on the London trading floor, with brokers surveying jobbers (the old name for market makers) to obtain the best quotes for their orders. In the screenless markets, brokers tend to telephone the market makers with whom they deal most frequently, then check the price with one or two others, with the result that the business becomes somewhat more focused.

With screen support, these markets have tended to progress through several phases. Initially, market makers entered competing quotations into a computerized system that redistributed them to market users, investors, and brokers. This enabled the latter to see at a glance all prices being quoted for a stock and identify the market maker offering the most competitive price before trading by telephone. This is the present state of affairs in London for SEAQ and SEAQ International and for NASDAQ in the United States.

At this stage, the markets are operating with a separation between the price discovery and trading processes (trading takes place on the telephone, price discovery primarily on the screen). Although it is difficult to predict precisely how these markets will evolve, it is clear that the potential for reducing cost per trade will lead to automatic execution of small orders, followed by screen-to-screen confirmation for larger trades already executed by telephone.

Although screen-to-screen negotiation of larger trades is but a short technical step beyond, there is a fierce attachment to telephone trading in larger sizes because of the vastly greater range of trading options and better flow of market information it supports and the "feel for the market" it imparts. There is a strong element of risk management in a telephone conversation in which a trader is assessing the counter party, trying to determine the true (as opposed to the disclosed) size of the order, the urgency of the trade, and whether the counter party "knows something." Systems have been proposed that will help to manage much of the risk and uncertainty surrounding large block trades, but it is unlikely that the telephone will be displaced. It might be more productive to enhance it with video and acknowledge the importance of trust and relationships in trading between professionals.

Wider Implications and Opportunities

In breaking down the old physical boundaries of the marketplace, electronic information and trading systems have broadened membership in markets by eliminating physical limitations to participation in the market. Prior to the Big Bang in London, the trading floor was limited to about 1,500 people. In the wake of the Big Bang, there are some 8,000 market participants trading by telephone and using the electronic market displays on the SEAQ system. Moreover, such systems have diminished the need to preserve a "clubbish" atmosphere in order to foster trust and good behavior, since everyone's behavior can be monitored electronically.

The professional competence and integrity of traders remain crucial for market credibility, but the need for greater capital backing and the ability to trade across national frontiers have fostered a trend toward external ownership of stockbrokers and the movement of large international banks into the securities industry. In some centers this has brought pressure to relax the traditional separation between stockbrokers and banks required by law in Japan and the United States.

London's Big Bang

London, having experienced a rapid series of changes since about 1985, provides an interesting case study of the way a market and its participants can react to the sorts of pressure described above. One cannot, of course, regard the London experience as anything approaching a clean, controlled experiment. There were many special factors operating, the effects of which can never be disentangled, and because the crash of 1987 occurred but a year after the "Big Bang," it is difficult to assess the effects of the two events independently.

The London Stock Exchange of the 1970s was a rather insular establishment. The foreign exchange controls, which inhibited the flow of investment funds into and out of the country, also provided a comfortable cushion against international competition and practice. The trading system entailed a strict "separation of capacity" between brokers, who acted for their clients, and jobbers, who traded for their firms as wholesalers. Neither class of member firm was permitted to perform the other's function. Brokers agreed to take all their client business for execution by jobbers, while jobbers agreed never to contact investors. This finely tuned arrangement engendered a high level of investor confidence, inasmuch as the broker was not tempted to "talk his own book." A fixed scale of minimum broker commissions was skewed so that private clients paid less and institutions more than true cost, an arrangement thought to be socially desirable and a way of offsetting the tax adantages enjoyed by institutional investors. Of some 15 jobbing firms, the largest four probably garnered four-fifths of the business. The gilts (U.K. government bonds) market worked the same way and ran on the same trading floor. Firms formed partnerships with unlimited liability and could not be controlled by outside interests. The Stock Exchange itself was an unincorporated association (the same legal entity as most golf clubs).

But things were changing. Early in the 1970s, the many stock exchanges throughout the United Kingdom and Republic of Ireland agreed to unify their governance and most of their administration, services, and regulation. Improved communications was making it increasingly wasteful to replicate facilities. Although a universal jobbing system for the United Kingdom (but not for Eire) was easy from a mechanical standpoint, the political achievement was considerable and was undertaken without government pressure. France only achieved the equivalent in 1990, Australia in about 1988, and Germany is still trying. It seems unlikely that U.S. exchanges will wish to unify at a national level, although the Midwest Stock Exchange in Chicago is already the result of a merger of smaller exchanges in the region.

U.K. exchange controls were removed in 1979, opening up the possibility of an active international securities market there. The Eurobond market developed rapidly, with London as its center, but with participants from many countries, including the United States, Germany, Switzerland, France, and, later, Japan. The market was, and remains, a dealer telephone market with no screen support for trading. It operates with a minimum of rules, and it is common for brokers to quote prices, take positions, and act as agents for their professional investor clients all in the same firm. Moreover, banks operate alongside more traditional brokers. Because most players were not members of The Stock Exchange and the rules of the game were totally alien to the single capacity system, the market operated in a fiercely independent frame of mind, with its own governing body, the Association of International Bond Dealers, based in Zurich.

The Stock Exchange had missed an opportunity to capture this business by liberalizing its rules for bonds. Active debate about how to do so without damaging the domestic market was halted in 1980 by legal action against The Exchange by the Office of Fair Trading. The Exchange had to choose between defending its traditional rules or agreeing to remove more than 100, which were alleged to be restrictive trading practices. The choice was easy, but as a consequence, change was halted for three years while the cases were prepared. When the deadlock was eventually broken in 1983, by an out-of-court agreement between The Stock Exchange and the government, a date was set three years hence for the implementation of key changes. With pressure for change dammed up all this time, the result was bound to be spectacular.

The agreement had required two key concessions by The Stock Exchange: the unfixing of minimum commissions, and the opening up of membership, including control of existing member firms, to outsiders. So fundamental were these concessions that The Exchange was forced to abandon single capacity, and with it the jobbing market system. After examining alternative market systems around the world, it decided to adapt the central concept of the U.S. NASDAQ, over the counter market system, the closest electronic equivalent to the jobbing system, which would support dual capacity market making. The resulting London trading system, called Stock Exchange Automated Quotations (SEAQ), collects, collates, and displays to market users the competing quotations of all market makers in each stock traded on The Exchange.

Ten days after the Big Bang in November 1986, the U.K. government passed the Financial Services Act, which provided a new regulatory structure for the securities industry under the Securities Investment Board (SIB). The SIB would license stock exchanges and supervise markets. It would also license independent self-regulatory organizations, which would regulate securities industry firms in terms of their business conduct, capital adequacy, professionalism, and client relations.

This brought under regulation for the first time all firms active in Eurobonds. In preparation for the change, these mainly foreign-based firms formed a self-regulatory organization (ISRO) to represent their special interests and style of business. In 1986, The Stock Exchange and ISRO negotiated an agreement under which the International Stock Exchange was formed, with half the council from the old Stock Exchange and half from the ISRO.

There were thus many changes to be assimilated in a very short period when the Big Bang came in October 1986:

- a new regulatory regime,
- a newly constituted International Stock Exchange,
- new entrants in the market,
- new owners of old firms,
- mergers between old firms,
- unfixed commissions,
- a new trading mechanism,
- a new trading support system, and, as it turned out,
- migration of trading away from the floor to screen and telephone.

But this was not all. The Bank of England decided to take the opportunity to restructure and regulate the gilts market, which, for many years, had been operated and regulated by The Stock Exchange. In the new structure, which was modeled on the U.S. Treasury bond system, a ring of primary dealers enjoying a direct relationship with the bank operated the wholesale market for new issues and trading and serviced a wider distribution network of brokers and banks.

Member firms were extremely active in the run-up to the Big Bang and adopted a range of different strategies. Some major firms, as well as a number of smaller firms, decided to capitalize on the demand for market access from banks and overseas brokers by selling off partnerships, inherited from previous generations of partners, for prodigious sums of money (agreeing, however, to ensure continuity of operations for at least a year or two). Some of these firms disappeared without trace—Hoare Govett into Security Pacific (purchased for £78 million), which withdrew soon after the Big Bang; Greenwells into Midland Bank (for £30 million), which dropped equity trading; and Scrimgeour and Vickers da Costa into Citibank (for £75 million), which later withdrew from the equities market.

Other firms merged broker with jobber and merchant bank.

Warburg, for example, bought Ackroyd & Smithers and Rowe & Pitman for £75 million; Barclays bought de Zoete & Bevan and Wedd Durlacher for £120 million; Kleinwort Benson bought Grieveson Grant for £44 million. These entirely U.K.-based conglomerates have all done rather well.

Other firms decided to remain in their chosen niche. James Capel, for example, which was bought by Hong Kong and Shanghai Bank for £100 million, pursued agency brokering in single capacity; Cazenove stuck to brokering and corporate finance; Smith New Court stayed with market making. These firms, too, have done well.

Most of the smaller brokers, including many outside London, that have continued to pursue their private client brokering businesses have not regretted their decision. There has, however, been a move to form large groups of retail brokers so as to gain economies of scale from systems and back office support. Among a handful of new specialist firms formed to fill specific niches are Winterflood, a market maker in less liquid stocks, and Sharelink, which makes extensive use of information technology to offer low-cost execution, especially for privatization stocks in small quantities.

Some American and Japanese securities houses elected to wait and join The Exchange in their own right after the Big Bang rather than buy an existing firm in anticipation. These include Nomura, Daiwa, Nikko, Yamaichi, Goldman Sachs, Merrill Lynch, Lehman Brothers, and Salomon Brothers.

In the wake of the somewhat frenzied jostling for position ahead of the Big Bang, rewards seem to have gone in the main to firms that kept cool heads when those about them were losing theirs. But one area in which nearly every firm got carried away was dealing room technology. Colossal sums of money were spent to equip the new dealing rooms that firms were setting up around the City of London. Estimates, though hard to verify, are that more than £1 billion may have been spent. Suppliers had a field day.

Because very little was spent on technology for efficient settlement, in the boom year after the Big Bang and before the crash, back office capacity could not match the trading capacity of front offices, resulting in a huge and potentially dangerous backlog of unsettled business in the equities market. The Exchange had to take serious disciplinary action to clear this backlog by degrees, even to the point of curtailing some firms' trading until their back office performance improved. Other firms imposed equivalent discipline upon themselves.

No review of the events surrounding the Big Bang would be complete without examining the creation of the SEAQ International market, a development that, in retrospect, probably did more to enhance London's position in the international securities industry than any other at the time. We have seen that there was dual capacity trading in non-U.K. equities going on in London, off The Stock Exchange, between Eurobond firms. By early 1985, nearly two years before the Big Bang, the volume of this trading had become so significant that Reuters had begun to provide pages on its worldwide information system to give dealers wider visibility to their clients. It was apparent that the foreign equities market might migrate to, and consolidate on, the Reuters network before The Exchange could offer it an electronic home on SEAQ, as it had planned to do after the Big Bang. But although the threat was immediate, the solution, SEAQ, was still nearly two years away. If foreign stocks could be traded with the help of Reuters, so too could U.K. domestic stocks.

The Exchange decided to act at once. It launched SEAQ International in June 1985, fifteen months before the Big Bang. The new market in foreign equities was nurtured over many months, and now trading volumes on some days exceed the value of domestic SEAQ trading. Leading stocks are traded from 21 countries, significant trading volumes having been won from the continental European bourses, notably Paris, Frankfurt, and Stockholm.

Success was possible only because The Exchange was able to assemble an effective system quickly from components already at hand. In response to the immediate threat, a screen market was developed in three months. Highly important to this effort was The Exchange's control of an information network of some 15,000 screens in the United Kingdom and United States and links with information vendors that facilitated an even broader dissemination of market information. Without this infrastructure, the international equity market would undoubtedly have joined the foreign exchange market on the Reuters global network.

Consequences of the Big Bang

More than five years after the Big Bang, and four years after the crash of 1987, we can take a measured view of immediate and longer-term effects and see how competitors have responded.

The cost to investors of using the market is one of the most visible external indicators of how the market has changed. The figures are telling (see Figure 6-1). For institutional investors, the rate of commission on trades done via brokers fell between 1980 (0.6%) and 1986 (0.4%), and then experienced an accelerated decline in the two years following the Big Bang (down to 0.25%). The level has since stabilized. But because institutions have been free since the Big Bang to trade "net" with market makers (i.e., for no commission) and the proportion of such trades has varied little from year to year, ranging between 27% and 34%, the average rate of commission being paid by institutions on all trades is about 0.175%. This is perhaps the best

Figure 6-1
Individual Investor and Small Bargain Commission Rates (UK)

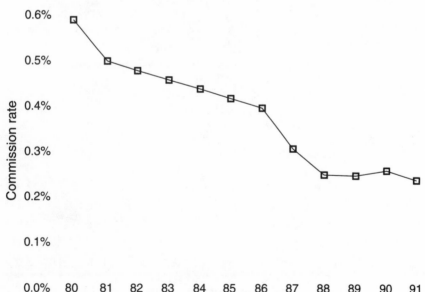

Source: London Stock Exchange Quarterly and *Quality of Market Reviews,* various years.

available measure of the value added by the broker for institutions, which have the option of by-passing brokers. This value reflects the cost of maintaining an institutional dealing and research capacity.

The cost to private clients presents a more complex picture (see Figure 6-2). Across all private client trades, the average commission fell from 1.1% in 1980 to 0.9% in 1986, then more steeply to 0.7% in 1988, where it stabilized. The pattern is similar to that for institutional trades. But for small trades, particularly very small trades of up to £600, the rates shot up following removal of the "institutional subsidy" from 4% to nearly 7%, and show signs of stabilizing at about 6.25%. At this level, the commission tends to be set in absolute terms to reflect the cost of handling a trade.

Figure 6-2
Estimated Institutional Commissions (excluding net bargains)

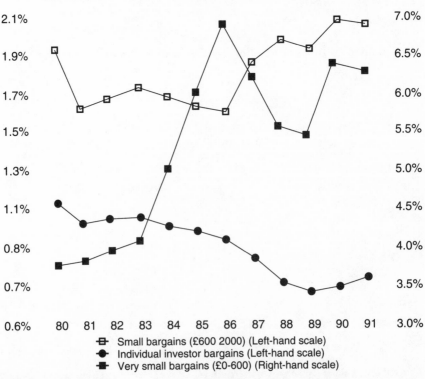

-⊟- Small bargains (£600 2000) (Left-hand scale)
-●- Individual investor bargains (Left-hand scale)
-■- Very small bargains (£0-600) (Right-hand scale)

Source: London Stock Exchange Quarterly and *Quality of Market Reviews,* various years.

By allowing market forces to operate freely, deregulation has clearly benefited institutions at the expense of small investors. During the period in question, the U.K. government has undertaken an enormous program of privatization with a policy of achieving very wide distribution of shares among the public. In 1980, there were only 3 million private shareholders, in 1986, 5 million, and in 1991, 11 million. But most of these 11 million shareholders are holding small amounts in only one or two shares, and there is still a net disinvestment in stocks by private investors of about £5 billion per year.

Banks are using branch networks to offer cheap dealing services to clients, and some company brokers are exploiting this special link to offer low-cost dealing arrangements. At present, however, no one has devised a means to reduce the cost of dealing in small amounts below about £12. Suggestions for using existing bank and electronic funds transfer networks to support self-service trading linked to automatic payment and electronic transfer of title remain possibilities for the future.

The level of competition between market makers before and since the Big Bang has been a point of interest, with regulators keen to encourage more market makers and improve the price spreads available to market users. Before the Big Bang, there were some 15 jobbing firms, of which two large and three small were active in the gilts market. Immediately after the Big Bang there were 29 market makers in U.K. equities, a number that has since fluctuated, up to 31 and down to 20, and presently stands at 21. In light of the massive falloff in market activity following the crash of 1987, this seems a real improvement. Figures published by The Stock Exchange in 1988, however, show that the top 25% of firms saw 80% of the equity turnover.

In the pre–Big Bang gilts market, large-size business was tightly held by two jobbers. The new market began with no less than 37 primary dealers. This number had fallen to 18 by the end of 1990, but only 13 recorded a profit. On closer examination, we find a sharp concentration of business, with the top four firms (Barclays de Zoete Wedd, Lehman Brothers, Greenwell Montagu, and Salomon Brothers) generating 80% of the profit from the entire gilts market.

In both these markets there has been serious overcapacity, and firms have dropped out following the market crash, but the number and ranking of market makers is not to be seen as unsatisfactory. Studies of competition in natural ecologies and in the high street have shown that it is usual for the number of direct competitors to be limited to between 7 and 15, and for market share (or the population of individuals in a species, in the case of the ecological study) to become skewed in just the way we see for market markers. It may not be realistic for the authorities to pursue a goal of larger numbers of competitors, or a more even spread of business between them, than occurs either in nature or the free marketplace.

One measure of market quality monitored continuously by The London Stock Exchange is "the touch," that is, the difference between the highest price at which any market maker will buy a stock and the lowest price at which any market maker (usually a different one) will sell, expressed as a percentage of the price. For the leading stocks, the average touch in the largest size quoted exhibits an interesting, but difficult to interpret, trend (see Table 6-1). The touch is an interesting measurement because it indicates the cost of market use to an investor, singling out just the pricing and trading mechanisms. In theory an investor could do a "round trip trade," buying shares at the lowest offer price and immediately selling them at the highest bid price. The touch indicates the percentage of his investment that he would lose in this hypothetical process, ignoring, of course, the cost of taxes, commissions, and settlement. By tracking the touch one can compare the quality of a market with other markets, and with itself from year to year.

The least cluttered picture compares the touch immediately before and after the Big Bang. It is fair to conclude that market quality was improved by the additional competition between market makers engendered by SEAQ in the Big Bang of 1986. Market conditions were similarly buoyant immediately before, and for a year after the Big Bang until the crash of 1987. The introduction of SEAQ therefore benefited investors.

Table 6-1
Average Touch as Percentage of Price

	Pre–Big Bang	*1987*	*1989*	*1990*	*1991*
% of price	0.97	0.91	1.28	1.67	1.53

Subsequently the touch has deteriorated. One interpretation is that the benefits of SEAQ have been masked by the effects of reduced market turnover. From the market's standpoint, the touch can be said to represent the collective position risk that market makers take when they trade at their quoted prices. This needs some explanation. A major determinant of a market maker's risk is market turnover, because he can trade his way out of an unwanted position more quickly in an active market. In an inactive market he widens his price quote to reflect his increased position risk.

Perhaps the most encouraging indication of the success of the Big Bang is seen in the response of other exchanges. Paris, for example, is talking of instituting its own block trading market in an effort to repatriate the order flow lost to London, and has unified its regional exchanges and introduced a computerized trading system. Germany, meanwhile, has begun to unify its nine existing exchanges into a single market and has introduced no less than three computer-based trading systems in Frankfurt.

Some encouraging statistical comparisons can be drawn with New York. Despite its admitted overcapacity, London's figures for member firms' profit per employee are consistently better than New York's. Table 6-2 shows their relative positions in 1989.

To summarize, it would generally be accepted that the London market is much more efficient than it was in terms of cost of trading for investors. But this inevitably means less revenue for member firms—a circumstance that was sustainable during the bullish year following the Big Bang, but that in subsequent years, with lower levels of market activity. has become unsustainable, causing firms to reduce capacity or drop out of the business. London has become a better market for investors, but a worse market for intermediaries.

Table 6-2
Member Firms' Profit per Employee

	London	*New York*
Profit of all member firms	$ 800 M	$1,800 M
Profit per employee	$35,000	$7,000

Opportunities and Challenges for Brokers

The same forces responsible for radical changes in The London Stock Exchange have opened up a variety of opportunities for market participants the world over. For securities houses, there is the opportunity to develop major international operations supported by their own data and voice communications networks. Firms allied to large retail organizations, including clearing banks, are in a position to internalize the order flow of their retail business. This practice, which is becoming widespread in North America and the United Kingdom, is a recognized means of building market share based on increasing customer loyalty and reducing unit costs. Barclays de Zoete Wedd, the securities arm of Barclays Bank, has become the leading exponent of this technique with its TRADE system. TRADE provides automatic on screen execution of small orders against BZW's market makers and takes advantage of the company's widespread distribution network and the wide range of securities in which it makes markets. Introduction of The Stock Exchange's own automatic small-order execution system, SAEF, was so delayed by policy arguments that TRADE was first into the market with superior technology. BZW consequently gained substantial market share, including the business of a number of smaller retail brokers to which it provides TRADE terminals free of charge, giving them an attractive solution and offering savings in dealing costs.

In the case of NASDAQ, the major retail brokers, including Merrill Lynch, stole a march on the market by linking their order routing systems directly into their own in-house automatic execution systems and guaranteeing to execute orders at the best price available on the NASDAQ screens.

Brokers clearly are having to cope with a tendency toward disintermediation: clients by-passing brokers. This trend will continue to test brokers in the years ahead as they look for new ways to add value for clients and reduce their costs below the level of the value added. In this context, some firms are beginning to look like miniature stock exchanges in their own right, although they continue to use central market prices. Were this tendency to go too far, say to the by-passing of the formal stock exchange price discovery mechanism by a major portion of the order flow, the price discovery process itself could be damaged to the ultimate detriment of the market and its users.

Opportunities and Challenges for Networks

The network operators and "quote vendors" who convey financial information and services have an opportunity to add value to existing information networks by providing transactional services for the routing and confirmation of orders and settlement instructions. Some of these networks are huge and worldwide in scope; Reuters claims 180,000 screens, ADP 80,000, and Quotron 55,000. Other network operators, including IBM, AT&T, and BT, keen to add value to their networks to avoid the downward competitive price spiral as raw communications capacity becomes a commodity, would be delighted to provide transaction processing services tailored to the securities industry worldwide.

When one examines the value chain of a stock exchange that has implemented electronic aids to trading, it becomes clear that the main value added is in the market system network and its links with the market maker, broker, and investor. The network is, of course, the medium for inbound and outbound logistics (in value chain jargon) and the value added at the center, in process terms, is minimal. This means that the exchange's users, whether they know it or not, are more dependent on the network as a means of communicating with one another than on the stock exchange as a consummator of trades. In other words, an alternative network provider could become indispensable to market users and (if it did the networking job better) displace the stock exchange in its central role in trading. One might argue that the stock exchange has other attractions that will ensure the loyalty of members and their clients, and so it has: investor confidence, regulatory authority, prices, and settlement (in some centers). But it turns out that investor confidence is increasingly being vested by national regulators in firms as well as exchanges, that large brokers linked to banks carry their own credibility, that regulatory authority is being taken closer to governments than to exchanges, that settlement services are open for trades done off the exchange, and that up-to-date and accurate dealing prices are readily available everywhere.

Stock exchanges thus have no choice but to be well equipped with networks. An exchange that does not own a network must develop a partnership with a network operator it can trust; an exchange that does not control the network it uses is at the mercy of the competitor that does.

Financial networks are potentially serious competitors for the electronic trading systems operated by exchanges. In some instances, we are seeing a convergence of these two businesses. Witness efforts to bring together and reconcile the core interests of exchanges with those of network operators, as in the Globex initiative discussed later in this chapter.

Opportunities and Challenges for Exchanges

Stock exchanges have an opportunity to free themselves from geographical constraints by going completely off the trading floor into the ether. Exchanges may now elect to position themselves as international trading facilitators, a direction in which both The London Stock Exchange and NASDAQ are moving. This is hardly surprising given that the customers and intermediaries of stock exchanges have for some time had an international outlook. Most of the leading listed companies have worldwide spreads of shareholders to match their worldwide customer bases. Major institutional investors, pension funds, and other fund managers are increasingly holding a significant portion of their funds in foreign securities, and, of course, there is a top tier of global securities houses, many of them members of several stock exchanges, that are able to operate around the clock in every developed country. The stock exchanges are the last to make the transition to internationalism.

Transformation of a domestic stock exchange into an international exchange poses a number of challenging problems, as the London Exchange discovered. The transition must be achieved while retaining the support of firms that remain predominantly domestic in outlook as well as that of the major international member firms. At the same time, The Exchange must come to terms with powerful network and system operators that can operate trading systems sans regulatory responsibilities, but currently lack market liquidity and credibility, without which no marketplace can operate effectively. Network and system operators can be either allies or competitors. Among the interesting examples of exchanges that have remained essentially floor-based while entering into partnership with a network operator in order to sweep up order flow from other time zones is the Globex link-up between the Chicago Mercantile Exchange and Reuters, which permits a form of order-match trading to be carried out between the close of the physical market and its opening the following day. Similar arrangements are being devised between the Chicago Board of Options Exchange and Reuters for equity options.

Where is all this change and activity likely to lead in five or ten years' time? Can we discern any general trends that will lend clarity to the murky crystal ball? Changes will probably continue for many years yet, but clear trends are in evidence.

In the equity markets, the key trends are disintermediation and segmentation. The ease and freedom of communication and ready availability of market information and trading systems to broker and investor alike are permitting investors to trade directly with counterparties, with little or no need for brokers. Already in London, some 30% of institutional equity orders are executed directly with market makers, with no broker and no commission paid; the U.S. Crossing Network of Instinet is facilitating a growing proportion of trades between institutions with no intermediation at all; and the services of Posit and Wunsch are making steady inroads into the New York Stock Exchange's market share of executions. Agency brokers no longer enjoy a protected niche in the old tidy ecology of the securities industry; they must examine and identify the value they add for clients and ensure that they can create and deliver it economically and competitively.

Alternative ways of performing the traditional functions of a stock exchange are challenging the role of the exchange itself. The challenges come from network operators, national regulators, international markets, off-exchange trading, and exchanges' own global member firms, many of which have retail networks, deep pockets, and systems capability. The process of putting buyer in touch with seller is now easily performed by a variety of systems and networks; Instinet, Posit, and Wunsch have already been mentioned. All over the world, exchanges are beginning to question what their long-term role should be.

The answer to this crisis of identity lies, as with any other business, in identifying clearly what customers value or require. Exchanges are not owed a living; they compete with one another and with other service providers and must earn their continuing role and market share. What investors, issuers, and intermediaries demand of an exchange are liquidity, credibility, access, and cost efficiency. By meeting and building on these needs, an exchange can define the services it should provide.

With international and professional securities trading increasingly servicing the global company and global fund manager, we are seeing a growing separation of this type of business. By contrast, traditional private-client brokering remains intermediated, domestic, and low value. Both sectors demand liquidity and market credibility, but at different levels. Similarly, access and cost considerations are widely divergent and levels of regulation need to be distinguished. To survive and succeed, exchanges will need to compete effectively in one or another of these sectors. There are competitors in both, and therefore there is a strong rationale for differentiated exchange services. Some exchanges will no doubt decide to specialize, with some domestic exchanges focusing entirely on the domestic private client business. Only the more adventurous and innovative will succeed in attracting and retaining professional and international business.

London certainly intended to be one of these, but to do so it will need to develop at least two sets of market services with differentiated facilities, branding, delivery, and governance. It is too early to see how this will be done, but The Exchange has made no secret of its intentions.

The next few years in the development of exchanges will be fascinating for observers and exciting for market users, but a matter of life and death for the exchanges themselves.

An Abstraction of the Impact of Telecommunications on an Information-Based Industry

It may be helpful to readers struggling to predict the implications of the telecommunications revolution for their own industry to draw some general observations from the perhaps rambling and disjointed story of the securities industry and London's Big Bang. I do not claim any special wisdom in this, but, as a physicist turned business manager with a tendency to look for the underlying pattern in an apparently chaotic series of events, I can begin to discern the hazy outlines of some general mechanisms that were at work, though we could not see them at the time. I do not know whether any of these ideas will fit other industries, or precisely what other factors were important in determining that things worked out the way they did, so the buyer must beware of building too uncritically on these theorems.

There seem to have been six effects of the telecommunications revolution on the securities industry. These are closely related to one another, but because the players in the game had to manage them separately, it will be convenient to prise them apart.

1. Competition between suppliers of similar services, for example, among market makers, was heightened as a consequence of the freer flow of information up and down, and across, the industry supply chain.

2. The old value chain—the industry production line, in which specialist players played a settled and well-established role—was thrown into confusion by the new, freer flow of information. The neat service supply chain of jobber, broker, institution, client was short circuited, first by information flows and then by business transactions. This had the effect of laying bare the value added by each step in the production line, leaving players whose charges were more than the value they added open to short circuiting or replacement. Players learned to recognize the value they were adding and either find ways to reduce their costs to that level or find new ways of adding value. This sometimes meant absorbing the roles of their traditional suppliers and/or customers. Competition began to come from unexpected directions.

3. Players were challenged to look at new ways to compete, as through:

   • relationships,
   • size, credibility, or comprehensiveness of service,
   • control of distribution channels,
   • specialization of function,
   • serving a regional customer base, or
   • internationalization.

4. Telecommunications eliminates geography as a consideration in business logistics. Firms can serve overseas customers more readily, but, by the same token, domestic firms can find themselves faced with competition from abroad. In the securities industry, there remained inhibiting factors to cross-border competition in the legal, regulatory, and cultural spheres. Interprofessional business flowed across borders more readily than retail business.

5. Massive structural change across the entire industry unearthed new and interesting ways to fail as well as to succeed! Among these were weaknesses in managing change
and cultural incompatibility, as between brokers and their
parent banks.

6. Industry changes and new technology enabled completely
new structures to emerge, such as SEAQ International and
Batterymarch Fund Management of Boston. The latter has
succeeded in using its institutional buying power, leveraged by technology, to turn the Wall Street industry supply
chain on its head. Fund managers decide what trades to
do, aided by a computer system that selects preferred
stocks and then, instead of giving the order to a broker and
waiting for execution, holds an auction among up to six
competing brokers, on a time deadline, and awards the
order to the best deal. Brokers who fail to win often enough
are automatically replaced by an eager hopeful on the
waiting list.

In this chapter, we have reviewed an international, information-based industry on which the impact of telecommunications
has been, and continues to be, profound and far-reaching. We
have dissected and analyzed the processes that are at work,
attempted some synthesis, and drawn some general conclusions.
It is hoped that these conclusions might provide rules of thumb
and rudimentary signposts for others in similar predicaments.

A major discontinuity such as that experienced by the securities industry poses both threats and opportunities for the players. We can see now that following London's Big Bang there
were only a few successful innovators. Some of the firms that
energetically seized opportunities are no longer in business,
while others that pursued policies of minimum change have sur-
vived and prospered by building on their established strengths.
Perhaps it is this observation that provides the wisest and most
surprising moral for others.

7

The Coordination of Global Manufacturing

Ramchandran Jaikumar and David M. Upton

Production capacity is now sufficiently flexible in some industries to be viewed as a commodity. Technological change has raised the prospect of global markets for a variety of types of flexible manufacturing capacity. This chapter outlines technological and commercial conditions under which markets for flexible manufacturing capacity are likely to arise, describes an industry in which a capacity market exists, and explores desiderata for such markets.

Conditions for Global Commodity Capacity Markets

Important changes in manufacturing technology have occurred in many industries. Machines for many processes are now very flexible, in that they may be programmed to perform a wide variety of manufacturing tasks and are able to accommodate diverse product characteristics while providing both high quality and low cost. Although the products manufactured by such technology are highly differentiated, the broad diffusion and standardization of the technology has made productive capacity comparatively common and indistinguishable. Indeed, for many highly differentiated products (metal-machined parts or socks, for example), the precise source of the product is becoming much less relevant since the technology of production allows consistent quality and cost performance regardless of source. This suggests a novel situation—one in which flexible capacity may be seen as a commodity—inasmuch as units of flexible capacity are comparatively lacking in distinguishing qualities. The large number of product variations that such capacity may effectively produce means that the primary input for the process is information, in the form of well-codified, often computer-readable product descriptions. Advances in global telecommunications mean that such information may be effortlessly transmitted between customer and source, making the precise location of the manufacturer progressively less important.

Along with advances in telecommunications, diffusion of the supporting manufacturing technology to an ever-growing range of processes has had far-reaching consequences, from the shop floor to the global structure of industries. We are seeing fundamental change in such basic elements of production as firm size, the nature and form of product and process specifications, transaction processing, and labor.

Factory Size

Why should factories be large? Companies have traditionally collected the machinery of production into large factories for two reasons:

- to gain economies of scale;
- to share overhead costs, such as maintenance, quality assurance, materials tracking, and so forth.

Technological economies of scale have never been strong in industries that produce highly differentiated products: machines in such industries are gathered together primarily to share overhead costs. With the new technologies, even this source of pressure to aggregate has been greatly relieved. Today's machines are highly reliable and require very little maintenance. What little is needed may be performed by operators. Because machining processes are under programmable computer control and are, in general, well understood and predictable, machines produce good quality output time after time, eliminating the need for separate quality departments to weed out defects. Finally, technological solutions make overhead due to information and material flow very small, regardless of the size of the operation. Minimum efficient scale for a modern manufacturing operation in many industries is a manufacturing cell of about six machines and fewer than a dozen people. Such a cell functions as a factory within a factory, effecting an entire production process under computer control, often including materials handling and inspection.

Product and Process Specifications

With computer-based manufacturing technologies, product and process specifications exist as computational procedures developed on specialized computer-aided design (CAD) systems. These procedures are transportable via standardized telecommunication links to the machine controllers that govern the manufacturing process. Moreover, to the extent that the people who write them are able to anticipate and solve every possible contingency, these procedures guarantee precise reproducibility, that is, every part made by any machine running a particular procedure will be exactly the same. These two characteristics of modern product and process descriptions—transportability and precise reproducibility—reduce the need in many industries to collocate engineering and design with manufacturing, except for pilot production. The standardization and predictability of the link between design and manufacturing weaken traditional dogma, which insists that design engineers be on hand during volume manufacturing to make design trade-offs as manufacturing problems occur. Technologies in many industries now anticipate and eliminate such problems systematically rather than on an ad hoc basis, allowing engineers to be absent from volume production and rendering the location of volume manufacturing less relevant. Indeed, manufacturing units need not necessarily even have their own engineering functions; in the context that is evolving, engineering and design can be effectively supplied by physically and functionally distinct organizations.

Transaction Processing

One economy of scale to which firms in the new manufacturing context do have access is in sales and distribution. With the right communication links, one marketing department can today serve the world.

The traditional firm-to-market scenario is depicted in Figure 7-1, the electronic marketplace in Figure 7-2.

Figure 7-1
Traditional Firm-to-Market Scenario

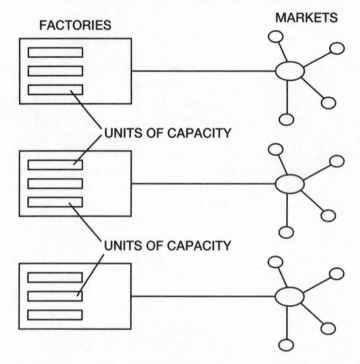

In the latter, we envision direct links between individual facilities of a firm and the buyers of their products. Contracts in the electronic marketplace would likely be many and small, and the market system would learn through repeated transactions, enabling it, over time, to arrange almost universally ideal contracts. The speed of the system would be such that contracts would be renegotiated dynamically in the case of nonfulfillment, utilizing surge capacity among the manufacturers. Such a system minimizes transaction costs by effectively automating transactions. The telecommunications basis for such a system exists; all that is required is sufficient speed, memory, and reliability. If the memory is structured well, the market functions could be performed without human participation.

Labor

The existence of standard flexible technologies has decreased the need for firm-specific training. A number of industries may

Figure 7-2
Electronic Marketplace

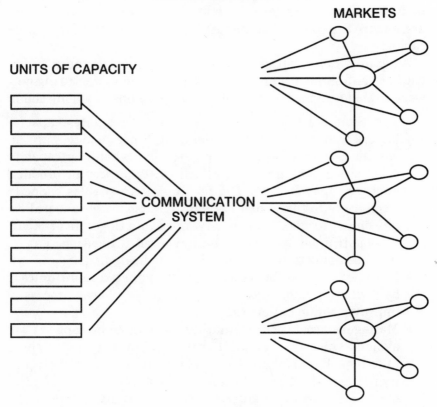

now draw from a pool of labor whose skill level is lower and more homogeneous. This, in turn, means lower costs for centralized training and personnel functions. For example, with standardized computer numerical control (CNC) machine tool technology, a person trained in CNC milling may very quickly learn CNC turning.

Summary

Collectively, these factors serve to substantially de-emphasize economies of scale and reduce absolute cost outlay at the plant level. Manufacturing concerns can now establish small, independent cells that operate effectively and economically with only a modest capital investment. Moreover, these small units of flexible capacity can be physically and organizationally separate from design, marketing, and engineering. Small minimum efficient scale, low capital requirement, and separability of volume manufacturing operations, by effectively lowering entry barriers, ensure the prospect of ample players in a market for flexible capacity.

Advantages of a capacity market. There are a number of distinct advantages to organizing an industry's manufacturing network so that providers of flexible capacity compete, among them:

- The pooling effect of the market better insulates capacity buyers from fluctuations in demand. Since products are diversified, it will often be the case that when one capacity purchaser's demand is high (for his/her particular product) another's may be low. The pooling effect enables capacity purchasers to take advantage of the disparate temporal requirement for flexible capacity and avoid the costs of capacity-constrained operation and low asset utilization that often face firms to which capacity is dedicated.
- Poor capacity performance can be combated more quickly by switching suppliers than through the slower process of improving internal operations.
- Managerial costs of coordinating and balancing capacity are avoided since market mechanisms perform many of these functions. For example, the difficult task of assigning capacity to the highest priority task can be performed by the price mechanism—when industry capacity is tight, it goes to the highest bidder. This saves the cost of bureaucratic internal groups having to juggle jobs inefficiently in order of apparent priority, without information that would enable them to reflect priorities accurately.
- Capacity can be bought in the short term, providing the buyer faced with a high degree of uncertainty can access capacity without committing to its continued use.

Commercial conditions. The factors listed above will be most beneficial when demand is highly uncertain, the managerial costs of coordinating proprietary capacity are high, and transactions are small and great in number. Provided the technological conditions described above prevail, we would expect to see markets for flexible capacity develop in industries that face such commercial conditions.

An Example: The Disintegration of the Textile Industry in Prato

Since the fourteenth century, the textile industry in Prato, Italy, has been the economic backbone of the Florence and Pistoia regions. Once, armies of artisans carded and dyed, spun and weaved. But with the technological changes that precipitated the Industrial Revolution, which brought increased economies of scale, firms grew in size and vertically integrated so as to be able to schedule and balance capacity in these various process steps. Because starving assets of input materials incurred substantial penalties, given the heavy required investment in production technology, great advantage accrued to coordinating the process steps directly to avoid such circumstances. Production equipment for the various process steps was collocated to facilitate coordination and the quick resolution of interprocess problems, and central marketing and design departments were maintained on-site to work with production and match customers to production capacity and capabilities.

Rediscovery of Small Economic Scale

Most Prato mills were integrated in this way in the early 1970s, with fiber production, dyeing, spinning, and weaving performed in the same company. But many of these companies had progressively become unprofitable. Lower market prices, global competition, and rising internal costs had gnawed margins to the bone. Meanwhile, new dyeing and finishing techniques were becoming available and the market was demanding an ever-broader range of products from these new methods.

Some mill owners recognized that their integrated mills were an encumbrance in the new regime. The processes had become so well understood, and hence specifiable, that the various steps were largely independent of one another, yet the flexibility of the individual processes remained constrained by the particular output of the upstream, and requirements of the downstream, steps. Capacity, such as weaving or spinning, had become cheaper and was now economical in much smaller units, eroding economies of scale. The increasing overhead burden and need to effectively coordinate production of the broader product ranges and take advantage of newfound flexibility in each of the process steps led firms to look very closely at the manufacturing structure that had been the industry paradigm for a century. In the face of extinction, firms began to change.

Many mills followed the example of the Menichetti family, which broke its mill into eight separate companies, one a realty company that leased space and services to the rest. As much as 50% of the stock in these companies, financed through profits, was transferred to employees. To ensure competitiveness, Menichetti insisted that each company find 50% of existing business outside the original business. At the same time, he established a New York–based marketing company to create new designs and match product with the best producer. This company was to provide no more than 30% of the business of any company in the Menichetti fold.

Within three years, all units of the disintegrated Menichetti mill were running at 90% utilization, product variety had increased tenfold, average in-process inventory was reduced from 4 months to 15 days, and attrition had reduced the labor force by a third while production had risen by 25% (largely because the satellite firms invested in new technology). By 1980, all but one of the Prato mills had undergone similar disintegration, turning a sluggish threatened industry into a thriving community of innovative flexible companies, each a world-class competitor. This process continued throughout the value chain (see Figure 7-3).

Figure 7-3

Firms in the Prato Network by 1975

Activity	Number of Firms
Wool scouring and combining	13
Spinning, twisting, winding, reeling	1,429
Weaving	7,013
Hosiery and knitwear	1,852
Waste reclaiming	491
Finishing	232
Total	11,030

The predicament of the textile industry, which found itself on the brink of an important global change, is by no means unique. Disintegration may have progressed further in textiles than in other industries, but the conditions outlined at the beginning of this chapter apply to a growing enclave of industries. Very similar circumstances prevail in small-batch metal machining, for example, with the flexibility of the machining cell and its small economic scale.[1] But the lack of standardization of parts programs, the existence of some remaining machine-tool specializations, and the indifference of machine tool producers to small manufacturers have so far prevented the production of parts-programmed machined products from following the example of textiles.[2]

Network Coordination and the Modern Impannatori

The key to the success of the Prato system lies in the role of the modern impannatori.[3] A throwback to medieval times, these agents provide central brokerage for the firms in the network, of which there are now between 15,000 and 20,000, employing some 70,000 people. Today, several hundred such brokers draw from a hierarchical network of these thousands of suppliers. Brokers' thorough knowledge of the capacity, capability, and loading of each of the producers loosely collected in their folds enables them to source production for customers, find customers for spare production capacity, and intermediate in the negotiation process.

Effective management of this complex information set, coupled with trustworthiness and honesty, are the hallmarks of the successful impannatori. Indeed, it is this trustworthiness that prevents the problems often resulting from contracts that are difficult to specify—the trust ensures that what is needed is provided without the constraint of legal specification. Many specifications are thus based on a tacit understanding of industry standards. The complexity of the capacity assignment problem is rendered manageable by the autonomy of the various actors in the system, who are able to concentrate on being effective in their specialties while contributing to the performance of the network as a whole. Assignments of capacity are made through the market mechanism and the impannatori, enabling the system to avail itself of the most appropriate vendor and thus the full flexibility of the market for each element in the value chain.

Globalization and Communication

Among the technological changes dramatically expanding and changing the textile industry is codification. Today, cloth required by the world market may be uniquely specified with a code of 50 digits. Computer-aided design systems permit rapid local prototyping of a fabric before sourcing to a volume producer. Most important, computers facilitate an electronic marketplace in which the complexity of the production hierarchy can be "managed." Global telecommunications and continued disintegration suggest the possibility of trading options on both products and production capacity. For example, a fashion manufacturer uncertain of the season's demand for a product that has not been precisely specified may ensure against a lack of supply by buying an option on the use of flexible capacity. Today, at least toward the end of the value chain, it is capacity, not product, that is a commodity. Units of flexible capacity are now relatively indistinguishable from one another and have the capability of producing myriad products. The products themselves, characterized by variety and customization to a particular fashion, are not at all commodity-like.

Manufacturing and Negotiation

Integration of advanced telecommunications and information systems holds promise for more fully automating the negotiation process in the Prato textile industry by speeding information flows and allowing requirements to be matched more quickly to supply. The extreme complexity of information flows, given the plurality of operators acting at different hierarchical levels (the top level comprising hundreds of impannatori splitting control to thousands of suppliers and manufacturers), makes control of an automated negotiation system highly strategic. Such a system would be capable of integrating single elements of the network; it would support real-time monitoring of the entire negotiation process and its related services, and provide the necessary control to achieve optimization. It would also enable the artisans and subcontractors, the largest group in the

Prato system, to "see" the market, to discern market trends and review other suppliers' capacities in order to react quickly to market demands. Access to such information would greatly stabilize the activities of the many small firms.

Conditions for the effective marshalling of resources in manufacturing systems that are coordinated using negotiation methods are currently of interest at many levels. As the flexibility of manufacturing elements increases and effective units become smaller and more independent, it becomes increasingly advantageous to permit entities to negotiate with one another.

Upton describes a negotiation system that functions within a plant.[4] In this system, the partly completed product (such as a raw casting) is provided with a miniature manufacturing computer physically attached to it. This computer uses artificial intelligence techniques to negotiate the manufacture of the product (step by step) with the various processing entities in the system, such as transport vehicles and machine tools. Machines bid for the right to provide processing for the product and the product selects the best bid at each step.[5] Bidding machines take into account their prevailing workloads, commitments, and capabilities. After successfully visiting all the necessary stations, the semifinished product (which might be a component for a large earth-mover, say) relinquishes its computer so that subsequent products may avail themselves of its experience, such as its knowledge about unreliable performers and optimistic bidders. Thus, the system slowly builds expertise about itself in the product stream. This system is able to adapt easily to the removal and addition of machines, since removed machines stop bidding and new machines are simply told to start. The technique solves many of the problems of centralized computer control in dynamic manufacturing systems.

At the intracompany level, Jaikumar has considered the optimal behavior of users and providers of processing capability within the firm.[6] He describes a negotiation system in which a firm's sales agents are the buyers of capacity and the production resource managers are the providers. Jaikumar shows that such a decentralized system can both be optimal for the firm and provide an efficient incentive system. At the level of global coordination, we are most interested in exploring how a global, decentralized negotiation system might best be constructed for manufacturing.

Issues in Systems Design and Objectives

A number of factors must be carefully considered in attempting to establish a structure for a Prato-like market, among them: reliability, management information, brokerage, and commodity-like transactions.

Reliability

Capacity must be reliable and there must be effective mechanisms for ensuring that unreliable suppliers discount appropriately. Information on the performance of previous contracts will enable the market to take into account both the quality and reliability of suppliers. The creditworthiness of buyers must similarly be assured. How might such information be promulgated and what recourse provided to suppliers and buyers for correcting inaccuracies? For example, suppliers might be required to specify the proportion of the last hundred contracts on which they were late, or in which there was a dispute concerning quality.

There will inevitably be transactions in which one party is aggrieved and assigns too much importance to one troublesome event. For example, a customer firm may suffer badly because of one instance of failure by its supplier and may feel the need to take some punitive measure. Of course, the consequences of a party's actions are not relevant in determining its ongoing performance, so the market should ensure that these kinds of occurrences are accommodated.

Management Information

What information does a supplier need in order to compete effectively in an automated market? Temporary differences in cost of capacity due to scheduling constraints are inevitable. Manufacturers currently making pink T-shirts, given sufficient demand, would very much like to continue doing so to avoid changeover costs; where should they seek buyers of such temporarily cheap capacity?

What internal information about changeover costs does a firm need? Decisions about what price to bid on a job rely on timely and accurate internal information. The advantage will go to players that are able to reliably predict their own performance for the purpose of determining their own bids as well as to ensure satisfactory acquittal of the contract.

Brokerage

Under what conditions is it advantageous to use brokers of capacity? Clearly if communications can be organized effectively in a distributed fashion, the need for a centralized hub is reduced. When information can be transmitted and received throughout a global network, the role of a central broker as a channel for information is less clear. Individual firms could begin to access the network to determine customer requirements and bid directly on jobs as they arise. Users of capacity could post requirements on the network (for products as well as for capacity options and futures).

Commodity-Like Transactions

Methods for limiting damage arising from nonperformance of contracts are essential. Some capacity providers will be able to provide insurance by maintaining spare capacity. A futures and options market in capacity would offer a hedge against increases in price, for example. Whereas product variety has previously limited such deals to commodity products, given the flexible capacity to produce commodity-traded products we expect to see commodity-like transactions.

Moreover, we need to explore the various methods by which different forms of capacity might be converted into financial instruments. Such forms would include futures and spot markets as well as options. The insurance of these instruments is also of interest, as is the entry and modus operandi of third parties in bilateral transactions, which might have a considerable effect.

The Growing Arena

The application of programmable computer control is likely to continue to broaden and increase in sophistication. As we learn more about the physics of various processes, it is becoming possible to automate them and allow a computer to control precisely the variants of the items they produce. This is true even of processes that have traditionally been craft-based and required tremendous skill.

An example of such a process is sheet metal spinning, in which a flat plate of metal is rotated on a lathe-like machine and forced over a metal die using a mandrel. This operation can produce many different shapes (it is most often used for the production of shades for industrial lighting). Sheet metal spinning has traditionally required very high skill on the part of the operator, since it is easy to push too hard and tear the metal, or too softly and leave the metal too thick. But now this operation may be carried out automatically under computer numerical control. Operators complain that the quality of the product is "not what we can do," but it will not be long until control has been refined to such an extent that a computer program will be able to produce dies and spin customized products to order.

The foregoing is an example of a process in the early stages of programmability; other processes are much further advanced and have been reliably programmable for a number of years. The chief constraint in such processes is no longer the physical manufacturing process, but the information required to tell the machine what to produce. For example, in the manufacture of electronic circuit boards, all manufacturing instructions may be completely specified by a set of computer programs, from drilling holes in the boards to the exact placement of surface-mount and through-hole components before soldering. What is more, these operations may be effected reliably and consistently by programmable machines running standardized programs. Despite the tremendous variation in electronic devices, circuit board manufacturing capacity is becoming a commodity. Many firms now produce boards for products ranging from modems to fashionable electronic toys in small facilities with only one or two programmable machines. They are often in competition with a large number of similar subcontractors using identical machinery.

Spring making has traditionally involved the precise cutting of cams and gears to control an automatic spring-making machine. This was a task requiring high skill and years of expertise. Some manufacturers were thus very much better than others and required substantial skilled machine shops to produce the appropriate cams. Today, springs can be produced under programmable computer control by small programmable machines that run a standardized program. Each machine is capable of interpreting the program and putting the appropriate kinks and hooks into any spring being produced. Such machines have dramatically changed the industry, and many small spring-making shops (often run by ex-employees of larger manufacturers) now bid readily on spring-making jobs for small electro-mechanical devices.

There are many other examples of industries in which the type of coordination described in this chapter is becoming practicable. Although the global computerization of such a market for flexible capacity has yet to be seen in practice, we believe that such markets will soon exist. As global telecommunications and information technology enable such manufacturers to compete efficiently, with standardized technology and minimal barriers to entry, sources of advantage for individual firms are hard to identify. This leaves small firms faced with the prospect of participating in such a global market for flexible capacity with a very important question: What is it now important to do well?

Notes

1. R. Jaikumar, "Japanese Flexible Manufacturing Systems: Impact on the United States," *Japan and the World Economy,* 1, no. 2 (1987): 113–143.

2. R. Jaikumar, Statement before the Subcommittee on Innovation, Technology and Productivity of the Senate Small Business Committee of the United States Senate, December 2, 1987.

3. The closest modern translation of this word is "rag-trader." Impannatori were coordinators of artisans during the Renaissance.

4. David M. Upton, "The Operation of Large Computer-Controlled Manufacturing Systems," Ph.D. diss., Purdue University (1988); Upton, "A Flexible Architecture for a Computer-Controlled Manufacturing System," *Manufacturing Review* (March 1992): 58–72.

5. The question of why machines should "want" to bid for the right to work results only from the anthropomorphic analogy, and not because this causes any inherent functional problem.

6. R. Jaikumar, "Resource Allocation in Automated Flexible Manufacturing Systems," Harvard Business School Working Paper 88026 (1988).

8
Quick Response in Retail/ Manufacturing Channels

Janice H. Hammond

Advances in telecommunications and information systems have sparked a revolution in the way the retail industry competes. Combined with related changes in the way manufacturers produce their wares, the growing ability of retailers and manufacturers to collect, transmit, and interpret data is enabling far-reaching changes in the fundamental buying and selling practices of retailers. Retailers that have learned to exploit these technological advances have made striking gains in sales, efficiency, and profitability. Similarly, manufacturers that have developed complementary skills in manufacturing and information management have seen sales soar.

What is the impact of the availability and use of these technologies on the structure of the retail industry? In a classic demonstration of Darwinian theory, natural selection is taking its toll among retailers: the weak languish and eventually fail as the strong thrive. Retailers such as Wal-Mart Stores, J.C. Penney, Toys 'R' Us, The Limited, Dillard's Department Stores, Home Depot, Nordstrom, and The Gap are combining innovative uses of information technology and strong merchandising programs to create an unprecedented gap between retail winners and losers.[1]

Moreover, retailers are gaining ground in their traditional power struggle with suppliers. The balance of power is shifting to retailers that can not only collect meaningful data, but also interpret that data and exploit their full power. Observes Lou Pritchett, former vice president of sales at Procter & Gamble:

As retailers began to significantly improve their internal and external communications systems and to install the technology that actually allowed them to *use,* not only *collect,* vast amounts of information coming from their scanners, they soon learned more about inventories and consumer preferences than the manufacturer—and learned it faster. Access to information has therefore tilted the balance of power away from the product/volume-oriented manufacturer to the retailer.[2]

Using information and telecommunications technologies, retailers can finally escape the need to choose between competing on scale and competing on local responsiveness. Larger retailers such as The Limited, Wal-Mart, and Toys 'R' Us can enjoy the scale benefits that result from massive product volume, and at the same time exploit their in-depth knowledge of local markets to provide products and services carefully tuned to local needs. Combining the purchasing muscle of a retail giant with the responsiveness of a local shop makes these retailers formidable competitors. But to exploit their knowledge of local and aggregate market trends, retailers must develop a crucial capability—the ability to respond quickly to changing market needs.

Channel Perspective

To fully understand how quick response capabilities can be efficiently and effectively achieved, it is necessary to analyze the development of these capabilities at both the firm and channel levels. Here "channel" denotes the global value chain—the sequence of firms that encompasses all activities from the acquisition of raw material to the delivery of product to the final customer. Thus, for example, in the textile and apparel industries, a channel might comprise a fiber provider, yarn manufacturer, textile manufacturer, apparel manufacturer, and retailer, as well as firms that supply supporting transportation, information, or distribution services to the companies that actually manufacture or sell the product (see Figure 8-1).

The channel perspective is critical; it is essential that we recognize quick response capabilities such as speed and flexibility as channel capabilities. Thus, for example, the set of capabilities a retailer offers its customers is very much the result of its suppliers' capabilities as well as its own. This suggests that companies must take far greater responsibility than is typical for the selection and management of the channels in which they participate. To efficiently achieve quick response capabilities, companies must choose and/or develop channel partners that

Figure 8-1
Industry Structure: U.S. Textile and Apparel Industries

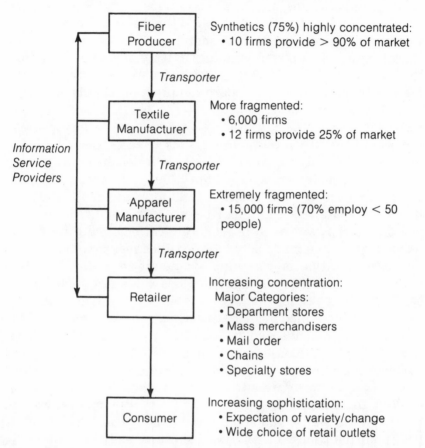

have the necessary capabilities and establish coordinating mechanisms that ensure the rapid flow of both product and information through the channel.

A global perspective is similarly crucial. Retailers and manufacturers that have succeeded in tightly coordinating their global supply chains have found that combining the speed and flexibility of a quick response system with the cost and variety advantages of a global supply network can give companies a commanding competitive edge. The Limited, Benetton, Levi Strauss, and Liz Claiborne are all formidable competitors who have effectively managed global channels to great advantage.

The Limited and Benetton manage global value chains with very different structures. The Limited restricts its retail activity to the United States; its supply-arm subsidiary, MAST Industries, has production offices scattered throughout the world that coordinate a global network of suppliers. Conversely, Benetton sources much of its apparel product in Italy, but sells its product through an expansive global network of stores. Levi Strauss and Liz Claiborne have built apparel empires on closely managed global supply networks.

Academics specializing in logistics have for years proclaimed the benefits of fully integrated logistics systems, the ideal being to manage the entire channel stretching from raw material supplier to final customer as a system rather than myopically managing the firms in the channel as individual elements. But only in recent years has this ideal begun to be realized, in large part because advances in telecommunications and information technologies have made possible the collection, communication, and interpretation of voluminous amounts of data. With this increasing technological capability has come acknowledgment of integrated channel management as a crucial management concern, accompanied by increased attention to the nature of the relationships, policies, and systems that span channel members.

This chapter discusses how quick response capabilities and partnerships affect the performance of manufacturing and retail channels. Examples are cited from a variety of industries, including an in-depth analysis of quick response approaches and results in the textile and apparel industries. The apparel industry has made concerted efforts to shorten lead times by using telecommunications and information technologies as linking technologies to coordinate its lengthy supply and retail channels. Although technology is by no means new to the industry, previous technological implementations have focused largely on cost reduction (by increasing productivity or efficiency) and improved product quality at the firm level, rather than on improved coordination between channel members and its impact on channel efficiency and responsiveness. We outline the essential components of a quick response strategy and discuss ways in which advances in telecommunications and information technologies can enable the supplier/retailer interface and, hence, the retailer/consumer interface, to operate more quickly, efficiently, and effectively.

An Example: The U.S. Apparel Industry Uses Quick Response to Regain Market Share Lost to Global Competition

The U.S. apparel industry offers a useful context in which to explore the changes in retailer/supplier partnerships enabled by technological improvements.[3] The industry is enigmatic: most of its segments compete primarily on low cost, yet the industry wastes an estimated $25 billion per year[4] through inefficient practices; its markets continually demand fashionable new products, yet it routinely takes more than a year to get new products to market. Because production must typically be planned so far in advance, production plans are invariably based on highly speculative forecasts. The time lags and errors inherent in the planning process result in staggering losses, primarily because of forced markdowns, stockouts, and high inventory levels. In an effort to avoid these losses, players in the industry have traditionally tried to shift risk either back to their suppliers or forward to their customers, thus reinforcing the adversarial relationships that have characterized the industry.

Industry Background

The U.S. apparel industry, like many U.S. manufacturing industries, has lost much ground in recent years to foreign-made goods. For the bulk of the market, this loss is largely due to the substantially lower labor rates that prevail in the Pacific Rim and Caribbean Basin countries, where many foreign competitors are located. (At the highest end of the market, the availability of top-grade fabrics such as those found in Italy and Japan and the availability of highly skilled labor are also important contributing factors.) In an industry that competes largely on a cost basis, the cost advantage foreign-made apparel products have over U.S.-made goods has had tremendous impact. For example, the share of the U.S. apparel market held by imported goods more than doubled between 1974 and 1985.[5] Total consumer retail expenditure for apparel in 1985 was estimated at $127 billion. Imports represented 44% of this dollar amount and nearly 50% of the number of garments sold.[6] The trade imbalance in clothing and textiles represented 12% of the total U.S. trade deficit in 1986.[7]

Despite the price appeal of offshore products, the combination of traditionally long procurement lead times for goods produced offshore and rapidly shifting market preferences has made retailers' attempts to match orders with eventual customer demand increasingly challenging. During the 10-year period from the mid-1970s to the mid-1980s, these factors combined with a sluggish U.S. economy, a saturated retail market, and declining consumer apparel expenditures to leave retailers with substantial apparel inventories that could be sold only through increasing price markdowns. A National Retail Merchants Association report found that store markdowns (both forced and promotional) on women's apparel rose from 16.3% of sales in 1976 to 28.2% of sales by 1984.[8]

The length of the apparel manufacturing chain and the time it takes finished products to work their way through the entire manufacturing process make planning risky and forecast errors costly. Estimates of the average length of time it takes for a new garment style to wend its way through the traditional apparel pipeline, from fiber production to retail presentation of a finished piece, range from 56[9] to 66 weeks,[10] with garments in actual production only 6% to 17% of that time. Long procurement lead times have substantial impact. Forced markdowns in the apparel channel are estimated to amount to 13% of net retail apparel sales (this amount comprises losses incurred at three levels in the channel: 8% by retailers, 3.5% by apparel manufacturers, and 1.5% by textile manufacturers). If losses throughout the system due to stockouts and inventory carrying costs (estimated at 6% and 5% of apparel sales, respectively) are added to the cost of forced markdowns, the total cost of inefficiencies throughout the apparel pipeline resulting from long lead times is approximately 24% of net annual retail apparel sales. Nearly two-thirds of these losses are experienced at the retail level.[11]

Genesis of the Quick Response Movement in the United States

In the mid-1980s, the "Crafted with Pride in the U.S.A." Council was created to address the domestic apparel industry's market share losses. The council's efforts to help domestic manufacturers exploit their locational advantage and increase their competitiveness led to the introduction of the quick response concept in 1985.

Simply stated, quick response is a strategy for linking retailing and manufacturing operations so that the supply channel is able to respond quickly to changing customer requirements. The strategy employs a combination of information technologies and supporting manufacturing and business practices designed to allow domestic manufacturers to capitalize on one of their strongest competitive advantages—proximity to domestic markets—by providing more suitable products, higher customer service levels, and shorter lead times than those offered by lower-priced foreign competitors. Quick response is intended to reduce overall inventory levels, increase inventory turns, and prevent forced markdowns and stockouts. By establishing production schedules close to the selling season and basing replenishment on actual, rather than forecasted, sales data, manufacturers and retailers can ensure that they have the right product available to the consumer.

By operating in quick response mode, retailers and apparel manufacturers eliminate much of the risk inherent in the traditional planning and production system. Forecast error is reduced by planning assortments much closer to the selling season and performing consumer preference tests and limited product introductions to pretest and fine-tune specific style, color, and size offerings. Inventory risk is reduced by producing smaller initial orders and re-ordering more frequently throughout the selling season based on point-of-sale data collected at the full stock-keeping unit (SKU) level (i.e., specific to style, color, and size). Ideally, the outcome is greater return on investment for the retailer resulting from increased inventory turns and reduced markdowns and stockouts. Many U.S. apparel and textile manufacturers are pursuing quick response strategies with the hope that these advantages will ultimately make their goods more profitable for retailers and thus more attractive than foreign-made goods. Although imported goods may cost the retailer much less initially, purchasing goods with the long order fulfillment times traditionally associated with offshore sourcing results in larger and more risky inventory investment. It is important to note, however, that some offshore producers are able to realize excellent quick-response capabilities. For example,

MAST Industries, the sourcing subsidiary of The Limited, can submit an order for certain new apparel products to its Hong Kong production office and have the appropriate textile material procured, cut, sewn, and air-freighted to The Limited's Columbus, Ohio, distribution center within a six-week period.[12] The Limited's global quick-response capability is a critical component of its competitive strategy and, together with the telecommunications and information technologies that support it, is largely responsible for the company's tremendous growth and profitability.

Quick Response Initiatives in the Apparel Industry

A number of companies in different sectors of the textile and apparel industries have implemented quick response programs. Some of these programs link only two partners in the supply channel (e.g., an apparel manufacturer and a retailer); others span a broader portion of the channel. Many were adopted first on a limited trial basis and then expanded as their benefits became apparent.

Benetton was an apparel industry pioneer in the quick response movement. In 1972, Benetton implemented a new production process in which knit garments were dyed after they were knitted, in contrast to the standard industry practice of knitting garments from pre-dyed yarn. This innovation allowed Benetton sales agents to change their preseason orders from unpopular to popular colors after witnessing demand at the retail level.[13] Luciano Benetton commented on the company strategy, "We have kept the same strategy all along—to put fashion on an industrial level. Most of the rest of Italian fashion is still on an artisan level."[14] Quick response capabilities provided the foundation for Benetton to implement this strategy—first in Italy, later worldwide.

In the United States, one of the first quick-response pilot programs to span the length of the apparel pipeline was the much-publicized implementation of the linkages initiated in 1986 among textile giant Milliken & Company, Seminole Manufacturing Co. (a major Mississippi-based manufacturer of men's slacks), and the discount mega-chain Wal-Mart Stores. Analysis of the results indicated that Wal-Mart experienced a 31% increase in unit sales on a same-store basis (900 stores were involved in the project) while its inventory turns increased 30%, from 3.7 to 4.8. On the basis of these results, Wal-Mart expanded the program in 1988 to include other major vendors.[15] Seminole Manufacturing, which prior to the pilot had reluctantly begun to produce some goods overseas in an attempt to reduce overall costs and remain competitive, brought some of this production back to the United States in 1988 when the technological improvements it implemented as part of its quick response program began to show positive results.[16]

Haggar Apparel Co., maker of menswear, was also an early quick-response entrant, with its H.O.T. (Haggar Order Transmission) system, which includes dual-technology, the universal product code (UPC and U-Line) product bar coding, electronic data interchange (EDI), and automatic electronic reordering, stock management, and replenishment functions. By mid-1987, Haggar's system was linked to more than 500 retail stores on one end and to textile suppliers such as Milliken and Burlington on the other. Haggar reduced its manufacturing cycle from 14 days to 7 using technological improvements in computerized cutting, materials handling, and fabric pressing, as well as a reconfigured assembly line and state-of-the-art distribution center that operates with just six employees.[17] To support Haggar's ability to manufacture smaller lot sizes, Milliken reduced its minimum order quantities from 5,000 or 10,000 yards to just 1,000 yards and developed the capability to deliver orders within a two-week lead time.

In the retail sector, many national chains (e.g., Sears and J.C. Penney), large department store conglomerates (e.g., Dillard's Department Stores and Dayton-Hudson), and mass merchandisers (e.g., K mart and Wal-Mart) have spearheaded the use of EDI and UPC product bar coding in anticipation of the significant advantages expected to result from the implementation of these technologies. Many of these retail companies are requiring their vendors to implement these technologies as a prerequisite for doing business with them. A notable example of a chain store that has successfully converted its vendors to these technologies is Mervyn's, the California-based subsidiary of Dayton-Hudson. Mervyn CEO Walter Rossi had a vision of receiving 75% of all incoming merchandise through electronically transmitted purchase orders in 1988, a goal he met; by the end of 1988, Mervyn's 220 stores were handling three-quarters of their $3.6 billion worth of retail merchandise through on-line systems. The company brought the remaining 25% of its vendors onto the system in mid-1989. Mervyn management estimated that the system was responsible for significant sales growth—for example, hosiery sales, previously a flat-growth category, increased 26%. Moreover, overall inventory levels were reduced even though the company opened 15 new stores.[18] (Figure 8-2 provides an overview of retail industry participants.)

Essential Elements of a Quick Response System

What would a system capable of inducing such profound changes necessarily entail? A quick response strategy involves seven key components:

- an effective, integrative information pipeline,
- shortened product development cycle,
- consumer testing to narrow product selections for specified market segments,
- effective forecasting and replenishment systems,
- rapid order fulfillment,
- short-cycle manufacturing, and
- transformation of corporate culture.

The underlying technologies associated with each of these components are described below and illustrated by examples of various implementations.

1. Effective Information Architecture across the Channel: Telecommunications and Information Technologies Associated with Quick Response

An effective information pipeline, characterized by information sharing and rapid information flow, is a vital component of a quick response system. Timely, accurate information benefits all parties in the channel. It allows them to plan production more accurately so that only goods for which there is likely to be consumer demand are produced, eliminate redundant quality control and distribution practices, reduce the amount of paperwork associated with ordering and inventory control, and ensure that changes made at one stage of production (e.g., a cost-reduction effort by a yarn manufacturer that results in the

Figure 8-2
Retail Firm Types

Department stores range in size and geographic coverage from single independent stores to larger independent companies with branches throughout a
given area (e.g., Hess's in Pennsylvania), stores that are members of department
store groups within a region (e.g., Mervyn's and Dillard's in the West), and
national chains (e.g., Sears, Macy's). Department stores offer both hard and soft
goods and generally carry a large number of nationally advertised brands.

Specialty stores can be either independent stores or chains. These stores
offer a more limited range of apparel and accessory items chosen to fit a particular theme, such as juniors (The Limited Express) or large sizes (Lane Bryant),
career apparel (Jos. A. Banks) or casual clothing (Casual Corner), premium
quality (Ann Taylor), or popular prices (Hit or Miss).

Discounters or mass-merchandisers are usually regional or national chains
(e.g., K mart, Zayre) whose strategy is to offer "everyday low prices" on both
hard and soft goods in a central checkout, self-service format. These stores have
begun to offer an increasing proportion of nationally advertised brands in their
merchandise selection, thus competing more directly with full-priced department stores.

Off-priced stores are regional or national chains (e.g., Marshalls, T.J. Maxx)
that offer designer-label and branded apparel at a discount, usually by purchasing excess inventory from manufacturers and retailers. Because they typically
rely on buying overstocks, these stores cannot offer full assortments of merchandise.

Mail order businesses offer merchandise either exclusively through catalog
sales (e.g., Lands' End) or through a combination of catalog and store sales
(e.g., L.L. Bean, Talbot's). In the latter case, catalog order-fulfillment centers
often have evolved into retail facilities open to the public.

Source: "Retailing: The Changing Game," *Bobbin* (January 1989): 56–57.

production of yarn of uneven diameter) do not impede the effectiveness of changes made later in the production process (e.g., a
cost-reduction effort by a textile manufacturer that results in
the installation of high-efficiency, automated looms that require
consistency of incoming fiber or yarn).[19]

Companies involved in quick response programs generally
make substantial investments in new technology to support
more efficient methods of designing, ordering, manufacturing,
and distributing products. These technologies are divided into
two classes: those that facilitate product identification and
tracking, and those that facilitate the transfer of data and/or
pictorial images.

Product Identification and Tracking

Bar coding, used in conjunction with barcode scanning equipment, allows product data to be recorded at the point of sale (POS), thereby facilitating merchandise tracking and inventory control at the most specific level of detail. POS data capture virtually eliminates pricing and cashier errors and greatly reduces the amount of time the retailer spends on ticketing activities, as barcoded labels containing all relevant information about a product are usually applied during the manufacturing process. Addition of a price look-up (PLU) function eliminates the need for reticketing when goods are put on promotion. The universal product code—a 12-digit merchandise identification code consisting of a unique 5-digit vendor number (assigned by the Uniform Code Council) and a 5-digit merchandise number (assigned by the vendor), as well as leading and trailing control digits—has emerged as the dominant bar coding standard. Scanning technology consists of an optical reading device that translates UPC bar codes into numbers that can be directly input into retailers' computerized sales-tracking systems.[20]

Shipping container marking (SCM) enhances the speed and accuracy of the merchandise distribution process. SCM requires bar code labeling on shipping containers to facilitate identification and processing at retail receiving facilities. A shipping container code supplied by the manufacturer identifies the vendor, order number, and destination and assigns a unique carton number to each container in a shipment. Levi Strauss & Co. was the first apparel manufacturer to apply the Uniform Code Council's "Code 128" bar code to all cartons delivered to its retail customers.[21] Used in conjunction with an electronically transmitted advance shipping notice (ASN) that details the exact contents of the container, SCM theoretically allows containers to be automatically received, verified, and sent to the sales floor without being opened. This will be feasible in practice, however, only if vendors can certify merchandise quality and verify the accuracy of their ticketing and packaging processes.[22] Currently, many distribution facilities lack sufficient control of their packaging processes to allow accurate tickets to be created.

Data and/or Image Transfer

Electronic data interchange facilitates business transactions by providing for electronic transmission of information formerly contained in paper documents (e.g., purchase orders, packing slips, invoices, and payment) and information hitherto considered too unwieldy to collect and/or exchange. Electronic transmission permits large volumes of data to be exchanged almost instantaneously. Moreover, because data do not have to be reentered at receiving locations, the use of EDI substantially increases accuracy and greatly reduces the amount of clerical effort associated with transactions.

Typically, either orders or point-of-sale data are transmitted via EDI to the vendor. A retailer that chooses to use its own forecasting and sales analysis systems makes sales forecasts based on its analysis of past and current selling trends and then constructs an appropriate set of order quantities to send to its vendors to be filled. This approach parallels traditional ordering practices. A more recent practice—rarely possible before the advent of EDI made it easier to gather timely, detailed data—is based on the transmission of retail point-of-sale data to appropriate vendors. In this scenario, manufacturers use their own sales analysis and forecasting systems to determine retailers' appropriate order quantities and automatically replenish retail stock. In general, such arrangements reduce the pipeline "whiplash effect" by allowing actual sales data to be transmitted to upstream channel partners.

An accurate, up-to-date database management system provides critical support for the organization, storage, and retrieval of necessary data. A unified database that makes available product information and order status, as well as current and past selling data, forms a crucial source of common information upon which well-founded decisions, made by parties from multiple functions within a firm or by multiple firms in a channel, can be based. MAST Industries' managers, for example, can log on to a terminal in any of the company's worldwide offices to obtain up-to-the-minute information about a host of matters, including selling trends, orders, and import quota status.

Isolated installations of EDI linkages are not sufficient to support the set of activities involved in the management of a retailer's supply and selling activities. To fully exploit today's technologies, these links must be consolidated into an integrated network of electronic linkages that supports the movement of product and information throughout the entire supply system, including retail outlets, transportation vehicles, and suppliers' and retailers' headquarters and warehouses. Abbott

Weiss, group manager of retail and wholesale at Digital Equipment Corporation, cites Toys 'R' Us as a particularly effective user of DEC's network management system. "Toys can continually pull sales information from their stores, trickle it back to their DCs for inventory replenishment, and then send that information back to headquarters," he explains. "So typically, within 15 minutes or a half hour, they know how a particular store was doing 30 minutes ago. This ability to manage their merchandise from a total systems point of view is a great advantage over the competition."[23]

An integrated system of EDI linkages and associated decision support systems forms an essential foundation on which all business transactions between a retailer and its suppliers can be based. Figure 8-3A illustrates how LeviLink, Levi Strauss's integrated quick-response system, incorporates multiple uses of EDI and other technologies to simplify and shorten the processes of analyzing sales, ordering, receiving, and stocking products, and maintaining inventories.

Radio frequency (RF) transmission—wireless communication between mobile units and a central computer—is used in warehouses and retail stores. RF units are regularly used in warehouse applications to facilitate two-way communication between warehouse personnel and a central database about the identities, quantities, and locations of products to be selected from warehouse shelves to fill customer orders. Some retailers use RF units for inventory and price verification. Caldor, for example, uses hand-held Telxon RF units that communicate with a Compaq PC to verify prices on file.[24]

Other technological advances have also had tremendous impact on the ability of individuals to communicate easily with members of their own and other organizations. Electronic mail (E-mail) and phone mail, for example, allow accurate messages to be quickly and efficiently transmitted without regard to simultaneity of schedules and without the need for additional personnel to take messages. E-mail differs from EDI in a number of ways. For example, E-mail allows the transmission of freely formatted messages, whereas EDI requires precisely defined formats, and E-mail messages typically cue recipients by means of an audio or visual signal, while EDI simply deposits messages in recipients' "mailboxes," to be located and retrieved when convenient.[25]

Figure 8-3A
LeviLink Components

Sell Through Analysis and Reporting System (STARS)

STARS analyzes raw point-of-purchase data to determine gross margin, return on sales, and specific product and geographic rankings for marketing.

Retailer Electronic Data Interchange Packages

An inventory control/financial analysis and reporting system designed to run on a personal computer to help expedite purchase orders and reduce stock-outs and overstocks for the small- to medium-sized retailer.

Electronic Invoicing

Levi's invoices, including product information, dates, and related information, are transmitted electronically to the retailer, reducing paper-handling costs and improving advance shipping information.

Electronic Packing Slip/Bar-Code Carton Tags

An electronic "packing slip" describing the contents of each carton in a shipment is transmitted to the retailer when the shipment is released from a Levi distribution center. Each carton is tagged with a bar coded label that enables the retailer to electronically match the carton with its contents upon arrival.

Model Stock Management

Retailers capture POS or inventory data using POS scanners or hand-held readers. These data are transmitted to the retailer's Levi sales representative, who compares current selling trends to model stock profiles and determines suggested order quantities.

Electronic Purchase Orders

LeviLink's electronic purchasing capability allows retailers to quickly submit orders to Levi, thereby significantly shortening order entry time.

Vendor Marking

Levi labels each of its items with a tag that identifies the item's style, color, and size. Each Levi tag is coded with multiple numbers (Levi's product number, a UPC bar code, and NRMA's UVM code) to support multiple standards for product identification. (Levi supplies a file that cross references the three product numbers to enable retailers to easily convert from one standard to another.) Levi estimates that, by avoiding the need to ticket merchandise, retailers using Levi's vendor-marked tickets eliminate 3 to 14 days from the time it takes to move merchandise from receipt to the selling floor.

Source: Levi Strauss & Co. documents.

Facsimile (fax) machines are widely used to transmit orders, selling data, and graphic or pictorial images among channel partners. Fax machines require minimal investment and transmission costs are simply the cost of the (long-distance) telephone call necessary to send the data. A shortcoming of fax machines (compared to EDI, for example) is the need to re-input data into the recipient's computer, thereby causing duplication of effort and increasing the likelihood of input error. Many personal computers are now equipped with fax modems that allow electronic messages to be sent and received without the need for a separate fax machine.

Digital camera images can be used to transfer detailed renditions of product samples to remote locations. These images provide a higher quality product likeness than a fax machine, but without the animation of television broadcasts.

Video conferences between widely dispersed employees can be conducted via satellite communication of television broadcasts. Video conferences enable managers to hold "face-to-face" meetings, display data trends or graphs, and show products without having to travel to a common location. J.C. Penney has replaced frequent buyer meetings in New York with video conferences, during which it uses satellite television broadcasts to display merchandise collections from a central location to individual store buyers and managers. Penney uses preliminary feedback about new products and order commitments from individual store managers to improve product designs and reduce ordering risks.

In January 1992, VF Corporation announced its Market Response Information System (MRIS), a multimedia communications system that combines IBM computer and videoconferencing technologies to link VF with its retailers. The system supports the exchange of data, sound, and images, and requires minimal retail investment; only an IBM PS/2 computer and camcorder are needed for the retailer to fully utilize the system.

High definition television (HDTV), which allows detailed, lifelike images to be transmitted to other parties, is in only limited use at present because of its prohibitive (for most companies) costs. MAST Industries has used HDTV to communicate with its Hong Kong production office. As MAST executive vice president Stephen DuMont reports, "HDTV gives a virtual three-dimensional image which gives the merchant much more of a feeling for the product."[26] HDTV's high expense is warranted only when image quality is critical to the evaluation and buying process, as for textile and apparel products.

2. Shortened Product Development Cycles

For short-life cycle products, short product development cycles are critical. Product development has typically been a drawn-out process characterized by little coordination between functional areas, sequential decision making and activities, and, frequently, poor results. Design, engineering, manufacturing, and marketing may have no sense of one another's priorities. Recent research reveals that product development processes in which functional areas overlap and managers in different functions make decisions jointly produce shorter, less costly development projects and better designs.[27]

Technological advances can also make significant contributions to the product development process. Computer-aided design (CAD) systems, for example, are increasingly being used by textile and apparel manufacturers to reduce from days or weeks to hours the lead times associated with planning new assortments and designing individual garments. CAD systems enable designers to experiment with a greater number of designs and respond more quickly to market changes, and they are capable of producing catalog-quality images that can eliminate the need to make sample garments. Limitations in the range of colors and the inability to convey differences in texture that characterized early CAD systems have been largely remedied by recent software advances. The Limited transmits design images via EDI between CAD terminals installed at its headquarters in Ohio and MAST Industry headquarters in Massachusetts, and designers for The Limited use the terminals to send preliminary designs to buyers who quickly feed back opinions and ideas. Once agreement is reached between designers and buyers, designs are electronically transmitted to a receive-only CAD terminal at MAST's international production offices, thereby triggering The Limited's renowned global supply network to spring into operation.

Similar technology has enabled J.C. Penney to improve its product development process. Penney uses Sony's "Still Image System" to electronically transmit detailed color photographs of new designs from its Texas headquarters to its overseas production offices in a matter of minutes. The manufacturer then creates samples that are sent to Penney headquarters for evaluation. Penney's centrally located buyers can solicit input from individual store managers by transmitting images of merchandise selections to store sites. The company's exclusive direct broadcast television system employs satellite transmission to send video images from Penney headquarters to more than 700 stores. Store units support video reception and two-way audio transmission, thus permitting real-time discussion of transmitted images between remote store managers and Penney buyers. After viewing the images, store managers transmit orders either directly to the production facility or to a Penney buyer who consolidates individual store orders and electronically places an aggregate order with the manufacturer. Use of this system improves new product designs by incorporating feedback from market-conscious store managers, dramatically reduces order lead times for new products, and greatly reduces uncertainty in buyer's orders. (Prior to the installation of the system, buyers placed orders with manufacturers based on forecasts of store needs, frequently resulting in wholesale-level overstock or understock.)[28]

3. Test Marketing

Test marketing of new product concepts plays a limited role when manufacturing lead times are long. End-customer feedback about a new product design may be considered irrelevant in fashion or other short product life-cycle markets if the product development and delivery time exceed anticipated product life. In such situations, designers often try to anticipate future consumer preferences with little feedback from those consumers.

The advent of quick response has made eliciting consumer feedback in the testing of new products and product concepts not only viable, but vital. When new products can be made available at retail in a matter of weeks, consumer test marketing becomes extremely beneficial. Test marketing of new product concepts allows more accurate forecasting of product demand prior to full production and significantly reduces manufacturers' and retailers' risk when new products are launched.

The Limited tests new product designs extensively. Upon completion of a preliminary design, the company sources and delivers "floor sets" of sample products to a few representative store locations. Limited buyers and merchandisers travel to the test sites to observe customer reaction to the new products and to elicit consumer feedback about potentially attractive improvements. Based on this feedback, The Limited orders large quantities of products with the strongest selling indications and lesser amounts of other promising products, specifies design alternatives for potentially popular products, and eliminates products that are expected to sell poorly. These test results are instrumental in indicating appropriate full production quantities and reducing ordering risk.

Benetton, prohibited by law from requiring POS terminals in its franchisees' stores, relies on 73 worldwide agents to gather information from stores, and electronically connects each agent's computer to a central system in Italy to rapidly capture demand and order information.[29] For product-testing purposes, Benetton has installed POS terminals in approximately 20 Benetton-owned outlets (less than 5% of its retail outlets are owned by Benetton) in carefully chosen, fashion-forward locations in Italy, other European countries, and the United States.[30] Benetton uses these sites to collect customer reactions to new products and, based on these early demand indications, is able to make better preliminary production plans and earlier commitments to raw materials, as well as help sales agents and store managers make better buying decisions.

J.C. Penney has expanded the use of its satellite-based direct broadcast system beyond communication between Penney employees to encompass consumer market research for test products. At research centers located in 16 major U.S. cities, selected consumers are invited to view new merchandise via satellite broadcast and answer questions about their reactions. Viewers sit at personal computers that record and electronically transmit their responses to Penney corporate headquarters in Plano, Texas. There, the results are quickly analyzed and summarized, enabling Penney to make merchandise commitments based on end-consumer feedback rather than on marketing forecasts.[31]

4. Effective Forecasting and Replenishment Systems

Merely collecting and transmitting data are insufficient to support the complexities of retail decision making. Effective decision support systems that incorporate current selling trends with existing sales history must be used to develop accurate demand forecasts and help buyers determine appropriate order quantities. Both informal and formal methods can be used to incorporate selling trends into ordering decisions.

For example, Ito-Yokado, the Japanese parent of 7-Eleven, has systems that support the timely use of selling information to plan replenishment of even the most perishable items. Using a POS system, 7-Eleven Japan employees can call up on the company's NEC computer full-color graphs that show the selling pattern of the same day's noontime sales of the store's fresh lunch boxes, with data organized by time of purchase or gender or age of buyer. Availability of these data in easy-to-interpret graphs supports local store managers' order-planning processes as well as market research performed at corporate headquarters. Portable store units that contain the same sales data can be carried through stores to take inventory and prepare orders.[32]

Automatic (or continuous) replenishment programs (ARPs) are becoming increasingly prevalent and highly effective mechanisms for determining appropriate replenishment quantities. An ARP is a decision support system that combines current and historical selling trends and designated customer service levels to determine appropriate stocking levels ("model stock profiles") at the SKU level for each product in each retail outlet. As new data are acquired, forecasts, model stock targets, and replenishment quantities are modified and retail stocks are replenished to the newly targeted levels.

Automatic replenishment systems can be operated by either retailers or manufacturers. Dillard's and Wal-Mart, for example, each have proprietary systems for interpreting sales data and creating and transmitting replenishment orders to the appropriate supplier. Manufacturers, too, are developing the capability to interpret retail sales data in order to determine appropriate replenishment quantities for their retail customers. Instead of placing orders, retailers that deal with such suppliers send them POS data and other information, such as planned promotions, relevant to future product sales. The manufacturer then updates its forecasts for each selling location, modifies retail model stock profiles, determines appropriate replenishment quantities, and delivers the appropriate quantity of product to the retailer. Levi Strauss has pioneered the use of automatic replenishment systems to help retailers manage their stocks at the SKU level. (Many manufacturers have expanded the use of such replenishment systems to their internal inventory and production planning processes. These manufacturers determine appropriate model stock levels for products to be held in their own finished goods inventory and periodically establish production replenishment quantities based on current selling trends.)

Although point-of-sale data capture and automated replenishment systems provide manufacturers with unprecedented amounts of information about end-consumer response to their products, some manufacturers have determined that sales and EDI data are not sufficient to transfer the full complexity of information available at retail. These manufacturers are placing their own employees at or near retail headquarters or stores. Procter & Gamble, for example, has developed a cross-functional team of 37 employees, which has relocated to an office in Fayetteville, Arkansas, a few minutes' drive from Wal-Mart headquarters in Bentonville, Arkansas.[33] Colocation has enabled P&G team members to better understand Wal-Mart's business and interact more easily with counterparts on a Wal-Mart team. The partnership has yielded impressive results: sales of disposable diapers doubled to more than $1 billion[34] and retail inventories of Tide detergent have been cut from one month to two days.[35]

Placing manufacturers' representatives at retail locations to collect and convey more subtle demand information is common in some retail environments. In Japanese department stores, for example, apparel manufacturers' employees often act as sales associates at in-store "boutiques" housing the manufacturers' garments. This practice enables manufacturers to gather detailed selling data as well as more subtle customer feedback (for example, why a customer chooses *not* to purchase an article of clothing). Manufacturers' in-store sales associates can also gather competitive intelligence by observing selling trends of competitors' products. This information can be promptly conveyed to the manufacturer to allow immediate redesign and remanufacturing of poorly selling items. In Japanese department stores, it is not uncommon to find these in-store agents equipped with fax machines that enable them to immediately dispatch sketches of popular competitor products to the manufacturing site.

5. Rapid Order Fulfillment

It is vital that manufacturers, once initial or replenishment order quantities are determined, rapidly fill the orders and deliver them to specified retail locations. Delivery times vary with the demand characteristics of products and the production disciplines employed by manufacturers. Many manufacturers, for example, hold limited quantities of a set of core products in inventory so that orders for these goods can be filled from stock. Fashionable items may be made to order, thereby adding the product's manufacturing cycle time to its order fulfillment time. Basic goods replenishment items may be ordered quite frequently—basic apparel items as often as once every week or two, and perishable items in Tokyo grocery stores, where available shelf space is limited by prohibitive real estate prices, as often as two or three times per day. (Figure 8-3B describes the operation of the order fulfillment process for Levi Strauss's Levi-Link system.)

6. Short-Cycle Manufacturing

Whether orders are filled from stock or to order, long manufacturing cycle times add significant risk to the manufacturing process. A number of manufacturing approaches have been developed to support rapid turnaround of new or replenishment products.

Flexible manufacturing practices, such as manufacturing cells ("modules") or unit production systems (UPSs), can significantly reduce apparel manufacturing lead times over the traditional "progressive bundle" system, in which garment pieces are tied into large bundles to be transferred between sewing stations and then untied and pressed to be worked on at the next stage of production. With cells and UPSs, lot sizes and work-in-process inventories are significantly reduced, resulting in shorter manufacturing cycle times, smaller finished goods inventories and minimum lot sizes, and improved quality due to reduced clutter, earlier feedback on quality, and general improvements in work force attitudes. Whereas product is typically moved manually in

Figure 8-3B
Levi Order-Fulfillment Cycle with K-G Retail

I. K-G stores track sales of products marked by Levi with UPC bar codes at the SKU (style, color, and size) level by point-of-sale scanning.

II. K-G stores use internal systems to generate demand forecasts and orders for Levi products. Orders for basic products are generated every two weeks.

III. K-G transmits EDI purchase orders to Levi via General Electric Information Service's value-added network (in VICS 850 format).

IV. Levi packs goods marked with UPC codes at the SKU level.

V. Levi marks cartons with bar codes (in standard Code 128 format).

VI. Levi ships cartons to individual K-G stores.

VII. As soon as the cartons leave the Levi distribution center, Levi sends K-G an advance shipping notice containing electronic packing slips relating each carton's contents and Code 128 serial number (the ASNs are sent in VICS 856 format).

VIII. K-G stores scan carton bar codes upon arrival at the loading dock.

IX. K-G's computer matches scanned carton bar-code numbers with Levi's electronic packing slips to update K-G inventory records.

X. K-G stores open cartons and place goods on store shelves. (Unlike most retailers of its size, K-G Retail does not maintain a warehouse; orders are shipped from K-G's suppliers directly to the destination store.)

XI. Levi sends K-G an electronic invoice (in VICS 810 format).

XII. K-G's computer verifies Levi's invoice against the electronic packing slip.

XIII. K-G's electronic funds transfer (EFT) program transfers funds via EDI from K-G's bank, Maryland National, to Levi's bank, First National Bank of Chicago (payment authorization is sent in ANSI X12 820 format).

Source: Levi Strauss and K-G Retail, as reported in "EDI Quickens Retail Responses," *EDI Executive* (November 1989): 1–3. K-G Retail is a Denver-based retailer with about $130 million in annual sales and 125 retail outlets. It was one of Levi's first EDI trading partners.

cells, UPSs automate the movement of garment pieces between sewing stations. Electronic pattern-making and laser-based cutting technologies also help to expedite manufacturing, improve accuracy, and reduce waste. Finally, computer-based monitoring systems help track the movement of finished goods through production and distribution,[36] and could eventually follow goods from the textile mill to the apparel manufacturer's cutting-room and sewing-room floors, and ultimately to the retailer's warehouse, facilitating inventory control and improving communication among all parties in the apparel channel.

7. Transformation of Corporate Culture

Perhaps the most important—and in many ways, most elusive—requirement for the successful implementation of a quick response strategy is the establishment of broad changes in corporate culture that support the strategy. MAST has effectively implemented changes in organizational focus to support its time-based competitive strategy; for example, MAST employees quote lead times in hours, instead of the weeks, months, or even years that most other apparel firms use. The more subtle benefits of quick response are rarely captured by standard company metrics, yet few companies employ time-based measurements and incentives that provide appropriate incentives and recognition for managers who reduce lead times.

Standardization of Quick Response Technologies

One of the biggest stumbling blocks to the implementation of quick response systems thus far has been lack of standardization of some of the key technologies that support them. Several different bar code conventions have been in use until recently, when UPC emerged as the standard. Incompatibility of EDI technologies and data transmission formats between companies has been especially problematic. A host of proprietary EDI technologies exist, and conforming to the requirements of one customer's or supplier's EDI system often renders a company's EDI capability incompatible with those of other potential quick-response partners. A 1988 survey revealed that while 63% of respondents in the apparel industry utilized established EDI standards, 91% also employed proprietary standards—evidence that most firms have been forced to invest in duplicate software development and implementation in order to support both standard and proprietary data interchange protocols.[37]

In an effort to remove these roadblocks and establish standards for quick-response-related technologies, a number of voluntary organizations have coalesced around representatives from different industry segments. In the apparel and textile industries, four oversight councils have been formed. Three of these facilitate ties between partners in the production chain (i.e., fiber-textile, textile-apparel, and apparel-retail); the fourth

Figure 8-4
Standards-Setting Organizations in the Fiber/Textile/Apparel Industries

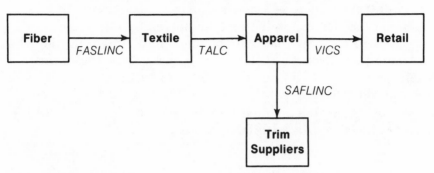

The organizations are:
FASLINC: Fabric and Suppliers Linkage Council. Established in 1987 with the goal of facilitating and improving communications between textile producers and their fiber suppliers.
TALC: Textile and Apparel Linkage Council. Formed in 1985 to discuss voluntary standards that would facilitate JIT deliveries between textile and apparel manufacturers. This group has established standards for roll identification, shade measurement, width/length measurement, identification of defects for flagging, flagging fabric defects, and EDI data transmission.
VICS: Voluntary Inter-Industry Communications Standards. A retail-based council concerned with established bar coding, EDI, and shipping container marking standards necessary to create the close ties between retailers and apparel manufacturers.
SAFLINC: Sundries and Apparel Findings Linkage Council. Formed in 1987 with representatives from 15 apparel companies and 50 trim suppliers, this group is concerned with establishing uniform formats for the EDI transmission of planning schedules, unique producer and product package identification, and shipping package identification standards. It has also determined vendor certification requirements for participation in EDI programs.

Sources: U.S. Congress, "The U.S. Textile and Apparel Industry"; "Staying in Tune with TALC," *Bobbin* (February 1988); Susan L. Smarr, "SAFLINC Trims EDI Rhetoric," *Bobbin* (July 1988).

links apparel manufacturers with trim suppliers (see Figure 8-4).

Although standards-setting bodies are important to the development of efficient pipelines between multiple users, standards-setting organizations, or the hardware or software companies that implement standards, have in a number of cases moved so slowly that they have been eclipsed by leading-edge companies acting outside of the agreed-upon standards. Software developers wanting to market multimedia products that require the digital transmission of voice, data, and video images over telephone lines, for example, were hampered by hardware providers, which were unable to implement in a timely fashion the standardized protocol (ISDN) for digitally decoding data from telephone lines. Eventually, a number of small software vendors developed software solutions that allowed their products to be used on regular telephone lines independent of the implementation of the complicated ISDN protocol.

Impediments and Challenges to
the Implementation of Quick Response

Implementation of a quick response program generally requires a broad range of intra- and interorganizational changes at both the manufacture and retail levels. A major stumbling block stems from the fact that quick response's requirements for increased flexibility, shorter production runs, and closer coordination among firms in different segments of the pipeline are antithetical to the way the industry has operated for decades.[38] Quick response requires radical change not only in the industry's operating procedures and technological base, but, more fundamentally, in its culture; short-term focus, weak or hostile interfirm relationships, inadequate attention to human resources, and a general dominance of mass production all must go.[39]

Believing that they stand to benefit most from quick response implementations—faster inventory turns, reduced markdowns, and decreased likelihood of stockouts—many retailers have readily embraced the quick response concept. Recent retail industry restructuring has created immensely powerful retailers. Many of them have pushed for quick response services before their suppliers, with more limited resources and perceiving fewer direct benefits, have been able to put the necessary capabilities in place. Many manufacturers can currently provide such service only by holding extra inventory and employing more expensive distribution methods. To develop effective quick-response programs, change must occur at both the manufacture and retail levels. Much of this change will require dramatic cultural transformations, which would seem to place larger, established companies, such as Sears and Penney's, at a disadvantage relative to younger firms, such as The Limited and The Gap.

At the manufacturer level, the requisite changes include:

- shifting focus from an emphasis on direct labor costs to bottom line and total product costs;
- focusing on timeliness and customer service in addition to cost as key elements of competitiveness;
- changing the planning process from one in which individual retailers and their suppliers plan separately to a system in which retailers and suppliers plan assortments together;
- replacing traditionally adversarial customer and supplier relationships with cooperative partnerships; and
- using currently available technologies (e.g., computer-aided design and point-of-sale data scanning) to make key product decisions closer to the retail selling season, thereby avoiding the risky practice of planning merchandise selections many months in advance based largely on speculative forecasts.

Needed changes at the retail level include:

- shifting retail buyers' focus from gross margin percentages to bottom line returns;
- changing the nature of the buying function from handling both buying and replenishment decisions to having fewer buyers handling initial purchasing decisions, with replenishment managers responsible for maintaining assortments at the store level;
- changing the planning process from one in which individual retailers and their suppliers plan separately to a system in which retailers and suppliers plan assortments together;
- replacing traditionally adversarial customer and supplier relationships with cooperative partnerships;
- planning assortments by individual store characteristics rather than by aggregate chain requirements;
- planning assortments and tracking inventory at the full SKU level;
- reviewing inventory more frequently and re-ordering based on actual data collected at the point of sale;
- managing inventory and re-ordering by store rather than by chain; and

• placing smaller initial orders and more frequent replenishment orders.[40]

Conclusion

An array of environmental changes have transformed the retail industry. Markets are fragmenting; less homogeneous buying populations cause national advertising to be less effective at the same time that declines in viewership are making national television advertising less efficient.[41] The retailer of the future will use telecommunications and information systems to capture microlevel market data, which will be used centrally to exploit the power of the consolidated data, and decentrally to understand trends and meet consumer needs on a micro basis.

As these changes occur, significant shifts in the division of responsibility and activities among channel members will follow. Suppliers are assuming responsibility for many functions— such as ticketing, sales forecasting, and in-store services—that have traditionally been the responsibility of retailers. Even the locus of decision making is changing as manufacturers decide upon the products and quantities to be sent to retailers. What are the implications of these changes? The manufacturer-retailer power struggle is intensifying. On the other hand, powerful retailers are inducing manufacturers to provide an unprecedented number of services in addition to the products they offer. On the other, some manufacturers, empowered by their increased forecasting and service capabilities, view the retailer of the future as little more than a real estate concern that will provide space for showing their wares and appropriate technologies to support the free flow of data. The roles of other parties in the channel, such as distributors and brokers, are also being challenged. Wal-Mart sent letters late in 1991 to many of its suppliers stating that it had "decided that our dealings should be directly with the principals of your company," rather than through third-party brokers, sparking tremendous resistance from brokers and manufacturing representative organizations. Wal-Mart maintains that its goal is not to eliminate independent sales representatives, but to develop closer partnerships with its suppliers so as to shorten lead times and ensure product availability.[42]

Who will survive these escalating power struggles? Who will

flourish? To a large degree, the answer is dictated by which channel members develop the ability to respond rapidly and efficiently to continuously shifting customer desires. To do so requires not only that companies learn how to gather and interpret data and undertake rapid product development and manufacturing, but also that they make the often transformational cultural changes that are needed to implement the necessary channel-coordinating mechanisms successfully.

Notes

1. Susan Caminiti, "The New Chaps of Retailing," *Fortune* (September 24, 1990): 85–100.

2. Ken Partch, "'Partnering': A Win-Win Proposition . . . or the Latest Hula Hoop in Marketing," *Supermarket News*, 46, no. 5 (May 1991): 29.

3. Portions of this section are drawn from Janice H. Hammond and Maura G. Kelly, "Quick Response in the Apparel Industry," Harvard Business School Case 9-690-038 (1990).

4. Robert M. Frazier, "Quick Response in Soft Lines," *Discount Merchandiser* (January 1986): 42.

5. Michael L. Dertouzos, Richard K. Lester, Robert M. Solon, and the Massachusetts Institute of Technology Commission on Industrial Productivity, *Made in America: Regaining the Productive Edge* (Cambridge, Mass.: MIT Press, 1989).

6. "Focus: Economic Profile of the Apparel Industry," *American Apparel Manufacturer's Association* (November 1987): 4.

7. Anne Imperato Tray, "Retailers Warm Up To Haggar's Hotline," *Bobbin* (April 1987): 90.

8. Christopher Sharp, "The Quick Response Gospel," *Women's Wear Daily* (March 1986).

9. W. A. B. Davidson, "Quick Response: Boon or Boondoggle?," *ATI* (May 1988): 56.

10. "Retailing," *Standard & Poor's Industry Surveys* (August 4, 1988): R62.

11. Frazier, "Quick Response in Soft Lines," 42, 44.

12. Ron Shulman, Presentation to the Harvard Center for Textile and Apparel Research, April 1991.

13. S. Signorelli and J. Heskett, "Benetton (A)," Harvard Business School Case 9-689-014 (1983).

14. Kenneth Labick, "Benetton Takes On the World," *Fortune* (June 13, 1983): 90.

15. "Why We Lose $25 Billion A Year," *Discount Merchandiser* (May 1988): 90.

16. Ralph King, Jr., "Made in the U.S.A.," *Forbes* (May 16, 1988): 108.

17. Tray, "Retailers Warm Up to Haggar's Hotline," 90–92.

18. Susan L. Smarr, "EDI: The Bandwagon Awaits," *Bobbin* (May 1989): 126.

19. U.S. Congress, Office of Technology Assessment, *The U.S. Textile and Apparel Industry: A Revolution in Progress—Special Report*, OTA-TET-332. Washington, D.C.: U.S. Government Printing Office (April 1987): 22–23.

20. Andersen Consulting, "A Study of Costs and Benefits to Retailers of

Implementing Quick Response and Supporting Technologies" (New York: Arthur Andersen & Co., 1988).

21. Levi Strauss company documents.

22. Ibid.

23. "Distribution Technology: The Seamless Pipeline Dream," *Discount Merchandiser* (April 1991): 49.

24. Gary Robins, "Ordering in the '90s," *Stores* (April 1991): 31.

25. Holly Haber, "Carter Hawley Hale, Levi Pioneer in the Use of Electronic Mail," *Women's Wear Daily* (April 24, 1989): 10.

26. Woody Hochswender, "How Fashion Spreads Around the World at the Speed of Light," *New York Times* (May 13, 1990): 4, 5.

27. Robert H. Hayes, Steven C. Wheelwright, and Kim B. Clark, *Dynamic Manufacturing: Creating the Learning Organization* (New York: Free Press, 1988): Chapter 11.

28. William Howell, "J.C. Penney's Competitive Technology," *Discount Merchandiser* (March 1990): 40, 44.

29. "The United Systems of Benetton," *Computerworld* (April 2, 1991): 70.

30. Interview with Giancarlo Chiodini, vice president of Logistics and Distribution, Benetton, May 1990.

31. Howell, "J.C. Penney's Competitive Technology," 40, 44.

32. James Sterngold, "New Japanese Lesson: Running a 7-11," *New York Times* (May 9, 1991): D1, D7.

33. Barnaby J. Feder, "Moving the Pampers Faster Cuts Everyone's Costs, *New York Times* (July 14, 1991): 3, 5.

34. Partch, "'Partnering': A Win-Win Proposition . . . or the Latest Hula Hoop in Marketing," 29.

35. Feder, "Moving the Pampers Faster Cuts Everyone's Costs," section 3, p. 5.

36. U.S. Congress, "The U.S. Textile and Apparel Industry," 26.

37. Stephen D. Sprinkle, "Sherlock Holmes Still Needed," *Bobbin* (July 1988): 100.

38. Kurt Salmon Associates, "Progress Report on Quick Response" (1988): 4.

39. Dertouzos et al., *Made in America,* 302.

40. Kurt Salmon Associates, "Implementing VICS Technology and Quick Response," a report for the Voluntary Inter-Industry Communications Standards Committee (1989): 7.

41. Feder, 3, 5.

42. "Wal-Mart Tries to Bypass Reps," *Television Digest,* 31, no. 49 (December 9, 1991): 13; "Wal-Mart Says Policy on Suppliers Aims Only to Ensure Stock," *The Wall Street Journal* (December 6, 1991): B6.

Part Four
Strategic Response to Structural Change

Introduction

In this section, we examine globalization, information technology, and competition from the perspective of the general manager who must assess what is going on and determine how to respond strategically. The appropriateness of strategic response clearly depends on a complex collection of factors that includes industry structure, drivers of change, strength of competitive position, likely competitor response, and so forth. Nevertheless, by stepping back we can categorize the types of strategic responses and gain insights by examining others' perspectives.

Newer firms, because they do not have the excess baggage of old hierarchical structures, that must be replaced with networks, have a distinct advantage. Moreover, we find that larger, established firms have a more difficult time changing than smaller and medium-sized firms do. Nevertheless, networking has an impact on all firms mandating significant changes that academics, such as Harvard Business School's Richard Nolan and Lynda Applegate, refer to as "transformational change."

The concept of being global has been a difficult one for managers to comprehend fully. Only a few years ago, many large companies that did business in more than one country were characterized as global. But most of these companies did not have highly integrated foreign operations and were dominated by the country and culture of the headquarters location. To be truly global, a company must achieve a high level of global efficiency and simultaneously provide excellent local service.

Globalization is a level of operation driven by a set of benchmarks or criteria. Local-global balancing, achieving global efficiency, and providing customized services to local markets and customers are among the most important of these benchmarks. Within the global context, it is important that a worldwide product/service line meet both global efficiency and local tailoring requirements. Moreover, a global firm's management system must reflect a global perspective. It must inform general managers about what is going on—what is working and what is not—and provide the information they need to conduct analyses and take corrective action at the appropriate levels in a timely manner.

With the blurring of traditional firm boundaries, new models begin to take form. One of these is the virtual corporation, which serves local markets in a way that makes customers think and feel the corporation is local when, in fact, its physical location might be anywhere in the world. The virtual corporation emerged in the United States as the ability to order goods via 800 telephone numbers. Often, the person who answers an 800 telephone number is in Omaha, which has excellent telecommunications support for such services and takes orders for many products offered by different companies. Customers, however, generally perceive this person as a representative of the company from which they are ordering the product. The virtual corporation is one version of the extended network organization that is emerging.

The chapters in this section focus on unique aspects of strategic responses to globalization, information technology, and competition. But they are unanimous in suggesting that all organizations ultimately will have to respond strategically to global networking. Some organizations are clearly better positioned to do so than others, but to the extent that all must respond, major organizational changes are likely to be involved. Rather than simply react, general managers should attempt to learn from organizations that have preemptively pursued networking as an integral part of their strategy—for example, Rosenbluth Travel, which responded to competitive pressures by creating a virtual corporation.

Information Technology and the Boundary of the Firm

In the course of his research on the role of information technology in competitive strategy, Eric Clemons of the Wharton

School has produced an economic framework for generalizing about which firms are likely to be winners, which losers, and which must engage in major changes or transformations as networking proceeds.

Changes in industry structure seldom benefit all parties equally. Who will win among manufacturers or service providers as a result of efficiencies gained from improved communications-based services is difficult to determine. In general, the winners will be competitors with complex value-added services, because the markets for their products and services are not likely to be eroded, and because it will be easier for customers to outsource services from them, leading to larger markets. Losers will include firms that have relied on customer search costs or other sources of friction or market inefficiency; those that have relied on short-term information advantages; and those that have relied solely upon economies of scale. Many other players, not as readily classified as winners or losers, will nevertheless find that they must change dramatically in order to survive.

The Nature of the Global Firm and Global Opportunity

Pierre Hessler, vice president and director general of marketing for services and operations, IBM Europe, relates the findings of a consulting study he sponsored to define the term "global" and determine what it means to "become a global firm." The study, which involved 10 of IBM's largest global customers, yielded not only a definition, but also an assessment of the key ingredients of being global. Hessler considers such aspects of being global as local-global balancing, servicing international customers, worldwide product lines, and appropriate management systems in light of the study's findings.

Saturn—The Making of the Modern Corporation

With all its reported competitive problems, General Motors is still the largest industrial firm in the world. Clearly, nothing is more important to GM than being a strong global competitor. The company has undertaken many initiatives to achieve this objective, but none so bold, so expensive, or so massive as the Saturn initiative. Saturn's mandate was to create a worldwide competitive automobile, building, in the process, a totally new organization from the ground up.

Saturn Corporation president Skip LeFauve and Sloan School professor and consultant to the Saturn project Arnoldo Hax explain how Saturn met its challenge. Their chapter is comprehensive, because building a worldwide competitive organization from scratch in the automobile industry is not done in a test tube but requires practical assessment of a host of organizational issues. This chapter is unique in reporting the processes involved in and reflecting on the experiment to date.

Information Technology and the Global Virtual Corporation

Rosenbluth Travel exemplifies the so-called virtual corporation. Since 1980, by establishing a series of alliances with leading independent travel companies in 34 countries, Rosenbluth Travel has grown from a $40 million regional travel agency to a $1.3 billion global travel agency. David Miller, vice president of global information technology for Rosenbluth Travel, was instrumental in the firm's global expansion, key to which was the development of the enabling technology. Miller, with Eric Clemons and Michael Row of the Wharton School, describes the process of preempting the competition by transforming a small regional travel agency into a major global travel organization through the creation of the Rosenbluth International Alliance. Although the firm's success is impressive, key questions revolve around the sustainability of that success.

9

Information Technology and the Boundary of the Firm: Who Wins, Who Loses, Who Has to Change

Eric K. Clemons

Information technology is having an increasingly important impact on the structure of firms and industries. The rapid, nearly instantaneous exchange of information made possible by global telecommunications networks is changing industries in ways that are complex and difficult to predict. The importance of economies of scale and scope, given the cost of modern production technologies, has been widely recognized; this has been a significant factor in the consolidation of many industries. Equally important, though less widely recognized, is the significance of the reduction in transaction costs yielded by IT; this implies reductions in the cost of coordinating with a supplier, or working with a customer, to accomplish something that would previously have been done within the boundaries of a single firm. The effect is so dramatic that it prompts us to refer to the combination of computers and telecommunications not as computing but as "coordination technology." This technology, or more specifically the change in transactions costs resulting from it, has led to the increasing, and increasingly visible, reliance upon cooperative efforts, including outsourcing, joint ventures, strategic partnerships, and variants upon them.

Changes in industry structure never benefit all parties equally. Who wins among service providers as a result of efficiencies created by improved communications-based services? The analyses need not be restricted to service firms: a key aspect of consumer packaged-goods manufacturers has been the service they provide to supermarkets and major retail accounts in the distribution and marketing of their products; they, too, will find their competitive position altered. In general, winners will be those service providers with complex value-added services, since their markets for these services are unlikely to be taken away, and since it will be easier than ever for customers to outsource these services from them, leading to larger markets. Losers will include those who have relied upon customer search costs, or other sources of friction or market inefficiency, as their principal source of adding value; those who have relied upon short-term information advantage; and those who have relied solely upon economies of scale. But many other players, not easily classifiable as winners or losers, will find that they have to change.

It is stylish to speak of the coming globalization of business. The October 1989 mini-crash on Wall Street occurred because a group of Japanese banks rejected the terms of a funding package put together by New York banks to support the friendly takeover of United Airlines by British Airways (BA). When the Japanese banks withdrew their support, BA withdrew its offer, United Airlines stock plummeted to the pre–takeover attempt price, and on Wall Street, when traders realized that the era of unlimited funding for takeovers was, at least for the moment, over, the prices of numerous other takeover targets went into the tank. When a crash in New York can be caused by Tokyo's rejection of funding terms for a London-based company's purchase of a Chicago-based competitor, it is meaningless to talk about coming globalization. At least in financial services, globalization has arrived.

Our investigations of various other industries, ranging from power generation and transmission to the sale of detergents, led us to conclude that globalization will continue, and will continue to accelerate. Legislative and regulatory changes, such as the 1992 accords leading to a single European market and the rationalization made possible by improved information technology, will be the drivers.

Rationalization enabled by information technology has not occurred uniformly. Consider Frito-Lay, which has matched competitors' products with such specialty items as white corn tortilla chips for the Southwest and crunchy thick-cut potato chips for New England. Distribution of these new specialty products is quite complex, as they are not manufactured in all plants and all geographic regions. Each handoff of stock, from plant to warehouse to bin to retailer, imposes a delay in information flow. Although the company's factories can respond extraordinarily rapidly to orders, the complexity of the distribution channel has introduced delay in order flow and necessitated the maintenance of considerable safety stock. Given the short shelf life of the product, additional rationalization of information flow, aimed at eliminating the need for this stock, appears to be essential.

In contrast to its many competitors in the numerous consumer packaged-goods categories in which it competes, Procter & Gamble (P&G) has developed a remarkably successful distribution system, so homogeneous that it is best described as "one size fits all." Whereas Frito-Lay's chips have a short shelf life and high package volume ("high cube" in the industry jargon, meaning the packages have high cubic volume and a great deal of air), P&G's Pringles potato chips, packed in high-density sealed canisters, are shelf stable. A board-level executive of a competitor said with a mixture of admiration and disdain that the principal difference between Pringles and Tide was that you eat Pringles and wash with Tide. This uniformity of product packaging no doubt facilitated some very successful distribution strategies for P&G. It remains to be seen how the company will respond and market effectively against more flexible competitors.

The remainder of this chapter explores how business will change as a result of improvements in information technology. What will change? Some changes are obvious: we will almost certainly see greater customization, service enhancements, and more efficient operations. But other changes are not so obvious—the shifting of boundaries in firms and industries, for example. Who will win and who will lose as a result of these changes? Finally, after the necessary framework is established, we conclude with the implications of information technology for global partnerships and examine factors that complicate their implementation.

The Complexity of Forecasting Effects of Change: The Example of Recent DOT Rule Changes for Reservation Systems

Changes in the rules governing computerized travel agent reservation systems (CRSs) proposed by the Department of

Transportation (DOT) in March 1991 illustrate the complexity of predicting the business changes that can result from changes in the technological environment. Four CRSs operate in the United States today, all run by one or more airlines, with market shares ranging from more than 40% to less than 10%. When these systems were first being developed, Sabre by American and Apollo (now called Covia) by United Airlines, competitors hardly took notice. Subsequently, they have become tremendously important. In many years, they have been more profitable than the airline businesses they support. Sabre, which accounts for only 5.5% of American's revenues, recently produced more than half of the airline's profits. The CRS business has become so profitable that it is said to divide airlines into haves and have-nots, carriers with and without successful CRSs.

Although the profitability of CRSs was not originally expected by their developers, and surely was not predicted by the carriers that chose not to develop one, it can readily be understood by looking at the structure of the distribution channel for air travel. Potential travelers cannot access air carriers directly. Given the complexity of schedules and airfares produced by deregulation, passengers rely on travel agents to provide expert advice. Nor do these agents attempt to contact carriers directly for fare information. During a period of peak activity, such as a fare war, carriers might enact hundreds of thousands, or even millions, of fare changes per week. Consequently, virtually all travel agents access airlines through computerized reservation systems.

CRSs are thus the airlines' conduit for making flight information available to travel agencies, the principal channel for booking flights. As most agencies use only one CRS, airlines that ignore a given CRS are shut out from close to 100% of the market that it serves. Each airline thus feels an economic need to participate in *all* CRSs, enabling even CRSs with small market share to earn considerable profits. In contrast, the provider and sole owner of a regional monopoly on an automated teller machine (ATM) network, with 100% of the market for interbank ATM services, has not been able to earn extraordinary profits. The primary point of contact with the banking system remains a customer's bank, not the ATM network, and banks that use contract ATM network services cannot be obliged to pay extremely high fees for services. The principal difference in the profitability of ATM services, when contrasted with CRS services, can be explained by the structure of the two distribution networks.[1] We summarize it thus: "Geometry is destiny!"

The Department of Transportation has recently proposed significant changes to the regulations under which CRS providers operate, as follows:[2]

- The agency is proposing that the closed black boxes—combined hardware terminals and specialized reservation systems software—provided by CRS vendors be replaced with open systems. Specifically, "[our] proposed rules would allow agencies to use third-party equipment and software in conjunction with a CRS as long as they are compatible with the system."
- More important, the agency is proposing to require that each CRS be accessible from any other. As their document states, "[we] also propose to allow agencies to use one terminal for access to all the systems, a step that should encourage more agencies to use all multiple systems."

The latter point is of particular interest, as it would change the geometry of the distribution channel and hence the destiny of the players. As no CRS would be assured 100% access to any agency and its customers, no CRS would be essential to participating airlines. An air carrier that felt a CRS vendor's participation fees were excessive could leave that CRS, confident that agencies could still locate its flights through ready access to the CRSs in which it continued to participate. Fragmentation of coverage would be an expected result: airlines would participate only in CRSs for which they chose to pay the fees, which would be those for which they felt the geographic coverage of agencies justified the cost of participation. This would certainly increase competition among CRSs and reduce the fees that airlines pay for the services they receive.

But what, truly, will be the effects of these proposed rule changes? We see no connection between these changes and the DOT's stated intention of increasing competition among airlines or improving customer service. One effect, as observed above, *is* predictable, and is probably an unstated objective of the DOT: a dramatic reduction in the market power and profitability of CRSs. But the unintended effects could be even more dramatic.

With the resulting fragmentation of CRS participation, scanning all available flights for the ones that best serve a customer's needs could no longer be done on a single screen. More important, agencies that provide corporate travel management services would need a completely new set of application programs. This is because most agencies have not written their own systems for corporate expense accounting: instead they piggyback off their CRS vendor's systems, which require that all bookings be made through a single CRS. Fragmentation of carriers' participation in CRSs, and the resulting fragmentation of agencies' bookings, will also necessitate development of additional software to consolidate reporting for corporate accounts. This software will, of course, be made available, but probably by third-party vendors, since with the profits of CRSs reduced, the incentives for CRS vendors to provide software to agencies will be dramatically altered. The result will be that agencies will have to pay for services that were previously made available to them at no cost. The added complexity and expense incurred by the DOT's proposals are also likely to have the unanticipated effect of precipitating considerable consolidation among travel agencies. Only the largest will be able to pay for or develop the systems needed to ensure that the level of service provided is comparable to that provided today.

To understand the competitive implications of technology for winners and losers among firms and industries, we need to understand the following:

- information technology and competitive strategy,
- industrial organization, transaction costs, and the structure of firms and industries, and
- the implications of improved information technology for changes in transaction costs and, hence, in the structure of firms.

We consider each of these areas in its own section, and conclude with some predictions for who will win and who will lose, and with guidelines for appropriate response.

An Introduction to Information Technology and Competitive Strategy

Systems can be strategic. They can even restructure firms and entire industries.[3] Of the numerous examples in financial services, perhaps the most striking is the experience following London's "Big Bang,"[4] the rapid deregulation of financial services in October 1986.

Industry Restructuring through IT:
London's International Stock Exchange

Among the changes associated with London's Big Bang were the following:

- Massive deregulation of the International Stock Exchange (ISE) in London. Notably, ownership was liberalized, allowing British and foreign banks and foreign securities firms to enter as members of The Exchange, and competition was increased by ending fixed commissions and increasing the number of firms that competed for customer business.
- New technology was introduced, the most important being the Stock Exchange Automatic Quotation (SEAQ) system, which enabled customers to determine instantly which of a dozen or more market makers was offering the best price for a security. This greatly intensified the competitive pressure on market makers.

The effects of these changes on The Exchange, its members, and its operation were rapid and dramatic. Most visible was the movement of virtually all trading activity off the floor into the well-equipped dealing rooms upstairs. On the floor, firms had access to information from SEAQ and from people nearby; traders upstairs had access not only to SEAQ information, but also to information from Reuters and other market information systems, to their sales and research staffs, to customers, and, of course, to detailed analytical trading support models. With hindsight, it is easy to explain the unexpected and rapid departure from the newly renovated exchange floor.

The changes brought about by the Big Bang produced some very attractive benefits for the ISE. Traders quickly discovered that just as a dealing room across the street was close enough, so was one across the Channel or even across the Atlantic. Turnover in foreign securities, which accounted for less than 2% of Tokyo's activity, and less than 5% of trading in New York, soon came to account for more than half of London's business. Electronic support of trading enabled the London exchange to consolidate its position as an international financial center, attracting nearly a quarter of the Frankfurt and Paris bourses' business. Sweden, which chose this inopportune moment to double its tax on securities transactions, effectively succeeded in moving 85% of the turnover in the most important blue-chip Swedish stocks away from Stockholm onto the London exchange.

But although it accomplished all that it was supposed to achieve for The Exchange, most member firms now view the Big Bang as anything but a triumph. Generations of hopeful MBAs and legions of novice traders have been instructed to "buy low and sell high." This presumes legions of obliging individuals who could be relied upon to take the other side, that is, to buy high and sell low. For generations, these individuals have existed, as the American customers and their U.K. equivalent clients. The nearly perfect market created by SEAQ rapidly became perfectly awful for securities firms, as institutional investors in transparent markets became as well informed, and traded as cleverly, as their service providers. In aggregate, London firms began to sustain appalling losses that are perhaps best explained by analogy. In Tom Wolfe's *Bonfire of the Vanities,* Sherman McCoy is a Master of the Universe, that is, a bond trader.[5] His wife, unimpressed, explains to their young daughter that this is not unlike managing a bake sale; when the state wants to raise money for a highway, or a hospital needs to raise money for a new wing, Daddy runs a bake sale, serves the cake, and gets to eat the crumbs. Prior to SEAQ, firms could profit handsomely from eating the crumbs, and even licking the knife. In the London market, SEAQ replaced the knife with a teflon chain saw. There no longer are any crumbs, and attempting to lick the knife is now extremely hazardous! This turn of events illustrates the potentially dramatic and unforeseen impacts of technological innovation and portends a clear and overwhelmingly depressing message concerning the future profitability of financial intermediaries.[6]

Strategic Necessity: McKesson Drug

Drug wholesaler and distributor McKesson Drug Company has made effective use of information technology to coordinate and rationalize its operations. As the primary mechanism for order capture within its distribution system, the company relies upon Economost, an electronic customer-driven order entry system. McKesson customers—managers of retail pharmacies or drug stores—can walk through their stores recording the numbers of items for which additional stock is required simply by waving a bar code reader at shelf labels. The following morning, with almost perfect reliability, the requested items will arrive, pre-marked with the customers' prices, and arranged in totes to conform to the layout of the store to facilitate shelf restocking. Client stores need not keep safety stock, and their managers report that the labor associated with inventory management and shelf restocking has been dramatically reduced.

McKesson uses the information it captures with Economost to improve and rationalize all aspects of its operations: McKesson inventory turns more than 13 times per year, enabling the company to ship product before it has paid its manufacturers. Because McKesson is the largest single customer for most of its manufacturers, it has been able to negotiate significant discounts by consolidating purchasing. Internal effects have been equally dramatic; warehouse worker productivity has sustained double digit improvements, compounded for a decade, and the field sales staff was halved and telephone order entry staff reduced from 700 to 15 in a period in which dollar volume increased sixfold.

The benefits McKesson has realized have been passed through to customers in the form of significant service improvements and major price reductions to drugstores that order through Economost. It is hardly surprising that the system has been widely acclaimed and nearly universally adopted by McKesson customers; electronic order entry now accounts for more than 99% of the company's order flow. Yet, in the first decade after Economost's introduction, there was no discernable improvement in McKesson's market share or margins, and reporters and business analysts still remark on how their stock continues to underperform the market.

Systems like Economost are not failures. All of McKesson's major competitors developed equivalent systems, and did so during approximately the same time frame in which McKesson introduced Economost. These systems became what we term "strategic necessities": companies that developed them retained parity among themselves, while those that failed to implement comparable systems are no longer in business. Strategic necessities do not confer advantage; nonetheless, they are critical to a company's survival.

Competitive Advantage by Leveraging Resource Differences: Barclays de Zoete Wedd's TRADE System

We have found systems that constitute strategic necessities to be far more common than applications of information technology that confer sustainable competitive advantage. The explanation for this is quite simple. The ideas behind strategic systems can rarely be kept secret, and even more rarely are patentable or otherwise protectable. The technology on which they are based is generally universally available to all firms at comparable prices. Thus, successful ideas are copied and the benefits competed away to customers.

Competitive advantage through information technology can be sustained if the technology is used to exploit critical resources not enjoyed by competitors. If a technology is used to leverage a firm's unique strengths and exploit existing structural differences that distinguish a firm from its competitors, duplication of the technology application will not erode the innovator's advantage. The operative differences can be scale of operation, market share, critical advantage in factors of production made more important by the innovation, or even strategy.

Barclays de Zoete Wedd (BZW), among the most successful of the integrated financial services firms to emerge in the wake of London's Big Bang, continues to operate profitably even in the current brutally competitive environment. Its TRADE system for automatic entry of small orders from brokers illustrates the value of structural differences. TRADE links BZW dealers to brokers throughout the United Kingdom and permits brokers to place customer orders for shares in companies traded on the International Stock Exchange. TRADE is built upon SEAQ's display of competing prices. Low-level clerks sitting at TRADE terminals key in the stock code of the customer shares to be traded and receive notification of the best price available in London through any of the competing securities firms. Next they enter the order size and designate whether the order is to buy or sell. The system then completes the trade and immediately confirms it with the broker. Personnel costs are reduced for both the broker and BZW and expensive errors are almost eliminated. BZW's margins have improved by about $15 per trade as a result of reduced costs, and its share of small orders has more than doubled since the system's introduction.

A publicly visible innovation that doubles market share while improving margins can be expected to attract competitors' attention. The hardware upon which TRADE is based is inexpensive and widely available to competitors; the software is neither complex nor expensive, and much of it was developed by an outside contractor. The explanation for TRADE's continued success lies in the structure of BZW, rather than in TRADE's technology. BZW makes markets in more than 1,800 U.K. securities;[7] its nearest competitor with significant small-order retail presence is Smith New Court with about 800 securities. The difference is significant. Brokers who use TRADE are almost assured that their clerks' requests for trades will be successfully completed at the best price available from any London market maker. A broker using a competitor's system would face a substantial probability that the order could not be filled, requiring the clerk to scan SEAQ or call around to fulfill the order. Such systems ride quite easily on top of existing market making, but they do not generate sufficient business to justify augmenting the scope of a firm's market-making operations. Thus, the differences between BZW and its competitors cannot readily be altered solely to allow other firms to match TRADE. Recognizing this, competitors have delayed or cancelled their plans to match TRADE with small dealing systems of their own. BZW's advantage thus appears sustainable.

Transaction Costs

Transaction costs are the costs of procuring goods or services in the market, outside the firm. They are distinguished from production costs, which are associated with manufacturing or obtaining goods within the firm's own hierarchy.[8] Transaction costs, like production costs, have many components, among them:

- the cost of placing an order,
- the costs of monitoring performance and ensuring that contractors do not shirk in terms of effort or quality, and
- the costs of maintaining sufficient safety stock to prevent

coordination problems caused by reliance upon outside suppliers.

Transaction costs economics (TCE) argues that the structure of firms and industries at a given time is chosen to minimize total costs, and represents a balance between production costs associated with producing goods or services and transaction costs associated with coordinating and arranging for production. Transaction costs are generally lower when goods are produced within a single firm, whereas production costs are generally reduced by procuring from an outside supplier that enjoys production economies due to scale and specialization.

Technology, most notably the telegraph and later the telephone, has clearly altered the balance over time. Readers of Chandler's management classic, *The Visible Hand,* are immediately struck by the degree of vertical integration that was the norm in late nineteenth century America.[9] The meat packer Swift, for example, owned the first refrigerated rail cars; brewers, such as Pabst and Anheuser-Busch, owned not only their own cooperages, but also the forests that supplied the raw materials for manufacturing kegs; and Singer Sewing Machine owned companies that trained would-be buyers in the use of, and provided financing for, their machines, as well as the resources needed to manufacture the iron and wooden components of the machines. Changing technology and reduced transaction costs have led to greatly increased use of marketplace procurement and considerable de-integration of firms' value chains.

We believe that transaction costs are best viewed as a combination of coordination costs and costs associated with transaction risk. TCE has traditionally focused on risk. For example, during many months of the year, it is simply not possible to ship fresh meat from Chicago to New York in boxcars that lack effective refrigeration. Thus, the risk associated with shirking or nonperformance is great: a supplier with rail equipment that fails to perform as promised poses an unacceptable danger to the shipper. TCE further holds that there is a greater danger, that of opportunistic renegotiation, or appropriation of benefits. Rail equipment suppliers, for example, no doubt aware of the critical importance of refrigerated boxcars, are in a position, come the arrival of the first truly hot days of June or July, to demand new rental contracts that ensure them almost all the profits the meat packers expect to derive from their shipments. Numerous factors—among them, the commodity-like nature of refrigeration technology today, the ability to monitor the location and availability of rental equipment, and the rapid exchange of information concerning the reputation of exploitive suppliers—have combined to reduce this risk and enable meat packers to rely upon railroads for refrigerated rolling stock.

According to transaction costs economics, investments to reduce coordination costs always increase transaction risk, producing strategic vulnerability. For example, locating a bottle manufacturing plant adjacent to a customer's brewery greatly reduces the total delivered cost of the bottles. But the bottlers investment in the new plant is clearly a sunk cost: plants are difficult and prohibitively expensive to disassemble and relocate. The brewer no doubt knows this, and knows that the bottler's next best use, selling to a distant competitor, will yield several mils per bottle less profit. Given the sunk investment in the plant and the difference between best and next best use of the investment, the brewer is in a position to demand (opportunistically misappropriate) several mils per bottle from the bottler.[10]

The value created by modern computing and communications technology in improving coordination and reducing integration costs is widely recognized.[11] We have argued that just as significant, though less well recognized, is the change this technology effects in the nature of transaction costs. Most notably, investments in IT may prove not to be specific to individual relationships, that is, not to represent sunk costs. Thus, IT can reduce coordination costs without creating significant transaction risk. IT facilitates monitoring of contractors' and suppliers' performance, for example, in maintaining necessary inventory in the appropriate locations. Open systems, standards, and widely available services such as electronic data interchange (EDI) can facilitate reduction in coordination costs without significantly increasing switching costs, relationship-specific investment, or their associated risk. This explains the failure of McKesson Drug to earn extraordinary profits despite the tremendous success of its Economost order entry system: it is just too easy for customers to switch to competitors' offerings, denying both McKesson and its competitors the opportunity to set high fees for their services. The improved ability to monitor the performance of outside vendors—combined with reduced risks associated with reliance upon outsiders—is resulting in increased use of outsourcing, and of cooperative ventures more generally. We see this as effectively changing the boundaries of firms and, ultimately, altering the structure of some industries.

Finally, enhanced communication can improve market efficiency. This was explored briefly in the context of London's Big Bang.

Reduced Transaction Costs and the Changing Boundaries of the Firm

Firms can produce essential goods and services themselves, or acquire them through outsourcing from contract service providers, develop them through joint ventures, or employ one of a wide range of available forms of corporate cooperation. For a variety of reasons, the norm for what is appropriate within the boundaries of a single firm has clearly changed over time. For example:

- meat packers no longer need to own refrigerated rail cars,
- brewers no longer own forests and foundries or make kegs,
- manufacturers, particularly in the automotive industry, are increasingly relying on parts suppliers,[12] and
- banks are increasingly relying on third-party processors for payroll and other accounting services.

Cooperative arrangements are once again on the rise. Among the reasons for this are the following:

- Cooperative ventures can facilitate rapid entry into a market, particularly overseas.
- Cooperative ventures permit sharing extraordinary costs or reducing risks, as evidenced in chip making and R&D consortia in the United States and Europe.
- Cooperative ventures permit companies with complementary resource needs to cooperate and succeed competitively.[13]

As always, the key trade-off is between risk and reward. Shared ATM service appears to be safe, and money access center (MAC) and New York Cash Exchange (NYCE) participants do not appear disadvantaged; reliance upon participation in competitors' CRSs to reach customers appears to be potentially quite expensive for airlines; outsourcing of commodity automobile components appears to be justified, although Ford's recent decision to outsource high-performance engines has become a subject of considerable concern to analysts who follow the automotive industry.

Who Wins

The analyses in the foregoing sections suggest some predictions about which firms will profit by riding the next wave of industrial restructuring. In general, firms that provide complex, scale-intensive, detachable services can be expected to benefit. Complex services that require expertise to deliver well offer the possibility of economies of specialization: specialist firms that learn how to deliver such services well will give their customers an incentive to outsource them. Scale-intensive services offer economies of scale; that is, given high fixed and lower incremental costs, an outside supplier with large market share can provide a service at a lower cost than a firm can provide it itself. This creates another incentive for outsourcing. But it is essential that such services also be readily detachable; that is, their complexity must be masterable by an outside contract service provider and it must be safe for companies to rely upon contractors for delivery of the services.

Post-deregulation corporate travel management, which meets all three of these criteria, has undergone tremendous growth in the past dozen years. Rosenbluth Travel, one of the first travel agencies to understand this, used its understanding to convert itself from a $40 million a year Philadelphia player to a $1 billion international powerhouse.[14] Travel expense management is clearly complex, with fares to manage, expenses to summarize and control, and the possibility for major players to negotiate preferred rates with airlines and hotels. It is also clearly scale-intensive, as are all software-based services. And it is detachable: Scott Paper and Du Pont can safely place travel expense management in the hands of an outside firm, but relying on contractors for product development, customer support, or marketing strategy would clearly pose intolerable risks.

As we saw in McKesson Drug's experience with its Economost distribution system, success does not assure profitability. Unless they are able to exploit some critical resource advantage, providers will at best enjoy limited and short-lived opportunities for profits.

Finally, firms that eliminate market imperfections will prosper. Thus, Quotron, Reuters, and Bloomberg Financial Markets can be expected to benefit, even as their services erode the profits of the financial services industry generally.

Who Loses

Although in general anything that improves efficiency can be expected to be good for the economy, changes certainly will not benefit all firms or all sectors equally. Losers will include firms that fail to change, to understand the implications of improved coordination technology, and to take necessary measures to adapt. Players in sectors that will be structurally disadvantaged by change can also expect to be damaged. This list is headed by firms that rely on market imperfections for competitive advantage. Thus, information technology will have a disruptive and painful impact on the securities industry, and on key players such as brokers and even stock exchanges, as we explained above.

Firms that rely on technological switching costs may also find their profits considerably reduced by regulatory changes and technological improvements in standards and open systems. Thus, the recent profitability of CRS vendors can be expected to be reduced with or without regulatory intervention.

Firms that gained competitive benefit by internally controlling all aspects of production will need to reexamine their decisions concerning the trade-off between production and procurement; they may find they need to undertake a difficult and expensive process of restructuring. Chrysler, faced with economic disaster, made such changes. Although General Motors has not yet adapted within its established divisions, its Saturn division may represent a more successful attempt to adapt and restructure than has been seen in any of its domestic competitors.

Finally, firms that rely solely on economies of scale created by superior size to provide and protect competitive advantage must adapt to avoid being damaged by the changes discussed above. Citibank's large New York branch network was a source of advantage when other banks had fewer branches. ATM services are different: a customer with an account at any participating bank can withdraw money from any NYCE machine. Citibank's failure to participate in NYCE, and its excessive reliance on the size of its own ATM network, has in recent years become a significant competitive disadvantage.

Who Has to Change

The category of who must change is more problematic than those of who will win and lose, including, as it does, nearly everyone else. Many of the most striking case studies are from the financial services sector, for obvious reasons: securities firms do not manufacture or ship any physical product; pure information processors, they are highly susceptible to alteration by coordination technology.

Nevertheless, a few illustrative examples from industries as diverse as snack foods and detergents suggest the breadth and degree of change that can be expected. Procter & Gamble, having proved itself to be an adaptive and successful competitor, would hardly seem to be a candidate for the category of potential losers, firms unwilling or unable to adapt. But in comparison with Frito-Lay's ability to respond to the demands of various markets by providing fresh specialized products, P&G's one-size-fits-all distribution system for Pringles, which relies on shelf-stable products that can be shipped and sold uniformly like detergent, is unimpressive. Clearly, in several markets P&G will need to change.

In some areas of distribution within the consumer packaged-goods industry, P&G is already at the forefront of change. Scanner technology has changed the supermarket check-out aisle from a simple expense for retailers to a potentially valuable point of contact between customer and distribution channel. Scanner data can be used to rationalize ordering and inventory management and to develop demand-driven, just-in-time inventory management relationships between retailers and key innovative manufacturers. As important, coupon-generating equipment installed at the check-out aisle can be used to issue targeted coupons, at low cost and with high probability of redemption. Coupons can be targeted at rewarding repeat users, developing potential new users, and even attacking the loyal customer base of competitors. No one really knows today how these new technologies will alter the balance of power in the distribution channel, but it appears that by increasing the value and importance of the check-out aisle, these technologies will increase the power of the retailers that control it. Through the emerging relationships with key retailers and suppliers of coupon-generating equipment, P&G has clearly signaled its intention to understand and exploit emerging trends in distribution.

How can executives predict the ways their firms will need to change in order to respond to the changing capability of coordination technology and its implications for the boundaries of their firms? The following three guidelines are helpful:

- Decide what can and should be outsourced, using the three criteria elaborated in the section on "Who Wins." Complex and scale-intensive goods and services should be outsourced or obtained cooperatively to the degree that they are readily detachable from the core value-adding functions of the business. Exclude from initial consideration for outsourcing only functions that are clearly part of the firm's core areas of competence.
- Decide what must be improved. Assess competitors' areas of competence and customers' key requirements. Determine where coordination technology offers you or your competitors new capabilities for cooperating with customers or suppliers.
- Understand that the necessary changes may themselves require additional changes to culture, process, and incentives in order to enable cooperative strategies and network-based competition. Rosenbluth Travel relies on Rosenbluth International Alliance, a cooperative network of independent affiliates, to provide international service to its corporate accounts. Its international vice president thus has no direct reports, no staff, and a minimal budget. Clearly, a new formula needs to be developed to set compensation in such environments.

The Global Implications of Increased Cooperation

Even a casual glance at a daily paper reveals a constant stream of information about global cooperation and partnerships: U.S. telecommunications companies are forging European and Asian cooperative ventures; airlines are forming trans-Atlantic partnerships; national computerized reservations systems are combining into larger global operating groups with multiple owners; IBM is working with Canon in PCs and with Toshiba in memory chips. Cooperation can be an especially effective strategy for globalization under a variety of conditions:

- When rapid implementation of a global strategy is necessary, and appropriate international partners are available.
- When the capital for a single-owner approach is not readily available.
- When there is a need simultaneously for different multi-domestic strategies and for effective global integration; small satellite operations may appear to provide the necessary points of presence in foreign markets, but may not be able to provide the quality of service demanded by customers or the market share necessary for profitable operations.
- When regulatory or national-interest barriers hinder a single player from effectively expanding into foreign markets.

While it would be misleading to suggest that these new cooperative agreements are driven entirely, or even largely, by information technology, the earlier sections of this chapter have suggested that information technology for coordination, monitoring, and control is essential to facilitate these agreements. Equally critical is the ability of information technology to mitigate the risk of global cooperative efforts. Technology permits performance monitoring, rapid detection of problems (whether because of intentional shirking by a partner or of unforeseen events), and rapid introduction of appropriate defensive measures. As we have seen above, investments in information technology tend to be more flexible than traditional physical investments in coordination and cooperation, and less committed to a single use; hence they are less likely to introduce strategic vulnerability.

The Rosenbluth International Alliance, explored above and in Chapter 12, is driven by the first three bullets. Hal Rosenbluth needed to achieve a global presence rapidly, lacked the capital to acquire foreign offices with necessary market share, and needed to be able to offer service quality abroad to an extent that would be difficult for a foreign player with small market share to achieve. Different global cooperative efforts are explained by different combinations.

MasterCard International operates as a global partnership comprising MasterCard, its European partner EuroCard, and its U.K. affiliate Access. MasterCard has equity in, but does not own or control, its European affiliates. Since the bulk of all bank card transactions are local—British usage in the United Kingdom, American usage in the United States, French usage on the Continent—it is critically important to have effective local presence, including good merchant acceptance, good consumer brand recognition, and the scale necessary for cost-effective operations. Of only secondary importance, but still critical, is the need for card holders to be able to use their cards abroad—Americans vacationing in Paris or London, British businessmen traveling in New York or Brussels. This does not require the launching of yet another card, but is best accomplished by linking existing domestic franchises, and thus building on existing merchant acceptance, consumer brand recognition, and economies of scale in operations. The structure of MasterCard International as a global partnership is thus best explained by the third bullet point. While this partnership has aspects that transcend information technology, authorization of card holder purchases, risk management for issuers, and settlement and clearing among members are all critically dependent upon interconnected systems.

Airlines have also demonstrated increasing interest in global cooperation. European carriers in particular have been scrambling to find partners; this is evidenced by the agreements between British Airways and USAir and between KLM and Northwest Airlines, both announced in the summer of 1992. These arrangements are driven largely by the last two factors. It is necessary for a trans-Atlantic airline to offer a large number of destination cities at both ends of its international routes; these domestic "feeder routes" are essential to achieving the load factors needed for profitability. Current regulations in the United States and in most European markets severely limit the ability of a nondomestic carrier to operate these feeder routes.[15] Regulations also ban purchase of a U.S. partner by a European carrier (non-U.S. voting ownership of a U.S. carrier cannot currently exceed 25%; total foreign ownership cannot exceed 49%). Hence, partnership is the best remaining alternative. Clearly these partnerships go beyond information technology: British Airways and USAir are coordinating their branding and marketing strategies, and BA is creating a major international gateway in Philadelphia, site of one of USAir's hubs. Similarly, KLM and Northwest Airlines plan to link most aspects of their operations to achieve "seamless" service for customers using the carriers for trans-Atlantic travel, perhaps leading to integration and common branding of the two airlines. Still, while these agreements affect marketing, strategic planning, and daily operations, this degree of cooperation would not be possible without linked information technology to coordinate reservations, scheduling, operations, and passenger service.

Complicating Factors

It would be wrong to assume that the progress of global cooperation and coordination will be smooth simply because there are good economic reasons for cooperative efforts and because information technology makes such efforts more effective and less risky. The following complicating factors will remain critical, and will need to be managed.

- *Human factors.* Ultimately, cooperation among organizations is determined by people, not technology. While technology can facilitate coordination, monitoring, and control in partnerships, and can reduce the risk of strategic reliance upon relationships, it is ultimately trust among partners that determines the success or failure of partnerships. Successful partnerships require careful selection of partners with similar cultures and similar objectives for the partnership. They require that each party have unique resources of critical importance to the success of the joint operations, so that each party will need the other; partnerships motivated solely by access to capital are unlikely to prove stable. Most important, success requires that actions be taken regularly to develop and retain confidence among the personnel of cooperating organizations.
- *Different objectives, different performance measures and incentive structures.* Partners with different objectives for their own organization are likely to have different expectations for the partnership, which can in turn place intolerable

strain upon cooperation. This problem can be exacerbated by national differences. One party may intend to develop market share, cutting down on operating expenses and improving long-term profitability; another party may need to show investors an immediate payoff from the cooperative venture. Such differences are likely to result in different performance measures and incentives in the two organizations, and to prompt each partner to take actions that the other views as counterproductive at best, and at worst as a betrayal of the partnership. Unless partners strive to improve and maintain personal contact and trust, such differences can place intolerable strain upon the partnership.

• *Different traditions.* It is likely that both partner organizations will have pride in their traditions, culture, and corporate history. Cooperation and acknowledgment of the different objectives of partners will, on occasion, require that the traditions of one organization be subordinated to those of the other. Again, without efforts to improve and maintain personal contact and trust, this is likely to place intolerable strain upon the partnership.

Conclusions

We have seen how IT is likely to produce significant changes in the relative importance of cooperation and coordination:

• information technology improves coordination and monitoring performance across the boundaries of firms, and
• unlike earlier investments in coordination, information technology investments are flexible, not restricted to a single use with a single partner, and thus do not increase strategic vulnerability.

We have also seen how the importance of global cooperative efforts is increasing, just as information technology makes such partnerships safer, more productive, and more cost-effective.

Finally, we have examined a number of complicating factors, which can limit the effectiveness of partnerships and, if not successfully managed, can ultimately lead to the failure of global cooperative efforts.

Acknowledgment

The assistance of my colleague, Michael C. Row, is greatly appreciated and gratefully acknowledged. Michael's thoughts, expressed in discussions before the writing of this and several other papers, have consistently informed my thinking and sharpened my presentation.

Notes

1. This is described in more detail in E. K. Clemons, "MAC—Philadelphia National Bank's Strategic Venture in Shared ATM Networks," *Journal of Management Information Systems,* 7, no. 1 (Summer 1990): 41–60.

2. Department of Transportation, Office of the Secretary (Docket No. 46949; Notice No. 91-6), RIN2105-AB47, Computer Reservation System (CRS) Regulations, Notice of Proposed Rulemaking.

3. Material in this section draws heavily upon E. K. Clemons, "Corporate Strategies for Information Technology: A Resource-Based Approach," *Computer,* 14, no. 11, IEEE Computer Society (November 1991): 23–32.

4. More detail can be found in E. K. Clemons and B. W. Weber, "London's Big Bang: A Case Study of Information Technology, Competitive Impact, and Organizational Change," *Journal of Management Information Systems,* 6, no. 4 (Spring 1990): 41–60; and in Chapter 6 of this volume.

5. T. Wolfe, *Bonfire of the Vanities* (New York: Farrar, Straus, & Giroux, 1987).

6. The impact of information technology on the future structure and profitability of financial services is described in more detail in E. K. Clemons and B. W. Weber, "Information Technology and the Changing Nature of the Financial Services Industry," *Proceedings of the IFIP TC8 Conference on Collaborative Work, Social Communications and Information Systems,* Helsinki, Finland (August 1991): 93–116.

7. A market maker trades with brokers or investors and meets customer demand to buy or sell shares by altering its own inventory position. A market maker's profits, unlike those of a broker, come from the difference in price at which it buys and sells shares rather than from commissions.

8. O. Williamson, *Markets and Hierarchies: Analysis and Antitrust Implications* (New York: Free Press, 1975).

9. A. D. Chandler, Jr., *The Visible Hand: The Managerial Revolution in American Business* (Cambridge, Mass.: Harvard University Press, 1977).

10. B. Klein, R. G. Crawford, and A. A. Alchian, "Vertical Integration, Appropriable Rents, and the Competitive Contracting Process," *Journal of Law and Economics,* 21 (October 1978): 297–326.

11. E. K. Clemons and S. O. Kimbrough, "Information Systems, Telecommunications, and Their Effects on Industrial Organization," *Proceedings, 7th International Conference on Information Systems* (1986): 99–108; F. W. McFarlan, "Information Technology Changes the Way You Compete," *Harvard Business Review,* 62, no. 3 (1984): 98–103; T. W. Malone, J. Yates, and R. I. Benjamin, "Electronic Markets and Electronic Hierarchies," *Communications of the ACM,* 30, no. 6 (June 1987): 484–497.

12. General Motors' own production has historically accounted for close to 70% of the value of its automobiles, while Ford outsources close to half, and Chrysler outsources closer to 70% of the value of their automobiles. Changes in transaction costs, and in the expense of internal production, have altered the optimal balance. Even GM's former chairman, Roger Smith, acknowledged the change, noting that what had once been a considerable source of competitive advantage had, somehow, become a "semi-disadvantage."

13. The examples most easily understood in this area involve small companies pooling their resources to match a threat from larger competitors. Thus, when Citibank in New York and Girard in Philadelphia launched proprietary ATM networks, their considerable size advantage over competitors provoked cooperative responses. Citibank was the largest retail bank in New York; Girard enjoyed a similar position in Philadelphia. Moreover, ATM service exhibits considerable economies of scale: it costs no more to write software to service a few hundred ATMs than to service a few dozen. Smaller banks recognized that individually they could not respond economically to the threats posed by these two competitors' proprietary ATM networks. In New York, a cooperative arrangement emerged (New York Cash Exchange, or NYCE), owned by all of Citibank's major competitors. In Philadelphia, the response took the form of a single-owner shared network (Philadelphia National Bank's *Money Access Center,* or MAC), which is now the sole ATM network in Pennsylvania.

14. More details can be found in E. K. Clemons and M. C. Row, "Information Technology at Rosenbluth Travel: Competitive Advantage in a Rapidly Growing Service Company," *Journal of Management Information Systems,* 8, no. 2 (Fall 1991): 53–79.

15. Rules against *cabotage* prohibit most foreign carriers from picking up passengers in one U.S. city and taking them to another. Thus, most foreign carriers operating in the United States will fly to their U.S. gateway city and then make one or, at most, two stopovers. These stopovers make the carrier more attractive by providing service to more U.S. cities, but since the load factor of these flights is frequently uneconomically low, they do so at considerable cost.

10
Being Global and the Global Opportunity

Pierre Hessler

IBM is interested in the topic of globalization for four reasons. The first is that IBM is a global company, deriving more than 60% of its revenue from outside the United States. The second reason IBM continues to study the emerging body of knowledge on "being global" is that its 500 largest international customers represent more than 20% of the company's revenue, more than $13 billion, and this customer base is growing approximately twice as fast as IBM's domestic base. The demands of these international customers are a powerful incentive. The third reason is that IBM's strategy is to cooperate with business partners, of which the company has thousands around the world. Working with our global business partners, many of which are intent on making use of IBM's international dimensions, has raised new and difficult issues that we have only partially dealt with in the past. The fourth reason is simply the business opportunity inherent in being global. IBM believes that globalization opens the field for new applications and services, which the company is eager to understand. These reasons, cited by more and more companies, are defining the 1990s competitive environment for most industries.

The IBM-Sponsored Global Study

The need to better understand global business opportunity is what led me to commission the "Becoming Global" study with the Nolan, Norton Institute.[1] This study, which involved ten major firms on four continents, eight of them among the top four in their industry in terms of revenue, reached three major conclusions that, although not revolutionary, proved to be of critical interest to IBM.

The first conclusion was that globalization is much more than a fad. All ten companies, while aspiring to become global, were struggling to define precisely what "being global" meant. They cited a number of driving trends in their quest to determine what globalization meant for them:

- Barriers to trade are dissolving, reshaping such aspects of business as logistics and sourcing.
- Technological advances are enabling worldwide information networks to emerge. (One company described how satellite television broadcasts of sporting events carried its brand name to places it was not yet prepared to serve.)
- Lifestyles are now transcending national borders as individuals travel more and move back and forth freely across national borders.
- Multicountry partnership arrangements and alliances are increasing dramatically.
- Corporate customers are increasingly becoming more global and expect suppliers to be able to meet their demands for consistent service anywhere in the world.
- Customer expectations for quicker response are putting pressure on companies to better coordinate activities worldwide.
- There is a growing emphasis on customizing "prime" products to meet local market needs.
- Customers expect companies to make their products or services increasingly information-intensive.
- Competition is itself becoming global.

One company suggested that there is a need to compress time and that a global strategy aims at eliminating the negative aspects of time and distance. This is an excellent description. But the workable definition that emerged by consensus among the companies studied, and that has subsequently been verified by a number of others, is: the global company is driven by a global strategy, which enables it to plan and treat all of its activities in the context of a whole-world system and, therefore, serve its global customers with excellence (see Figure 10-1).

The working definition of a global company developed by IBM

Figure 10-1
Definition of a Global Company

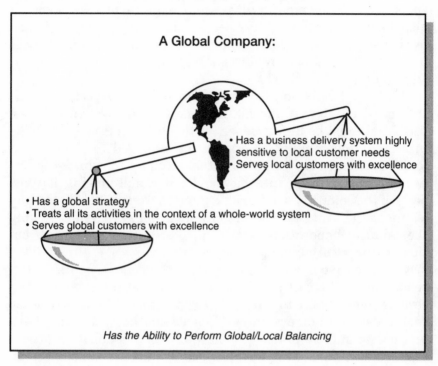

A Global Company:

• Has a business delivery system highly sensitive to local customer needs
• Serves local customers with excellence

• Has a global strategy
• Treats all its activities in the context of a whole-world system
• Serves global customers with excellence

Has the Ability to Perform Global/Local Balancing

in collaboration with the executives of the ten companies reflects a convergence of three views. The first is that globalization is a business concept involving a global strategy that enables a company to have a worldwide plan for products, marketing, manufacturing, logistics, and research and development. Companies that are furthest along in being global view these activities holistically and treat them as being driven by the mind-set of a global system. A global company has low, or no, boundaries, and undertakes mission-critical business activities where they make the most sense (e.g., research and development might be carried on wherever the talent physically exists). Internal decisions, such as the location of headquarters, are transparent to the market or individual customer. Being global means extending a company's reach and presence within its sphere of influence—in other words, having a scope that is broader than its actual facilities.

Second, a global company must have a business delivery system that is highly sensitive to local customer needs and able to support local customers with equal degrees of excellence. A global company takes a basic set of values, principles, and business systems and tailors them to the areas in which it does business. Being global requires a high degree of cultural diversity and understanding.

Third, a global company learns to balance aspects of itself that must be viewed and planned as a global system with aspects that must be highly sensitive to local requirements. Organizational power must be effectively managed to ensure that local requirements are appropriately attended to, while simultaneously maintaining integrity and not compromising key aspects of the company's integrated global systems. This balancing is one of the toughest aspects of being global. It is not simply the balance of operations—it is the distribution and redistribution of power throughout the organization.

One executive in the study captured the general sentiment in remarking, "The culture of the people within the company is a serious impediment to our realizing our global vision. It is too centered on our home country." Echoed another: "We must have an understandable philosophy to establish globalization principles and convince all our employees so that the principles can become actual practice."

The second conclusion pertains to the process of becoming global. The concept of being global is far more easily described than implemented. The process of becoming global is integral to what Richard Nolan refers to as fundamental business transformation.[2] Nolan describes business transformation as a multi-year process, driven by the vision of achieving a fundamentally different state than the current one, and involving simultaneous changes in just about every aspect of the business.[3]

IBM, like other companies, has struggled with the magnitude of change associated with Nolan's concept of transformation. Neither our company nor others in the study have experienced managing change at the level and magnitude suggested. Yet there seems to be no other way, and it is clear that being global cannot be achieved with traditional approaches to managing change incrementally.

In the context of transformation, the executives in all the companies studied indicated that, although they are making progress in translating the concepts of globalization into reality, they are still far from their objective. It was something of a surprise to find that companies in different industries (services, manufacturing, banking) in different parts of the world (Japan, Europe, the United States) face similar issues associated with transformation, and that the steps they see as necessary to becoming global are very much the same. The homogeneity is striking.

The study's third conclusion identified six major ingredients in an effective transformation process for becoming global. This list might not be complete, and refinements will undoubtedly be made, but these six ingredients provide a basis for a company to undertake a global initiative.

Ingredient 1: Shared Global Vision

The first key ingredient in the globalization process is the sharing of a global vision and creation of a so-called global mindset in all employees. Most executives in the companies studied had a vision, but none were certain that their vision was shared to any significant degree by their employees. It is very difficult, indeed, to ensure that such concepts are shared throughout a large organization.

In an interview in the *Harvard Business Review,* Percy Barnevik, president and CEO of Asea Brown Boveri, among the most successful of global companies, described the importance of a shared vision. Barnevik termed his company the "overhead" company in reference to the use of transparencies to communicate his vision to his executives. He personally travels with more than 2,000 overheads that he uses to explain his vision for the company and what that vision means.[4]

Figure 10-2 illustrates what one of the companies in the research study identified as the global strategic imperatives needed to make the global vision "real" in employees' eyes.

If it is to be shared, a vision must go beyond slogans and transcend the semantics of a company's country of origin. To determine whether it is shared, it is necessary to test the impact of the vision and truly determine the "buy-in" of employees. IBM is working very hard on something it calls "market-driven quality." IBM actually measures employee buy-in, and this measurement appears on the top sheet of its key corporate perfor-

Figure 10-2
Global Strategic Imperatives and the Shared Vision

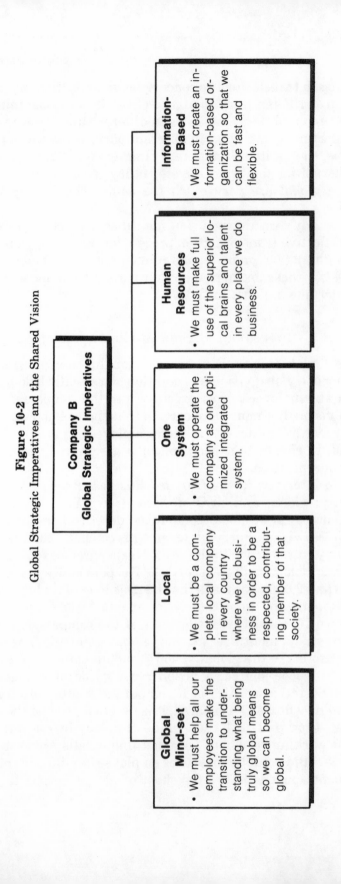

**Company B
Global Strategic Imperatives**

**Global
Mind-set**
• We must help all our employees make the transition to understanding what being truly global means so we can become global.

Local
• We must be a complete local company in every country where we do business in order to be a respected, contributing member of that society.

**One
System**
• We must operate the company as one optimized integrated system.

**Human
Resources**
• We must make full use of the superior local brains and talent in every place we do business.

**Information-
Based**
• We must create an in-formation-based or-ganization so that we can be fast and flexible.

mance measurements, immediately after the customer satisfaction and quality measurements. The number of people who recognize the concept and can do something with it (expressed as a percentage) is thus the third piece of information the chairman sees when the IBM monthly results are presented.

Ingredient 2: Measurement

The second key ingredient in the process of becoming global is the ability to set priorities and measure progress toward globalization. If the globalization process takes 10 years, there will be dozens of reasons during those years to forget the strategy. I heard a top executive of a large bank, who was completely convinced of the necessity of working on a globalization plan, remark that "we are going to start next year because this year is very difficult." It is critical to establish objectives and measurements at the outset, link them to long-term plans, and translate them into short-term actions that yield immediate results, which can, in turn, be used to further the global design and global project outcome that executive management wants.

Ingredient 3: Local-Global Balancing

Developing the tools and methodologies useful for balancing global integration with locally sensitive activities is the third key ingredient of the globalization process. Striking the "right" local-global balance is highly dependent on individual companies and their managements.

IBM has chosen to use its business processes to achieve this balance. The company has defined 15 enterprisewide processes that lead from understanding customer needs to delivering products and services. Front-end business processes, that is, those relating to customers, are candidates for a high degree of local tailoring. Back-end activities, on the other hand, which are typically of a more general nature, are subject to a more institutionalized global view. This analysis of the business process points to many reengineering opportunities, from local streamlining to corporatewide surgery.

Ingredient 4: Information Technology (IT)

Nine of the ten companies in the study listed IT as one of five factors essential to accomplishing their global objectives. The tenth company stated that IT is "critical to our survival." With the continued trend toward globalization, we can expect a new wave of IT infrastructure expenditures, as well as specific systems investments on an unprecedented scale.

IT planning for global objectives exhibited a number of common characteristics.

- Using global planning frameworks to understand the linkage of IT to business strategy by identifying key areas where IT can add long-term value.
- Initiating an IT architecture process with outputs that include blueprints of the structure of technology for doing business globally.
- Identifying the opportunities offered by global IT portfolios (product and process support, and coordination and control systems).
- Understanding the difference between global and local IT infrastructure requirements and applying this concept to achieve a rational balance.
- Developing a global IT resource allocation and deployment strategy.

Ingredient 5: Understanding Global Customers

The fifth ingredient is to determine whether the global company has customers with truly global needs, and then find a way to understand those needs as precisely as the company understands the needs of local customers. This was a major purpose of the research study, and it uncovered some very interesting business opportunities that IBM is in the process of pursuing.

Ingredient 6: Alliance Partners

The sixth key ingredient of the process of globalization has to do with alliance strategy. Two needs were recognized by virtually all participants in the study. The first is for a more rigorous selection process for alliances, involving a truly worldwide search for partners. The second is to pursue appropriate alliances at the local, national, continental, and worldwide levels.

In terms of global alliance partners and service partners, the companies studied shared several characteristics, among them:

- processes for scanning the environment to identify and study key players that can affect the industry,
- programs for educating internal management about the potential role of partners, and
- capabilities for getting deals done quickly in lieu of long drawn-out negotiations.

IBM and Globalization

IBM is not exactly a "new kid on the block" with respect to globalization. The company began its globalization process more than 60 years ago. In 1929, IBM founder Thomas J. Watson, Sr., said that he expected to see the day when more than 50% of IBM's revenue would come from non-American sources. Having chosen the name International Business Machines in 1915 is in itself quite impressive.

Watson and his successors emphasized a common culture, even a common language. IBM "THINK" signs hang in just about every company office around the world. Very early, the concept of a worldwide product line led to the centralized management of research and development, with laboratories around the world. IBM subsequently established manufacturing on a continental basis by linking and synchronizing production across three plants on three continents. From a marketing and services perspective, IBM's expansion occurred country by country, with nationals leading and shaping the subsidiaries. Although an obvious approach today, it was not so obvious 50 or 60 years ago.

Initially, the subsidiaries were managed from a highly centralized base. For many years, for example, the head of corporate marketing was writing the compensation plan that determined the salaries and benefits of the IBM sales force around the world. It was joked that countries had complete freedom to translate the plan "without a single change."

Over time, the IBM companies created in different countries

became substantial economic factors (with more than 20,000 employees in Japan, for example) and, as a consequence, more autonomous. This movement has been noticeably accelerated by the industry drive toward services, which are both manpower-intensive and, by definition, local. Expectations of governments and customers competing with the needs for national and regional division partnerships have reinforced the emphasis on local services.

IBM came to fit the definition of a global company almost without realizing it; perhaps this is the least painful way to become global. IBM achieved the model of a "local presence worldwide" some time ago, and is quite satisfied with it. But this does not mean that the company is in a stable and comfortable situation.

The local-global balance described in the study as a key characteristic of global corporations is constantly being rocked and runs the risk of being destroyed. Two conflicting movements account for this instability. Decentralization, or the localization of activities, needs to be and, in fact, is being accelerated. In the past, this acceleration was experienced in countries that were becoming more autonomous. Today, it is seen even in more local organizations. Until recently, for example, IBM had 12 areas in the United States. Today, it has about 70 trading areas, each striving for the highest degree of freedom it can achieve.

This strength and increasing autonomy of local organizations is underscored by dramatic changes in the measurement system: in the way a company prices its products, invests, and concludes alliances. This freedom breeds incredible diversity across the constituent autonomous organizations.

At the same time, there is enormous pressure from customers and business partners on an international level to increase the level of homogeneity in the company. They want uniformity around the world, not differences from one city to another. Management, concerned about the company's identity and fearing that too much local autonomy could introduce fragmentation and dissolution, also exerts pressure for homogeneity. With tough global competition, controls that ensure an understanding of the company's competitive situation around the world are critical.

These two opposing forces can generate considerable tension in a firm. Because both are "musts" for a company's evolution, it is essential to invent methods for reconciling them and to pursue new and constantly changing balances within the company.

Local-Global Balancing

Three aspects of a company are particularly important to achieving local-global balance: serving international customers, maintaining a worldwide product line, and developing an appropriate management system. Each is discussed briefly below.

Serving International Customers

In terms of international customers and business partners, IBM's main challenge is to adapt its activities and structures to the way its customers want to conduct their businesses internationally. There is no single model. An autonomous organization fits the needs of companies (or functions within companies) that want to be highly autonomous within their respective countries. Other companies want to be centralized. For these, IBM is creating "logical organizations" that precisely match the way they want to be organized. IBM has created a new institution, the "ex-territorial authority," that affords local managers in charge of the headquarters of global companies the power to influence the related activities of IBM worldwide. The company has found that giving national managers both local and worldwide responsibility changes their mentality profoundly. IBM currently has about 50 cases being managed this way and is seeing very good results from them. Although these customer-specific organizations, or "micro-global entities," do not ensure a local presence worldwide, they do provide a global presence in every town. IBM believes this is a major step toward globalization.

Worldwide Product Line

IBM's worldwide product line was a simple concept some years ago and a very satisfying one because it provided the best possible "glue" for the corporation. Today, for a couple of important reasons, the company is in a phase of profound redefinition of its concept of the worldwide product line.

First is a need for some local products to become world products. The best example is Japanese language-handling personal computer systems. IBM was quite surprised to find in the United

States some 2,000 customers for these systems—not subsidiaries of Japanese companies, but 2,000 good, solid American-based customers. The same is true for Europe. IBM expects these American and European customers to want access to its personal computer systems in the next two or three years, probably for use in corresponding with Japanese subsidiaries. Thus, what was a local product must now be integrated into the worldwide product line.

Second, locally defined services carry a threat of fragmentation. Services defined and developed locally in countries around the world are unlikely to correspond to a worldwide picture. Customers around the world that demand at least equivalent services must be included in some form in the worldwide product line.

In the face of these two developments, the product line becomes too large and cannot be provided effectively around the world. Hence, it is necessary to create a subset of the product line for which it is possible to guarantee fulfillment for international or global customers. Such changes in the worldwide product line, though very difficult to manage, are extremely important, and IBM will be working at them for many years.

Management System

The traditional way to decentralize a company such as IBM, termed "powers reserved," holds that autonomous managers do what they want, save for certain corporate powers reserved to the center. But such a decentralized approach is not sufficient for globalization. Consequently, IBM has developed a complementary system of "obligations," to which local IBM organizations must adhere in practice and in spirit. Everything, of course, cannot be specified in black and white. But managers of autonomous entities are expected to respect both general and specific rules of the game, for example: to fulfill an obligation to ensure the availability of products and services the corporation offers to international customers, to respect IBM's code of ethics, and to participate in the company's worldwide alliance. These obligations will be administered not by a central staff, but by the local organization, subject perhaps to a corporate audit from time to time to reinforce accountability. Failure or noncompliance will mandate swift action.

Being global requires a strong central authority focused on a few critically important powers. Altogether, it is enough to make one long for the good old days of simple, central authority before these kinds of obligations were conceived.

Conclusion

On the subject of globalization, it is easy to oscillate between enthusiasm and skepticism. Globalization invites skepticism, for example, because it cannot be an objective per se but must be linked with a company's other objectives to make sense. Globalization could well be just another name for the obvious management issues of a large multinational company. Perhaps it is the ultimate platitude. Clearly, a worldwide company must make decisions on a worldwide basis, as well as accommodate local needs.

Globalization can also be an ambiguous concept. For example, to deal with its Japanese customers around the world, IBM employs Japanese assignees to help its local organizations. Is this globalization or, to the contrary, is it a failure to "go the whole nine yards" toward globalization?

It is also possible to push globalization too far or treat it simplistically, ignoring the deep-rooted importance of nations and perhaps even of regions. The notion of a world dominated by global managers, without risk, without culture, without even a language beyond elementary English, is truly frightening. Hence, we must move beyond enthusiasm and skepticism to refine our concept of globalization and translate it into reality in a powerful but subtle way. IBM believes that its competitiveness depends upon doing so.

Notes

1. Although this study is company confidential, the key concepts related to becoming global are described by John L. Daniels and N. Caroline Frost in "On Becoming a Global Corporation," *Stage-by-Stage* 8, no. 5 (Boston: Nolan, Norton & Co.); 1–14.

2. See Richard L. Nolan, "The Strategic Potential of Information Technology," *Financial Executive* (July/August 1991): 25–27.

3. Ibid.

4. William Taylor, "The Logic of Global Business: An Interview with ABB's Percy Barnevik," *Harvard Business Review*, 69, no. 2 (March–April 1991): 104.

11
Saturn—The Making of the Modern Corporation

Richard G. LeFauve and Arnoldo C. Hax

The Origins of Saturn

The Saturn Corporation grew out of the need to effectively respond to the intensifying competition in the global auto industry in the early 1980s. In 1981, GM was coping with financial losses, a prolonged U.S. recession, and escalating loss of market share to foreign competitors. Among other things, the company laid off nearly 170,000 GM/UAW employees and began to scrutinize its American automobile production.

In June 1982, GM's Advanced Product and Design Team was asked to answer the question, "Can GM build a world-class-quality small car in the United States that can compete successfully with imports?" The team subsequently initiated a "small-car project" embracing a "clean sheet" approach, avowing that it would not be restricted by traditional thinking and industry practice. It hoped that approaching problems with an unobstructed mind would yield new approaches and solutions. Lost-foam casting and high-speed machining techniques were among the concepts evaluated as high risk but considered as possible solutions to problems.

Meanwhile, another team was forming. Alfred S. Warren, vice president of GM's Industrial Relations Staff, and Donald Ephlin, UAW vice president and director of the General Motors Department, both increasingly dissatisfied with the labor relations climate, decided to bring together a handful of people to try to figure out if there might be a better way to do business. The group quickly realized the enormity of the problem and reached out for assistance. The result was an unprecedented alliance of GM and UAW personnel—plant managers, superintendents, union committeemen, production workers, and skilled tradesmen, as well as UAW and GM staff. This team, which represented the collective knowledge of 55 General Motors plants and 41 UAW locals in the GM system, became known as "The Group of 99."

These two teams then spent two months visiting 49 GM plants and 60 benchmark companies around the world. Together, they made more than 170 contacts, traveled approximately 2 million miles, and devoted some 50,000 hours to study.

During these fact-finding visits, the teams observed several common threads in the successful companies.

- Quality is a top priority for maintaining customer satisfaction. The customer, whether the next group to receive parts (the internal customer) or the person who receives the final product (the external customer), is number one.
- Everyone in the company shares in the ownership of its failures and successes.
- Equality is practiced, not just preached.
- Barriers to doing a good job are eliminated.
- Total trust is a must.
- People are the company's most important asset.
- People have the requisite authority to do their jobs.

With this background work behind them, team members focused on two concepts that were new to General Motors. The first was a conflict resolution process that relied on consensus to arrive at outcomes. As practiced, key stakeholders in a conflict are given all information relevant to the decision and, putting aside hidden agendas and focusing on each party's needs, strive to reach a consensus that is a win-win solution for all. Consensus is deemed to be reached when at least 70% of participants are in agreement with a decision and each commits 100% to its implementation.

The second concept to emerge was the need for a new organizational structure. The Group of 99 concluded that the integration of technology and resources required a partnership of Saturn management and UAW people at all levels of decision making. The group also recognized that workers will support an environment they help create. These insights produced a Memorandum of Agreement, separate from the GM-UAW national contract, that, unlike traditional agreement, was but 11 pages long. It avoided the list of forbidden fruit common to most labor contracts, focusing instead on the Saturn philosophy and experimental structure for making world-class cars.

After the small-car project identified the technology required to produce a small car and The Group of 99 evidenced the willingness of UAW and GM management to work together, General Motors' chairman Roger Smith pledged that if a labor agreement could be written that would support the integration of the needed technology, he would create a separate company. Smith suggested that marketing be included so that a new approach to selling cars might be considered as well. On January 7, 1985, the Saturn Project emerged as a separate subsidiary, known as the Saturn Corporation, charged with developing an entirely new approach to the way the automobile business is run. The new company would not utilize technology for technology's sake, but instead would blend technology and people to optimize overall business performance.

The Massachusetts Institute of Technology International Motor Vehicle Study cited Saturn as an initiative of great strategic importance to GM for at least three very valid reasons.

First, for GM it is the last chance to compete with Japanese manufacturers in the small-car market. This is a critical market in the automobile industry because most first-car purchases are made in this segment; by having no market presence, a firm risks losing a customer who could subsequently become a satisfied Japanese car owner for the remainder of his or her life. Thus, although Saturn is a quintessential American initiative, it represents a response to global competitive challenges, pitting it directly against the Honda Civic and the Toyota Corolla—the most attractive Japanese cars in the small-car segment in the United States.

Second, for the UAW it represents a unique opportunity to show that its members can produce a world-class car and add value to the process.

Finally, Saturn provides an unparalleled opportunity in recent American business history to build a modern organization where the concepts of empowerment and teamwork can be tested.

The Mission

The mission statement developed by the founding team had two distinct components:

1. to market vehicles developed and manufactured in the United States that are world leaders in quality, cost, and customer satisfaction through the integration of people, technology, and business systems; and
2. to transfer the resulting knowledge, technology, and experience to General Motors.

Fundamentally, Saturn's mission was to prove that Americans could be competitive in the small-car market by manufacturing world-class cars engineered and designed in the United States. Most important, Saturn did not limit itself to being successful in building cars, but wanted to transfer its managerial and technological innovations to its parent, and thereby effect a transformation within GM. It was a challenge of immense proportions being met by people willing to take risks and to draw ideas from all over the world and adapt them for their own ends. Their goal was to create a new approach to car making that integrated people, technology, and business systems. We find such a goal particularly powerful in a modern organization whose people, technology, and systems are the key ingredients to achieving competitive advantage.

The Philosophy

Saturn's mission was complemented by a statement of corporate philosophy that identified critical stakeholders—customers, members, suppliers, dealers, and neighbors—and defined how Saturn was to fulfill its responsibilities toward them.

Saturn's philosophy reads as follows:

We, the Saturn Team, in concert with the UAW and General Motors, believe that meeting the needs of customers, Saturn members, suppliers, dealers, and neighbors is fundamental to fulfilling our mission.

- To meet our customers' needs:
  —Our products and services must be world leaders in value and satisfaction.
- To meet our members' needs:
  —We will create a sense of belonging in an environment of mutual trust, respect, and dignity.

—We believe that all people want to be involved in decisions that affect them.
—We will develop the tools, training, and education needed for each member.
—Creative, motivated, responsible team members who understand that change is critical to success are Saturn's most important asset.
- To meet our suppliers' and dealers' needs:
  —We will create real partnerships with them.
  —We will strive for openness, fairness, trust, and respect.
  —We want them to feel ownership of Saturn's mission and philosophy.
- To meet the needs of our community neighbors:
  —We will be a good citizen and protect the environment.
  —We will seek to cooperate with government at all levels.

By continuously operating according to this philosophy, we will fulfill our mission.

This wording was arrived at after long and serious reflection by the founding team, and became the guiding framework for Saturn's decision-making process. The philosophy statement sounds simple and straightforward. In fact, it represents a fundamental commitment not to be compromised or undermined by decisions that might be attractive in the short term, but that would lead the organization off course in the long run. The test every decision must pass is whether it fits Saturn's philosophy. This provides the sense of coherence and strong character essential to a firm that believes people want to be involved in decisions that affect them and attempts to push responsibilities down into the organization.

Core Values

The founding team concluded its task of defining the organizational principles of Saturn by enunciating its core values:

- commitment to customer enthusiasm,
- commitment to excel,
- teamwork,
- trust in and respect for the individual, and
- continuous improvement.

These five core values are deceptively simple: put your customer first, pursue an unrelenting commitment to excellence, embrace teamwork and trust as the essence of management style, and strive constantly for continuous improvement. Sadly, one must recognize the urgent need for these core values in the context of the American auto industry, where complacency in the 1970s and early 1980s resulted in a significant loss of competitiveness. Saturn is perhaps the most visible and creative effort of a U.S. car manufacturer to regain public confidence and recover competitive advantage.

Saturn's mission, philosophy, and core values constitute an unalterable foundation. The orientation and training of every new Saturn employee begins with learning and serious reflection focused on the philosophical base that constitutes the focal point of Saturn's leadership.

Partnership at Saturn

If one word can summarize the heart of the Saturn culture, it is partnership. The "clean-sheet" approach to management was born of the conviction that old formulas were not responding to the new challenges facing the American auto industry. It was thus deemed necessary to start de novo, defining the new values needed to compete effectively and striving to attract highly qualified people—both from GM management and the UAW rank-and-file—willing to meet the challenges that had been identified and assume the risks associated with them.

Central to creating this new environment for constructive work was the effort to develop a close partnership between the UAW and GM, which would involve union leadership in all managerial decisions of a strategic, tactical, and operational nature. This was a unique undertaking: sharing decisions and building mutual trust between parties that traditionally had been confrontational and suspicious of one another.

The way Saturn has chosen to illustrate the GM-UAW partnership approach is presented in Figure 11-1. The overlapping area of the ellipses suggests an area of congruency. What is evident from the figure is that most decisions fall within this so-called partnership arena, the areas in which union and management have nonoverlapping interests being relatively small and peripheral. Areas in which GM managers and UAW representatives are jointly fully involved include site selection, process design, choice of technologies, supplier selection, make-versus-buy decisions, dealer selection, business planning, training, business systems development, budgeting, quality systems, productivity improvement, job design, new product develop-

Figure 11-1
The GM-UAW Partnership Approach

Partnership
Arena

Union
Role

Management
Role

- Strategic Planning
- Tactical Planning
- Operational Planning/Performance

ment, recruitment and hiring, maintenance, engineering, and transportation. The mere listing of these common areas of decision-making concerns reveals the vastness of the partnership arena.

Moreover, the gap that remains between management and union roles is growing narrower as the two groups become more comfortable with one another and the partnership arena expands to include all of the most important issues facing Saturn, including quality of the product, quality of work life in the plant, and concern about the long-term strategic success of the business.

Paramount to the success of this partnership is the development of an educational process that will help union leaders to become more business-oriented and managers to understand how employees at all levels feel about the business and its direction. Saturn has used the strategic planning process as the vehicle for bringing union and management people together and reeducating them. The strategic planning process has become a powerful communication and coordination mechanism that enables people to participate in such business concerns as defining the mission of the business, recognizing industry trends, understanding competitors' moves, determining what actions the firm must take to establish a strong competitive position, and identifying the roles that must be played by all the members of the organization. Taking both employee and management perspectives into account in every business decision that is made leads to a much better strategic business plan and stronger commitment to implementation.

Saturn's partnership process is not limited to UAW and GM managers. It extends to dealers and suppliers, as true and legitimate partners in the business venture, and includes teamwork—with its associated individual involvement and consensus management—as a key element of the partnership approach.

Self-Directed Teams

The cell of Saturn's organizational structure is referred to as a work unit—a group of about 15 people integrated as a team around consensus decision making. Ideally, work units become self-directed teams. The normal evolution follows a four-phase sequence, the behavior of which is illustrated in Figure 11-2.

Team structuring begins with the forming phase, which resembles a conventional type of team activity with two significant exceptions. One, every team relies on the support of two external advisers: a UAW and a management adviser, representing the two critical perspectives of Saturn's work. These advisers are shown outside the circles representing the team in Figure 11-2. Two, a "charter team member" assumes the responsibilities traditionally assigned to a superior or foreman depicted at the center of the team in Figure 11-2. Charter team members hire the other members of the team, teach them Saturn's mission, philosophy, and core values, and ensure that members develop the skills, abilities, and knowledge needed to accomplish team tasks. In the initial phases of team development, the UAW and management advisers interact directly with the charter team members.

The second phase of team development, the storming phase, is characterized by an increasing amount and degree of group interaction (represented in Figure 11-2 by the lines connecting

Figure 11-2
Team Development at Saturn

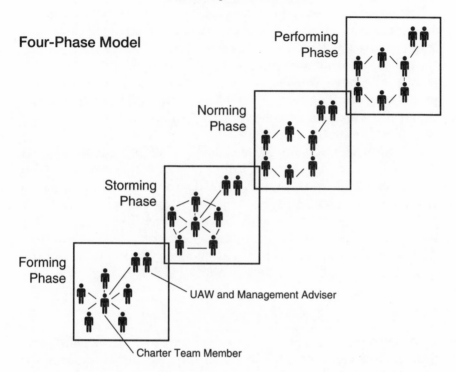

Four-Phase Model

Performing Phase

Norming Phase

Storming Phase

Forming Phase

UAW and Management Adviser

Charter Team Member

team members, which signify an increasing amount of direct communication among them). In the third, or norming, phase, the charter team member moves outside the team center, but continues to be the conduit for interaction with the team and its advisers. Only in the last phase, the performing phase, when the adviser acts with the group as a whole, is the team completely self-directed. At this point, the charter team member becomes an equal team participant.

Full transition is a lengthy process, typically occurring over two to three years. Often, when a team experiences a significant change, as when two or three new members are added, it is common to regress temporarily to the third phase.

The responsibilities of the work units cover a very broad range, including producing to schedule and budget, quality, housekeeping, safety and health, maintenance, material and inventory control, training, job assignments, repairs, scrap control, absenteeism, supplies, record keeping, personnel selection and hiring, and work planning and scheduling.

Team members spend between 250 and 750 hours in an intensive educational and training program to prepare for their jobs. These figures become even more impressive when one realizes that these are not newcomers to the auto industry. Most are people who have worked at GM or other auto manufacturing plants for 5 to 25 years. Moreover, a large part of this educational effort is spent on behavioral subjects that emphasize leadership and team development.

A final academic point. The concept of adaptive team players is an old one in the organizational behavior literature. In fact, Tuckman (1965) was first to identify the four stages of team development adopted by Saturn: forming, storming, norming, and performing. However, the ways in which these stages have been internalized at Saturn represent a creative contribution. Although the names of the stages given by Tuckman have been retained, much of its content is a unique Saturn response.

Organizational Structure

Saturn's organizational structure is so dramatically different from the conventional, hierarchical organizational form that it cannot be explained or represented with traditional organigrams and organizational charts. Instead, Saturn uses circles to explain interactions among working units and their participation in Saturn's businesses. These circles are nested within the overall structure of the Saturn organization. Beginning at the work unit level, work units charged with tasks that need to be coordinated are grouped into a work unit module (see Figure 11-3). The outside circle of this module, referred to as the decision circle, includes all charter team members of participating work units and the associated UAW and management advisers. Advisers normally oversee 4 to 6 teams, all of them part of the module. The decision circle can also contain temporary or permanent resource people needed to advise the work unit module. For example, one such module could be the cooling system of the car. The decision circle might work on ideas for cost reduction and quality improvements, job content and rotation, and so forth.

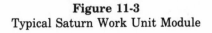

Figure 11-3
Typical Saturn Work Unit Module

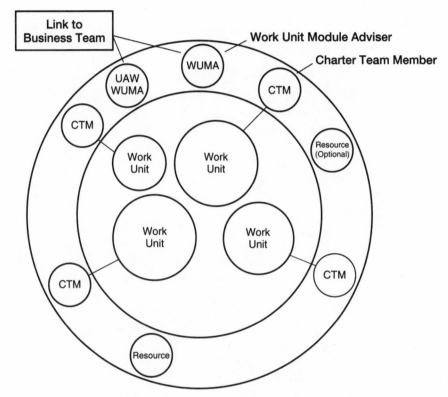

Taking the structure a level higher, work unit modules become part of a business unit within the Saturn structure (as
portrayed in Figure 11-4). For example, the manufacturing and
assembly activities are executed in the 4-million square foot
manufacturing complex in Spring Hill, Tennessee. There are
three distinct business units in this complex: power train, which
makes castings from a central foundry into fully dressed engines
and transmissions; body systems, which stamps, fabricates, and
paints complete sets of body panels; and vehicle systems, which
assembles and builds the final car. These three business units
are overseen by the Manufacturing Action Council (MAC),
which makes decisions that affect the entire manufacturing operation. The MAC organizational circle is depicted in Figure
11-5.

Figure 11-4
Typical Saturn Business Team

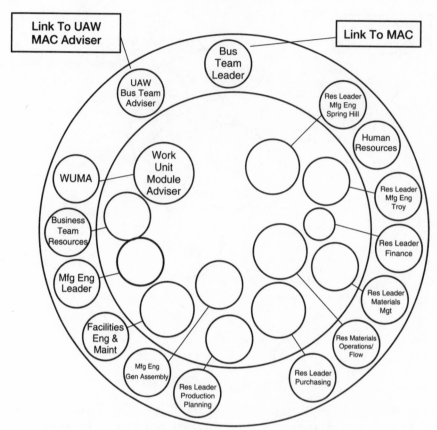

There are, in addition to MAC, two other functionally oriented high-level councils at Saturn: the Technical Development Action Council (TDAC), which coordinates advanced engineering and design, and the Customer Action Council (CAC), which includes two Saturn dealers and focuses on sales, service, and marketing. At all levels of decision making, both a Saturn manager and a UAW manager advise the teams. The vice president of manufacturing and the president of Saturn's UAW, for example, are the corresponding members of the MAC manufacturing adviser circle.

MAC, TDAC, and CAC come together in the Strategic Action Council (SAC), which oversees the organization and sets strate-

Figure 11-5
Saturn's Manufacturing Action Council (MAC)

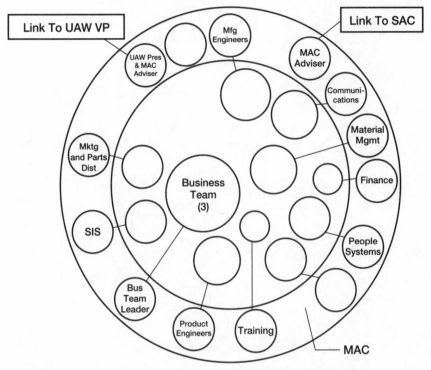

gic directions. The councils, which have a number of critical resource teams to assist them (see Figure 11-6), operate much differently than traditional staff functions, which tend to become centralized entities at the corporate level. The councils are more flexible, fluid, and involved than would be possible in a conventional functional structure. Resource Teams, as their name implies, are highly qualified groups of professionals that move from business team to business team, bringing their capabilities and actively participating in the decision-making process as required.

Rewards System

Another remarkable departure from conventional U.S. auto industry practice is the agreement established by Saturn and the UAW, whereby both share in the rewards of overall com-

Figure 11-6
Top Organizational Councils and Resource Teams at Saturn

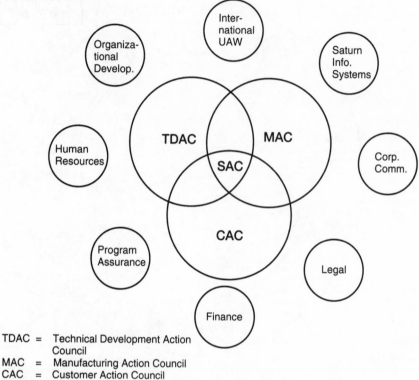

TDAC = Technical Development Action
         Council
MAC = Manufacturing Action Council
CAC = Customer Action Council

pany performance. To reach this agreement, UAW had to put something at risk—20% of workers' wages go back into General Motors if certain predetermined performance goals are not met. These goals, which are negotiated each year, involve such targets as quality, number of cars produced, and productivity. When the established goals are exceeded, workers can earn in excess of 100% base salary. The base pay is the domestic auto industry's, not just General Motors', average base.

The 20% pay-at-risk concept contributes to the creation of a climate of teamwork and continuous improvement. By focusing everyone involved on common goals, risk, and rewards, this compensation system creates a "win-together" environment. It pulls an already close group even closer together; every team member is compelled to be supportive of every other.

It is important to emphasize that the targets that determine superior performance are set at the broadest level—they are Saturn's goals, not individual or group performance objectives. This total Saturn reward system prevents the parochialism that often puts one group in an organization in conflict with another.

Suppliers

The same spirit of partnership that characterizes Saturn's internal activities is reflected in its relationships with suppliers. Saturn's goal is to establish a long-term partnership with only one supplier per input. This relationship is to be based on mutual trust, high standard for quality, just-in-time delivery, and continuous improvement.

To determine which materials are to be sourced, Saturn drafts members of the organization with different expertise—manufacturing, engineering, finance, materials management, quality management, and UAW technicians—into a Product Development Team (PDT).

A PDT first visits different facilities of prospective suppliers to consider whether these candidates will be able to meet the company's needs on a timely basis and determine how well they run their own organizations. Then, after establishing the necessary lead-time requirements and narrowing the list of candidates, the team members select by consensus the supplier they believe will best serve the organization. Upon agreement with the leadership, the candidate recommended by the PDT becomes a Saturn partner. But the process does not stop here. Even more important is that the PDT continues to work with the supplier after the partnership is formed to ensure continuous improvement.

Saturn was the industry leader in developing an electronic data interchange (EDI) system to communicate with its suppliers, using the Automotive Industry Group standards approved by the National Bureau of Standards. Saturn currently uses EDI for materials flow, just-in-time inventory control, and its payment process. EDI enables Saturn to communicate regularly with suppliers about planning and shipping schedules, and inventory and payment advice. Overall, Saturn's use of EDI has reduced order-cycle and clerical-processing time, postal service expenses, and costs, while increasing accuracy (since most transactions are electronic).

Saturn currently uses EDI to communicate with more than 300 direct suppliers about materials planning and shipping schedules, and uses electronic funds transfer (EFT), a "money" form of EDI, to pay more than half of these suppliers. Saturn is using standardized forms of EDI to communicate electronically with as many organizations as possible. It is also sharing interest in and use of these standards with other GM organizations.

Dealers

Saturn dealers are referred to as retailers. The people partnership embraces all members of the Saturn network—including the retailer, Saturn's direct contact with the end-customer. A vital participant in the Saturn organization, the retailer must not be threatened by a spirit of competitiveness from other Saturn retailers, which has proven counterproductive in the automobile industry generally. Instead, Saturn retailers are assigned designated market areas and lend a helping hand to other regions as needed. Perhaps this sounds like an ideal, but if so, it is an ideal reflected in the Saturn philosophy and mission statement. Framed and hanging on retailers' walls, these statements are daily reminders of how to make decisions, just as they are at Spring Hill.

Saturn has developed a state-of-the-art business system to integrate its retail network. Each Saturn retailer is equipped with an IBM AS/400 system provided with satellite communication for two-way data and one-way video information exchange. This arrangement affords retailers instant access to vehicles in the production pipeline for purposes of order change and status. It also facilitates rapid location of service parts, since Saturn has its finger on each dealer's inventory 24 hours a day, and early detection of product problems, as all vehicle repair information is transmitted nightly to Saturn for analysis.

The efficacy of this early detection process is demonstrated by the recall of 1,800 Saturn vehicles that were shipped with a defective Texaco cooling liquid. A sudden increase in water-pump changes was observed within three days of initial occurrence through information transmitted by the dealer network. All affected cars were recalled within two weeks, averting a major calamity in the field. Normally this defect would not have been detected until warranty claims began to materialize. These vehicles were crushed to keep them from ever reaching the public and help ensure Saturn's reputation for quality.

Information technology has also benefited operations within the retail outlet. The sophistication of the systems enables retailers to reduce their personnel costs by eliminating the need to order vehicles and service parts and reducing the handling of the same data by multiple people.

Technological Initiatives at Saturn

The central challenge facing industry today is the ability to integrate people and technology in a fast-to-market environment. With increasing consumer demands and a greater number of competitors in the field, companies must react more quickly than ever if they are to survive.

Very often, the missing ingredient in a company's equation for success is people. Many corporations fail on this level because they implement high technology without a structure to help the work force keep pace. The investment in the most technologically advanced piece of equipment in the world is wasted if it is not easy to use and if employees struggle with the machinery rather than concentrate on doing quality work. At the same time, technology is no enemy. It is vital to getting to the marketplace fast.

Some traditional companies lack the systems to integrate people and technology. Saturn is built around them. The company uses an equilateral people-technology-systems triangle to describe its mind-set about technology. Systems forms the base of the triangle, supporting people and technology equally. Within this structure, people and technology can grow at the same rate.

Mutual growth is the foundation of the continuous improvement process and the cornerstone of the company's people and technology philosophy. If people and technology needs can be interrelated and simultaneous growth maintained, Saturn can be successful in a fast-to-market world.

Saturn has made a number of important technological innovations in American car building, including the plastic external panel and the use of the skillet system method of assembly. Saturn was also the first U.S. automobile manufacturer to build both automatic and manual transmissions on the same line, an unusually flexible operation in the manufacturing industry. These accomplishments were possible in part because Saturn secured the total involvement of team members in the design stage of the new technologies and gave them a strong voice in the design of their work environment. Saturn puts people first, and lets them drive technology. The balance is accomplished through business systems.

Business Systems Development at Saturn

Saturn's business systems, like its other important activities, are the product of a clean-sheet approach based on the following guiding principles:

- functional applications would process on a single corporate platform,
- database structure would be relational,
- data entities would be defined in a central repository, and
- rigorous standards would be established for data presentation and modeling.

These principles enabled Saturn to achieve a level of integration unheard-of in most industries. They eliminated the inefficiency of interfaces between systems and made available accurate real-time data for all critical business needs.

Electronic Data Systems (EDS), the data processing company GM acquired from Ross Perot, provided most of the expertise and equipment that enabled Saturn to integrate its business systems. Given Saturn's many differences—including new staff, new business processes, new technology, new car, and new culture—EDS had a unique opportunity to develop a totally new systems approach. To ensure that every new system was ideally suited to Saturn—in terms of cost, integration, and operations—the Business System Action Council (BSAC) was created. The BSAC, which reports to the EDS member of the Strategic Action Council, is charged with ensuring consistency in Saturn systems. Every decision is agreed upon by the members of the group, which includes all functional areas of Saturn. The partnership between Saturn and EDS guarantees EDS involvement in all key decisions. Thus, EDS is not just a provider of information technology, but a critical resource team.

Saturn's EDS manager has used the slogan "from art to part"

to describe the integrated nature of Saturn's systems. Every element of the car is first designed on computers, which inform purchasing, manufacturing, and other departments what must be done to achieve an orderly production schedule. Suppliers and dealers are also integrated electronically to process their financial and physical transactions.

The following list of applications provides a more detailed account of the business systems Saturn has implemented to support each of its managerial functions.

Human Resources

- Member Roster—identifies and maintains all demographic, people-related data and is the sole source of people information for all Saturn systems.
- Education Tracking—tracks and maintains training plans and history for all Saturn employees (including those not yet hired but identified as needed).
- Represented Applicant Tracking—tracks the applications received to fill the plant floor and other openings and supports searches to match for open positions.

Product Engineering

- Business systems have achieved a level of integration unmatched in GM, resulting in significant cost savings and elimination of redundant data.
- 100% of Saturn's in-house product design is done electronically using CAD/CAM/CAE.
- In line with Saturn's initial vision to be paperless where appropriate, the Saturn office environment is tailored for a computer-literate work force; electronic mail and EDI are the foundation for inter- and intra-corporate communications.

Manufacturing

- The total manufacturing planning process is an integrated solution with product engineering, material systems, and dealer order processing.
- The systems maintain document information on current and future processes and integrate it with the CAD system.
- The systems identify tool gauges and machinery and relate them to the process in which they are used.

Materials Management

- Every part is ordered every day and delivered using pre-planned routes and scheduled dock times.
- EDI is used to communicate weekly planning quantities and daily shipping schedules.
- Material is paid for based on units produced, and these counts serve as the basis for replenishment scheduling.

Sales, Service, and Marketing

Vehicle Distribution:

- An allocation system that establishes monthly allotments agreed upon by both dealers and manufacturing.
- An order management system that computer-generates dealer orders based on individual retailer sales and seasonality.

Service Parts:

- The system is integrated with product engineering for service parts releasing and integrated with materials management for part scheduling

Service:

- Service applications are designed around a national vehicle history to support the following activities:
    Dealer service operations
    Product engineering/manufacturing
    Warranty administration
    Saturn assistance centers

Retailer (Dealer)

- The Saturn retailer system was developed in partnership with Saturn and its retailers to provide the following applications:
    Sales—Integrated finance and insurance, vehicle inventory, and prospecting
    Parts—Locator, inventory, invoicing, and replenishment
    Service—National vehicle history, diagnostics integration, service merchandising and invoicing
    Business—Automated delivery reporting, financial
    Reporting—AR/AP, payroll and purchase order

Communications—Satellite technology for data and video, integrated with Saturn Corporate Systems

Financial

- Use of electronic funds transfer is standard.
- An on-line time reporting system supports the entire work force.
- One disbursement activity handles all purchasing activities: direct, indirect, freight, services, and so forth.
- The financial database is integrated to communicate with dealers and suppliers.

Corporate Communications

- EDS installed full-motion teleconferencing equipment between its Michigan and Tennessee facilities to expedite communications and thereby reduce travel time and save money.
- EDS installed a media center for the Tennessee site that provides sitewide video distribution, video production and edit capabilities, conference audio/visual needs, and satellite receive capability.

Early Results

The early results are extremely promising. By the end of 1992, the Tennessee plant reached full capacity, and a third crew will be added for 1993 which will significantly increase capacity. Further, Saturn opened 144 retailers in 1991, and plans to have approximately 250 by the end of 1992.

It is not too early to examine Saturn's significant accomplishments in terms of customer satisfaction and dealer performance. Figure 11-7 presents the Dealer Satisfaction Index (DSI) in 1991 as reported by J.D. Power and Associates, based on its Dealer Attitude Study. Saturn, as can be seen, is surpassed only by Lexus and is ahead of Infiniti, two of the most successful recent entrants in the luxury car market.

The J.D. Power and Associates Sales Satisfaction Index (SSI) locates Saturn well ahead of the industry. The firm appears in sixth place behind Lexus, Cadillac, Infiniti, Lincoln, and Mercedes-Benz, the top nameplates in the luxury car segment, which cost tens of thousands of dollars more than a Saturn (see

Figure 11-7
1991 DSI Top Performers (by nameplate)

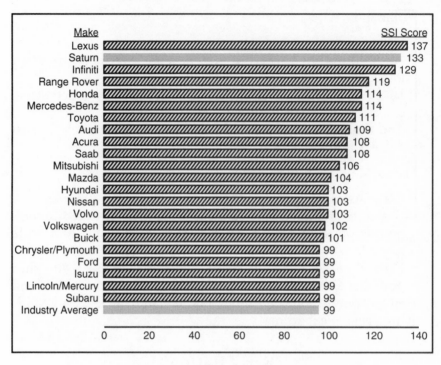

Source: J.D. Power and Associates, "The Power Report," February 1992.

Figure 11-8). When ranked against the top-five basic small performers that are its direct competitors, Saturn's SSI score, which measures owners' overall satisfaction with their sales and delivery experience, is far superior (see Figure 11-9).

These results have led J.D. Power and Associates to state that "Saturn, Lexus and Infiniti are raising traditional standards of customer satisfaction in the automotive marketplace. The degree to which new-car buyers respond to these efforts could determine whether or not every other manufacturer will be forced to change as well."[1]

The 1991 Estimated New Vehicle Profit Performance by Franchise, also reported by J.D. Power and Associates, ranks Saturn third, after Lexus and Infiniti, in total new vehicle gross profit per dealership. The top ten performers are listed in Figure 11-10.

Figure 11-8
Satisfaction Elite: Top Makes in 1991 SSI

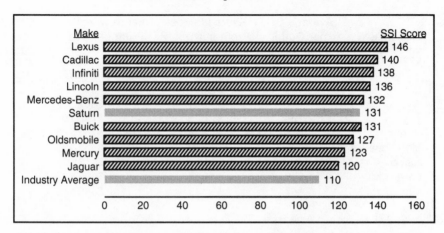

Source: J.D. Power and Associates, "The Power Report Special Saturn Issue," 1992.

Further, *Business Week* provided some new measurements of Saturn's success. In a cover story appearing on August 17, 1992, it reported that Saturn was the third car in customer satisfaction, rating right after Lexus and Infiniti—cars that belong to the luxury segment and sell for as much as four times the price of the Saturn. All in all, an amazing performance! These results are shown in Figure 11-11.

Figure 11-9
Top-Five Basic Small Performers in 1991 SSI (by model)

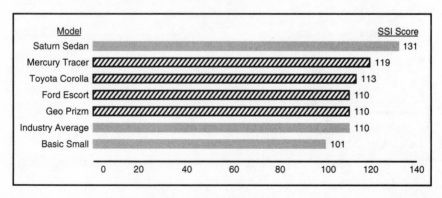

Source: J.D. Power and Associates, "The Power Report Special Saturn Issue," 1992.

Figure 11-10

1991 Estimated New-Vehicle Profit Performance by Francise

Franchise	Average Sales per Outlet 1	Average Gross Profit per Unit 2	Total New-Vehicle Gross Profit per Dealership
Lexus	565	$4,390	$2,480,350
Infiniti	391	$3,429	$1,340,739
Saturn	694	$1,292	$896,648
Acura	482	$1,831	$882,542
Toyota	784	$1,006	$788,704
Honda	676	$1,138	$769,288
Mercedes-Benz	145	$4,539	$658,155
Nissan	493	$1,041	$513,213
Ford	519	$963	$499,797
Mitsubishi	387	$1,145	$443,115

Source: J.D. Power and Associates, "The Power Report," February 1992.

All of these indicators evidence an impressive debut for Saturn in the area of customer satisfaction, the central criteria for its strategic positioning.

Lessons Learned

We have tried to communicate the basic principles that guide the Saturn organization in an attempt to regain competitiveness in one of the most critical and contested segments of the automo-

Figure 11-11

1992 Customer Satisfaction Rating: J.D. Power Report

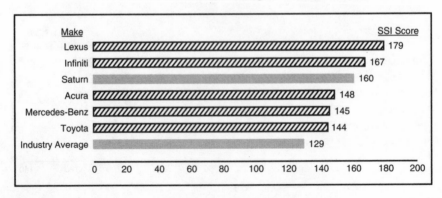

Source: Saturn Cover Story, *Business Week,* August 17, 1992.

bile industry. What we have learned from this effort can be summarized in three fundamental lessons.

Involvement. The cornerstone of Saturn's leadership philosophy is that people want to be involved in the decisions that affect them. Involvement translates into better understanding of the business and supports a powerful learning process throughout the organization.

Commitment. Involvement also leads to a sense of ownership and a personal sense of responsibility to make the decisions work. Implementation occurs much faster and in a more logical manner than it otherwise would.

Quality over quantity. The strongest and most unbending change is the pursuit of the highest quality standards in the auto industry. Saturn is creating a culture in which everything that is done has a quality stamp on it.

These appear to be simple lessons. Their impact, however, promises to be of tremendous importance.

Note

1. J.D. Power and Associates, "The Power Report Special Saturn Issue," 1992.

Reference

B. W. Tuckman, "Developmental Sequence in Small Groups," *Psychological Bulletin,* 63, no. 6 (1965): 384–399.

12

Information Technology and the Global Virtual Corporation

David B. Miller, Eric K. Clemons, and Michael C. Row

Today one of the five largest travel agencies in the United States, Rosenbluth Travel, was in 1980 a regional agency with annual sales of $40 million. Its growth to a national giant with sales over $1.3 billion has been characterized by:

- rapid and creative innovation driven by closeness to its market and a clear vision of its corporate customers' changing needs, and
- aggressive use of information technology (IT) to build infrastructure for the delivery of services and to form a platform for continued innovation.

These characteristics have enabled the company to ride the wave of change that swept across the travel industry after the deregulation of the airlines in 1978—change that included dramatic growth in the corporate travel market, in terms of services offered and size of market segment, as well as extensive restructuring and consolidation. A decade of sustained growth in market share and improvements in service quality have afforded the company both strategic positioning and the critical resources needed to sustain its competitive advantage.[1]

The travel industry, like many other industries, is coming under increasing pressure to globalize. Rosenbluth offers global travel services in an effort to keep pace with its customers, which have globalized their operations in response to market pressure, competitor actions, and changing supplier relations. As the company demonstrated domestically in its pioneering program of negotiating superior rates with hotels and airlines based on its commanding market share advantage, there are benefits to scale.

But it is difficult for service organizations to globalize. Global expansion through acquisition is usually expensive, and expansion through internal growth is time-consuming, and sometimes impossible in markets that are not actively growing. Rosenbluth now believes that these traditional routes to global expansion may even be inappropriate for service industries that must preserve local responsiveness through local presence and expertise, as well as expand. The company believes that, although integration of local markets will improve, it will always be necessary to base global service on local expertise.

Consequently, Rosenbluth chose a unique structure for globalization, the Rosenbluth International Alliance (RIA). Rather than rely on expansion through development of its own offices abroad and attempt to develop the requisite local travel management expertise and capture the necessary shares of foreign markets, the company chose to work with the best foreign partners it could find. RIA, a cooperative alliance of independent agencies initiated in 1987, today comprises 32 partners spanning 37 countries. The approach has resolved Rosenbluth's global dilemma admirably.

- Even for multinational corporate clients, the bulk of travel is regional or local, requiring local expertise. RIA's structure reflects this.
- When necessary, local markets can be linked. Providing service for traveling executives and resolving unanticipated problems requires more than presence; it requires local expertise coupled with global access to information. RIA's structure reflects this as well.
- The need for global coordination is expected to increase as clients demand consolidated reporting of travel patterns and global travel management services. RIA's structure, being flexible, can evolve as global travel support needs change.

The creation of RIA did not entail either the resources or delay that would have been associated with alternative strategies. The organizational form, which we term a "global virtual corporation," relies on IT to structure and restructure itself, combining local partners meeting local needs to service global accounts with global needs.

The structural changes set in motion by globalization are as fundamental and far-reaching as the structural changes experienced in the United States following deregulation. The RIA is positioned to enable Rosenbluth to repeat its successful U.S. domestic strategy on a global scale. Specifically, the company is:

- anticipating changes in service needs caused by increased globalization,
- anticipating the impact of these needs on the operating economies of travel agencies and the resulting industry structure, and
- aggressively using IT to build an infrastructure that will enable RIA to ride the new wave of change and restructuring that will accompany globalization.

IT enables the coordination of travel services throughout the world. Information on clients and travelers is available to agents worldwide to provide superior support to traveling executives. Information can be globally consolidated in order to coordinate decision making and leverage global purchasing power. IT's role in supporting coordination has long been recognized,[2] but coordination among independent organizations introduces new challenges. Trust, for example, is implicit in placing service for key customers in the hands of other service providers. IT cannot build this trust, but it can help provide information that promotes trust, such as near real-time monitoring and assessment of service quality levels. IT can also support performance-based incentives that can contribute to mutually beneficial cooperative relationships.

Company Background

Rosenbluth was the founder and principal architect of RIA. To understand RIA, it is necessary to first understand the domestic strategy and remarkable success of its founder and principal architect.

Deregulation and Domestic Growth

When the airline industry was deregulated in 1978, Rosenbluth was a strong, family-owned regional travel agency centered in Philadelphia, Pennsylvania.[3] Hal Rosenbluth, a fourth-generation executive with the company, anticipated and set out to exploit three major implications of deregulation:

- the increasing importance of corporate travel,
- the increasing importance of economies of scale and scope, and
- the critical role of IT for providing value-added services and achieving operating economies in the new environment.

Prior to deregulation, travel agents could do little more for corporate accounts than deliver tickets. Fare structures were simple and unchanging and route structures were fixed. But in the wake of deregulation, fares became highly volatile. Fare wars produced hundreds of thousands of fare changes per week, and carriers were free to add or drop routes as desired. In this increasingly complex and dynamic environment, travel agents began to function as informed brokers, obtaining for their corporate clients the best posted fares and most convenient flights. Rosenbluth's strategy focused on capturing a substantial share of this growing market segment through innovations and superior service. Travel being perhaps the only market in which the best commercial customers pay higher prices than individuals, Rosenbluth sought to exploit its information advantage to negotiate preferred rates for its corporate accounts.

Under Hal Rosenbluth's leadership, the company accumulated a long string of industry "firsts."

- It was the first agency to introduce a corporate reservation center to improve service and exploit economies of scale.
- It developed proprietary front-end support systems to improve service and maintain quality control. READOUT enables agents to sell flights based on cost, rather than rely on computerized reservation systems (CRS) listings based on departure times. PRECISION introduced scripts into the CRS to guide and improve the accuracy of the sales process, thereby improving agents' service and ability to enforce client companies' travel policies.
- Rosenbluth also developed proprietary back-office support systems. VISION automatically captures information at the time reservations are ticketed and consolidates it overnight in order to apprise client companies in near real-time of

evolving travel patterns throughout the United States. This information is also used to produce a variety of travel management reports. USERVISION supports flexible, on-line access to travel information almost immediately and allows this information to be downloaded for further analysis on client systems.

- It was the first agency to introduce route-by-route fare negotiation with carriers. Rosenbluth enjoys a commanding presence in some of its markets and can move substantial market share among competing carriers. It developed the reporting systems necessary to identify high-volume routes, demonstrate to carriers what a special fare program could do for them, and monitor the benefits of the program for both carriers and clients. The company uses its PRECISION system to ensure that share actually moves to the service provider affording the client improved rates.

As the corporate travel market has grown more competitive and price sensitive, economies of scale have become more important, both to reduce the costs of providing service and to consolidate the purchasing power needed for rate negotiation. Rosenbluth used innovative IT applications to provide superior service and capture market share; it used the market share advantage to secure better prices and provide superior service for clients, which further increased its market share. The company's share advantage also supports its technology-based strategy, inasmuch as the cost of IT software development is largely independent of market share, thus benefiting larger players. Rosenbluth has cascaded its IT applications into an integrated IT infrastructure, continuously "upping the ante" for competitors and using its size to create barriers to the duplication of its success.

Rosenbluth's success is unambiguous. It has enjoyed dramatic growth in revenues for the past decade, from $40 million to more than $1 billion annually. Almost all of this growth has been generated and funded internally, through increased business rather than by merger or acquisition. Consequently, the debt burden incurred has been limited and there has been no dilution of the owners' equity. Rosenbluth is today a mega-agency, one of the largest travel providers in the United States, and the gap between the megas and other agencies continues to grow.[4]

Hitting the Wall—Limits to Growth

By the late 1980s, Rosenbluth had begun to experience pressure to offer global services. Major U.S. clients were increasingly demanding support for their global travel needs as a pre-condition for contracting with an agency. Hal Rosenbluth believed that continued growth in the forces for globalization would create new opportunities for agencies that could provide global service first and thereby create new markets for leveraging his company's infrastructure and expertise.

Rosenbluth believed that a global solution should be consistent with his company's domestic strengths: customized client service, continuing innovation, and reliance on IT. But global service introduced new problems.

- Global support required that a company be present in all major markets, but this omnipresence was not consistent with Rosenbluth's limited financial and managerial resources.
- Differences in local markets and difficulties associated with trying to compete with local companies (if Rosenbluth was perceived as a U.S.-owned competitor) necessitated reliance on local agencies for local support, but lack of an effective integrating infrastructure made it difficult to rely on those local agencies for support of global accounts.

The principal problem was to develop an organization able to seamlessly coordinate travel management of global accounts, when travel management was based upon largely autonomous heterogeneous markets that needed to remain so and were difficult to integrate. The RIA was formed and structured to implement Hal Rosenbluth's vision of the global arena.

IT's role in implementing global strategy was viewed as twofold:

- to integrate autonomous partners that would continue to provide local service to largely local markets, while allowing RIA affiliates to offer uniformly superior global service to the most demanding global executives, and
- to enable alliance members to consolidate and exploit their purchasing power to negotiate preferred rates.

IT must perform additional roles in cooperative relationships not often required when employed by a single company. It must provide monitoring and control to enable partners to assess the quality of service they are receiving from independent affiliates, as well as support cooperative incentive structures and communications to foster more stable relationships.

Globalization of the Travel Industry

Industries are restructuring in response to increased competition for common markets; economies are becoming more interdependent, precipitating changes in competitive, cooperative, and supplier relationships; the restructuring of Europe, both east and west, is proceeding apace; the Pacific Rim has established itself as the fastest-growing region in the world; and cross-border investments and instruments to protect against changing foreign exchange rates have increased dramatically in importance. In short, business is becoming more global.

Client Pressure for Globalization

Travel agencies are being driven to globalize by their key corporate accounts. Gerry Ephraim, manager of travel and fleet services for Eastman Kodak Co., is delighted with the domestic service he receives from Rosenbluth. But Kodak is becoming increasingly global and, accordingly, Ephraim recently created a Japanese travel management function. When asked if Kodak would have remained with Rosenbluth without the ability to service Japanese travel, he responded: "That's a very interesting question. I've asked it myself. Fortunately, we didn't have to answer it!"

The travel manager of a European multinational chemical manufacturer was more specific in explaining the importance of global travel and his reasons for working with an RIA member. "It is important," he observed, "that we know we can reach everywhere we need to go with comparable levels of service, and that we can assure that our people are making the best use of available service providers. We want a global agency with buying power for negotiation and with technology to make certain we take best advantage of these deals."

Rosenbluth believed that if his firm's key accounts were going global, it would be necessary to become more global to support them. This strategy was aimed less at increasing domestic market share than at protecting existing relationships. Ron Millette, senior vice president of corporate travel for Canada's Marlin Travel,[5] expressed a similar belief. Many of Marlin's corporate clients, subsidiaries or affiliates of U.S. corporations, were beginning to demand a more global approach to travel management. "It was necessary for us to respond, or risk losing business," Millette claims.

International travelers are often companies' most senior officers and agencies' most demanding customers. Such travelers require a local presence for making itinerary changes, handling emergencies, and providing local expertise. The ability to provide this support is increasingly a factor in attracting and retaining large domestic corporate clients. Many clients have favorite stories of special services that RIA has provided for them, from allowing their executives to clear the wait list on sold-out flights to truly extraordinary efforts during the Gulf crisis to check on the condition of executives being held in Kuwait City.

Many companies believe that the principal benefits of working with a global travel management company will be negotiation and implementation of special travel programs based on a firm's global volume. "The name of the game is negotiating the best service and rates," explains Kodak's Ephraim. "This requires detailed on-line data with accurate volume and market share figures, so that we can show the providers our ability to move market share." It also requires "that we can help our travelers exploit these rates, and that we know when our travelers are not taking advantage of the best opportunities." These capabilities, according to Ephraim, figured prominently in Kodak's decision to work internationally through the RIA.

Significant obstacles to the globalization of travel remain, among them the following.

- Most corporations naturally grant foreign subsidiaries considerable autonomy in making local travel arrangements. These units need to be induced to cooperate, but globalization cannot be mandated or forced by U.S. headquarters.
- Much of the infrastructure to support integration of travel services does not yet exist.

These obstacles had a significant effect on the structure and governance of the RIA.

Agency Pressures for Globalization

In addition to pressures from major accounts, travel agencies are subject to many of the same forces that are driving their accounts to globalize, including:

- threats from foreign competitors expanding into the United States,
- the need for new sources of business,
- the need to continue to expand so as to increase purchasing power and be better able to negotiate with service providers, such as airlines and hotel chains, and
- the need for continued growth to support capital expenditures, particularly for IT.

The last two are especially important; the largest agencies have been the most effective in negotiating preferred rates, making them more attractive to clients. This need for scale economies has been a factor in the continued growth of the largest U.S. agencies. As limits to domestic growth are encountered, agencies will begin to rely on foreign sources for increased sales volume. Agencies also play a critical role in consolidating travel information for their largest accounts, enabling them to negotiate preferred rates and services for these accounts. Increasing globalization of travel is demanding a more integrated, global approach to rate negotiation. The development of systems to support global integration can be quite expensive. But as agencies discovered domestically, much of this IT expense is a fixed cost, largely independent of the scale of company operations. Thus, IT interacts with and augments the trend toward globalization. Once companies begin to invest in systems to support foreign operations, the economies of scale present in the required systems lead to full globalization rather than limited exploratory foreign expansion.

Competitors' Globalization Moves

Rosenbluth is not alone in moving toward globalization. All the large U.S. travel agencies are developing global organizations and products, and large foreign agencies are making inroads into the U.S. market. The strategies that agencies are following vary considerably, but all show consistent recognition of the importance of global operation.

The U.S. standard-bearer in the globalization of the travel industry is undoubtedly American Express. With an established network of more than 1,400 offices and affiliates worldwide, Amex is positioning itself as the established veteran of globalization. The company has begun to use the advanced proprietary communications network that links its offices to integrate travel reporting and support, as well as provide traditional financial services. Amex recently announced the ability to consolidate travel reporting worldwide.[6]

Carlson Travel Network, the second-largest player in the U.S. market, has established a global network in 20 countries. Its strategy combines acquisitions (e.g., Britain's A.T. Mays) and affiliates, with a strong emphasis on eventual equity control. Lifeco, another large U.S. player, relies heavily on acquisitions. Acquisition strategies are largely based on global standardization and control. Both Amex and Lifeco have installed their own computer systems and business processes in acquisitions.

Other large players are following a strategy of cooperation. Consortia and franchise networks such as Woodside Travel and Hickory have long had international members, but were not focused on global coordination and service. Rosenbluth's RIA was the first global cooperative network focused on global service and technology. A number of large U.S. agencies have followed Rosenbluth's lead in the four years since the RIA was founded. IVI Travel Inc. formed the Business Travel International network with a few large foreign partners, and Maritz recently reorganized its international affiliate group, Internet, along similar lines. All of these cooperative approaches are aimed at tapping into existing foreign strength rather than bringing American-style services to the world.

According to Rosenbluth vice president of international development, Carl Nurick, many large players, in scrambling to establish a global presence, are underemphasizing the importance of coordination in providing global service.[7] Nurick believes the key ingredients for global service are technology and people. "The technology is critical," he explains. "You need accessibility for all data from point A to point B. But without consistency and interaction, the technology is worthless. The greatest strides of the RIA are due to the attitudes of the people in the alliance; a commitment to the client and to each other."

The Rosenbluth International Alliance

Formed in 1988 as Rosenbluth Travel's primary mechanism for achieving a global presence, the Rosenbluth International Alliance now includes 32 partners operating in more than 1,200 offices in 37 countries. The RIA has a local presence in virtually every major travel market around the world and gross annual sales of more than $6 billion. Rosenbluth adopted a cooperative approach for several reasons. Most important, it perceived an overriding demand for local responsiveness, which argued strongly for using established local players with a high degree of autonomy. Moreover, the cost and time involved in a global acquisition strategy were prohibitive.

Foreign markets can differ radically in customs, supplier relationships and ways of doing business. Consider the following as a dramatic example. During the recent Gulf crisis, two Chevron employees were trapped in Kuwait. All phone lines into the country were inoperative and all efforts to ascertain the status of the two men met with failure. Nancy Godfrey, Chevron's manager of travel services, contacted Rosenbluth and Nurick, who, in turn, contacted Kanoo Travel, the RIA partner in Saudi Arabia. Through a private business line still in operation, Kanoo was able to locate the businessmen and determine that they were unharmed. Kanoo even offered to send people across the border in disguise to retrieve the travelers, who eventually returned safely. "Nobody else could find out anything," recalled Godfrey. "The RIA member had the local relationships to help. They knew the people. They knew the system. Clearly this is service beyond the call of duty."

Fortunately, most of the benefits of local presence are more mundane than the Chevron example. A local agency's supplier relationships can be critical in helping stranded travelers. "For a client stranded in Toronto at midnight without a hotel room," explains Marlin Travel's Millette, "we stand a better chance of helping than an 800 line to Philadelphia. There is always some slack in the system, and a good local agent can find it for you."

This is not just in Toronto and not just for hotels. The ability to find the slack is important, and is possible only with strong local supplier relationships.

Patterns of corporate travel also suggest a need for local presence. One travel manager of a global firm estimates that two-thirds of all travel for any client location is domestic, but that the one-third that is international is typically by higher level managers with extremely high service needs. Moreover, international travel accounts for more than half the cost of travel. A network of cooperating local players can supply high-quality service to traveling executives, while continuing to provide cost-effective and high-quality domestic travel support.

The overriding needs for local presence argue strongly for using established local players rather than attempting to open new offices. Rosenbluth could have obtained some local presence through acquisition, but such a strategy was inappropriate for several reasons. An independent foreign national has a significant marketing advantage when selling to foreign multinational corporations. Whereas companies such as American Express are viewed as U.S. companies serving U.S. clients, the RIA can adapt to local conditions. "It is difficult to sell a foreign company a U.S. system," explains Nurick. "The RIA has the advantage that it looks like a global American company to an American client and a global Austrian company to an Austrian client." A global alliance can thus strengthen local players, rather than force them to serve as satellites in the context of a single national strategy.

Rosenbluth lacked the capital for expansion through widespread acquisition, which would have been prohibitively expensive and time-consuming, and, as a privately held business, it had no desire to lose autonomy through massive equity or debt financing. Thus, it was impossible for the agency to build a truly global service through an acquisition strategy. "Global service requires omnipresence," observes Nurick. "It is simply not enough to be in one or two major markets." Cooperation had the added advantage of being relatively quick to implement; a firm pursuing an acquisition strategy is constrained by financial and managerial considerations to proceed slowly and incrementally.

The benefits of cooperation were clear to Rosenbluth. But cooperation is difficult in any situation, particularly where the cooperating parties span nations and cultures. Moreover, cooperation has yielded uneven results in the travel industry. The dominant cooperative organization in the United States, the consortium, has generally failed, beset by problems of organization, coordination, and control, as well as volatile and ultimately declining membership. Consortia are typically organized around a separate headquarters with considerable overhead and, frequently, separate profit-making responsibility. Although consortia profits are shared among members, the high overhead costs and incompatible incentives foster an "us against them" mentality that limits coordination. Moreover, consortia tend to be managed in a top-down fashion, limiting their ability to develop a shared vision. Thus, although a number of domestic consortia had international affiliates, Rosenbluth believed that existing cooperative structures were inadequate to implement its global strategy. To make cooperation work, a different organizational model was required. The result, the alliance concept, was based on two principles: the importance of selection, and cooperation among equal partners.

The Structure of the Rosenbluth International Alliance

The alliance is an alliance of independent organizations bound by a common interest. Each member retains its own identity and autonomy, and all areas of cooperation are voluntary. To make this arrangement work, members had to be selected that "fit" Rosenbluth's global vision, with a service orientation and culture compatible with those of the agency. Rosenbluth looked for service innovators and leaders in each national market. Members did not have to be dominant in their markets, but did have to have strong management and financial histories and demonstrate a technological responsiveness that would support Rosenbluth's view of IT's role in global travel management.

The importance of member selection is reflected in the effort devoted to the process. Rosenbluth conducted careful competitive analyses of each local market, employing consultant and trade press reports and extensive discussions with clients and suppliers. Meetings were held with potential members, both in their own countries and in the United States, to establish mutual interest and compatibility. By all accounts, the selection process paid off. David Whittaker, managing director of RIA's U.K. partner, The Travel Company, and chairman of the British Guild of Business Travel Agents, remarked: "There is an uncanny synergy between RIA members. I've never seen this before. It must come from the selection process." Paul Howard, director of RIA's Australian member, Austravco, noted, "The RIA can serve international clients through independently owned 'local' organizations of similar types of business mix with a philosophy of providing excellent service and professionalism. We have a distinct advantage over global organizations such as Thomas Cook and American Express that become distracted by bureaucracy and corporate politics."

To support cooperation, members do not compete in any markets. Decision making, as much as possible, is by consensus. To ensure that smaller members remain committed and that positions and decisions are global rather than regional or national, each member, regardless of size, is permitted one vote.

There is little overhead or centralized bureaucracy in the alliance. RIA liaison offices are maintained in Philadelphia, London, and Singapore to provide same time-zone support and coordinate communications among alliance members and between the alliance and global clients.

Most of the work of the alliance is accomplished through committees. There are standing committees for hotel program implementation, for negotiating programs with suppliers, for standardizing global business practices, and for IT. Participation is voluntary and costs are borne primarily by participants.

The resulting organizational structure is more of a dynamic network than a traditional, centrally directed hierarchy. Decision making is decentralized among autonomous units that coordinate as needed through direct, lateral communication. The nature of and mechanisms for coordination (e.g., committees and relationships) shift over time as environmental conditions change. This type of dynamic network has been recognized as an important and emerging organizational form.[8] Bartlett and Ghoshal maintain that many firms operating in international markets are beginning to exhibit the characteristics of such networks, which they term "transnational" organizations to distinguish them from the traditional centrally directed or totally decentralized organizational approaches to globalization that have been common in the past.[9]

RIA Client Services

Although the centerpiece of the RIA is global travel support, the alliance can provide other services. It has instituted a number of programs that leverage its purchasing power to realize savings for its clients. Perhaps more important, the RIA has established an infrastructure that supports global consolidation of clients' travel information.

The RIA desk maintained by each RIA member is the key to the alliance's global service. The RIA phone (typically toll-free) is answered in English by an agent with complete access to the local member's resources. If authorized, the agent has immediate access to the traveler's itinerary and travel preferences as well as information on the corporation's travel policies. Agents also have electronic access to other RIA members for help in resolving problems, and to RIA proprietary databases containing information on hotels and special rates. The RIA desk can provide complete support from changing itineraries to handling medical emergencies.

Among programs for harnessing the alliance's purchasing power to the benefit of clients is the RIA Executive Traveler Hotel Program, which provides RIA clients with special rates in hotels around the world. Rates are negotiated by the local RIA member using the combined volume of the alliance. The RIA infrastructure enables this information to be accumulated and reported to support negotiations and monitor program performance. This is significant because it enables RIA to substantiate the program's costs and benefits to the hotel. Recently, the RIA introduced special programs for airfare and car rental. As with the hotel program, savings and services are negotiated with suppliers based on total RIA volume. All special programs are made available to RIA clients throughout the world through the RIA desks.

Perhaps its most important emerging service is the alliance's ability to support worldwide consolidated travel reporting. Such reporting enables global clients to leverage their total volume in negotiating better rates and fares. The ability to negotiate fares has been a strong driver of consolidating travel through a single agency in the United States. Rosenbluth, which pioneered this capability, believes the opportunities for worldwide negotiation are tremendous. "We need buying power for negotiating deals and technology for directing people to those deals," explained one RIA travel manager.

Kodak, which is also pursuing opportunities for global consolidation, implemented its first international negotiated program with Japan in the fall of 1991. The airlines, Ephraim explains, are typically organized by country and do not yet have the capability to consolidate a firm's travel volume. Consolidating information through the RIA gives Kodak an information advantage in dealing with suppliers. Suppliers are reacting quickly, however; British Air, for example, is taking steps to allow consolidated reporting and to adjust incentives and negotiation processes to better support global programs.

Incentives and Stability

Cooperative approaches introduce considerable risk. Participants are sometimes in a position to exploit other partners opportunistically, either through underperformance or by unilaterally renegotiating the arrangement after one party has already committed unrecoverable investment.[10] If an arrangement collapses, participants stand to lose a considerable amount of money and critical time. The issue of incentive compatibility—structuring the relationship so that the benefits of cooperation exceed the benefits of opportunistic exploitation or defection and the related risk—thus becomes of extreme importance. What does Rosenbluth get out of the RIA? What do other members get? Is the relationship stable?

The RIA's greatest benefit to members is the ability to offer clients global services. As internationalization proceeds apace, global service is becoming increasingly critical to securing corporate accounts, even if true global service is not yet required. The need for global service was the driving force behind Rosenbluth's organization of the RIA and remains the most important client service enabled by it. This is a strong incentive for other RIA members. Millette of Marlin Travel points out that many businesses in Canada are subsidiaries of U.S. firms. Being allied with Rosenbluth in the United States has been a significant advantage in securing corporate accounts from these firms.

Other RIA services improve members' competitiveness in obtaining corporate accounts in their local markets. The special savings programs that rely on global purchasing power both attract clients and improve member profits. And the ability to consolidate worldwide travel reporting and support supplier negotiations will be critical in selling business in the future.

RIA members also benefit from opportunities for technology transfer. "The United States is the most innovative and advanced market in the world for travel services," explains Millette, "and Rosenbluth is the most innovative and advanced firm in that market. Rosenbluth's problems today are our problems tomorrow."

Rosenbluth is working with Marlin to enhance the latter's ability to perform automated quality assurance, including auditing and reporting for lowest fare, wait list clearing, and checking for information completeness and consistency. Millette views this technology as critical to building and maintaining Marlin's business in the Canadian market. Digby Collis, managing director of Franco-Asian Travel, RIA's member in Singapore and Malaysia, echoes this sentiment. "What do we get from Rosenbluth?" he asks. "Insights into the workings of a mega-travel company, access to excellent training programs, exposure to state-of-the-art travel technology, possibilities for joint business, and valuable friendships!"

Rosenbluth has also been the driving force in the development of the RIA's IT infrastructure. However, just being a member of the RIA and having the opportunity to exchange ideas with other RIA firms is itself a considerable benefit. "There has been an increase in revenues generated by RIA members," explains David Moxness, international development manager for the Rosenbluth/RIA liaison office in Singapore, "and at least some of this can be attributed to the learning and sharing of mutually beneficial ideas and working together in a concentrated, global effort."

Nurick is quick to point out that Rosenbluth in turn has benefited considerably from its members' expertise. He likens the situation to that of Sir Edmund Hillary and his Sherpa guide in their ascent of Mt. Everest. "Sir Edmund knew how to climb mountains," he explains, "but Tenzing Norgay knew Mt. Everest, its crevasses, its peaks, its ridges, its danger zones. Without him, Hillary would never have reached the top. We Americans know much about travel management services, but in the international environment, we need the help of the 'Tenzing Norgays' of each country—if we hope to succeed."

Alliance members also benefit from opportunities for joint business and cross-selling. To date, this has been most significant in the area of package deals for meetings and vacations, typically high-margin business where working directly with a local alliance partner in a destination eliminates the middleman. Moreover, RIA is increasingly generating referrals. "The trend I have noticed the most," reports Kris Engle, international development director of the London Rosenbluth/RIA liaison office, "is the recent interest the RIA clients seem to have in networking with other members. Since February of this year, five or more Rosenbluth clients or their European divisions have requested proposals, started working with RIA members, or are in the process of doing so."

Is there risk involved? The alliance appears to be mutually beneficial to all parties. Is this likely to change? One important source of stability appears to be that RIA members are in non-competing areas. This may change, particularly as Europe is unified after 1992, possibly forcing RIA members into direct competition. RIA members in Europe recognize this possibility, according to Nurick, but he believes it is leading them to forge closer ties, including equity transfers, instead of threatening stability.

Nurick views the alliance's tremendous flexibility as its primary source of stability. He cites by way of example the situation in London—the territory of the RIA member, The Travel Company—where many clients have demanded a Rosenbluth office. The solution: a Rosenbluth office run by The Travel Company, with revenues shared. "There are no entrenched interests," explains Nurick. "We will do anything together that is legal, ethical, moral, benefits the client, and makes money for both of us."

There is little doubt that RIA membership, with attendant technology transfer, increases member agencies' value. There is some risk that competitors will appropriate this increased value through takeovers, but it is minimal. Most RIA members are privately held, and their owners are heavily committed to their business and to the alliance. Moreover, much of the alliance's benefit is systemic, and is lost when cut off from its base.

The Role of IT

IT has played a critical role in the success of the RIA. It supports coordination, enabling global access to client itineraries and profiles and to RIA preferred rate programs and providing global consolidation of travel information. IT also facilitates monitoring and control of alliance performance on global accounts and special rate programs.

Despite the importance of IT, there is no massive, integrated proprietary computer system. Rather, IT has enabled RIA to offer global products and services before any integrated global infrastructure existed. The global market is characterized by fragmented, uncoordinated systems—islands of technology. RIA is exploiting the capabilities of existing systems, such as the various CRSs that span the globe and members' own back-office systems. Its success lies in linking these islands of technology to offer seamless integrated services. The RIA, like Rosenbluth in the United States, is attempting to lead the industry's evolution. As Hal Rosenbluth says, "There will eventually be an integrated industry infrastructure centered around two or three worldwide CRSs, but in the interim, there's tremendous opportunity for getting it right now, in today's imperfect environment."

Today, the RIA relies for its basic infrastructure on the Apollo CRS offered by Covia in the United States, Mexico, and Japan, by Gemini in Canada, and by Galileo in the rest of the world.[11] Members have access to the Apollo CRS for RIA business, but may use a different CRS to record reservations. This often occurs in markets that are dominated by closed, airline-supported systems.

A number of proprietary applications have been built on the Apollo system, which is collectively termed the RIA Global Distribution Network (GDN). All major CRSs permit the development of proprietary programs and databases and allow their integration with CRS functions. Rosenbluth and the RIA have been very aggressive users of this capability. Through the GDN, RIA members have access to an on-line directory of RIA partners as well as a messaging system for member communication.

The RIA Executive Traveler Hotel Program, which gives RIA members access to preferred rates at hotels around the world, is implemented as a proprietary application on Apollo. The system has been augmented with marketing information about the hotels to assist clients in making decisions. The proprietary application interfaces with Apollo's hotel management system to enable reservations to be booked and confirmed electronically at the negotiated rates on the hotels' systems. A record of all reservations is automatically routed through Apollo to Rosenbluth's back-office system, VISION, to support the consolidated monitoring of the program's performance that is essential to negotiating preferred rates.

The major CRSs can now be accessed through flexible and powerful workstations that can be programmed to customize the user dialogue with the CRS and proprietary applications. Again, Rosenbluth and the RIA have aggressively used this technology to provide integrated access to RIA's GDN applications and the reservations process. This capability has been used by some members to integrate RIA access to Apollo with normal access to their primary CRS through a Microsoft Windows application.

Authorized RIA members can now access global client profiles and itineraries directly through Apollo. The alliance worked actively with Covia to develop this capability, and is the first agency to utilize it aggressively. This capability enables a traveler originating in Philadelphia but needing service in London to be serviced by the U.K. RIA partner.

The Apollo CRS also serves as a backbone for global consolidation of travel information for multinational clients. Any transaction for a global client placed through Apollo by any RIA member can generate a record that can be transmitted to the member that manages the global account. To continue the earlier example, if our London traveler makes changes or additional reservations, a record of those transactions can be automatically routed to Rosenbluth in Philadelphia for consolidated reporting. It is this process that is currently used to monitor the hotel program worldwide.

This so-called front office consolidation, though clearly the ideal, is currently limited to transactions placed through Apollo. As noted earlier, Apollo is not well enough established in many markets to be useful as the local agency's primary CRS. Moreover, many smaller CRSs are not completely integrated for hotel room and car rental bookings. For these situations the RIA has implemented another approach called "back-office" consolidation, whereby each member providing service posts transactions for global accounts to its own back-office system. The formats and information to be included are established by prior agreement among members. Periodically the information is sent directly to the RIA member managing the global account for consolidated reporting. To accomplish this integration, the alliance is implementing proprietary linking systems built on X.25 packet switching standards.

The fragmented islands of technology will not remain isolated forever. The emergence of truly integrated global CRSs will eliminate many of the integration problems, making front-office consolidation practical for many clients. In the meantime, RIA views its ability to integrate now as a significant advantage. "Ultimately, global infrastructure will be a commodity," Hal Rosenbluth observes, "but by then our global advantage should be entrenched."

Rosenbluth is working closely with the Galileo/Covia/Gemini federation to shape the emergence of the global infrastructure and incorporate the latest capability into its own service and support offerings. Concurrently, RIA is working to develop a consistent back-office client MIS capability for all its members. The vision for the future is the capability to transfer information seamlessly across CRSs and RIA members to meet any foreseeable client need.

Analysis and Conclusions

Experience with RIA leads to three conclusions widely applicable to service providers that desire to expand globally.

- Cooperative relationships and cross-border partnerships will become increasingly common and increasingly important.
- IT is essential to coordinating these cooperative relationships.
- It is crucial that cross-border partnerships be based on similarity of objectives, style, company culture, trust, and on growing relationships; no amount of IT, and no array of contracts negotiated by attorneys specializing in international law, will make a partnership succeed unless these factors are held in common.

Cross-Border Cooperation

Cross-border cooperation may be the most effective way for service providers to achieve global scale and scope.

- Most service companies lack the financial and managerial resources needed to become truly global. It may be possible to enter some markets through growth or acquisition, but it will almost certainly not be possible to enter enough to provide full service.
- Many service markets are highly idiosyncratic. The expertise needed to practice law, deal in securities markets, or operate in the travel industry differs greatly among countries. In many travel markets, it will be necessary to have a local player, with well-established relationships with airlines and other service providers, in order to provide quality service under extraordinary conditions.

Both sets of circumstances argue for globalization through partnerships using local affiliates rather than opening one's own offices.

The Role of IT in Cross-Border Cooperation

Cooperation requires a complex balance of coordination and independence, monitoring and trust.[12] Common functions must be coordinated to benefit from economies of scale and facilitate technology transfer. Data must be consolidated to support global rate negotiation or, more generally, to exploit the purchasing power inherent in the union of partners. Innovation and best practice must be readily transferable among members, and global service must be synthesized out of a collection of independent agents performing in their local markets.

This degree of coordination, across continents and oceans, in real time, is only achievable through IT. RIA makes use of IT for a host of activities, including:

- sharing of customer profiles, company policy, and travel itineraries to enable service to follow executives without interruption as they travel around the globe, from one RIA member's home market to another's;
- consolidation of travel data for rate negotiation; and

- transfer of account management software from Rosenbluth to RIA members.

Finally, IT makes it possible for corporate clients, and for RIA members that initiate global account relationships, to assess the quality of service given and received almost immediately. If RIA relationships were not working successfully, it would readily be apparent.

The Role of Similar Objectives

No amount of IT reporting on the quality of partners' fulfillment of their reciprocal relationships, and no amount of legal contracting, would be sufficient to assure effective cross-border cooperation without common objectives and corporate cultures among the partners. Thus, members must be chosen carefully and an organization and infrastructure established that support cooperation. Cooperation works when the objectives of the parties are consistent and the incentives each sees are compatible.

A Model for the Future

RIA can usefully be viewed as a model for future efforts at cross-border expansion. When rapid expansion is necessary and significant differences among markets argue for reliance on local service providers, the RIA model appears to be the best way to meet the needs of globalization. Differences in local markets will also serve to protect each player from possible predatory attacks by defecting affiliates, reducing the risk of transferring expertise. The RIA model, among other things, accomplishes the following.

- It leverages the best available practice and rapidly transfers it among members.
- It achieves effective coordination through IT.
- It uses cooperating independent service providers to achieve seamless integrated global service.

That is to say, it has become an example of the emerging global virtual corporation.

The emergence of the global virtual corporation has interesting implications for achieving competitive advantage through IT. We have argued elsewhere that competitive advantage derived from IT is extremely difficult to sustain unless it exploits some unique resource advantage of the innovating firm.[13] Rosenbluth Travel discovered a novel way to sustain advantage domestically—by cascading each innovation and investing the results of short-term advantage until sufficient differentiation was achieved to ensure sustainability.[14] The very considerable size advantage Rosenbluth achieved by using IT to deliver superior service, for example, enabled the company to use technology to offer additional services, such as fare negotiations, which cannot now be offered by many smaller competitors. With RIA, Hal Rosenbluth has once again employed information technology for sustainable advantage, using IT in a cooperative manner to leverage both assets in which his firm enjoys an advantage (U.S. market share, technological skill, expertise in managing corporate travel) and assets his firm does not own (local expertise and presence throughout the world). This cooperative use of IT to coordinate assets not under direct ownership or control is a particularly timely and exciting way to gain competitive advantage.

Notes

1. Eric K. Clemons and Michael C. Row, "Ahead of the Pack through Vision and Hustle: A Case Study of Information Technology at Rosenbluth Travel," *Proceedings, 24th International Conference on System Sciences* (January 1991): 287–296; Clemons and Row, "Information Technology at Rosenbluth Travel: Competitive Advantage in a Rapidly Growing Global Service Company," *Journal of Management Information Systems,* 8, no. 2 (Fall 1991): 53–79.

2. Jay R. Galbraith, *Designing Complex Organizations* (Reading, Mass.: Addison-Wesley, 1973).

3. Clemons and Row, "Ahead of the Pack through Vision and Hustle" and "Information Technology at Rosenbluth Travel."

4. "Business Travel Survey," *Business Travel News,* May 13, 1991.

5. Founded 25 years ago to arrange fishing tours, Marlin Travel is a remarkably successful Canadian agency with 267 offices and current revenues of Cn\$ 650 million (a 12% market share). Marlin is still independently owned and operated and, in its home market, shows remarkable similarities to Rosenbluth Travel.

6. "Business Travel Survey."

7. Nurick is responsible for Rosenbluth's global strategy and implementation and was the primary architect and organizer of the RIA.

8. J. Carlos Jarillo and Joan Enric Ricart i Costa, "Sustaining Networks," *Interfaces,* 17, no. 5 (September–October 1987): 82–91; Raymond E. Miles and

Charles C. Snow, "Organizations: New Concepts for New Forms," *California Management Review,* 28, no. 3 (Spring 1986): 62–73; Hans B. Thorelli, "Networks: Between Markets and Hierarchies," *Strategic Management Journal,* 7 (1986): 37–51.

9. Christopher A. Bartlett and Sumantra Ghoshal, "Organizing for Worldwide Effectiveness: The Transnational Solution," *California Management Review,* 31, no. 1 (1988): 54–74.

10. Benjamin Klein, Robert G. Crawford, and Armen A. Alchian, "Vertical Integration, Appropriate Rents, and the Competitive Contracting Process," *Journal of Law and Economics,* 21, no. 2 (October 1978): 297–326; Oliver Williamson, *Markets and Hierarchies: Analysis and Antitrust Implications* (New York: Free Press, 1975).

11. Covia, Gemini, and Galileo have formed a federation to offer a global distributed CRS. Each is currently offering access to Covia's Apollo worldwide, but will eventually offer its own core system. All federation core systems will be fully integrated throughout the world. Galileo's system is currently being rolled out.

12. Eric K. Clemons and Michael C. Row, "Information Technology and Industrial Cooperation: The Changing Economics of Coordination and Ownership," *Journal of Management Information Systems,* 9, no. 2 (Fall 1992): 9–28; Thomas W. Malone, Joanne Yates, and Robert I. Benjamin, "Electronic Markets and Electronic Hierarchies," *Communications of the ACM,* 30, no. 6 (June 1987): 484–497.

13. Eric K. Clemons and Michael C. Row, "Structural Differences Among Firms: A Potential Source of Competitive Advantage in the Application of Information Technology," *Proceedings of the Eighth International Conference on Information Systems* (December 1987): 1–9; Clemons and Row, "Sustaining IT Advantage: The Role of Structural Differences," *Management Information Systems Quarterly,* 13, no. 5 (September 1991): 274–292.

14. Clemons and Row, "Ahead of the Pack through Vision and Hustle."

Part Five
Competing with Technology

Introduction

Enabling technologies are clearly critical to the way the competitive landscape develops. But the power of traditional providers of information technology, especially computers and telecommunications, to dictate the rate of enabling technology appears to be waning. Customers increasingly drive the technology, looking for seamless solutions to the problems that keep them from competing more effectively in highly competitive global industries.

For example, over the past 10 years IBM's power and dominance has been eroded to the point that it is unclear whether the company can retain its traditional role of establishing de facto industry standards. If it cannot, and many now believe this to be the case, how will this role be filled? AT&T has similarly provided de facto standards for telecommunications in the United States and, to a large degree, in the rest of the world. With the deregulation of much of the telecommunications industry, AT&T no longer has absolute power in the United States, although it still plays a very significant global role. What organization, if any, might assume AT&T's traditional role remains an open question. Given the highly competitive, evolving industries in which they are being asked, these are important questions and they must be answered.

Current responses of manufacturers of both computers and telecommunications equipment suggest that the traditional hardware leaders will be unable to meet their customers' needs in a timely manner. Given that hardware's inflexibility is proving to be a problem, it makes sense to reduce hardware to a standard form and make its production as efficient as possible, achieving the requisite flexibility through software. This appears already to be the direction of the computer industry, and the telecommunications industry may respond similarly.

The leaders in computers and telecommunications, being large established companies, simply cannot respond to market demands as fluidly as smaller, more flexible software firms. Hence, we expect leading software firms, such as Microsoft, Novell, Borland, and Lotus, to play an increasingly significant role in the Networking Era.

As we examine the key characteristics of networks, it becomes clear that not only connectivity, but what is communicated, is important. One type of networking technology is required to communicate by telephone, a very different type to communicate via still or video images. The notion of broadband communication is an important element of the network organization.

The three chapters in this section attempt to address the technology issues associated with enabling the network and assess the key players likely to serve this growth market. The message is that the network organization is serious business. Not only is the network organization manifest in successful organizations, but the major providers of information technology are attempting to understand the network organization and how to serve the market opportunities associated with it.

Competing Globally in Telecommunications

Massachusetts Institute of Technology professor Jerry Hausman is one of the leading academics studying the economics of the telecommunications industry. His chapter is a careful analysis of the industry and how it has evolved and is likely to evolve in the future. In particular, Hausman explains why the strategies of major telecommunications competitors are designed to expand globally. He assesses which competitors are likely to be most successful in their global expansion and in which technologies. Finally, he reviews the responses of various governments to the new global competition and makes some recommendations for effective government policy. Hausman concludes that over the next decade globalization will likely fundamentally alter the way telecommunications services are provided.

Seven Technologies That Matter

MicroAge chairman Alan Hald and Emory University professor Benn Konsynski discuss the key information technologies that will have an impact on organizations and competition over the next decade. First, the authors address information technology trends that are contributing to the notion of "information intensity" in organizations. Then, they consider the key information technologies responsible for information intensity and suggest that companies must monitor the evolution of these technologies in order to be able to forecast their impact on their respective industries.

The Broadband Society

Bill Marx, president of AT&T's Network Systems, addressed colloquium participants on the issue of building the broadband society, which AT&T has concluded is the end point for current trends in networking. Consequently, the company has set its sights on specifying this environment. Marx identifies how customers' needs, which in the past lagged technological innovation, are now driving technology, and relates his vision of what technology in the next century will be able to accomplish and the role AT&T will play in providing this new technology.

13

The Bell Operating Companies and AT&T Venture Abroad While British Telecom and Others Come to the United States

Jerry A. Hausman

For most of their history, the Bell operating companies (BOCs) and their corporate parent, American Telephone and Telegraph (AT&T), confined their operations to the United States. In the past five years, however, the BOCs have become involved in operating telecommunications networks in Europe, Latin America, Asia, and New Zealand, while AT&T has recently announced an agreement to provide telecommunications network equipment and to operate joint telephone networks in part of the former U.S.S.R. At the same time, British Telecom has made sizable investments in cellular telephone and data networks in the United States. NTT (Japan) and France Telecom are also planning international telecommunications networks for large corporate customers. This chapter first describes the historic changes in ownership and regulation of telecommunications service providers throughout the world that have led to this increase in international operations and competition, then goes on to consider the economic and business strategy reasons that have led previously all-domestic telecommunications operators to expand abroad in such an aggressive manner. After describing some recent examples of international expansion, we analyze the prospects for the success of these large international investments. We consider market evaluations of these investments as well. Lastly, we discuss appropriate government policy responses to the changes in telecommunications competition and requirements of large corporate customers.

Changes in government regulation can create increased competition among telecommunications providers, resulting in less expensive and higher quality services for users. Removal of trade barriers in telecommunications services should lead to increases in economic efficiency and economic welfare, as have other reductions in trade barriers over the past 30 years throughout the world.[1]

Historic Provision of Telecommunications Equipment and Services

Between World War I and about 1980 very little competition existed in the international telecommunications industry. AT&T in the United States and government-run operations in England, France, Germany, and Japan provided local and long-distance telephone service with little or no competition. These telephone operations also provided all the telephone equipment used in their networks and by their customers. AT&T manufactured equipment, while the non-U.S. telephone operations typically bought almost all of their equipment from one or two domestic suppliers, called "country champions." Thus, international competition was almost completely absent; for instance, AT&T did not attempt to sell its technologically advanced network equipment to telephone operators in other countries.

AT&T in the United States

Prior to its divestiture in 1984, AT&T was almost the sole domestic provider of telecommunications service and equipment, providing about 80% of local telephone service lines in the United States and an even larger percentage of long-distance service. Output of its manufacturing company, Western Electric, was sold almost entirely to local Bell operating companies and AT&T Long Lines (AT&T's former provider of long-distance services).[2] Thus, the pre-divestiture Bell System was to a large extent a self-sufficient organization, neither importing nor exporting services or manufactured products.

AT&T's international involvement was limited by a 1920s agreement with the U.S. government not to compete abroad.[3]

At the time of divestiture, AT&T provided most international service to and from the United States through agreements negotiated with foreign PTTs (postal and telephone and telegraph companies that provide domestic and international telephone service), but it did not provide telephone service within any foreign country. More important, AT&T did not manufacture or export telecommunications equipment abroad after the mid-1920s.[4]

ITT in the Rest of the World

Founded in 1920, International Telephone and Telegraph (ITT) was the U.S.-based competitor in international telecommunications.[5] AT&T, prohibited by a commitment to the U.S. Department of Justice from making further acquisitions, agreed in 1925 to a division of the world market whereby it would compete only in the United States and ITT would compete throughout the rest of the world.[6] ITT was a fully integrated telecommunications company that operated entirely outside the United States, providing domestic telephone service in a number of countries in Latin America and Spain and manufacturing telecommunications equipment in Europe, South America, China, Australia, and Japan.

Over a two-year period in the 1940s, ITT was forced to sell its two largest telephone service operations to national governments: to Spain in 1945 and Argentina in 1946.[7] But the company retained a monopoly or near-monopoly position to provide equipment for these repatriated telephone companies and, together with traditional competitors Ericsson and Siemens, remained an important competitor in international telecommunications markets up to the mid-1980s, when NEC and other Japanese companies entered the picture. But ITT was unable to make the transition to computer-controlled telecommunications switches and, in 1987, merged all of its equipment manufacturing operations in a joint venture controlled by the state-owned French company Cie. Générale d'Electricite (CGE).[8] Although the new company, Alcatel, achieved moderate success, ITT gradually withdrew from the telecommunications equipment manufacturing market. In March 1992, ITT sold off what remained of its holdings in Alcatel, thus completing its exit from the telecommunications industry.

Telephone Operations in Europe and Japan

The U.S. pattern, in which a single domestic entity provided essentially all domestic telecommunications services, was emulated by many other developed countries. One important difference, however, was that in most of these other countries, including England, France, Germany, and Japan, a government entity, the PTT, provided telecommunications services along with postal services.[9] PTT provision of telecommunications services, saddled with raising large cross-subsidies to support postal services, tended to be quite inefficient compared to that of the U.S. system. Foreign domestic telephone companies also bought most of their telecommunications equipment from a domestic equipment provider closely affiliated with the telecommunications service provider.[10]

Privatization and Competition Come to Telecommunications

During the 1980s, two extremely important changes occurred in the international telecommunications industry. First, the divestiture of AT&T considerably reduced the size of the base organization. The AT&T that remains provides domestic and international long-distance services and manufactures telecommunications equipment and faces competition in both of these areas. The BOCs provide local telecommunications services and cellular services. Competition is increasing for the BOCs, but it has not reached AT&T's level of competition. In Europe and Japan, the former nationalized telecommunications providers were privatized, and in some countries, have begun to face significant competition. At the same time, the BOCs and AT&T have begun to compete abroad while British Telecom (BT) and other foreign providers have begun to compete in the United States and other countries. In this section, we discuss the economic and business reasons for this expansion of international competition in telecommunications: (1) the ability to use expertise in telecommunications and apply it in foreign countries—economies of scope, and (2) the strategy of "following your customers abroad," which has become increasingly important as large multinational companies create corporate telecommunications networks that merge their computer networks and telecommunications networks into integrated worldwide operations.

Traditional Telecommunications Services

The 1982 Modification of Final Judgment (MFJ) led to the divestiture of AT&T, the primary U.S. telecommunications provider. The firm was divided into AT&T, which provides long-distance services and manufactures telecommunications equipment, and seven independent regional Bell operating companies (RBOCs), which provide local telecommunications and cellular telephone services. Long-distance competition among AT&T, MCI, Sprint, and a host of smaller long-distance companies became firmly established during the 1980s. Indeed, the competitive pressure from MCI and Sprint has become sufficiently intense that the Federal Communications Commission (FCC) has decided to eliminate price regulation for AT&T's long-distance service to businesses.[11] The RBOCs, which provide local basic exchange services and some intrastate long-distance services, also face increasing competition. Competition for residential services remains quite limited, but competition for other large user services has increased greatly. In large U.S. cities, for example, competitive access providers (CAPs), such as Teleport and Metropolitan Fiber System, provide fiber-optic local services for larger customers and government agencies that compete directly with BOC-provided services.

When the U.K. government privatized British Telecom in 1984, it permitted a competitive long-distance provider, Mercury, to enter the market.[12] Shares of BT were floated, with wide public participation in purchases of the company. In 1991, the U.K. government opened competition to unlimited entry and introduced a liberal policy for foreign holding of the cable franchises that had begun to compete with BT at the local level.[13] These moves have made Britain's by far the most competitive framework for competition in telecommunications in Europe.

France, Germany, Sweden, and other European countries have separated their telecommunications providers and postal services, but the resulting entities (e.g., France Telecom) remain state-owned companies. Moreover, only Sweden has permitted more than limited competition in traditional voice telecommunications services. Cross-subsidies, and, consequently, economic inefficiencies in provision of telecommunications services are likely to remain for the foreseeable future.[14] Harmonization of markets, beginning in the European Economic Community (EEC) in 1992, will have only limited effect on domestic telecommunications service provision unless current regulations are significantly modified.

Japan has followed a pro-competitive approach to telecommunications, privatizing both its main domestic (NTT) and international (KDD) service providers. Japan has permitted three domestic long-distance carriers to compete with NTT for business in the Osaka to Tokyo corridor, in which much of Japanese industry is located; and provision of a competitive fiber-optic ring for local services has created competition for large businesses in Tokyo. An international competitor for KDD has also inaugurated service. Indeed, in 1993, Japan was the only country in which a call from the United States was more expensive than a call in the opposite direction.

Competition in Cellular Telephones

Competition in cellular telephones began within the original regulatory framework in the United States. In 1980, the FCC decided to have two cellular carriers compete in each cellular market rather than allow only a single provider as AT&T had recommended.[15] The largest U.S. provider of cellular service is currently McCaw, which had no previous telecommunications experience before entering the industry. An extremely dynamic and rapidly growing service in the United States, cellular telephone's average annual growth has exceeded 50% per year since the service's inception in 1983.

The U.K. government also adopted the duopoly framework for cellular telephones, with BT and Racal competing to provide service.[16] In 1989, the United Kingdom granted three additional licenses for mobile telecommunications firms to establish personal communications networks, which are currently under construction and expected to be delivering service during 1993.

Many other countries initially allocated cellular telephone service solely to their domestic telephone service providers. But Germany, Sweden, Norway, Japan, and New Zealand subsequently adopted the competitive duopoly framework that prevails in the United States and United Kingdom.[17] Competition is thus well established in cellular telephone service throughout North America, Japan, and Europe.

Limited Entry by Foreign Providers

In each of the situations discussed so far, all competitive entry was by domestic companies. MCI and Sprint and all the non-BOC cellular providers are U.S. companies; Mercury and Racal are U.K. companies. This competitive approach has an important limitation in that it precludes competition by foreign firms involved in providing similar services abroad.[18] Experience gained in providing a telecommunications service in one country can often lead to cost efficiencies in providing the same service in another country—economies of scope. That economies of scope can be an important economic factor is demonstrated by the U.S. experience with cellular service providers, which have expanded geographically far beyond their original service territories by acquiring other cellular providers. Consolidation in the U.S. cellular industry continues, with the expectation that joint ventures among cellular providers will become more important in the next few years.

Countries that have permitted competition in cellular services have permitted foreign interests to contribute expertise by forming joint ventures with domestic companies. Pacific Telesis, for example, owns 26% of the cellular telephone provider, Mannesmann Mobilfunk GmbH, that competes with the German telephone company, Deutsche Bundespost Telekom. The U.K. government similarly permitted non-U.K. companies to join the consortia that bid for personal communications network (PCN) licenses.

Many countries nevertheless continue to limit the amount of foreign participation in telecommunications service provision. In the United States, for example, the proportion of foreign holdings permitted in a telecommunications company is limited to 25%. National security, often discussed in conjunction with limitations on foreign participation, seems an outmoded concern for such nonessential services as cellular telephones and for services, such as long distance, for which multiple sources of supply exist. A further anachronism of the pre-competition framework of telecommunications is the practice of "giving away" franchises for mobile telecommunications through awards instead of through competitive bidding or some other economic approach.[19] Spectrum is a scarce resource, and competitive bidding would ensure that it is used in an economically efficient manner.

Incentives for Foreign Expansion by U.S. Companies

The MFJ bars the Bell operating companies from providing many telecommunications services within the United States.[20] BOCs have been permitted to provide cellular service outside their home regions since 1986, and have competed quite successfully with other cellular providers. Because the MFJ allows them almost unlimited foreign activity, BOCs clearly have an economic incentive to employ their expertise and economies of scope to expand their operations abroad.[21] Consequently, the BOCs have pursued aggressive expansion policies in Europe, Latin America, and New Zealand, providing local, long-distance, and cellular telephone services. Success in these foreign ventures will require massive cultural change for these previously all-domestic companies. The economic and regulatory environments the BOCs will encounter will be radically different from the highly legalistic regulatory frameworks of the FCC and state commissions.

AT&T also has significant economic incentives to expand abroad, particularly in its telecommunications equipment manufacturing division, now called AT&T Network Systems. Telecommunications equipment manufacturing is today characterized by extremely high fixed costs, mainly for software development, and much lower variable costs of manufacturing, particularly for central office switches, the computers that control telecommunications networks.[22] Thus, AT&T has established joint ventures to provide central office switches in the Netherlands, Spain, and Italy. Eastern Europe and the former Soviet Union, given their limited and antiquated telecommunications networks, represent the next great opportunity for telecommunications equipment manufacturers. AT&T announced in January 1992 that it will provide central office switches in the Ukraine, as well as become a 39% partner in the domestic telephone service provider, effectively reentering the local telephone service industry outside the United States.[23]

"Following Your Customers Abroad"

Given the increasing globalization of foreign competition, large corporations will want to set up corporate telecommunications networks that integrate their own computer equipment with the public networks in each country. Companies like Volvo and General Motors, for example, will want telecommunications networks that can operate in many countries without having to customize the local part of the network to each country's regulatory framework. Significant economic advantage will arise for any telecommunications network provider that has the ability to interact with a single point of contact rather than with each domestic telecommunications provider. This international corporate network expansion represents another important incentive for foreign expansion for BT, France Telecom, NTT, KDD, AT&T, MCI, Swedish Telecom, and other domestic providers.

These same providers are establishing joint ventures and other forms of partnerships in an effort to follow their major customers abroad. BT, though it has been particularly aggressive in pursuing joint ventures, has made only limited progress to date. Its Atlanta-based Syncordia Corporation, which provides global facilities management, international private line services, and international telecommunications outsourcing services for large corporations, as well as multilingual customer service, custom designs for networks, and assumed service levels, has reportedly signed up only one major customer so far.

Other telephone companies have also begun to establish international network services for their large customers. AT&T has announced a similar international service, Accumaster Management Service, to provide worldwide integrated operations for large multinational corporations. AT&T, however, has already encountered regulatory problems. In the United Kingdom, AT&T can manage both voice and data services because of the outcome of the duopoly review discussed above. But in the rest of Europe, AT&T cannot manage voice networks; instead it is limited to data networks only. This restriction arises because European countries, apart from the United Kingdom, still do not permit competition with their monopoly telephone companies on voice networks.

France Telecom and Deutsche Bundespost Telekom have also announced a joint venture to provide international network services. The partnership, called Eunetcom, will compete with BT's Syncordia and AT&T's Accumaster to provide worldwide voice and data services. To some extent, Eunetcom is a defensive response to BT's Syncordia. An important future development will be the choice of a partner by NTT, the Japanese provider. A possible favorable outcome from these new joint ventures will be deregulation and increased competition for voice services in France, Germany, and eventually the remainder of the EEC. As Eunetcom and its partners attempt to expand internationally, they are likely to be met with demands to deregulate their own home territories.

With rates controlled by national governments and only limited competition permitted, international telephone service has been extremely profitable. The U.K. regulatory agency for telecommunications, OFTEL, has estimated rates of return to capital of about 80% to 85% on international services for BT during the years 1989–1991.[24] However, given modern technology, a call originating in London and destined for New York can be placed going in either direction. The existence of a significant price differential for calls in either direction creates an incentive for economic arbitrage. Furthermore, the aggregation of traffic onto unswitched bulk facilities (e.g., DS-1 or DS-3) provides an additional opportunity for customers to escape paying the high international MTS rates. If BT has account control over a U.K. company's network, instead of EDS control of the network, BT is likely to achieve a higher return on international traffic.

These formerly domestic telecommunications providers will find themselves competing with systems integrators, such as EDS, which will offer similar services to large international corporations. It is not clear that domestic telecommunications providers will have a competitive advantage when they venture abroad to provide network services to large companies. Highly regulated companies that face limited competition in their domestic markets may find it difficult to compete, although pre-existing links with other domestic telecommunications providers may offer some competitive advantages.[25]

BOC and BT Acquisitions Abroad: Some Examples

The BOCs' penetration of foreign and BT's penetration of U.S. telecommunications services markets through acquisitions has increased rapidly over the past few years, with no drop-off in activity as has occurred in other international acquisitions during the 1991–1993 period. Many of these acquisitions (e.g., in cellular and personal communications networks) are associated with extremely dynamic technologies, which present investment situations likely to deteriorate much less than acquisitions in less dynamic industries. Moreover, the political situation has changed fundamentally in numerous Latin American countries, such as Mexico and Argentina, creating new opportunities for U.S. investment. Similar opportunities for investment are emerging in Eastern Europe and the former Soviet Union as a result of the fundamental political changes of the past two to three years. In this section, we offer some recent examples of international investment in telecommunications service markets by the BOCs and BT, then consider economic and business strategy evaluations and stock market evaluations of the prospects for success of these investments.

Cellular Telephones

Pacific Telesis joined a consortium led by a German company without telecommunications experience in order to enter a bid to become West Germany's second cellular provider. The country's current provider, the German telephone company, Deutsche Bundespost Telekom, had not expanded cellular service at rates near the growth rates in the United Kingdom or Scandinavia. The consortium, Mannesmann Mobilfunk GmbH, was awarded the contract at the end of 1989, beating out two other consortia, both of which also had other BOCs as partners. Since reunification, the license has been extended to cover the whole of Germany. Because the license required the consortium to provide cellular service over all of Germany, it has been forced to make an extremely large investment; but the attendant opportunities hold great promise. Cellular service may, for example, provide a cost-effective substitute for regular telephone service in the former East Germany, with its antiquated telecommunications infrastructure. Moreover, as the technology being used in Germany by Pacific Telesis is the "next generation" digital standard planned for use throughout Europe, a successful network operation in Germany could yield future opportunities for the company in other European countries.

Bell South has been awarded licenses throughout Latin America. In 1988, it participated in a consortium that received a license in Argentina; it added Mexico in 1990, and Venezuela in 1991. Bell South also successfully bid for the second cellular license in New Zealand and is currently constructing a cellular network to compete with that of the existing provider, formerly the national telecommunications provider, which has been privatized and sold to U.S. and European companies.[26]

Bell Atlantic was awarded a cellular contract for Czechoslovakia in 1990, and U.S. West has been awarded contracts in both Hungary and the former Soviet Union. Numerous additional cellular contracts can be expected to be awarded in the former Soviet Republics over the next few years.

Personal Communications Networks

The United Kingdom's Department of Trade and Industry licensed three consortia to provide personal communications networks at the end of 1989. Each of the three partnerships comprised one or more U.K. companies, but all had foreign partners as well, among them Pacific Telesis and U.S. West.

PCNs, sometimes referred to as the "next generation" cellular technology, are designed to use advanced signaling systems to support "personal phone numbers" that will permit communications independent of a subscriber's geographical location. PCNs are also designed to be within the microwave region of the radio spectrum (cellular is in the UHF television range) and to employ many low-powered transmitters to achieve greater reuse of the spectrum and possible subscriber base than current cellular systems.[27]

PCN technology, a new digital technology that will push the limits of digital radio, is considerably riskier than the analog technology used in cellular systems, which was at least 25 years old when deployed in the United States. The investment will be considerable, given the requirement to provide nationwide U.K. coverage. Indeed, Pacific Telesis sold its share of the consortia in 1991, in part because of the high investment costs and the company's concentration on its cellular operation in Germany. The FCC is currently allowing experiments with PCNs (called PCSs in the United States) and is likely to take action during 1993 (the U.K. network is expected to begin operation this year).

While the future role of PCSs in the United States is not clear, most BOCs attempted to become involved in the technological development of PCNs in the United Kingdom because they saw it as potentially the next important telecommunications technology.

Cable Television

Until October 1991, the information services restriction of the MFJ prohibited BOCs from providing cable television service within the United States. That restriction has now been lifted, the Cable Act of 1984 still bars BOCs from providing cable television within their own regions. Although the FCC is currently proposing that the cable provision be modified to permit BOCs to provide "video dial tone," congressional action is highly uncertain given the enormous financial stakes, which have led both groups to hire teams of lawyers and lobbyists.[28]

Cable television has the potential to provide significant competition in local telephone service. As cable networks change from coaxial cable to fiber-optic-based systems, they gain the ability to carry large amounts of voice and data, unencumbered by the network architecture. In the United States, cable networks, quick to recognize this potential opportunity, are developing experimental systems to explore PCSs. Cox Cable and TCI, two of the largest cable companies, have also bought from Merrill Lynch a substantial share in Teleport, a provider of competing local telephone services to large businesses.

Cable television is much less developed in Europe than in the United States, where it passes over 90% of all residences with about a 62% subscription rate. Among those taking advantage of the resulting opportunity are NYNEX, which has bought cable television systems in a number of U.K. cities; Southwest Bell, which has also purchased systems in the United Kingdom, though less extensively than NYNEX; and U.S. West, which has bought systems in both the United Kingdom and Hong Kong. An economic question arises as to how successful cable will be in the United Kingdom, given satellite competition, which is already well developed. Nevertheless, the BOCs are planning to offer voice and data telecommunications services over their U.K. cable networks, perhaps to determine how competitive the technology might be in the United States.

Telephone Networks

The BOCs' greatest potential competitive advantage lies in operating telephone networks abroad. The technology has become common across countries, with the same models of computer-controlled central office switches used in the United States, Europe, Japan, and South America. BOCs have also developed numerous computer-controlled systems for maintenance and planning that might be used abroad. Given the privatization of national telecommunications companies and the desire to import foreign technology to bring national telecommunications networks up to Information Age standards for globally based companies, the BOCs have a natural competitive advantage.

Bell South bought a major stake in New Zealand Telecom when it was privatized and sold to investors. Indeed, New Zealand has perhaps gone further in the privatization of its telecommunications network than any country except the United States, where companies historically have been privately owned. Telephone, cellular, and television have all been affected by New Zealand's privatization program.

Latin America has provided the other major opportunity for the BOCs. Southwest Bell, selected by the Mexican government to run much of its telephone network, has quadrupled its investment since assuming a financial interest in the system, and GTE has a major stake in, and will provide assistance in operating, the Venezuelan telecommunications network.[29] Both the opportunities and risks of participation in Latin America are great. The Salinas government clearly wants change in Mexico, but the successor government may be much less pro–free trade and friendly to U.S. involvement in its economy, and the failed coup attempt in Venezuela in January 1992 demonstrates the potential for political instability. Yet another potential problem is the tradition of corruption, often enforced in part by the labor unions, associated with telecommunications in virtually every Latin American country. The Foreign Corrupt Practices Act of 1977, enacted in part in response to activities of ITT, attempts to limit bribery by outlawing payments to foreign officials that result in a distinct change in operations for Latin American telecommunications companies.[30] Providing telephone service to large portions of the population without monopoly prices could greatly aid economic development throughout much of Latin America.

BT Investment in the United States

British Telecom has made significant investments in the United States. It bought a 20% stake in McCaw, the largest cellular provider in the United States (BT already operates one of the largest cellular networks in the world in London), and is a partner with McCaw in a number of the largest U.S. cities, including New York, Los Angeles, and San Francisco. BT also bought Tymnet, the second-largest value-added (data) network in the United States (value-added networks, VANs, have enjoyed extremely fast growth rates in the United States). Its investment may reflect an effort to gain experience in VANs, since competition in VANs is expected to grow in the wake of European integration in 1992. VANs are not nearly as restricted in competition with the national telecommunications providers as are traditional voice networks within the EEC. Moreover, the expected future integration of data and voice with full digital technology may enable BT to add significant value to its U.S. operations. The recent decision to allow BOCs to enter information services in the United States makes the future success of Tymnet less certain. Competition in VANs can be expected to grow, but with the BOCs still barred from providing long-distance services, VANs may receive increased traffic as new BOC information service offerings shift the demand curve outward.

Prospects for Success

None of these foreign investments are guaranteed to be successful. Indeed, critics have claimed that BOC diversification efforts have been largely unsuccessful and that the public would be better served if the BOCs concentrated on providing high-quality local telephone service in the United States.[31] But given the economic incentives to apply their telecommunications network and cellular expertise, continued BOC investment abroad is likely.[32] The areas in which prospects for success seem brightest are cellular and network services.

Cellular services. To date, all countries except New Zealand have awarded their cellular licenses "free" in a duopoly (two-provider) framework. Since neither costs nor extreme price competition should pose profit problems, the major factor for success is whether sufficient cellular demand exists in Europe and Latin

America. Although commuting by automobile is much less prevalent in Europe, even in the United States portable sales now comprise about 50% of cellular sales. Latin America, with its poorly developed public transit, is closer to the United States in terms of dependence on the automobile. Hence, BOC investments in cellular service are likely to be successful overall.

Network services. Network services is the other category of BOC investment likely to be successful. Here the success criterion will be economies of scope, which will support the shift of knowledge and expertise to Latin America and Eastern Europe. Political risk, particularly in Latin America, remains an important consideration given the high visibility of the telephone network. But the increasing importance of globalization and trade should lead most governments to think twice before expropriating U.S. or other foreign investments. The uneven development of many Latin American countries, with limited modernization outside major cities, may be problematic, insofar as it incurs obligations to provide modern telephone service to rural areas through enforced cross-subsidies. Overall, however, the prospects seem favorable for network service investments by BOCs.

Personal communications networks. Technological uncertainty puts the future success of PCNs in question. Nevertheless, the technology has the potential to be an important competitor in the field of mobile telecommunications, in which the BOCs now have a favorable position. If the FCC keeps BOCs out of PCNs because of their presence in cellular service, BOCs may use their U.K. experience to develop expertise that they can subsequently apply in other countries. A potentially more important reason for BOCs to participate in PCNs in the United Kingdom is the possibility that they might eventually compete directly with local network service, which is the BOCs' core business in the United States.

Cable television. The most problematical category of BOC investment abroad may well be cable television. BOCs lack experience with cable, and cable lacks economies of scope with other BOC operations. Nor do BOCs have experience in programming, considered a crucial aspect of successful cable operation. Nevertheless, experience with cable television may serve BOCs well by preparing them for two eventualities: cable as a competitive threat to their core networks, and congressional reversal of restrictions on the BOCs' full participation in cable.

Preliminary Measurement of Prospects

Prospects for the success of these investments can be measured in a preliminary way using a methodology termed an "event study." An event study measures how much the price of a stock changes at the time of an announcement. Although only estimates, event studies are widely used in empirical finance studies to anticipate effects of changes in regulations, outcomes of acquisitions, and so forth. Adjustments to stock price changes are required, for example, when the awarding of a contract becomes public knowledge before it is announced or when changes in a stock price are unrelated to the awarding of a contract. These adjustments are made using the capital asset pricing model, which is widely used in financial economics to account for market changes at the time of an award.[33]

Cellular investments have been received very favorably by the stock market. The 8.5% increase in Pacific Telesis's stock that accompanied its award of the German cellular contract represents a gain of hundreds of millions of dollars to Pacific's shareholders.[34] Similarly, Venezuela's award of its cellular contract to Bell South increased the market value of Bell South by about 5%, again a substantial gain in market value.

BT's investment in McCaw, however, has not paid off to date. Although it paid a significant premium for its stock in McCaw, BT did not gain corporate control, which is usually the reason for paying a premium. Market price to date has not reached a level to make the investment particularly successful, and it is unclear how the McCaw investment fits BT's strategy, since it is not consistent with the "following your customers abroad" strategy discussed earlier. Furthermore, BT has no special expertise in operating cellular networks that can add value to McCaw's operations.

PCN awards have also been favorably viewed by the stock market; Pacific Telesis stock, for example, increased by 3.1% upon its winning the U.K.'s PCN contract.

The stock market has also been receptive to telephone network investments. Southwest Bell's stock increased by 4.8% when it was awarded the contract to operate the Mexican telephone network. Subsequent experience has also been favorable; to date, the value of Southwest Bell's investment in the Mexican phone company has approximately quadrupled. Similarly, Pacific Telesis's investment in the IDC trans-Pacific network precipitated a 2.9% increase in its market value.

Investments in cable television have been viewed less favorably. Pacific Telesis's market value decreased by about 1% with its U.K. cable investment, and Southwest Bell's stock decreased by 0.6% with its investment in U.K. cable television operations. Cable is not perceived to have anything close to the profit potential of other BOC investments; this perception is consistent with the view that BOCs lack a competitive advantage in running cable networks.

Government Policy Response

Telecommunications will continue to globalize and to accommodate increased international trade and the geographic dispersion of corporate operations. Competition among telecommunications providers seems bound to increase as companies export their expertise and attempt to follow their large domestic customers abroad. But telecommunications has traditionally been highly regulated, often to the point of governments' operating the telephone network. Will governments decrease trade restrictions on telecommunications services in keeping with the elimination of trade barriers for products and equipment?

The U.K. government is by far the most progressive in terms of allowing foreign investment in telecommunications. Its PCNs all have foreign partners. Moreover, in its duopoly review in 1991, the U.K. government removed remaining restrictions on telecommunications competition, opening the door to U.S. long-distance companies such as U.S. Sprint, which has announced it is seeking a license to join BT and Mercury as the United Kingdom's third major carrier.[35]

Most other European countries lag the United Kingdom considerably in permitting privatization, competition, and foreign investment in telecommunications (excluding cellular service). Many European governments continue to view their telecommunications networks as an element of basic infrastructure that has traditionally been provided by government. These attitudes may change with the harmonization of the EEC beginning in 1992. But for the present, domestic telephone service is largely insulated from EEC regulations. Thus, competition for large businesses and toll service may not occur soon. As improved telecommunications make headquarters locations for businesses become increasingly mobile, governments may ease regulations somewhat. However, neither privatization nor significant competitive deregulation is likely in the near future in most of Western Europe.

For its part, the U.S. government should consider removing the historic 25% restriction on foreign ownership of U.S. telecommunications companies. Were BT to acquire all of McCaw, for example, how would the national interest be hurt? As another cellular provider would continue to exist in each of McCaw's cellular markets, national security interests would be unaffected. Nor is national security a particularly persuasive argument with respect to local exchange and toll services. National security concerns should be receding in importance, and the government operates much of its network privately anyway.

Another consideration is strategic. The United States has a comparative advantage in providing telecommunications services, as the contract awards discussed previously demonstrate. Some might argue, therefore, that the United States should make bilateral deals as a lever to force foreign markets open, for example, in Western Europe. This strategy is not likely to gain much for the United States since some countries, e.g., the United Kingdom, have less restrictive markets. Were the United States to reduce its restrictions now, domestic competition would likely increase, with subsequent benefits to both businesses and consumers. Given increasing globalization and the "follow your customers" strategy, foreign entry can be expected to increase in the United States. Such entry might well be via joint ventures or partnerships, but foreign companies should not be subject to restrictions that would constrain future increases in their financial interest in the venture.

Conclusions

Globalization is likely to change fundamentally the provision of telecommunications services over the next decade. The trend toward privatization and competition has spread from the United States to a number of countries. Improvements in providing telecommunications services will enable globalization to occur more quickly, in numerous other industries, which, in turn, will foster globalization in the telecommunications industry.

Countries such as Singapore have partly designed their industrial strategy around the provision of world-class telecommunications. Given the United States' significant comparative advantage in providing telecommunications services throughout the world, U.S. government policy should eliminate undue obstacles to foreign investment by U.S. providers. Dismantling U.S. trade barriers is likely to benefit both domestic consumers and domestic businesses.

Notes

1. Research funds for this project were provided by the Massachusetts Institute of Technology Telecommunications Economics Research Program.

2. Infrequently, AT&T sold telecommunications equipment to independent telephone companies, such as Rochester Telephone, and Bell operating companies purchased small amounts of telecommunications equipment from companies other than Western Electric, such as NEC and Northern Electric. However, the large majority of BOC equipment purchases were from Western Electric.

3. AT&T, through International Western Electric, manufactured telephone equipment in Europe until after World War I, when the latter company's assets were purchased by ITT. The early history of the Bell System and its various agreements with the U.S. government are described briefly by Peter Temin in *The Fall of the Bell System* (New York: Cambridge University Press, 1987): 9–13.

4. AT&T, until the mid-1970s the clear technological leader worldwide in telecommunications equipment, licensed its technology to foreign companies, such as NEC and Northern Telecom.

5. For a history of the early ITT, see R. Sobel, *ITT* (New York: Times Books, 1982).

6. ITT purchased the international manufacturing assets of Western Electric in 1925, after the U.S. government strongly recommended that AT&T divest itself of those assets. At the same time, AT&T agreed not to compete overseas and ITT not to compete in the United States. Further discussion of ITT's early history and its dealings with AT&T can be found in Sobel, *ITT*, 41–44.

7. ITT received substantial payments for both companies, so in no sense were they expropriated by the national governments.

8. See J. Hausman and E. Kohlberg, "The Future Evolution of the Central Office Switch Industry," in S. P. Bradley and J. Hausman, eds., *Future Competition in Telecommunications* (Boston: Harvard Business School Press, 1989) for a discussion of ITT's exit from telecommunications equipment manufacturing in the late 1980s.

9. In Japan, domestic and international services were divided between two companies that did not compete with one another.

10. The country champion framework is discussed at length in Hausman and Kohlberg, "The Future Evolution of the Central Office Switch Industry."

11. The FCC continues to regulate, albeit in a more flexible manner, AT&T's long-distance service to residential customers (see FCC, "Competition

in the Interstate Interexchange Marketplace," CC Docket no. 90-132, September 16, 1991).

12. Mercury is a corporate affiliate of Cable and Wireless, a U.K.-based company that has provided telephone service in Hong Kong and other former British colonies for many years.

13. OFTEL, "Modifications of the Conditions of the License of British Telecommunications PLC," September 1991.

14. Cross-subsidies continue in the United States, but have become smaller since divestiture. In France, in contrast, equipment manufacturers receive cross-subsidies, and the government recently proposed that the French computer company, Bull, also be cross-subsidized by France Telecom.

15. *Notice of Inquiry and Notice of Proposed Rulemaking,* 78 FCC 2d 984 (1980).

16. There is an important difference between the United States and other countries that have adopted the competitive framework for cellular service. The United States has awarded 733 different licenses that correspond to different metropolitan and rural service areas, whereas all other countries have awarded nationwide licenses.

17. Hong Kong is the only nation to date to permit more than two cellular service competitors.

18. A new domestic competitor can overcome this limitation to some extent by hiring personnel away from the existing domestic company. But management systems and technology remain limited by the framework.

19. To date, only New Zealand has adopted competitive bidding for telecommunication licenses (although both the United States and United Kingdom are considering changes to their licensing frameworks). See, for example, U.S. Department of Commerce, NTIA, *U.S. Spectrum Management Policy,* Chapter 4 (U.S. GPO, 1991).

20. The BOCs were limited by the 1984 MFJ to providing essentially only local, nearby toll, and cellular services. In 1991, BOCs received permission to provide information services as well. But they continue, with minor exceptions, to be barred from providing long-distance, toll, and cable TV services.

21. The BOCs face a significant disadvantage in manufacturing telecommunications products or being partners in joint ventures that manufacture such equipment abroad, since almost all telecommunications equipment markets are now international. Because the MFJ forbids them to sell foreign-manufactured products in which they have a financial interest in the United States, BOCs are unlikely to be involved in either R&D or manufacturing efforts abroad. For further discussion, see J. A. Hausman, "Joint Ventures, Strategic Alliances, and Collaboration in Telecommunications," *Regulation* 14, 1991: 69–76.

22. This economic situation developed in the 1960s with the change from electromechanical to computer-driven central office switches. See Hausman and Kohlberg, "The Future Evolution of the Central Office Switch Industry, for a discussion of increased global competition in central office switches.

23. AT&T will face competition from Siemens, Alcatel, and Ericsson, the major European manufacturers of central office switches. Lack of tradable currency may limit the modernization of telephone networks in Eastern Europe and the former Soviet Union in the short term, but modernization can be expected in the medium term, with a significant foreign presence in each country.

24. OFTEL, "The Regulation of BT's Prices" (January 1992): 31. Calculation of these types of regulatory rates of return are notoriously unreliable;

nevertheless, the magnitude of the rate of return is likely to signify a profitable service.

25. AT&T, BT, France Telecom, and KDD have jointly agreed to provide expedited service with a single point of contact to improve service for global corporate telecommunications networks.

26. New Zealand put its cellular license up for bid; all other countries have awarded licenses on the basis of proposed networks, without fees for use of the radio spectrum.

27. In London, New York, and Los Angeles conventional (analog) cellular networks are beginning to approach their practical capacity limits. The introduction of digital cellular systems over the next few years might increase capacity by a factor of between 3 and 8.

28. Under the video dial tone proposal, a BOC could provide common carriage for TV programs, but not own separate cable channels or originate programming. The BOCs' aim is to be allowed to provide common carriage over part of the available cable channels (upward of 150 on fiber-optic cable) and programming on some other fraction of the channels.

29. GTE, since its acquisition of Contel in 1991, is the largest provider of local telephone service in the United States. Though not a descendent of the Bell System, GTE purchases most of its telecommunications equipment from AT&T.

30. Public Law 95-213 [S. 305], December 19, 1977.

31. These critics often confuse their own economic interests with the interest of BOC shareholders. Such confusion is endemic in regulation proceedings in the United States.

32. Whereas both the BOCs and GTE have invested abroad in telephone and cellular, McCaw, the largest cellular operator in the United States, has made no investments abroad (perhaps because of its extreme indebtedness, which may well constrain its actions).

33. See, for example, R. A. Brealey and S. C. Myers, *Principles of Corporate Finance,* 4th ed. (New York: McGraw-Hill, 1991): Chapters 8 and 9.

34. All of the subsequent stock price changes are adjusted by the CAPM for market changes.

35. *Network World* (January 13, 1992): 27–28. The initial investment was announced to be between $200 and $300 million.

14
Seven Technologies to Watch in Globalization

Alan Hald and Benn R. Konsynski

Trends in globalization lead to new organizational strategies that, when properly executed, transform the coordination and control systems, management practice, and organizational structure of the global enterprise. Coping with ambiguity is a natural part of the internationalization of business, with its diversity and information intensity. Changes in traditional modes of competition in the emerging global business environment present significant opportunities for leveraging information technologies to transform business and management processes. The resulting management challenges create "emotional stress" in the marketplace and in management practice. Key managerial challenges that give rise to a review of the role of information technology include:

- *Coordination.* To compete effectively, at home or globally, firms require significant coordination skills that address value-chain management and relations with public sector entities.
- *Time-to-market.* Market and product innovation often involve cooperation and partnership across a diverse and geographically dispersed set of industrial entities.
- *Management control.* As time, costs, distance, and other factors undergo radical change, it requires significant effort for decision makers to comprehend new technology and control its evolution in the organization.
- *Organizational learning and talent/skill retention.* Two major challenges to management in the 1990s will be to acquire and keep internal talent (people, skills, core competencies)

and build key relationships in the market (external talent) that provide important scale factors without ownership.

It is this emotional stress that will set the direction and pace of development and assimilation for many emerging information technologies. Here we present factors that influence both the institutional and technical innovation needed to address these new organizational challenges, and we explore the evolution of several emerging technologies deserving attention— among them, wireless communication neural networks, multimedia interfaces, electronic linkages, and virtual realities. Finally, we review the alignment of strategic institutional requirements and these emerging "base" technologies.

In the decades following World War II, a number of factors changed the manner of competition in the global business community. Specific catalysts for globalization and evolving patterns of international competition vary among industries. Among the causative factors are growing similarity in available infrastructure, distribution channels, and marketing approaches and a fluid global capital market that supports large flows of funds between countries. Additional causes include falling political and tariff barriers, increasing incidences of regional economic pacts that facilitate trade relations, and the growing impact of the technological revolution on the restructuring and integration of industries. Widespread globalization is also evident in a number of what were once largely separate domestic industries, such as software, telecommunications, and services. Political changes in the former Soviet Union and Eastern European countries and the evolution of the European Economic Community have led to growing international competition, as have changes in the economic dynamics of the Pacific Rim area—Hong Kong, Japan, China, Taiwan, Korea, and Singapore—and the reentry of nations such as Vietnam to the global economic community.

Whereas organizational learning historically focused on implicit adaptation in a firm's internal environment, in the global enterprise it involves recognizing turbulent competitive/political and complex internal environments. Today the education of people and institutions is often influenced by the available information-technology platform. Internal and external policies need to be modeled to reflect the effective adaptation of systems of control and coordination in the global enterprise.

An understanding of the administrative options available to general managers in a global environment is necessary in order to derive a strategy for developing and assimilating a new information-technology infrastructure.

The Management Challenge—Changing What *Should* Be Done

Management is traditionally challenged to deal consistently and effectively with coordination, time-to-market, management control, and retaining organizational talent under one roof and within a common corporate culture. Often, the "blowtorch" approach prevails; management puts heat on the aspect of the organization that is not performing well. This approach typically fosters a fire-fighting mentality, encouraging management to ignore fires in other parts of the organization until they, too, develop serious problems.

Quality improvement programs that focus on team empowerment, education, work as a process, and adherence to client requirements are being adopted by companies throughout the world. Although intellectually driven by philosophies first articulated in the United States, the concepts were most effectively applied in Japan in the 1960s and 1970s. The concepts were embraced by U.S. businesses in the 1980s and 1990s as a matter of competitive survival, rather than as a means to achieve commercial leadership in the global environment.

Talent and access to technology will determine the ongoing competitive capacity of commercial organizations in today's economy. Talent, particularly in advanced economies, tends to concentrate around areas of opportunity and superior quality of life. In developing economies, talent typically lacks mobility because of socioeconomic constraints, while developed technology lacks effective transfer mechanisms. Globally competitive businesses will need to tap global centers of talent and technology to leverage their efforts.

The challenge is to cope with coordination, time-to-market, management control, and organizational learning/talent retention in a cross-cultural and geographically distributed context. Each culture finds unique ways to communicate and develop relationships and has its own temporal sense (the pace at which things *should* change). Cross-cultural, global standards for conducting business are emerging from the adoption of innovation.

Business processes, such as the order fulfillment cycle, are being accelerated as a result of the emergence of interdependencies that virtually integrate service and manufacturing organizations (and primary suppliers) subject to international competitive pressures. This acceleration, in turn, is driving the development and adoption of standardized information and communications technologies deemed necessary to implement these processes.

Information technologies play a significant role in coordination:

- they increase interlinkage in the competitive environment,
- they foster interplay between clusters and foundations to engender a positive growth cycle that may, in turn, lead to a concentration of talent and knowledge, and
- they drive the development and adoption of processes that increase the rate of product/service innovation, rapidly diffusing processes through linkages and consulting organizations composed of individuals who experienced the development of the processes.

Businesses that can adopt a variety of forms for coping with change have become topics of popular books on management. Studies of productivity in the late 1970s and the 1980s indicated that business-process changes had yielded significant productivity gains and, at times, major competitive advantage. These process changes are closely coupled with an organization's ability to change the way it operates and employs information and communications technologies.

The increasing pace of innovation by competitors has driven businesses to strengthen linkages, further accelerate the flow of information, intensify competition, and decrease the innovation cycle until virtually all waste time within the cycle is squeezed out. How much can be squeezed out depends on the limits of the technology application. More important is the adoption (change) rate of the organization and its trading partners.

Customers demand tailored, specialized products and prefer a high degree of self-selection coupled with quick delivery at low cost. The historic assumption is that customers buy value at the best price. Information intensity in the product and in the manufacturing and delivery processes signals a strong role for information technology in the differentiation of end products.

Businesses are being driven to increase internal/external integration. Control is shifting from physical asset management to virtual control (influence over the interdependencies that exist between clients and suppliers).

Information Intensity: Changing What *Can* Be Done

As organizations become more information-based and information from internal and external sources becomes electronically available on demand, traditional corporate functions, such as planning, marketing, technical support, documentation, and publishing will be dramatically transformed or even eliminated. In turn, the organization shifts from being paper driven to being electronically driven. Several important trends are accelerating this organizational shift to high information intensity.

High-capacity and high-reliability optical scanning and character recognition. What is not in electronic form now probably will be in the near future. New multipurpose copiers, scanners, and facsimile machines will act as high-capacity data-capture and -conversion devices. Already there are inexpensive multifont and multicolumn optical character-recognition machines that achieve impressive and practical levels of performance.

Availability of external and internal information in electronic form. Most major newspaper and magazine publishers now make their publications available in electronic form. Many organizations are also doing this for the information they share beyond their organizational boundaries. Desktop and electronic publishing, groupware, electronic mail, local area networks, and word processors are accelerating the availability of internal information in electronic form.

Document format standards and automated recognition. With the support of virtually all computer vendors and the aggressive endorsement of the U.S. Department of Defense, an International Standards Organization standard for the markup of technical documents—the Standard Generic Markup Language—has been adopted. Products that automatically scan technical documents and insert the appropriate markup terms have been developed. These developments will vastly improve the speed and efficiency of technical documentation preparation as well as facilitate the automated classification and retrieval of complex technical and legal documents.

Hypertext and hypermedia. Hypertext products link parts of different documents according to their content. These products, among the first to exploit the accessibility and malleability of text in its electronic form, can be extremely effective educational tools.

Software integrated circuits and knowledge codification. Advances in object-oriented programming make it possible to encapsulate knowledge and software functions in independent modules that can be "plugged in" and combined with other modules as if they were integrated circuits. These techniques could make it feasible to assemble software applications from standard components. Simple knowledge-codification techniques borrowed from the expert systems area make it possible to capture and distribute certain forms of routine knowledge as a corporate asset.

Automated indexing and routing techniques. Intelligence agencies and vendors of financial information have developed, and will soon deploy, artificial-intelligence-based systems for the indexing and routing of real-time textual information.

Inexpensive and high-capacity distribution channels. Methods for distributing information products and services are proliferating in the form of high-capacity private corporate networks, inexpensive one- and two-way satellite dishes, fiber optics, high-density compact disk/read-only memory, high-density erasable and writable optical disks, removable high-capacity secondary storage, audiotext, FM broadcast, and high-speed telephone lines. Dow Jones & Co., for example, through its Dow Vision service, is offering direct high-bandwidth links to corporations for the bulk downloading of business information.

Bulk pricing of corporate information purchases. Information vendors are beginning to recognize that usage-sensitive pricing and onerous royalty agreements are inhibiting demand for their services and preventing the resale and republishing of their products. Customers are demanding the right to reuse and combine external sources. We can expect the same open-architecture mind-set now prevalent in the workstation industry to spread to the information industry.

On-line and distributed management. The advent of networked organizations, groupware, and other ways of coordinating and directing work in globally distributed firms will not only increase the volume and velocity of information within organizations but will also require new business techniques for managing on-line and distributed data.

Electronic data interchange. Interorganizational systems for integrating many of the marketing, logistics, and distribution functions of buyers, sellers, manufacturers, and suppliers are growing at an enormous rate. These systems, in turn, are creating enormous volumes of data and information that have transactional, managerial, and analytic value. Not only can companies more effectively tie in to their suppliers, they can also use data from their operations to monitor and improve their performance and relationships.

High-performance platforms. A respected pioneer in computer architectures estimates that the price/performance ratio of processors is increasing at a rate of 70% annually. Reduced instruction-set computing architectures and multiprocessing techniques promise to deliver 100 million instructions per second (MIPS) to the desktop within the next two to three years, with high-IQ capacity servers achieving performance levels in the range of 500 to 1,000 MIPS.

Trends: Seven Technologies to Watch

Interorganizational systems, groupware, document-based processing, information refineries, executive support systems, and other information technologies and applications have a fundamental impact on coordination and control. Each of these technologies offers significant potential to catalyze changes in decision and business processes in the global enterprise. There are many opportunities for using new technology initiatives to expand a company's range of technology options. Although further research is needed to evaluate the effects of technology on business processes that may be unique to new organizational forms, we can offer some predictions about critical technologies that have earned our attention.

1. Notebook/Palm-Tops, Personal Digital   (Now–1995)
   Assistants
2. Multimedia/Interactive Media   (Now–1995)
3. Neural Network/Fuzzy Logic   (1993–2000)
   (AI Learning Process)

4. Wireless Technology	(1993–2000)
5. Interoperability Standards (EDI, Unix, and so forth)	(Now–2000)
6. Object-Oriented Programming Systems (OOPS)	(Now–2000)
7. Virtual Reality	(1996–2000)

Notebook/Palm-Top Computers—Personal Digital Assistants

The "personal" aspect of these technologies lies in their service to the individual; the portable aspect lies in the relaxation of normal constraints of weight, location, connection, and power requirements. We can expect these technologies to transform the nature of work, to change patterns of management control and interchange, and to augment present and emerging forms of work and leisure. How are tasks transformed via the application of these technologies? Are organizations subject to radical structural changes that diminish temporal and geographical constraints? What management challenges related to control and coordination arise in the transformed environments? How will information flows be altered by the introduction of technologies that change patterns of communication, move the locus of decisions, and create new models of storage and relations within and across organizational boundaries? How will logistics and personal communications be transformed by global positioning systems and global point-to-point communications?

Hand-held systems are, as the name suggests, designed to be held in one's hand while one enters information for particular applications.[1] A major gas utility, for example, uses hand-held systems for a dispatching application. Frito-Lay salespeople use a hand-held system to enter orders at a customer's location. In the case of Frito-Lay, hand-helds are plugged into a printer bay in the delivery truck to print an inventory/pick list used by the salesperson to replenish the customer stock, with the data stored for later transmission to the home office. At Federal Express, drivers use a hand-held terminal to log packages received and delivered. Package information is then batch-transmitted to a centralized computer when the driver returns to the office. In all three cases, the hand-held terminal was introduced to reduce paperwork and improve operations. Initially domestic efforts, these innovations are likely to be diffused globally through assimilation in the multinational and global enterprises of the firms that own them.

Although they share common features, these three examples exhibit many differences when we consider their tasks, form, quantity, and volatility. The tasks performed by all three applications primarily involve communications. The primary task for the gas utilities is dispatching information to service personnel, for Frito-Lay it is communicating orders to the home office, and for Federal Express it is communicating package locations to the company's centralized systems.

The form of the information is also similar in that all three systems interface with a central computer. The gas utilities' dispatchers work from a single dispatching center that stores customer data electronically. Frito-Lay's order information must eventually reach the corporate system in Texas for processing and order fulfillment. Federal Express package information is stored centrally to facilitate tracking and retrieval.

Although the quantity of information on the central computer is large, the amount to be transmitted to or from field personnel is relatively small. Thus, the hand-held systems, with their presently limited viewing screens and keyboards, suffice as both input and output devices. Federal Express drivers enter the package information via a light pen scanner to minimize entry error.

These applications differ in the immediacy of the information transmitted, as is reflected in the specific hand-held chosen by each company. Dispatched information must reach a service person immediately or it is useless. To re-route service people effectively, the company needs to know where they are at all times and be able to reach them at any time. Hence, the gas-utility hand-held has a radio transceiver built in for real-time communication.

The growth of personal digital appliances will accelerate. Key to these initiatives is the availability of low-power, high-speed, high-density, high-capacity processors and storage units with new forms of interface (pen point and speech) and communications (e.g., local infrared and radio frequency, wide area cellular satellite and global positioning systems). A renewal of attention to investment in information technology in support of mobile work and mobile leisure is occurring.

The global caravans of materials and information will increase. Independence from location, wires, power source, language, and other factors that serve as barriers to global coordination and control are essential trends. With these capacity increases comes the opportunity to increase the personalization of the systems. These appliances will be independent of the constraints that have homogenized the systems of the past. The ultimate customization and adaptation of software to the individual user is a trend correlated with the personalization of the hardware.

Multimedia/Interactive Media

Computer-based blending of graphics, sound, and video is a rapidly growing area in hardware and software development. The implications for ease of use and increased functionality are tremendous. In the global arena, the opportunity to leverage multiple media holds enormous potential for facilitating communication and overcoming the negative effects of distance and cultural diversity. Multimedia technology supports communication and interaction that transcends traditional language-based and culturally biased communication forms because more senses are addressed; higher economies of space are available through the leverage of multimedia technology.

In the 1980s, "multimedia" meant interactive video to most people. The focus of discussion was on audiovisual content that was easily accessible and could be stored and retrieved in an object database. Technically, this involved personal computers connected to video-disk players and hard disks to support the retrieval of audio and video clips used in data and image presentation. This was a first step in moving away from linear presentation and access for image and motion, demonstrating the high-capacity use of image-storage systems for data. Application areas that emerged were in interactive, video-based training and merchandising—for walk-up kiosks at Florsheim's Shoes, for example. This hybrid technology involved the confluence of several available technologies toward a first test of multimedia concepts.

The first wave of multimedia technology had many problems and limitations. The information bases on video-disk had to be designed in advance, as the disks were permanent storage. The forms of interaction with the information (audio, image, motion) had to be scripted and lacked the benefits of advanced interfaces (voice, touch, projection).

Currently the evolution of compact-disk technology is setting the pace for the availability of multimedia. CD-ROM drives are now available in the $200 to $400 range. Access times and transfer rates will approach those of current hard disk drives (30 ms). Hundreds of CDs are available containing books, encyclopedias, music, images, hypermedia, and other forms of software. The Grolier Electronic Encyclopedia CD carries all the text from 21 printed volumes, 250 maps, thousands of color and black and white images, and digitally stored sounds. With digital video interactive (DVI) technology, one can store an entire hour of video on a single disk. New forms of compression will increase these capacities and decrease access time by orders of magnitude.

Neural Network/Fuzzy Logic

Neural networks are attempts to model biological neural networks. The biological network of the human brain is, of course, naturally capable of remarkable feats of pattern recognition, decision making, and logical inference. To date, most attempts to emulate the native capabilities of the human brain using computers have employed the rule-based logic evident in the conventional theories of artificial intelligence. These attempts at modeling human intelligence have hinged on what might be called the "psychological approach" to machine intelligence. They have significant limitations, leading some to dismiss the rule-based approach as degenerative research.

In contrast, neural-network technology is a "physiological approach" to artificial intelligence. It involves designing a network of electronic circuits that resemble those in the human brain. In fact, neural networks are designed to have behaviors similar to those of their biological counterparts. Like their biological counterparts, they consist of large numbers of small processing elements called "neurons." Biological and artificial neurons are very similar. The artificial systems permit the modification of network performance by adjusting values and relations. To some degree, this approach is similar to the electrochemical behavior that occurs at the junctions between biological neurons.

As a tool in decision processes,[2] the variable nature of the networks is seen to provide a variety of benefits unique to neural networks: adaptation to changes in problem specifications, compensation for faults in the network, and improved performance over time. Although the properties attributed to it may vary, the single neuron is generally deemed capable of processing its inputs on an elementary level in order to generate outputs. Applications are growing in areas of speech and character pattern recognition, classification problems,[3] learning environments, and other situations that defy rule-based logic approaches. Language, semiotics, and adaptive communications are natural concerns in the global business environment. We can expect that this class of technologies will play a significant role in resolving these challenges.

Wireless Technology

Personal portable technologies will permit actualization of the "anytime, anywhere" philosophy. Motorola has a model that links global to local communications. In the 1996–1997 period, Motorola plans to launch the Iridium communication system (owned by a global consortium), which is composed of 144 low-polar-orbit communication satellites that will allow point-to-point cellular-phone-like conversations and data exchange between any two places on earth. Individuals will employ Iridium hand-held phones, linked via cellular or central office systems, to engage in wireless communication anytime, anywhere, for about three dollars per minute (see Figure 14-1).

Personal communication services (PCSs) will emerge as the successor to today's cellular phone. PCS technology will have a massive impact on home and satellite office communications in the next decade. While millions are buying cellular phones even though the government has yet to resolve issues involving the allocation of rights, PCS promises to be a more versatile technology and clearly reduces the cost of wireless communications. Many complain that the price of cellular service is excessive and does not reflect true costs. PCS technology, with its low power requirements and ability to work inside buildings and tunnels, offers the potential for a new wireless infrastructure. We believe the PCS network will grow to augment, and possibly replace,

Figure 14-1
Wireless Communication 1990–2000

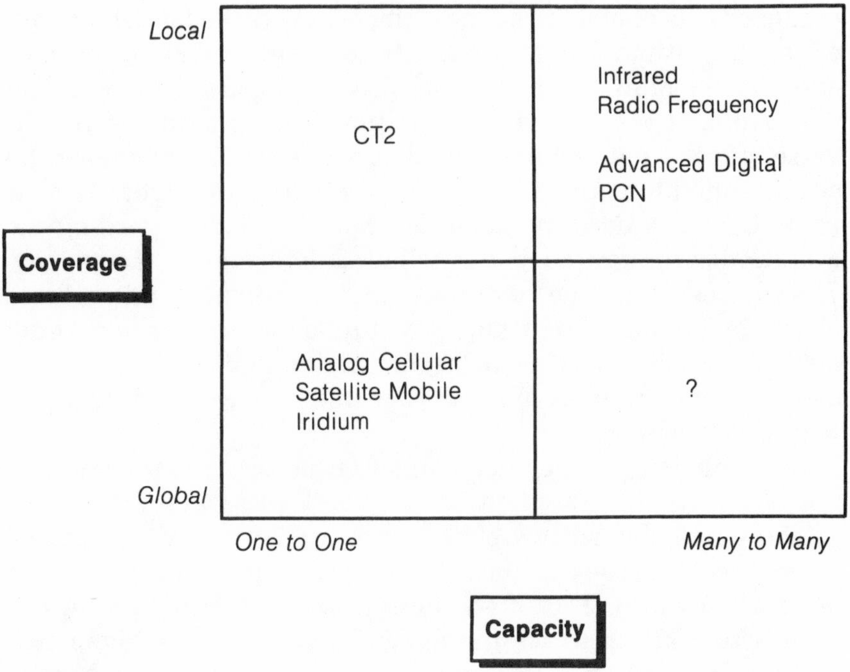

Local	

some of the communications technologies emerging on the existing infrastructure associated with telephone, cable-TV and other metropolitan cable networks, communications over power lines, and cellular links.

Increased workstation power, particularly graphics capacity (driven in part by RISC/CISC competition in the early 1990s), will improve visualization capability. Graphic representations and animated simulations will replace text when appropriate, while the ability to manipulate graphic representations of processes rather than verbal abstractions will enhance cross-cultural communication. A globally dispersed, culturally diverse team that shares a common methodology (e.g., process management) will be able to visualize its efforts in a manner consistent with the methodological approach (e.g., a simulated process) and will be able to communicate directly through the methodology.

Interoperability Standards

Managing the growing information technology capability in organizations is one of the most important tasks facing managers as they attempt to influence the strategic directions of their enterprises. Management is faced with the need to establish effective controls over the acquisition and structure of the diverse information technologies that are becoming available. Issues of individual and organizational productivity enhancement have thus far eluded managers in their decisions regarding the evolution of integrated, yet distributed, information technology. These issues must be addressed in the future to allow firms to create architectures that take full advantage of emerging technologies, as well as to highlight an important objective: global interoperability of networked heterogeneous workstation and server devices.

The popularity of the microcomputer has spurred the publication of an assortment of how-to articles. Topics range from analysis of particular software packages (e.g., word processing or spreadsheets) to the evaluation of new user interface techniques (e.g., windowing). Too often these articles concentrate on the trees while failing to see the forest. In other words, given current trends, the key issue in future years will not be which word processor is best, but rather how large amounts of incompatible hardware and software can be made to communicate and share data.

As is to be expected with any new product, the computer's current environment is characterized by fragmentation, and often incompatibility. Specifically:

- hardware and software from different vendors do not communicate.
- hardware and software for communicating between micros and mainframes—a must for applications that need the power of the mainframe—are still in their infancy.
- data frequently cannot be shared between packages—although, as discussed later, this problem is being addressed through the development of an integrated package.

These problems exist mainly because the popularity of single-function applications, together with the lack of coordinated acquisitions, has biased the market toward locally optimal solutions. Clearly, the microcomputer will not reach its full potential until we can provide a global plan for microcomputer compatibility.

What does "compatibility" mean? Basically, it is the ability of different software packages running on heterogeneous devices to communicate over heterogeneous networks. We refer to this as "interoperability," or common functionality across devices, packages, and vendors. In addition to the many side benefits that would attend interoperability (e.g., transparent devices or consistent keystrokes that would reduce learning time), the standards developed to define communications, storage, and functionality protocols would promote sharing of resources both within and between workstation environments.

Interoperability is clearly a worthwhile goal, but achieving it is a tall order. The approach we suggest has two phases. First, the major issues to be considered in building an interoperable environment (i.e., which operating system, hardware, and interface protocols to select) must be outlined in detail. From this analysis, an architecture can be developed to provide guidelines for analyzing the organization's existing micro usage, project future needs, and develop a migration plan for the future evolution of the current inventory of stand-alone micro systems that support a degree of interoperability. This approach enables the organization to take advantage of differences in vendor alternatives, while at the same time providing the highest degree of homogeneity in function and operation. In effect, the first phase provides a framework for working on the second phase: developing an architecture.

This characterization helps us outline capability and performance objectives for an interoperable architecture.

- *Global interoperability.* Devices should interconnect in a manner that is transparent to the user. Multiple sites should be able to communicate and pass files. Long-distance digital networks and other network facilities should be accessible to the user in a transparent fashion.
- *User environment commonality.* Physical and functional interfaces should be common across the system environments. Dialogues, keyboards, and keystrokes should be common across environments and applications. The same or similar keystrokes should be available in different applications, such as word processing, communications, and spreadsheets.
- *Multivendor environment.* Hardware and software should be

available from multiple distributors. Few organizations will find all needed functional capabilities available from a single vendor.

- *Evolutionary growth.* A function- and feature-phasing schedule that accounts for the evolving technologies (e.g., window management tools, such as DESQ) should be developed. A timing schedule or workload threshold may define the transition between environments.
- *User friendliness.* The user should never have to interface at the operation systems level. The system might infer the standard features and interfaces, minimizing keystrokes and retaining the user's place when moving between applications.
- *Minimization of cost per user.* Cost per user, given the functions available, should be minimized. Cost sharing should be exploited where function performance is not compromised.

OOPS

OOPS is an acronym for object-oriented programming systems, a term that refers to a number of systems development tools, computer languages, and design methods that are coming into use as a design philosophy for information systems. It enables profoundly new approaches to describing models that make information technology more accessible to general management.

Object-oriented programming might be shrugged off as yet another buzzword coined by the computer science types to confuse harassed managers, except that business systems users and developers now realize that object-oriented programming enables business systems designers to develop complex systems in a fraction of the time it would take using traditional approaches. Users and developers also support OOPS as a possible solution for finally getting rid of the applications development backlog that has been plaguing MIS groups since computers descended on the business world. Moreover, such well-known toolsmiths as Borland and Microsoft have introduced object-oriented features into their best-selling computer languages. The new graphical user interfaces, such as Windows 3.0 and the newer versions of Macintosh and Next computers, also come with object-oriented development environments.

This is all very well, but why should a general manager be interested in OOPS? The answer lies in the use this new paradigm might have in modeling organizations and building the business and management processes that directly support an organization. OOPS enables technology to finally approach the language and concepts of business and organizations. Systems are described in terms of actors, roles, responsibilities, behaviors, relations, and other terms and concepts common to traditional business environments. By permitting the use of business terminology in the description of system requirements, OOPS enables managers and other business-oriented individuals to participate more actively in the design process.

OOPS is an emerging design paradigm that focuses both on the interaction of behaviors among system objects (rather than on scheduled events) and on the conditions and responses of the entire system. The central principle of object-oriented programming is that systems, rather than being "lists" of things for a computer to do, are descriptions of the objects that compose them and of the relationships among those objects. Most object-oriented programming systems contain a large number of standard, predefined objects. Programming in the system largely consists of choosing the right set of objects, modifying them as needed, and defining the way in which they should interact.

There are three essential terms in object-oriented programming: objects, classes, and inheritance.

Objects are elements that possess information about their own state (instance variables) as well as snippets of code (methods) that enable them to respond to requests (messages). Messages, which might be requests for information about the instance variables or instructions for changing them, come from other objects. Thus, an object contains not only data but also the means of accessing and manipulating it. A third element is the meaning for the object (e.g., when is a warehouse "full" and what does it mean for an order to be "acceptable"?).

Classes are prototypes of objects. A class exists in a hierarchy of classes; it usually has a superclass and might have subclasses. Object-oriented programming systems generally come with a bewildering number of classes; systems development generally consists of constructing new classes, either by modifying existing classes or writing new ones from scratch (i.e., making a subclass of the top class).

Inheritance refers to the ability of classes (and objects, of course) to inherit properties from their superclasses. An object usually has methods specific to itself, as well as methods similar to those of its superclass. An object, when receiving a message, will look first for a corresponding method in its own set of methods; if one is not found, it will look in the set of methods of its superclass.

Software reusability, the ability to construct new classes by redefining (subclassing) existing classes, is one of the major benefits of object-oriented programming. To construct a new class requires no new code except for the modifications and additions that set the new class apart from its superclass. This makes prototyping, once one is familiar with the OOPS library of classes, an extremely fast process. Actual time improvements vary, but estimates of 80% to 95% reduction in development time are frequently reported by impartial observers. The library of classes will generally remain stable as organizations gain experience with OOPS. In other words, after a learning period, the reuse of objects and classes in the organization will rapidly increase.

Virtual Reality

Virtual reality is a way of interacting with real or imagined "environments." In the user-transparent case, it involves using a computer in such a way that all consciousness of using a computer disappears. To date, this technology has been available only to a small group of computer hackers and researchers. The costs and nature of the equipment needed to place one in a "whole new reality" currently preclude access for the average individual.

Yet many of us have seen various forms of these technologies. Commercial airlines and NASA use simulators to place pilots and astronauts in an environment intended to give them a feel for the flight process and the situations they will encounter. The Air Force uses simulated environments for fighter pilot training that place several aircraft in the same simulated space for combat-performance training and evaluation. And for some years, children have played video games that, in a modest way, place them in a different world that includes dragons, aliens, and other objects that seem alive.

Our traditional forms of entertainment (literature, movies, television, and so forth) have exercised our imagination through the employment of a limited set of senses (usually visual and auditory). These forms of interaction require significant concentration, in part because of the extraneous interference and "noise" around us. We are periodically reminded that we are not really "in that world" as other senses and reality intervene (glancing away from the book, seeing the room beyond the television screen, recognizing our inability to interact in a movie). These are not limits of our imagination, but rather limits on our ability to place ourselves in a new reality, and block out sensory interventions that might interfere with our acceptance of the new reality.

A virtual reality system affords the user a feeling of being *in* the environment, like a fighter pilot in a flight simulator system. This is done by stimulating more than one sense at a time, using natural movement as input and locking out external stimuli.

A computer normally relies on the user's sight (and occasionally hearing) to make interaction possible. A virtual reality system can stimulate hearing more effectively (by employing realistic sound effects or using binaural sound) or feeling (by using joysticks and other devices) to give the user a feel for the computer-generated objects being manipulated.

Using natural movement as input. In the example of an architect and customer, neither gives explicit commands to the computer to tell it that they are moving in a certain direction in the virtual building. Instead, they are "walking" in that direction, and the direction and speed are picked up by a treadmill on which they are walking or by infrared sensors that sense their spatial positions. The designer uses a device that lets her grip the computer-projected camera using exactly the same movements she would have used if she were gripping a real camera.

Locking out external stimuli. When the architect and the customer are "walking" around in the building-image built by the computer, they do not see anything but that building. Since the computer-generated image is the only stimulus received, that image will be what the mind perceives as real. This is done through wide-angle stereoscopic projection (a lot of our sensing of room and place is done by what we see out of the corners of our eyes) and binaural sound (sound that has been recorded with two microphones placed on each side of a sound-blocking device, as our ears are placed on our heads). When this sound is played back through earphones, according to inventor Eric Howlett, it gives one "an eerie feeling of being there."

For the person without access to the latest in computer technology and research labs, virtual reality might seem far away. One can, however, get a flavor of virtual reality from a video game called "Hard Driven." There are two versions of this game: one in which the player stands up, and the other in which the player is seated. The sit-down version employs a large video screen, realistic sound, and a wheel and gearshift that simulate reality; as one drives through a curve, the wheel becomes difficult to move, certain gearshifts are more difficult than others, and so forth.

While most virtual reality initiatives deal with rendered realities, organizations like Leep Systems of Waltham, Massachusetts, also work in the area of telepresence. In telepresence, the subject deals with reality, but with a reality remote to the subject's location. The blurring of reality and rendered realities offer significant opportunity to shape new applications that challenge our assumptions about people, time, location, visualization, and attention.

Shifts: Broad Evolutionary Patterns

The technologies we have just discussed reflect a series of individual evolutionary paths. Yet, if these describe the velocity of evolution, what can we expect in terms of acceleration? There are clear meta-trends that transcend the evolution of individual technologies. In this section, we consider several of these "trends in trends," and relate these social, political, and technical shifts to issues that involve management challenges in the leverage of information technology to business service delivery.

Technology Simplification with Increasing Local Intelligence

In the early 1990s, increasing systems complexity, as a result of extensive networking and use of the client/server distributed-processing model, will drive manufacturers to simplify the installation of complex networks. Although interoperability standards will exist among diverse systems, administrators will have to make many complex systems design and maintenance decisions. Artificial intelligence application approaches will be applied to design "self-adaptive" systems, which self-configure and re-configure as needed to adapt to changes presented to the system. By the turn of the century, this design approach will initiate a series of evolutionary improvements supported by corresponding changes in systems architecture (parallelism-neural/fuzzy logic or other AI-enhancing logic designs). Later, very dramatic changes in the nature of large-scale computers will refocus processing back to a central system capable of sustaining a dynamic real-time model of the organizational processes and interaction with the environment.

Complex Integration ———————————————— Now
  Self-Adapting Systems ———————— 1995–2000
    Self-Partnering Systems ——————— 2000–2010
      Self-Conscious Systems ————————— 2030

Processors to the People

Computer technology, which leverages the individual mind, and communications technology, which leverages the collective mind, will be the driving technologies for the next 50 years. Computer technology is often measured in millions of instructions per second (MIPS). MIPS are typically evaluated as MIPS/$, but a more important figure may be MIPS/person. The current generation provides 3 MIPS/user (386 technology). By 1995, this per-user figure will rise to more than 50 MIPS and by the end of the decade to more than 600 MIPS. The ubiquity of processing capacity and connectivity permits consideration of new arrangements for the distribution of functionality and form. This empowerment of the individual and the collective opens new possibilities for the redesign of work and leisure.

The Rise of Human Literate Systems

Applications of technology are being simplified, natural interfacing will provide alternatives to keyboard entry, and pen-based notebook tablets may revolutionize the personal organizer and automate the last link in the logistic chain between field representative and client. Consider the impact of pen-based systems with fax/cellular modems and wireless LAN capability, or IR/RE technology, on the ability to handle "electronic paperwork" anytime, anywhere. Such technology, widely deployed, would allow the use of computer-based group process applications (brainstorming, prioritizing, decision making, surveying, and so forth)[4] and facilitate virtual team meetings at the convenience of the team members.[5] It could support "intelligent agents"[6] that collect and review information and meet with other agents. The near-term focus will be on increasing convenience while conserving resources. Conjuring up Apple's image of the *Knowledge Navigator* or Microsoft's *Information at Your Fingertips* leads one to reflect on the ever-present paradox of the Industrial Age—how to reconcile the desire to make life more convenient with the need to conserve physical resources. The Information Age may resolve this paradox.

In the area of dialogues and natural interfaces, continuous recognition of handwriting and speech remains a major challenge. The confluence of powerful learning technologies (neural networks, other AI) and powerfully adapted but cheap processing engines in the late 1990s should render these capabilities more common. Voice-to-command, voice-to-text, and handwriting-to-text should emerge as commonplace. Even advanced keyboard entry is subject to evolution. One company has developed a keying system based on finger movement that increases the throughput of the traditional "Qwerty" keyboard typist by 50% with ten hours of training. The next level is to eliminate the physical interface, at least in the perception of the user; in effect, to directly extend the mind of the user into the system's virtual world. Before the end of the decade, the virtual reality interface should become economically practical as a workstation tool, about as practical as today's high-resolution monitor and keyboard.[7] It is possible to go on at length—and many have—concerning the implications.

Underlying all the externally perceived simplicity and human literacy will be a conceptually layered organizing environment that in itself simplifies the process of developing and supporting applications. OOPS and the object-oriented philosophy are the beginnings.[8] The challenge is to manage the complexity growing from networking and information proliferation. Expert systems (and novice systems for nonexperts) that learn from humans, and learning systems (neural networks, fuzzy models, and so forth) that learn from experience may help.

Ultimately, individuals, organizations, and entire societies will struggle to capture, store, organize, retrieve, and present information in meaningful, useful ways. By the decade's end, NASA will each year handle twenty-nine times the information stored in the Library of Congress's 15 million volumes. We call this the "taxonomy of knowledge" problem. It may be one of the most significant challenges of the late twenty-first century.

Conclusions

The future global environment will place increasing demands on the evolution of our information technologies to facilitate new forms of human and systems interaction. It is incumbent on the general manager to pay attention to these tendencies, trends, and shifts. No longer do the issues of technology options follow the study of strategic options. Indeed, the changes brought about by the leverage of information technology innovations change strategic possibilities.

The individual, group, organizational, industrial, social, and global entities that will participate in the future information-rich global marketplace face many more challenges than merely automating, informating, or even redesigning current business practices. Fundamental changes will occur in roles and responsibilities that will transform the global marketplace. Emerging information technologies must address even broader demands in the coming decades. They must help us to thread our own unique pathways through bodies of knowledge, organize information in personally useful ways, and recognize patterns that exist beyond our current threshold of perception.

Although the major challenges of humankind and society are not technical challenges, the concerns and aspirations of business and society will be resolved only by leveraging the many existing and emerging information technologies. The emergence of the global enterprise is related to the challenge of the barriers to coordination and cooperation among independent cultures and business and management practices. Only by challenging traditional assumptions and assertions that have prevented the emergence of the global enterprise can we leverage these new information technologies to create new global business practices.

Notes

1. B. Konsynski and K. Ostrovsky, "Personal Portable Technologies: Doing Business Anywhere," Harvard Business School Working Paper, 1991.

2. E. Stohr and B. Konsynski, *Information and Decision Processes* (Los Alamitos, Calif.: IEEE Press, 1992).

3. G. Elofson and B. Konsynski, "Only Diamonds Are Forever: Caching Knowledge for Episodic Classification Problems," in *Current Research in Decision Support Systems,* eds. R. Blanning and D. King (Los Alamitos, Calif.: IEEE Press, 1992).

4. J. Nunamaker, L. Applegate, and B. Konsynski, "Computer-Aided Deliberation: Model Management and Group Decision Support," *Operations Research,* 36, no. 6 (November–December 1988): 826–848.

5. E. Andersen and B. Konsynski, "Virtual Reality and the General Manager: Toys Becoming Tools," Harvard Business School Case 192-090 (1992).

6. G. Elofson and B. Konsynski, "Delegation Technologies: Environmental Scanning with Intelligent Agents," *Journal of Management Information Systems,* 8, no. 1 (Summer 1991): 37–62.

7. Ibid.

8. E. Andersen and B. Konsynski, "What the Hell is OOPS, Anyway?," Harvard Business School Case 192-104 (1992).

15

Building the Broadband Society

William Marx, Jr.

Advanced information technology is being unleashed in the global marketplace, transforming businesses from national to multinational companies and revolutionizing virtually every aspect of doing business in the modern world. Whatever the business, in whatever industry, instantaneous information has gone from luxury to necessity. Those in search of a strategic edge in the global marketplace of the 1990s are increasingly finding solutions in the form of computers lashed together with telecommunications lines joined to a worldwide network.

This chapter explores the information revolution's role as a catalyst for global expansion of businesses and industries, and examines the technologies likely to accelerate the pace of change. Customer needs, which once lagged technical innovation, are now out front, pulling technology. This may be the most important development of all, because it calls for new relationships among customers, suppliers, and competitors.

Customer demand is today the most potent catalyst for change in telecommunications. But equally important is the globalization of commerce, which has been spurred by political and social changes occurring in Europe and the Far East. Add the blurring pace of technological advance and it seems logical to conclude that we are on the verge of a historic era.

The New Global Economy

The war in the Gulf briefly deflected our attention from broader changes in world affairs. But it is worth noting that, although it had considerable impact on international business travel, the war had very little effect on business transactions.

Thanks to the global network, one does not have to "be there" to make a deal.

In this fast-paced world, the Gulf War quickly became a historical footnote. Shortly after the last shot rang out in the desert, the world's attention shifted back to events even more dramatic: Western Europe's preparations for a borderless market, Germany's struggle to reunify and the implications of its efforts for world trade, the rise of nationalism and movement toward free enterprise economies in Central Europe and the former Soviet Union, the continued economic success of nations in the Pacific Rim, and the awakening of the former "sleeping giant" of South America. Latin America receives little attention against the backdrop of sweeping change in other parts of the world, but the vast human resources and market potential of its nations cannot be ignored.

The transition to market economies will no doubt stimulate the spread of free trade, which, in turn, should spark growth in the world economy. With information having become to the Information Age what steel was to the Industrial Age, telecommunications will clearly be a catalyst in the transformations at hand.

The trade routes of the new world are hair-thin glass fibers. Cargo moves along these routes as tiny pulses of light. Like the trading ships of the past, the machines that load, route, and distribute this ephemeral cargo are today's critical assets.

Speed is everything today. The business world, intent on minimizing production time and maximizing the flow of raw materials into finished goods, employs just-in-time systems for inventory, ordering, manufacturing, and management, all designed and implemented on a global scale. Information that is not instantaneous is worthless. The world marketplace sees all and demands what it sees, no matter who produces it or where it is produced. Benetton sweaters and Levi jeans are as common on the streets of London and Tokyo as they are on those of New York and Rome, and even residents of Moscow can find the familiar golden arches to satisfy a "Big Mac attack."

Not long ago, products and services had to be produced where they were consumed, without regard to cost or strategic advantage. That has changed. In a *Harvard Business Review* article titled "Who Is Them?," Robert Reich surveyed the changing business landscape that faces the global manager. Reich cites several examples of products assembled from components designed and manufactured in several different nations. Mazda's newest sports car, for example, was designed in California and financed by Tokyo and New York, its prototype was created in Worthing, England, and it was assembled in Michigan and Mexico, using advanced electronic components invented in New Jersey and fabricated in Japan.

That is not a rare occurrence. On the contrary, it is becoming rare to find all the components of any complex product designed, manufactured, and assembled in one place.

Growing Telecommunciations Demand

Telecommunications has made it possible to build and assemble products with components that are manufactured wherever it makes sense to manufacture them. As geography has become irrelevant, modern communications networks have become crucial to nations that want to remain competitive. No nation without a solid communications infrastructure can hope to attract or retain world-class companies. At present, nations are trailing many companies when it comes to applying information technology.

Today's global companies are using information systems to meet the needs of time-sensitive operations and be more responsive to their customers. They are connecting R&D to manufacturing, inventory to suppliers, sales to service, and even themselves to their customers. With instant communication essential, telecommunications traffic today tends more often to be computer-to-computer and fax-machine-to-fax-machine than person-to-person, especially where differences in time zones come into play. More than 50% of the telecommunications traffic across the Pacific Ocean takes the form of facsimile messages. More than 3.7 billion fax pages transit the AT&T network each year, and fax service is expected to grow by some 250% over the next five years. AT&T projects that by 1995, about half the traffic carried by its network will be some form of data communications.

Under constant pressure to offer new capabilities and applications that combine multiple services, in 1991 AT&T launched AT&T EasyLink, a new business created to market advanced global messaging services. EasyLink services, such as electronic mail, electronic data exchange, enhanced fax, and video-conferencing, were high on customer shopping lists from EasyLink's first day in business.

Customer-Demand-Driven Technologies

As the war in the Gulf heated up and people got edgy about traveling, AT&T's video-conferencing volume grew by almost 400%. Technology has driven down the cost of the equipment necessary to support video-conferencing, and broadcast costs, thanks to digital technology, have plunged sharply as well. The pre-1988 cost of a one-hour coast-to-coast video conference was between $500 and $800. Today, the same video conference costs as little as $30 per hour. Moreover, video-conferencing is no longer just a domestic service. Technological advances and cooperation among PTTs have given us international switched digital service. Progress in video compression technology has enabled AT&T to offer one hour's worth of international video-conferencing for about $300, which compares with about $2,500 for the use of a dedicated wide-band circuit.

Video-conferencing can be an invaluable communications tool. I have held three-way video conferences with AT&T personnel in Hong Kong and Holland from my office in New Jersey, and I once conducted an employee telecast from Taiwan using a video-conferencing set-up.

The market for global messaging services is explosive. AT&T estimates that global messaging worldwide will be an $11 billion market, twice its current value, within five years.

Readers of this book will likely be using multimedia global messaging by the end of the decade, perhaps much sooner. They will retrieve from an electronic mailbox personal messages that might have originated anywhere in the world, and they will be able to convert faxed messages into computer-synthesized speech and voice messages into text.

Speech recognition technology will render keyboards, telephone dials, and keypads obsolete for effecting electronic transactions. Users will simply tell a communications device what they want. That is where users are pushing the technology.

Whatever device is used for communication will be the gateway to the global network, and the intelligence it calls upon will be stored in a remote part of that network. Integrated services digital network standards, better known as ISDN, will be in place globally. Already, AT&T provides ISDN connectivity to 10 countries.

Technology for the Twenty-First Century

The last major gap in the global network, broadband switching capability, will be filled by the turn of the century. Users are already demanding it. Microelectronics propelled telecommunications through the past two decades; photonics, or lightwave, will thrust the information revolution beyond the 1990s. Optical fibers—hair-like strands of ultrapure glass through which information is transmitted as pulses of light by lasers so tiny that two million of them fit on a chip the size of a fingernail—are replacing copper wires beneath streets and oceans around the world. The information-carrying capacity of optical fiber is virtually unlimited. Even at today's impressive transmission speeds, we are using less than 1% of the theoretical capacity of these information raceways.

The overall capability of lightwave communications systems is measured by multiplying the transmission data rate by the distance a signal can travel before it needs to be regenerated. Today, we can transmit signals commercially at 3.4 gigabits per second over 50 kilometers. At this speed, the entire *Encyclopedia Britannica* could be transmitted in less than one minute. This compares to five days for a voiceband circuit operating at 2,400 bits per second.

Lightwave transmission systems handled 242,000 calls simultaneously in 1989. Today, these systems can handle twice as many. This kind of progress could continue for another two decades at the same pace before we hit the wall of fundamental physical limitations. This leaves room for a thousandfold improvement over the capabilities of today's most advanced lightwave systems.

The information-carrying capacity of one fiber lightguide cable is equivalent to that of 155 reels of copper cable. Moreover, a 28-mile stretch of fiber cable requires only 100 two-way repeaters. A copper system of equivalent capacity would need about 20,000. The disparity in these numbers will only be made greater by recent improvements in lightwave capability. Optical amplifiers that strengthen lightwave signals will eliminate the need for high-speed electronics to convert and then regenerate signals. Moreover, because it is not confined to specified bit rates, the optical amplifier will boost signals carried by many different wavelengths, or "colors," of light. For example, a single two-way path at one gigabit per second could be upgraded to accommodate several simultaneous signals at four or even ten gigabits each. An undersea cable equipped with such amplifiers at regular spacings can be upgraded merely by changing the electronics that feed it from both shores. The tenth TransAtlantic cable will incorporate optical amplifiers, together with state-of-the-art fiber cable systems.

Bell Laboratories' researchers are working on the final bridge across the broadband gap—an optical switch. The capability has already been demonstrated. Using techniques similar to those employed for integrated circuits, an optical switching circuit has been created on the surface of a lithium niobate crystal. The switch is designed to accommodate 16 input and 16 output lines at the ultrahigh data rates associated with future optical transmission systems. AT&T could have an optical switch ready for the network market by the end of the decade. Such switches could fundamentally change the way we access and use information.

Switchings being computers, and vice versa, development of an optical switch obviously has implications for computing. The development of an optical computer, very likely early in the next century, is tantamount to reaching the Holy Grail of computer technology. Such a computer has the potential to be hundreds, perhaps thousands, of times faster than today's electronic computers. An optical switch no larger than a doctor's bag could someday handle all the voice and data traffic between France and Germany.

Beyond heretofore unheard-of capacity, optical switches will provide new capabilities that will put more information within our grasp. Most of today's telecommunications customers use single voice channels, each with a capacity of 64,000 bits per second. Future needs will demand hundreds of times this bandwidth. To accommodate the dramatic growth in data speeds, broadband ISDN line rates are approximately 150 megabits per second and optical fibers are replacing metal conductors in transmission. Tomorrow, we will need optical devices.

Breakthroughs in photonic communications are driving down

costs and increasing capacity and flexibility. Continued progress on a commercial optical switch will edge us toward yet another quantum leap in global network capability.

Private versus Public Networks

Some major companies are demanding private networks on a global scale. Such a network being developed for General Electric and British Telecom will be the largest private network ever built. When it is completed, any GE employee will be able to pick up a telephone and dial a seven-digit number to reach a colleague in any of the company's 1,400 offices in 25 countries on six continents. More important, GE's digital network will carry data, images, and video, and support private video conferences between senior executives and managers around the world.

Some companies will choose to manage their own global networks. But others, lacking the requisite expertise or simply not wanting to divert energies from their core businesses, are increasingly outsourcing the development and management of their telecommunications networks to international carriers.

In turn, many of these carriers—including AT&T—are extending their global networks both in quantity of facilities and range of services. AT&T, for example, now offers its software defined network (SDN), a virtual private network, or VPN, that is easily reconfigured to meet customers' changing needs and employs shared circuits to reduce costs in 12 countries. Given the flexibility and cost advantages of these networks, carriers can expect increasing pressure from customers to provide VPNs.

Countries as well as companies are reassessing their telecommunications infrastructures in light of customer demand for global communications capabilities. The U.S. Department of State, for example, is planning a global network similar to that being built by GE to connect U.S. government offices, embassies, and consulates in 42 countries. More important, this demand is the driving force in the rush to liberalize and privatize telecommunications agencies around the world. Untested by competition, many of these agencies have become inefficient bureaucracies operating outdated networks. In many underdeveloped countries, telephone line density is fewer than 10 lines per 100 people, compared to 50 lines per 100 people in the United States, and the wait for a consumer line is often measured in years. In addition to fostering a bureaucratic quagmire, Europe's former communist countries intentionally constrained the growth of telephone lines to limit the free flow of information, though not terribly successfully, as history has shown. Even in many developed countries, the continued prevalence of analog lines hampers the development of advanced telecommunications services.

Thus far, liberalization has been largely confined to permitting competition in value-added services, such as private networks for data communications. This satisfies the needs of multinational companies. But the United Kingdom has taken a significant further step in opening up local voice service to competitors. It remains to be seen just how open competition will be, but the U.K. government's move could presage intracountry competition in communications services in other nations.

Some countries are attempting to speed network modernization through privatization. Over the next five years, some 25 governments are expected to sell their telecommunications networks to private interests.

Restructuring for the Global Marketplace

AT&T has responded to customer demand for transformation of the communications industry by undertaking a major overhaul of its business structure. AT&T today has 20 business units with clear lines of accountability and responsibility for profits and a broad strategy to globalize its entire business with the goal of generating half its revenues from sources outside the United States by the end of the decade.

AT&T's commitment to broadening its focus from a domestic to a global market is underscored by several recent organizational changes. An AT&T vice chairman has been given oversight of international planning, development, and operations for worldwide services and products and responsibility for speeding up the globalization process.

Inasmuch as it made no sense in a company going global to preserve artificial walls and artificial distinctions that might impede decision making and interface with customer responsiveness, the company's international services division has been absorbed into organizations that serve business customers and consumers. To lend a local cast to global decision making, AT&T is experimenting in Spain with the designation of a country president to assume responsibility for integrated strategic and business plans, an approach the company hopes will provide a model for sharing accountability between in-country and global business unit management. Finally, AT&T has established a global affairs office that reflects the political realities of doing business abroad. Because foreign governments tend to play a larger and more direct role in economic development than the U.S. government, telecommunications companies must develop public affairs as well as marketing strategies tailored to individual countries.

AT&T, like many other companies, is facing the challenge of expanding to a transnational company while trying to satisfy the information needs of client transnationals, a difficult juggling act reminiscent of the task of dismantling the Bell System while continuing to provide telecommunications service to U.S. customers. Although the latter task was a monumental undertaking, often compared to taking apart and reassembling a 747 while in flight, it was arguably a new direction in familiar territory. AT&T's globalization task is a new direction in new territory.

AT&T's Global Progress

Global progress is measured not in miles, but in revenues. AT&T's rate of progress varies with business line. Some units are in the passing lane, others have just left the on ramp. AT&T's international services business is among the former. It has a long tradition and strong reputation in the world's telecommunications market.

In telecommunications products, AT&T, viewed as a newcomer in the 1980s, is picking up speed. Early in the decade, product sales topped $1.5 billion, as total international revenues reached nearly $6 billion.

AT&T has been using direct investments, partnerships, alliances, and joint ventures to establish itself in the global market. It has struck partnerships with strong companies in Europe and Asia and reexamined its entire global marketing effort, country by country, to determine what kinds of changes will be required to be successful in the decade ahead. AT&T has deepened its roots in Europe, opening state-of-the-art factories in Spain to produce electronic components and switching systems, making the Netherlands a center for its international network equipment business, and entering into a partnership with Italtel to expand the Italian network, a joint venture to rebuild the Ukrainian network, and contracts with other emerging democracies of Central Europe, such as Poland, to manufacture network equipment. AT&T now manufactures products in Europe, Asia, and Latin America. Working through its ISTEL subsidiary in the United Kingdom, the company is beginning to offer enhanced services, such as value-added networks, software applications, and electronic messaging, throughout Western Europe.

Meanwhile, AT&T is building a full information and management capability and acquiring the pieces needed to complete this puzzle. The acquisition of NCR and its networked computing capability was an important piece of this puzzle.

Inasmuch as AT&T's mission and role involve facilitating global connectivity, the company will at times enter into partnerships with PTTs and large companies engaged in providing telecommunications services. But on the equipment side, AT&T may well find itself competing with these same partners. Indeed, AT&T may find itself a customer, partner, supplier, and competitor of the same company at the same time.

How well AT&T balances its businesses and manages its complex role will determine how successful it will be in the 1990s and beyond. The global information market is expanding rapidly. It is estimated that the world will spend more money on network infrastructures in the next 10 years than in the 115 years since Alexander Graham Bell invented the telephone. The worldwide network investment, more than $50 billion in 1989 and expected to average $60 to $70 billion per year throughout this decade, is just part of the market AT&T is pursuing. The market for services will be even more lucrative. Businesses everywhere will be seeking whatever strategic edge they can get and demanding information capabilities that put them one up on their competitors. Demands to link operations within and between nations will intensify as companies expand their operations around the world. Customers will want more of what they are already demanding—interconnected information systems, simplified terminals capable of sending and accessing information in any form, voice, data, or image—much the same capabilities that GE's private global network will provide.

Eventually, the public switched network will be able to provide the kinds of innovative service only large companies can now afford, and at a much lower level of investment. But just as companies in other industries must deal with trade barriers and local rules and customs, so, too, will global service providers, such as AT&T.

Standards as Barriers

Common worldwide standards for communications technologies continue to elude us. Although international standards bodies such as the ITU and CCITT have made some progress in recent years, compatibility problems continue to plague providers and users alike. The root of the problems lies in the different paths along which telecommunications and computers evolved. Whereas the telephone system was designed to be interconnected, computers evolved as closed systems designed to meet specific data needs ranging from payroll to inventory. As telecommunications and data processing requirements began to merge, the lack of compatibility took center stage. The cry for common standards went out, not only from industry competitors, but from customers who saw the implications of combining their isolated islands of information into single, powerful knowledge networks.

The stakes are too high for common standards not to emerge in the near future.

The Broadband Society

We are moving toward a "broadband society" in which every individual will have access to virtually unlimited information. Universal access to information and the relatively inexpensive cost of transmitting it offer the potential to create a worldwide entrepreneurial revolution to rival the one that followed the personal computer. Universal telephone service, the goal of the past era, will be replaced by universal information services; global video tone will become a reality; much of future communications will emanate from a "wireless" world, with cellular radio joining advanced microelectronics technology to free us from reliance on the wall plug.

The technologies fueling global business developments will also change the home as consumers demand more communications options that deliver entertainment, news, and even work-at-home business capabilities.

Those involved in the global marketplace will find it much

easier to understand and respond to customers' needs. Managers will have more information at their fingertips and more control and flexibility in responding to the demands of the marketplace. If they act first when new information technologies appear, they will be able to move their companies ahead of the competition and, equally important, keep them there.

Exactly where the information revolution will lead us is difficult to predict. There seems to be no question that the marriage of computers and communications will go a long way toward democratizing information and, with it, people. The political and economic changes we have recently witnessed can be attributed, at least in part, to the free flow of information. As other barriers begin to collapse and trading is thrown open, vast opportunities will greet those who are prepared. And those who are prepared will be armed with information technologies that are one step ahead of those of the competition.

Most of the current trends in global communications point to continued high demand for telecommunications products and services for the next decade and beyond. Technological progress, propelled by consumer demand, will continue to accelerate, bringing new communications capabilities and increased user-friendly applications.

Those who will ride highest on these trends will be the people and organizations that are flexible enough to adapt as new technologies and market shifts produce constantly moving targets of opportunity in global commerce.

The importance of liberalization in clearing away the debris from the path of the Information Age cannot be overstressed. The liberalization of trade and of regulation and the formulation of policies that bolster market-based economies will hasten the expansion and modernization of global networks and at the same time deliver to individuals, companies, and governments the full benefits of information technology.

We are at a moment in history when technological, social, and political trends are converging to produce tremendous opportunities for securing a more peaceful and prosperous world. Telecommunications technology helped bring the world to the brink of this new age. Information technology will help us finish the journey.

About the Contributors

Stephen P. Bradley is the William Ziegler Professor of Business Administration and faculty chairman of the Executive Program in Competition and Strategy at the Harvard Business School. His current research interests center on the impact of technology on industry structure and the competitive strategies of firms. He has written numerous articles and four books on operations research and competitive strategy, including *Future Competition in Telecommunications* (co-edited with Jerry A. Hausman). Professor Bradley received his B.E. in electrical engineering from Yale University, where he was elected to Tau Beta Pi, and his M.S. and Ph.D. in operations research from the University of California, Berkeley. He is a member of the board of directors of the Controlled Risk Insurance Company, Ltd., an associate editor for strategy of *Interfaces,* and a past member of the editorial board of the *Harvard Business Review.*

Dr. Eric K. Clemons is associate professor of decision sciences and of management at the University of Pennsylvania Wharton School, and project director of the Reginald H. Jones Center's Sponsored Research Project in information systems, telecommunications, and business strategy. His research and teaching interests include strategic information systems, the use of information systems in international securities markets, and the impact of information technology on the distribution channel. He specializes in assessing the competitive implications of information technology and in managing the risk of large-scale implementation efforts. His education includes an S.B. in physics from the Massachusetts Institute of Technology and an M.S. and Ph.D. in operations research from Cornell University. Dr. Clemons is currently a member of the editorial boards of the

Journal of Management Information Systems, Information and Management, and the computing practices section of *Communications of the ACM.* His recent publications include "Evaluating Strategic Opportunities in Information Technology" and "Information Technology and the Changing Boundary of the Firm: Implications for Industrial Restructuring."

Robert G. Eccles is professor of business administration at the Harvard Business School. His undergraduate education was taken at the Massachusetts Institute of Technology where he received two bachelor of science degrees, one in mathematics and one in humanities and social science, in 1973. He received an A.M. and a Ph.D. in sociology from Harvard University. Professor Eccles's research and teaching interests are in the field of organizational design and management control systems. He is the author of *The Transfer Pricing Problem: A Theory for Practice* and co-author of *Doing Deals: Investment Banks at Work* and *Beyond the Hype.* Professor Eccles currently teaches in the executive education program and is chairman of the Organizational Behavior/Human Resources Management areas at the Harvard Business School.

Vice chairman of the board and co-founder of MicroAge, Inc., **Alan Hald** has been a pioneer in marketing microcomputers for business applications since opening Arizona's first computer store in 1976. He has helped MicroAge grow from a single location to a sales network of more than 1,200 franchised and affiliated locations. Mr. Hald has been honored by *Computer Reseller News,* and five times has been ranked in the list of the top 25 most influential people in the industry. A former chairman of the board of ABCD, he currently serves on the boards of directors of the Arizona Museum of Science and Technology and the Enterprise Network, and on the advisory board for COMDEX. He is also president of the Arizona Innovation Network and a member of the Governor's Science and Technology Council. Mr. Hald graduated from Rensselaer Polytechnic Institute and has an M.B.A. from Harvard University. He, his wife, and their six children live in Phoenix.

Professor **Janice H. Hammond** is an associate professor at the Harvard Business School, where she teaches courses in Technology and Operations Management, Business Logistics, Decision Support Systems in Logistics, and Quantitative Methods, in the M.B.A. and Executive Education programs. Her current research focuses on how manufacturing and logistics systems develop the speed and flexibility necessary to respond quickly and efficiently to changing customer demand, primarily in the packaged consumer-products and textile and apparel industries. Professor Hammond holds an S.B. in applied mathematics from Brown University and a Ph.D. in operations research from the mathematics department at the Massachusetts Institute of Technology.

Jerry A. Hausman, MacDonald Professor of Economics at the Massachusetts Institute of Technology, received his doctorate in economics from Oxford University, where he was a Marshall Scholar. In 1985, Professor Hausman received the John Bates Clark Award from the American Economics Association for the most outstanding contributions to economics by an economist under 40 years of age. He is currently director of the MIT Telecommunications Economics Research Program and a special consultant to Cambridge Economics, Inc. Professor Hausman has conducted research and done extensive consulting in the field of telecommunications economics and is co-editor of the book, *Future Competition in Telecommunications* (with Stephen P. Bradley), which considers evolving competitive issues in telecommunications services and equipment both in the United States and worldwide.

Dr. Arnoldo C. Hax is the Alfred P. Sloan Professor of Management and a Leaders for Manufacturing Professor at the Massachusetts Institute of Technology Sloan School of Management, where he served as deputy dean from 1987 through 1990. A native of Chile, he received his M.S. from the University of Michigan, and his Ph.D. from the University of California, Berkeley. He has published extensively (as author or co-author of seven books and more than eighty articles) in the fields of strategic planning, management control, operations management, and operations research. An accomplished teacher, Dr. Hax is the recipient of the Salgo Award for Excellence in Teaching at the Sloan School. He is also strategic management editor for *Interfaces,* and a former editor of *Operations Research* and

Naval Research Logistics Quarterly and serves on the editorial boards of the *Journal of Manufacturing, Operations Research,* and the *Journal of High Technology Management Research.*

George A. Hayter is best known in the securities industry as the man who led the transformation of the London Stock Exchange's trading and information systems throughout the 1980s, and especially in the run up to the Big Bang in 1986. After graduating in 1962 from Queen's College, Cambridge, with an M.A. in physics, and after two years as a control engineer in military avionics, he gravitated to the newly emerging field of business systems, joining a pioneering British computer manufacturer. Later at BOAC and British Airways he headed the development team for the global passenger reservation system, which he also helped install at several other airlines around the world. At the London Stock Exchange he headed the electronic information and trading services during a period of unprecedented development between 1976 and 1990. When he left the Exchange at the end of 1990, he was the managing director of the Trading Markets division. More recently, he has been a consultant to emerging stock exchanges and other businesses where the strategic deployment of technology is key to their success. He is a director of Bankinter Madrid, The Critchley Group, Cognotec Services, and Synergo Technology.

Pierre Hessler joined IBM in 1965 as a sales representative in Switzerland, where he held several managerial posts until he was named director of operations in 1980 for IBM Europe in Paris. In 1983 he came to the United States as an administrative assistant in the office of the vice president and group executive, Information Systems and Communications Group (IS&CG), and was named IS&CG director of software strategy the following year. In 1985 he returned to IBM Europe, Paris, as a general manager, area north, and in 1987 became EMEA vice president of market development. He was appointed IBM director of marketing and services in January 1989, and became a corporate vice president in November 1990. He was appointed directeur general du marketing, des services et des operations, IBM Europe in January 1991 and appointed to his current position, IBM vice president, in September 1992. A citizen of Switzerland, he is a graduate of the University of Lausanne with degrees in law and economics.

An authority on the management of computer-integrated manufacturing, Professor **Ramchandran Jaikumar** of the Harvard Business School has more than 20 years of industrial experience in the management of advanced manufacturing systems and establishing technology strategies. His current research interests include the design and analysis of operating systems using advanced manufacturing technologies and the restructuring of firms in a multiplant environment and where vertical integration has played a major role. Professor Jaikumar is widely published and has served as adviser to the Congressional Office of Technology Assessment and U.S. Senate subcommittees on Science and Technology, and a number of National Research Council committees. He has helped a number of firms restructure their operations worldwide and is working on industrial restructuring in Russia and Eastern Europe. Professor Jaikumar received his undergraduate degree in engineering from the Indian Institute of Technology and his Ph.D. from the Wharton School at the University of Pennsylvania.

Jahangir Karimi is associate professor of information systems at the University of Colorado College of Business at Denver. He received his M.S. and Ph.D. in management information systems from the University of Arizona in 1978 and 1983, respectively. His research and teaching interests include information systems modeling, analysis, and design; information systems strategy, planning, and management in national and international environments; and software engineering. He has published in *IEEE Transactions* on software engineering, *Management Information Systems Quarterly, Communications of the ACM, Journal of Management Information Systems,* and in a number of conference proceedings.

Benn R. Konsynski is George S. Craft Professor of Business Administration and area coordinator for Decision and Information Analysis at the Emory Business School, Emory University. Dr. Konsynski served six years on the faculty at the Harvard Business School, where he taught in M.B.A. and executive programs. Prior to arriving at Harvard, he was a professor at the

University of Arizona, where he was a co-founder of the university's multimillion dollar group decision support laboratory. He received his Ph.D. in computer science from Purdue University. His early research involved work on tools and methods in software engineering, model management, and group decision support. His current research involves domestic and international field work on interorganizational systems, electronic data interchange, channel systems, electronic integration, information partnerships, and the electronic marketplace. Other ongoing research involves work on information refineries, intelligent agents, and virtual reality and visualization. Dr. Konsynski has published books and papers in both technical and managerial areas. He serves on several boards of directors and has senior management advisory responsibilities.

Richard G. "Skip" LeFauve was appointed president of Saturn Corporation on February 3, 1986. In this capacity, he heads a unique effort to design and manufacture small cars in America to successfully compete with imports. Prior to joining Saturn, he was vice president of manufacturing operations for GM's Buick-Oldsmobile-Cadillac Group and in 1985 was named a vice president of General Motors Corporation.

A native of Orchard Park, New York, Mr. LeFauve earned a B.S. in mechanical engineering from Case Institute of Technology in Cleveland and attended the Senior Executive Program at the Massachusetts Institute of Technology. In 1957 he joined the U.S. Navy and earned his wings a year later. Following six years of active duty, he became a lieutenant commander in the Naval Reserve. From 1963 to 1983 he held various positions at the Packard Electric manufacturing organization, including those of plant manager, manager of production engineering, director of manufacturing engineering, and general manufacturing manager. Mr. LeFauve has also served as general manager of the Diesel Equipment division, general manager of Rochester Products division, and general manufacturing manager of Chevrolet Motor division.

Thomas W. Malone is the Patrick J. McGovern Professor of Information Systems at the Massachusetts Institute of Technology Sloan School of Management and director of the MIT Center for Coordination Science. His background includes a Ph.D. from

Stanford University and degrees in applied mathematics, engineering, and psychology. Professor Malone's research focuses on how computer and communications technology can help people work together in groups and organizations, and how organizations can be designed to take advantage of the new capabilities provided by information technology. Before joining the MIT faculty, he was a scientist at the Xerox Palo Alto Research Center, where his research involved designing educational software and office information systems. Professor Malone is on the editorial boards of *Human Computer International, Management Science, ACM Transactions on Information Systems,* and *Organizational Science.*

William Marx, Jr. heads a group of AT&T business units serving the telecommunications and electronics industries: AT&T Network Systems' equipment business units manufacture, market, and install a full line of network telecommunications equipment worldwide; AT&T Microelectronics manufactures and markets electronic components for AT&T and original equipment manufacturers around the world. Mr. Marx earned a bachelor of mechanical engineering degree from Union College, and a master of science degree in management from Stanford University's Sloan Program. He began his AT&T career as an engineer at Western Electric, where he has since held a number of positions, including those of director of engineering, executive vice president, and director of Teletype Corporation. In 1986 he assumed the duties of group vice president—computer systems, and in 1987 returned to Network Systems as executive vice president before becoming chief executive and president in 1989. He is a director of the Massachusetts Mutual Life Insurance Co., a member of the Junior Achievement National Board of Directors, New Jersey Chairman of the Greater New York Blood Program, and a member of the Stanford Sloan Alumni Advisory Board.

David B. Miller is one of Rosenbluth Travel Agency, Inc.'s 12 senior executives, currently holding the position of vice president, Global Information Technology. His primary responsibility is to develop the technological infrastructure required for the Rosenbluth International Alliance by leveraging the experience gained from the development of Rosenbluth's domestic technology platform. Since he joined the firm in 1986, Mr. Miller has spearheaded a number of technological innovations. Under his direction, Rosenbluth Travel developed the world's largest real-time integrated travel detail database and became the leader in consolidating travel data for U.S. corporations. Mr. Miller received an M.S.S. in social research from Bryn Mawr College and a B.S. in engineering and social science with distinction from Cornell University. He is active in many community and civic organizations such as the administrative board of the First United Methodist Church of Germantown, the mid-Atlantic board of the Appalachian Mountain Club, and the executive council of the Cresheimbrook Condominium Association.

Richard L. Nolan, professor of business administration at the Harvard Business School, is currently course head and teaches in the Information, Organization and Control Systems area of the M.B.A. program. He received his B.A. in operations research, M.B.A. in organization, and Ph.D. in business administration from the University of Washington in 1962, 1963, and 1966, respectively. Professor Nolan's research interests center on the role of information technology in business transformation. He is the former chairman and co-founder of Nolan, Norton & Co., a leading international organization of counselors, focusing on the effective management of computer-based technologies. The author of several books and numerous articles on information resource management, he continues to consult with organizations such as IBM, Metropolitan Life, and Ericsson Telecom AB. Professor Nolan is the originator of the States Theory for analyzing computer growth, a theory he researched and developed while an associate professor at the Harvard Business School.

John F. Rockart is the director of the Center for Information Systems Research and a senior lecturer at the Sloan School of Management, Massachusetts Institute of Technology, where he has taught and conducted research on the management and use of computer-based information systems since 1966. He is best known for the development of the critical success factors method for information and information systems planning, which served to initiate the field of executive support systems (ESS). His current research interests include the extension of ESS concepts into management support systems, business process redesign, and new software methods and tools for more effective systems development. He is the author of several articles and co-author of three books as well as the 1989 nonfiction winner of the Computer Press Association Book of the Year Award. Dr. Rockart serves on the boards of directors of five organizations and consults and lectures for several major companies.

Michael C. Row is a senior research associate in the Decision Sciences department of the University of Pennsylvania Wharton School and works with the Reginald H. Jones Center's Sponsored Research Project in information systems, telecommunications, and business strategy. His education includes a B.B.A. in accounting and computer science from the College of William and Mary and an M.B.A. in strategic planning from the Wharton School. Mr. Row has been a director of information systems at The MAC Group and a senior analyst in the management information consulting division of Arthur Andersen & Company.

A member of the Harvard Business School faculty since 1989, **David M. Upton** has taught the first-year M.B.A. course Production and Operations Management, the second-year M.B.A. course Operations Strategy, and Manufacturing in the Corporate Strategy in the executive education program. He has undergraduate and graduate degrees in engineering from Cambridge University and is a chartered mechanical engineer and registered European professional engineer. Upton completed his Ph.D. in industrial engineering at Purdue University. He also holds qualifications in accounting and finance. Professor Upton has worked in engineering, sales, and production at Tube Investments, Ltd., as a production engineer at TI Raleigh, Ltd., and carried out extensive consulting work on microcomputer operating systems. He has consulted at numerous corporations and taught executive programs on flexible manufacturing, robotics applications, information systems, and operations management. His current work explores the sources of flexibility in manufacturing through field-based research. He has written numerous journal and book chapters on computer-integrated manufacturing.

Index

ABB. *See* Asea Brown Boveri
"Account control," 24–25
Accumaster Management Service, 321, 322
Acquisition strategies, 292
Adhocracies, 47–49. *See also* Network organizational structures
Advanced Micro Devices (AMD), 25
Advance shipping notice (ASN), 196
Airline industry: *cabotage* rules, 242*n;* community networks and, 116; consolidated reporting and, 298; cooperative strategy in, 238–239; global logistics system and, 90
Airline reservations systems, 41, 87, 105, 233, 234; DOT rule changes for, 221–224; Rosenbluth International Alliance and, 301–303
Amadeus Coalition, 87
American Express, 119, 139, 292, 294
American Hospital Supply, 20, 46, 128–129
Andersen Consulting, 30
Answer networks, 51, 52
Apollo system, 301–302, 303
Apparel industry, 189–194; industry background, 189–190; quick response system and, 17, 192–194; standards-setting organizations and, 208–210
Apple Computer, 131, 140
ARPs. *See* Automatic replenishment programs
Artificial intelligence, 345–346, 355, 356
Asea Brown Boveri (ABB), 19, 124, 139, 247
ASN. *See* Advance shipping notice
ATMs. *See* Automatic teller machines
AT&T: Accumaster Management Service, 321, 322; broadband environment and, 311, 359–370; competitive advantage and, 22, 134, 138; cooperative approach at, 367–368; foreign markets and, 27; globalization and, 27, 314–315, 316, 320–322, 366–369; integrated services and, 7; Modified

Final Judgment and, 7, 317; NEC and, 20; restructuring at, 366–367; technology-based supplier competition and, 23; telecommunications standards and, 28, 309
AT&T EasyLink, 361–362
AT&T Network Systems, 320
AURORA system, 146
Automated indexing, 340
Automated recognition, 339–340
Automatic replenishment programs (ARPs), 204–205
Automatic teller machines (ATMs), 119, 132–133, 222–223, 235, 242*n*
Automation, 9–10

Bakos, Yannis, 46
Banking industry, 35, 90, 116, 119. *See* Financial services industry
Barclays de Zoete Wedd (BZW), 47, 162, 228–229
Bar coding, 196, 208
Barnevik, Percy, 247
Bartlett, Christopher, 33, 57–59, 65, 66, 82, 124
Bellcore, 28
Bell Laboratories, 364
Bell operating companies (BOCs): AT&T divestment of, 7, 316; competition and, 7, 314, 316, 326; foreign markets and, 320, 322–326, 327–330; standards and, 28
Benchmarks, and globalization, 215–216
Benetton, 122, 128, 140, 187–188, 192, 203
Bidding consortia, 130–131
"Big Bang." *See* London Stock Exchange
Bloomberg, Michael, 22, 134
BOCs. *See* Bell operating companies; Regional Bell operating companies
Bonfire of the Vanities (Wolfe), 226
Boundaries of the firm, 109, 232–233. *See also* Industry structure
Bradley, Stephen P., 3–32, 13, 110, 113–142

British Airways, 238–239
British Telecom (BT), 322, 365; U.S. market and, 313, 316, 321, 327, 329–330
Broadband society, 311, 359–370
Broadcasting industry, 119–120, 139, 325
Brokers: of manufacturing capacity, 181; securities, 162
Brynjolfsson, Erik, 46
BT. *See* British Telecom
Business environment, and global firms, 89–91
"Business process redesign," 136
Business strategy: differences in, and cooperative strategy, 239–240; at Du Pont, 101; global enterprise structures and, 82–87; global information system and, 98–106
Business systems. *See* Electronic Data Systems; Saturn Corporation
Buyer relationships, 128–130
BZW. *See* Barclays de Zoete Wedd

Cable News Network (CNN), 120
Cable television, 325, 328, 329
CAD. *See* Computer-aided design
CAE. *See* Computer-aided engineering
CAM. *See* Computer-aided manufacturing
Capital budgeting, 140–141
CAPs. *See* Competitive access providers
Carlson Travel Network, 292
Carlye, Richard, 89
Cash management account (CMA), 19, 126, 133
Caterpillar Tractor Company, 19, 125, 138
CATS system, 149
"C&C" strategy, 20, 126
CD-ROM technology, 345
Cellular telephones, 318–319, 323–324, 327–328, 329
Centralization versus decentralization: coordination-intensive structures and, 49–51; in hierarchical versus networked organization, 63; levels of design approach and, 68, 72, 78; local-global balancing and, 254–255; multinational strategy and, 83
Centralized remote meter reading, 117
Chandler, A. D., 37, 230
Channels, 186–188. *See also* Distribution channels
Chicago Board of Options Exchange, 165
Chicago Board of Trade, 146
Chicago Mercantile Exchange, 164

Chief information officer (CIO), 76, 99–101
CIM. *See* Computer-integrated manufacturing
Cincinnati Stock Exchange, 149
CIO. *See* Chief information officer
Citibank VISA, 139
Classes, in OOPS, defined, 351
Clemons, Eric, 18, 21, 216, 218, 219–242, 283–307
CMA. *See* Cash management account
CNN. *See* Cable News Network
Collis, Digby, 299
Colocation, 205, 231
Community networks, 14, 116
Competitive access providers (CAPs), 317
Competitive advantage: based on market inefficiency, 45; in future information technology industry, 30–31; global systems at Du Pont and, 102–103; key threats to, 21–23; leveraging of resource differences and, 228–229; in retail industry, 185–186; versus strategic necessity, 136–141; sustainability of, 21–23, 46–47, 110–111, 131–136; threats to, 132–136
Competitive environment: before and after "Big Bang," 159–160; DOT rule changes for CRSs and, 223–224; globalization of travel industry and, 291–293; integrated services and, 6
Competitive strategy, 5–6. *See also* Competitive advantage: change in basis of competition and, 24–25; early-mover advantages and, 137–138; formulation of, and self-design, 70; IT networking and, 18–21, 123–126, 224–229; strategic necessity and, 138–140
Competitor retaliation, 138
Comp-U-Card, 46
Compu-Store, 46
Computer-aided design (CAD), 16, 88, 114, 275; manufacturing industry and, 121, 171; quick response system and, 201; retail industry and, 17, 129–130
Computer-aided engineering (CAE), 88, 114, 275
Computer-aided manufacturing (CAM), 16, 88, 275
Computer hardware manufacturers. *See* Hardware industry
Computer-integrated manufacturing (CIM), 125, 138
Computerized reservation systems (CRSs). *See* Airline reservations systems

Computer-mediated decision networks, 53
Conferencing systems, 48–49. *See also* Video-conferencing
Consensus, 258, 296
Consortia, 295
Cooperative strategy. *See also* Rosenbluth International Alliance: airline industry and, 238–239; boundaries of the firm and, 232–233; competitive advantage and, 139–140; complicating factors for, 239–240; global implications of, 236–239; incentives and, 298–300; IT networking and, 126–131; objectives of partners and, 239–240, 305; process of globalization and, 250–251; service industries and, 284, 303–306; telecommunications industry and, 321–322
Coordinated federated organizational structure, 85–87
Coordination-intensive structures. *See also* Quick response system: adhocracies and, 47–49; market efficiency and, 44–47; shift toward use of, 42–44
"Coordination technology," 12–13, 38, 219
"Core competencies," 64–65
Corporate culture: cooperative strategy and, 240, 262–273, 305; IBM and, 251; quick response system and, 208; use of new technologies and, 48
Corporate philosophy, at Saturn, 260–261
COSMOS, 123
Countries, telecommunications infrastructures in, 365–366
Country managers, 100–101
Coupon-generating equipment, 235–236
Credit card industry, 119, 139, 238
Cross-border cooperation, 303–306. *See also* Rosenbluth International Alliance
Cross-border trading, 146–147
CRSs (computerized reservation systems). *See* Airline reservations systems
Customer demand: DEC and, 26–27; improved information technology and, 41–42; improved transportation technology and, 39–40; IT industry structure and, 30–31; local-global balancing and, 253; strategy formulation and, 70; technology development and, 311, 338, 359, 362–363
Customer lock-in, 25
Customs systems, 104–105. *See also* TradeNet

Daimler-Benz, 127–128
Databases. *See also* Value-added information service industries: Du Pont's management strategy for, 102; information management strategy and, 96–98; quick response system and, 197; superordinate-designed infrastructures and, 65
"Data channel" strategy, 25
Data Processing Era, 9–10, 61
Data transfer, 196–201
DEC. *See* Digital Equipment Corporation
Decentralization. *See* Centralization versus decentralization
Decision framing, 70–73, 78
Decision making, 53, 70–73, 82, 258, 296
Decision support systems, 203–205
Deregulation, 138, 285–287. *See also* Modified Final Judgment; London Stock Exchange and, 15, 118–119, 152, 159, 225
Deutsche Bundespost Telekom, 321–322, 323
Digital camera images, 200
Digital Equipment Corporation (DEC), 24, 26–27, 124, 198
Digital video interactive (DVI) technology, 345
Dillard's Department Stores, 185, 204
Distribution agreements. *See* Nonequity collaborations
Distribution channels, 220–221, 340; CRS service profitability and, 222–223; quick response system and, 186–188; Saturn and, 272–273, 276–277
Doing Deals (Eccles & Crane), 35
Domestic distributed systems versus global information systems, 89, 98, 100
Domestic market, 30–31
DOT. *See* United States, Department of Transportation
Dow Jones: Dow Vision service, 119, 340; news retrieval service, 116–117, 138; strategic necessity and, 138, 139
DP Era. *See* Data Processing Era
Drucker, Peter, 60
DuMont, Stephen, 200–201
Du Pont, 60; global systems at, 101–103
DVI technology. *See* Digital video interactive technology

Early-mover advantages, 137–138
Eastern Europe, 333*n*
Eastman Kodak Co., 289, 290, 298

Eccles, Robert, 35; organizational network structures and, 13, 57–80
Economies of scale and scope: competitive advantage and, 233, 234–235; global manufacturing and, 170–172, 173; horizontal relationships and, 19, 125; new industries and, 118; size economies, 137; standards and, 28; telecommunications industry and, 319
Economost distribution system, 226, 231, 233
EDI. *See* Electronic data interchange
EDS. *See* Electronic Data Systems
EFT. *See* Electronic funds transfer
EIS. *See* Executive information system
Electronic data interchange (EDI): contrasted with E-mail, 198; customer relations and, 114; Federal Express and, 22, 133, 139; Norwegian customs system and, 104; organizational change and, 341; quick response system and, 196–198, 208; retail industry and, 17, 193; Saturn and, 271–272, 276; value-added/managed data networks and, 116
Electronic Data Systems (EDS), 14, 30, 116, 135, 274–277
Electronic funds transfer (EFT), 272
Electronic mail (E-mail), 47, 66, 116, 198
Electronic markets, 46, 49, 51–52
E-mail. *See* Electronic mail
Employees, and shared global vision, 247–249
Engle, Kris, 300
Ephlin, Donald, 257
Ephraim, Gerry, 289, 290, 293
Equity collaborations, 86–87. *See also* Interorganizational systems
Eunetcom partnership, 321–322
European Community (EC), 318, 327
European companies, and multinational strategy, 83
Executive information system (EIS), 42
Expert systems, 356–357

Fabric and Suppliers Linkage Council (FASLINC), 209
FASLINC. *See* Fabric and Suppliers Linkage Council
Fax service, 22, 133, 139, 200, 361
Federal Express: competitive advantage and, 22, 133, 137, 138, 139; IT networking and, 18–19, 123; technological innovation at, 342–343
Financial networks, 163–164
Financial Services Act (U.K.), 153
Financial services industry. *See also*

Banking industry; London Stock Exchange; Securities markets: competitive advantage and, 139, 234; effects of telecommunications revolution on, 166–168; opportunities and challenges in, 162–166; pressure for change in, 144–145; restructuring of, 14–15, 111, 118–119, 148–168
Financial staff, 74–75
Flexible manufacturing capacity, 16, 121. *See also* Global manufacturing: advantages of capacity market, 174; as commodity, 169–170, 181; design issues, 180–181; growing arena for, 181–183; Prato textile industry and, 175–179; quick response system and, 206–207
Ford Europe, 11–12, 136
Ford Motor Company, 20–21, 127–128, 136, 140, 233
Forecasting systems, in retailing, 203–205
France Telecom, 313, 321–322
Franchises. *See* Equity collaborations
Frito-Lay, 42, 220–221, 235, 342, 343
Fuzzy logic, 345–346

Galileo Coalition, 87
GE. *See* General Electric
GEIS. *See* General Electric Information Systems
Gemini system, 301, 303
General Electric (GE): "business process redesign" and, 136; cooperative strategy at, 130; medical imaging, 124–125; private network, 365; quick response system and, 17–18; Wal-Mart and, 17–18, 137, 139
General Electric Information Systems (GEIS), 14, 116, 130
General manager. *See also* Management challenges; Senior management: alignment of business and information systems strategies and, 98–99; management challenges, 335–336, 337–341; meta-trends and, 354–357; technological trends and, 341–354
General Motors (GM), 135–136, 234, 242n. *See also* Electronic Data Systems; Saturn Corporation; UAW-GM cooperation
Ghemawat, Pankaj, 21, 132, 135, 137
Ghoshal, Sumantra, 33, 57–59, 65, 66, 82, 124
Global economy, 359–361
Global enterprise. *See also* Global information system; Information management strategy; Transnational firm:

components of globalization process, 247–251; concept of being global and, 215–216, 217, 243–251; definition of, 245; local-global balancing and, 246, 249, 252, 253–255; need for global information system in, 87–91; structures and strategies in, 82–87

Global information system (GIS), 87–98. *See also* Information management strategy: business environment and, 89–91; business strategy and, 82; defined, 88–89; versus domestic distributed systems, 89, 98; at Du Pont, 101–103; management options for, 91–94; public sector role in design of, 104–106

Globalization: alliance strategy and, 250–251; catalysts of, 336; concept of, 215–216; customer needs and, 250; domestic market and, 30–31; IBM and, 20, 26–27, 217, 251–253; information technology planning and, 250; ingredients in process of, 247–251; local-global balancing and, 249, 252; management principles and, 4–5; measurement of progress and, 249; obstacles to, in travel industry, 290; present reality of, 220; for service industries, 284, 303–306; shared global vision and, 247–249; technological innovation and, 3–8; in telecommunications industry, 313–334

Global manufacturing: design of coordination system for, 180–181; factory size and, 170–174; labor and, 172–173; management information and, 180–181; manufacturing cell and, 170–171; market conditions and, 169–170; Prato textile industry and, 175–179; product and process specifications and, 171; programmable computer control and, 181–183; transaction processing and, 171–172

Global messaging services, 362

Global strategy: organizational structure and, 83–84; process of globalization and, 247–249

GM. *See* General Motors

Godfrey, Nancy, 293

Government policy. *See also* Regulation: design of global information systems and, 104–106; foreign investment in telecommunications and, 330–331

Greene, Judge Harold, 7

Haggar Apparel Co., 193

Hald, Alan, 30, 310, 335–358

Hamel, Gary, 64

Hammond, Janice, 16–17, 111–112, 185–214

Hardware industry. *See also* Telecommunications industry: competitive environment, 24–26, 309–310; critical technological trends in, 341–354; future IT industry structure and, 30–31; high-performance platforms, 341; optical switching and, 364; standards formation and, 27–29

Hausman, Jerry A., 3–32, 23, 310, 313–334

Hax, Arnoldo C., 21, 218, 257–281

Hayter, George, 15, 111, 143–168

HDTV. *See* High Definition Television

Hessler, Pierre, 20, 27, 58, 217, 243–255

Hierarchical organizational structure. *See also* Organizational structure: impact of the computer on, 59–77; versus network, 33–35, 47–48; networks floating on, 59, 60, 62, 68–69

High Definition Television (HDTV), 200–201

Holdup, 22–23, 134

Home base country, 89–91

Hong Kong, 90

Horizontal relationships, 19–20, 125–126

Howard, Paul, 296

Human literate systems, 355–357

Human resources, 66, 75, 76–77, 275

Hypermedia, 340

Hypertext, 340

IBM: Apple and, 131, 140; competitive environment, 24, 243; competitive strategy, 24–25, 137; cooperative strategy, 131, 243; customer demands, 26–27, 243; globalization and, 20, 26–27, 217, 251–253; integrated services and, 7; local-global balancing and, 252, 253–255; Microsoft and, 131, 137; Nolan, Norton Institute study, 243–251; organizational slack and, 136; PS2 PCs, 25; Rohm acquisition, 20

IBM standard, 25, 27–28

IDN. *See* Integrated digital network

Image transfer, 196–201

Imitation, 21–22, 132–133, 138

Impannatori, 177–178

Incentives: cooperative approaches and, 298–300; for use of new technologies, 48

Indexing, automated, 340

Industrial Economy, 37–39, 62–63, 70–71, 109, 360

Industry structure: channel perspective and, 186–188; IT networking and, 14–18, 115–122; winners and losers from changes in, 217, 219–220, 233–235

"Informated organization," 10

Information capture, cost of, 61

Information-driven industries, 14, 29–30, 166–168. *See also* Multimedia; News retrieval services; Value-added information service industries; Video-conferencing

Information Economy, 37–39, 62–63, 70–71, 77

Information intensity: emergence of, 29–30, 335–337; management challenges and, 337–341; organizational design and, 61–62, 339–341; trends in, 339–341

Information management strategy: alignment with business strategy, 98–106; data architecture and, 96–98; global structures and, 91–94; network architecture and, 94–95; standards and, 95–96

Information networking services, 14

Information Resources, Inc., 117–118

Information systems, 36

Information systems staff, 75–76

Information technology: achievement of desires and, 54; automobile defect detection and, 272–273; effects of improvement in, 40–44; financial market opportunities and, 162–166; key technologies, 311; management challenges and, 335–336, 337–341; market efficiency and, 44–47; in process of globalization, 250; reshaping of organizations and, 34–35, 37–56; return on investment in, 140–141; role in global enterprise, 87–98; superordinate-design and, 65, 67–68, 76; transaction costs and, 231–232; travel services and, 285, 288–289, 301–303, 304–305; trends in, 310–311, 335–358, 363–365

Information technology industry, 7, 27, 30–31. *See also* Hardware industry; Software industry

Information technology (IT) networking. *See also* Integrated services: competitive strategy and, 18–21, 123–126, 224–229; cooperative strategy and, 126–131; industry structure and, 115–122; strategic applications of, 115–131; sustainability of competitive advantage and, 110–111, 113–115, 131–136

Infrastructure, 64–68, 71–73

Inheritance, in OOPS, defined, 352

Instinet, 165

Insurance industry, 116

Integrated digital network (IDN), 91

Integrated services. *See also* "Coordination technology"; Information technology (IT) networking: competitive environment and, 6, 7–8, 24–26; competitive strategies and, 18–21; demand for, 6, 8–13; industry structure and, 14–18, 115–118; organizational impact of, 12–13; producer/user interface and, 26–27; Stages Theory and, 8–13; suppliers and, 6–7, 17–18, 20–21, 24–26; sustainability of competitive advantage and, 21–23

Integrated services digital network (ISDN), 28, 91, 210, 362–363, 364

Intel, 25–26

Intelligent products, 10–12

Intel standard, 25–26, 28

Interactive media, 344–345

International Stock Exchange (ISE), London, 15, 152–154. *See also* London Stock Exchange

International Telephone and Telegraph (ITT), 315

Interoperability standards, 348–350, 354–355

Interorganizational systems (IOSs), 13, 86–87. *See also* Equity collaborations; Nonequity collaborations

Investment banking industry, 35

IOSs. *See* Interorganizational systems

Iridium communication system, 346

ISDN. *See* Integrated services digital network

ISE (International Stock Exchange). *See* London Stock Exchange

IT networking. *See* Information technology (IT) networking

Ito-Yokado, 204

Jackson, Kenneth, 54

Jaikumar, Ramchandran, 16, 111, 169–183

Japan: competition in telecommunications and, 7–8, 316, 318; department stores in, 205–206; National Bicycle Company, 129

J.C. Penney, 185, 200, 201–202, 203

J.D. Power and Associates, 277–279

Joint production economies. *See* Economies of scale and scope

Joint ventures, 131, 134. *See also* Cooperative strategy; Equity collaborations

Jones, Daniel, 135

Kaleida, 131
Karimi, Jahangir, 13, 36, 81–108
KDD (Japan), privatization of, 318
Kennedy, John F., 63
KLM, 239
Knowledge codification, 340
Komatsu, 138
Konsynski, Benn, 13, 30, 36, 81–108, 335–358

Labor market, internal, 52–53
LANs. *See* Local area networks
Laptop computers, 50–51. *See also* Microcomputers
Latin America, telecommunications in, 326
"Leadership through Quality" program at Xerox, 128
Leep Systems, 354
Le Fauve, Richard G., 21, 218, 257–281
LeviLink, 198, 199
Levi Strauss & Co., 187–188, 196, 198, 199, 205, 207
Lexus/Nexus, 116–117, 138
Licensing arrangements. *See* Nonequity collaborations
The Limited, 122, 185, 187–188, 192, 201–203
Liz Claiborne, 187–188
Local area networks (LANs), 11
Local-global balancing, 246, 249, 252, 253–255
London Stock Exchange, 45, 118–119, 164: consequences of "Big Bang," 157–161, 225–226; dealer markets and, 149–150; events surrounding "Big Bang," 151–156; participation on, 151; "the touch" measure, 160–161; unification of U.K. exchanges and, 152–153

McCaw, 327, 329
The Machine that Changed the World (Womack, Jones, & Roos), 135–136
McKesson Drug Company, 226–228, 231
Mainframe computing, 9–10, 25, 27–28
Malone, Thomas W., 12–13, 34–35, 37–56
Management challenges, 335–336, 337–341. *See also* Information management strategy
Management control systems, 69–70, 78
Managing Across Borders (Bartlett & Ghoshal), 33, 57–59, 65, 66, 82
Mannesmann Mobilfunk GmbH, 323

Manufacturers' representatives, and retail stores, 205–206
Manufacturing cell, 16, 111, 121, 170–171, 206
Manufacturing industry. *See also* Apparel industry; Flexible manufacturing capacity; Global manufacturing; Textile industry: negotiation and, 178–179; quick response system and, 211; restructuring in, 15, 111, 120–121
Manufacturing process, 275
Market efficiency, 34–35, 44–47, 160–161
Marketing agreements. *See* Nonequity collaborations
Market Response Information System (MRIS), 200
Markets, and coordination of economic activity, 44–47, 93
Marlin Travel, 290, 293, 298, 299, 306n
Marx, William, Jr., 27, 311, 359–370
Massachusetts Institute of Technology International Motor Vehicle Study, 259
MasterCard International, 238
MAST industries, 188, 192, 197, 200–201, 208
MCI, 317, 319
Mead, Thomas, 101
Medical imaging, 15, 120, 124–125
Menichetti family, 176
Merrill Lynch, 19, 22, 126, 133, 134, 162
Mervyn, 193–194
MFJ. *See* Modified Final Judgment
Microcomputers. *See also* Laptop computers; Personal computers: in consumer products, 10–12; informating and, 10; interoperability standards, 348–350; trends in, 342–344
Micro Era, 10–11, 61
Microsoft, 28, 131, 137, 140
Miller, David, 21, 218, 283–307
Millette, Ron, 290, 293, 298, 299
Milliken & Co., quick response system and, 17, 43, 127, 192, 193
Minority equity investments. *See* Equity collaborations
MIPS (millions of instructions per second), 355
Modified Final Judgment (MFJ), 7–8, 28, 317–318
Motorola, 46, 346
Moxness, David, 299
MRIS. *See* Market Response Information System
Multimedia, 200, 344–345, 362
Multinational strategy, 83

NASDAQ, 148, 150, 153, 162, 163
National Bicycle Company (Japan), 129
National competitive posture, 92, 106–107
NEC, 7, 20, 23, 126
Negotiation system, in manufacturing, 179, 180–182
Network architecture, 82; at Du Pont, 101–102; information management strategy and, 94–96; quick response system and, 194–201
Network Era, 11–12, 310
Network organizational structures, 5, 13, 34. *See also* Organizational structure: design of, 35; investment banking industry and, 35; IT industry structure and, 30–31; relation to hierarchy, 59, 60, 62, 68–69; self-design and, 68–69
Neural networks, 345–346
New industries: competitive advantage and, 138; IT networking and, 14, 115–118
News retrieval services, 14, 116–117
New York Cash Exchange (NYCE), 233, 235
New York Stock Exchange, 148, 165
Nolan, Norton Institute study, 243–251
Nolan, Richard L., 3–32, 35, 57–80; concept of transformation, 246; Stages Theory, 8–13
Nonequity collaborations, 86–87. *See also* Interorganizational systems
Northwest Airlines, 239
Norway, 104
Notebook computers, 342–344, 355–356
NTT (Japan), 313, 318, 321, 322
NUMI, 135
Nurick, Carl, 292–293, 294, 299–300
NYCE. *See* New York Cash Exchange
NYNEX, 325

Object, in OOPS, defined, 351
Objectives: cooperative strategy and, 239–240, 305; in traditional versus networked organization, 63
Object-oriented programming (OOPS), 350–352, 356
Ohmae, Kenichi, 120
OOPS, 350–352, 356
Open systems, 27–29, 231
Optical switching, 363–365
Order-driven financial markets, 148–149
Order fulfillment process, in retailing, 206, 207
Order routing systems, 148
Organizational design: self-design and, 59, 62–63, 68–70; superordinate design and, 64–68; two levels of design approach to, 62–70, 78
Organizational learning, 335–336
Organizational power, coordination-intensive structures and, 49–51
Organizational slack, 23, 134–136
Organizational structure. *See also* Coordination-intensive structures; Hierarchical organizational structure; Network organizational structures; Organizational design: coordination-intensive structures and, 42–44; framework for design of, 62–70; global strategy and, 83–84; improved information technology and, 42–44, 51–53; improved transportation technology and, 39–40; multinational strategy and, 83; network versus hierarchy and, 33–35; Saturn and, 258–259, 266–269; self-design and, 68–69; transnational strategy and, 85–86
Orlikowski, Wanda, 48–49
Otis Elevator Company, 41
Otisline system, 41
Outsourcing, 46–47, 102, 233, 236. *See also* Suppliers
Overnight organizations, 51–52
Oxford Analytica, 117, 138

Pacific Telesis, 323
Palm-top computers, 342–344
PCNs. *See* Personal communications networks
PCSs. *See* Personal communications networks
PDT. *See* Product Development Team
Performance measurement, 66–67, 247, 249
Perot, Ross, 274
Personal communications networks (PCNs), 319, 324–325, 328, 329, 346–347
Personal computers (PCs), 25–26, 28–29. *See also* Microcomputers
Personal digital assistants, 342–344
Phillips Petroleum, 50
Phone-mail, 66
PLU. *See* Price look-up
Point-of-sale (POS) data analysis: quick response system and, 196, 197, 204; retail industry and, 17, 117–118, 122, 191
Pollock, Alex, 59
Porter, Michael, 30–31
POS. *See* Point-of-sale data analysis
Posit, 165
Prahalad, C. K., 64
Prato textile system (Italy), 16, 39, 43–44, 121, 175–179

Price look-up (PLU), 196
Pritchett, Lou, 185–186
Private versus public networks, 365–366
Procter & Gamble, 17, 43, 127, 205, 235–236
Prodigy, 22, 117, 138
Producer/user interface, 26–27
Product development cycle, 201–202
Product Development Team (PDT), 271–272
Product differentiation, 24–25
Product identification, 196
Product line, worldwide, 253–254
Product tracking, 196
Programmable machines, 16, 181–183
Project tasking, 66
PTT (Post, telephone, telegraph), 90, 315, 316, 317
Public sector, global information systems design in, 104–106
PWAF ("Plant with a Future") project at Caterpillar, 125

Quick response system. *See also* Coordination-intensive structures: channel perspective and, 186–188; components of, 194–208; corporate culture and, 208; defined, 191; forecasting and replenishment systems, 203–206; genesis of, in U.S., 190–192; implementation of, 210–212; information architecture of, 194–201; product development cycle and, 201–202; product identification technology, 196; product tracking technology, 196; rapid order fulfillment, 206; retail industry and, 16–17, 121–122, 185–214; short-cycle manufacturing, 206–207; standardization of technologies in, 208–210; test marketing, 202–203
Quote-driven financial markets, 149

Radio frequency (RF) units, 198
RBOCs. *See* Regional Bell operating companies
Regional Bell operating companies (RBOCs), 22–23, 117, 317
Regulation: competition in telecommunications and, 8, 321–322; global firms and, 90–91; U.K. financial markets and, 153–154, 159
Reich, Robert, 360–361
Relationships, 137. *See also* Buyer relationships; Cooperative strategy; Horizontal relationships; Rivals, relationships among; Suppliers; Vertical relationships
Reliability, 180

Replenishment systems, in retailing, 204–205
Resource allocation, 67
Response lags, 138
Restructuring of industries. *See also* London Stock Exchange: IT networking and, 14–18, 118–123, 225–226; manufacturing industry and, 15, 111; retail industry and, 16–18, 111–112; securities industry and, 111; strategic necessity and, 139–140; winners and losers from, 217, 219–220, 233–235
Retail industry. *See also* Saturn dealers: competitive advantage in, 185–186; computer-aided design and, 129–130; cooperative strategy in, 127, 128; electronic markets and, 46; participants in, 195; quick response system and, 16–17, 121–122, 185–214; restructuring in, 16–18, 111–112, 121–122
Return on investment, 140–141
Reuters, 139, 156, 163, 164–165
Reward system, at Saturn, 269–270
RIA. *See* Rosenbluth International Alliance
RINET, 116
Rivals, relationships among, 130–131
Rockart, John F., 12–13, 34–35, 37–56
Roos, Daniel, 135
Rosenbluth, Hal, 237, 286, 301
Rosenbluth International Alliance (RIA), 22, 43, 218, 236, 237–238; client services, 297–298; creation of, 284, 288, 293; incentives and stability in, 298–300; local presence and, 293–295; role of information technology in, 301–303, 304–305; structure of, 295–296
Rosenbluth Travel, 21, 43, 218, 233, 236. *See also* Rosenbluth International Alliance: cooperative approach at, 293–295; deregulation and, 285–287; pressure for globalization at, 288–290
Rossi, Walter, 193
Routing systems, 148, 340
Row, Michael, 21, 218, 283–307

SAFLINC. *See* Sundries and Apparel Findings Linkage Council
Saturn Corporation, 135, 217–218, 234; accomplishments of, 277–280; business systems development at, 274–277; cooperative strategy, 21, 130; core values, 261–262; corporate philosophy, 260–261; dealer relationships, 272–273; fundamental lessons

Saturn Corporation (Continued)
from, 280–281; mission statement,
260; organizational structure, 258–
259, 266–269; origins of, 257–259;
partnership strategy at, 262–273; re-
wards systems at, 269–271; self-
directed teams and, 264–266; sup-
plier relationships, 271–272;
technological initiatives at, 273–274
Saturn dealers, 272–273
SBUs. *See* Strategic business units
Scanner technology, 235, 339
Schlumberger, 125–126
SCM. *See* Shipping container marking
SDN. *See* Software defined network
SEAQ. *See* Stock Exchange Automatic
Quotations
SEAQ International, 156
Securities firms, and London's "Big
Bang," 154–156
Securities Investment Board (SIB), 153
Securities markets. *See also* Financial
services industry: future directions
in, 165–166; impacts of information
technology on, 145–151; order-driven
systems, 148–149; order routing sys-
tems, 148; physical versus virtual
trading floor and, 145–146, 147–148;
quote-driven systems, 149; restructuring of, 111, 143–168; telephone trading and, 150
"Self-designed networks," 59, 62–63,
68–70; decision making and, 70–73;
superordinate-designed infrastructures and, 66, 68
Self-directed teams, 264–266
Seminole Manufacturing Co., 17, 43,
127, 192–193
Senior management. *See also* Chief information officer; General manager;
Management challenges: changing
role of, 73–77, 78, 98–101; decision
framing and, 70–73; superordinate information structure design and,
64–68, 78
Service industries, globalization for,
284, 303–306
7-Eleven, 204
Sharing of knowledge: database infrastructure and, 65; incentives and,
48–49
Sheet metal spinning, 182
Shipping container marking (SCM),
196
SIB. *See* Securities Investment Board
Singapore, 89–90
Single business applications of IT networking, 123–124

SITA. *See* Société Internationale de
Telecommunications Aeronautique
Size economies, 137
SKU. *See* Stock-keeping unit
Slack, 23, 134–136
Sloan, Alfred, 60
Smith, Roger, 242*n*, 259
Société Internationale de Telecommuni-
cations Aeronautique (SITA), 116
Society for Worldwide International
Funds Transfers (SWIFT), 91, 116
Software, and integrated services, 7,
29, 30–31
Software defined network (SDN), 365
Software industry, 26
Sony Corporation, 19, 123–124; "Still
Image System," 201–202
Speech recognition technology, 362
Spring making, 182–183
Sprint, 317, 319
SQL. *See* Structured query language
Stages Theory, 8–13
Standards. *See also* Open systems:
AT&T and, 28, 309; formation of, 27–
29; global information management
and, 95–96; Intel and, 25–26, 28; in-
ternational, 27, 28; interoperability,
348–350, 354–355; personal comput-
ers and, 25–26, 28–29; quick re-
sponse system and, 208–210; for tech-
nical document formats, 339–340; in
telecommunications, 27, 28, 91, 369
Standards-setting organizations,
208–210
The Stock Exchange. *See* London Stock
Exchange
Stock Exchange Automatic Quotations
(SEAQ), 15, 150, 153, 156, 160–161,
225–226
Stock exchanges, opportunities for,
164–166. *See also specific exchanges*
Stock-keeping unit (SKU), 191
Strategic business units (SBUs), 60
Strategic control, defined, 89
Strategic necessity, 138–140, 226–228,
235–236
Strategy. *See* Business strategy; Com-
petitive strategy; Global strategy; In-
formation management strategy
Structured query language (SQL), 91
Substitution, 21–22, 39, 40–41, 133
Sundries and Apparel Findings Link-
age Council (SAFLINC), 209
Supermarket check-out aisle, 235–236
"Superordinate design," 59, 64–68
Suppliers. *See also* Channels; Outsourc-
ing: Du Pont network management
and, 102; integrated services and,

6–7, 17–18, 20–21; IT networking and, 6–7, 17–18, 20–21, 127–128; number of, and market efficiency, 46–47; Saturn and, 271–272; technology-based competition and, 23–31; value of local relationships, 293–294

SWIFT. *See* Society for Worldwide International Funds Transfers

Syncordia Corporation, 321, 322

Systems integrators, 30

TALC. *See* Textile and Apparel Linkage Council

Taligent, 131

"Taxonomy of knowledge" problem, 357

TBDF regulations. *See* Transborder data flow regulations

TCE. *See* Transaction costs economics

Technological innovation. *See also* Information technology; Telecommunications: company demand for, 6; customer demand and, 311, 338, 359, 362–363; globalization and, 3–8; at Saturn, 273–274

Technology transfer, 299

Telecommunications industry. *See also specific companies:* cable television and, 325, 328, 329; cellular telephones and, 318–319, 323–324, 327–328, 329; competition in, 7–8, 24, 316–322; foreign telephone networks and, 326, 328, 329–330, 365–366; globalization in, 313–334; standards and, 27, 28, 91, 369

Telecommunications industry, foreign: competition in, 7–8, 315–322; incentives for foreign expansion, 321–322; privatization and, 316, 317–318; software demands of globalization and, 27

Telecommunications industry, U.S.: competition in, 7, 314–315; incentives for foreign expansion, 320

Telecommunications technology: growing demand for, 361–362; restructuring of securities industry and, 111, 148–168; superordinate-designed infrastructures and, 67–68

Telephone networks, foreign, 326, 328, 329–330, 365–366

Telepresence, 354

Test marketing, 202–203

Textile and Apparel Linkage Council (TALC), 209

Textile industry. *See also* Prato textile system (Italy): channel perspective and, 186, 187; codification and, 178; coordination-intensive structures

and, 42–43; restructuring of manufacturing in, 16, 39, 121; standards-setting organizations and, 208–210

Toronto Stock Exchange, 149

Toyota, 84

Toys 'R' Us, 185, 198

TradeLink platform, 90

TradeNet platform, 89–90, 104

TRADE system, 162, 228–229

Trading systems, 41, 47, 118–119, 147–151. *See also* London Stock Exchange; Stock Exchange Automatic Quotations

Transaction costs, 219, 229–233

Transaction costs economics (TCE), 230–231

Transborder data flow (TBDF) regulations, 91

"Transformational change," 215

Transnational firm. *See also* Global enterprise: Asea Brown Boveri as, 124; coordination-intensive structures and, 49; design of global information systems and, 36, 59; framework for organizational design, 62–70; key characteristics of organization, 57–58; organizational structure of, 33, 36

Transnational strategy, 85–86

Transportation technology, 39–44

Travel industry. *See also* Airline reservations systems; Rosenbluth International Alliance; Rosenbluth Travel: globalization of, 289–293; information technology and, 285, 288–289, 301–303

Tuckman, B. W., 266

Turner, Ted, 120

TVINN system, 104

UAW-GM cooperation: management at Saturn and, 262–264; origins of Saturn and, 257–259; rewards at Saturn and, 269–270

United Kingdom. *See also* London Stock Exchange: competition in telecommunications and, 7–8, 316, 317, 318, 319, 322, 324–325, 366; financial markets in, 151–166

United States: Department of State, 365; Department of Transportation, 221–224; foreign participation in telecommunications in, 319; regulation of GISs in, 105

Unit production systems (UPSs), 206–207

Universal product codes (UPCs), 17, 193, 208

UNIX framework, 26

UPCs. *See* Universal product codes
UPSs. *See* Unit production systems
Upton, David, 16, 111, 169–183
USAir, 238–239

Value-added information service industries, 116–118, 134. *See also* Databases
Value-added/managed data networks, 14, 22, 116
Value-added networks (VANs), 327
VANs. *See* Value-added networks
Vertical relationships, 19, 124–125, 230
VF Corporation, 200
VICS. *See* Voluntary Inter-Industry Communications Standards
Video-conferencing, 12, 117, 200, 362
Videotext systems, 14, 117
Virtual corporation, 218, 283–307
Virtual private network (VPN), 365
Virtual reality, 352–354, 356
The Visible Hand (Chandler), 230
Voluntary Inter-Industry Communications Standards (VICS), 209
VPN. *See* Virtual private network

Wall Street crash of 1989, 220
Wal-Mart, 122; competitive advantage and, 137, 139, 185; General Electric and, 17–18, 137, 139; quick response system and, 17–18, 43, 127, 192–193, 204, 212
Warbelow, Arthur, 45
Warren, Alfred S., 257
Watson, Thomas J., Sr., 251
Weber, Max, 59, 60
Weiss, Abbott, 197–198
Welch, Jack, 130, 136
Westinghouse, 129
Whittaker, David, 296
Wireless technology, 346–347
Wolfe, Tom, 226
Womack, James, 135
Workstation industry, 26, 28
Workstations, 69–70, 347
Wriston, Walter, 109
Wunsch, 165

Xerox, 20–21, 135; "Leadership through Quality" program, 128, 135, 139–140

Zuboff, Shoshana, 10